Nature, Bureaucracy and the Rules of Property

Regulating the Renewing Environment

Earl Finbar Murphy
Professor of Law
Ohio State University

1977

NORTH-HOLLAND PUBLISHING COMPANY
AMSTERDAM · NEW YORK · OXFORD

Library of Congress Catalog Card Number 77-15455
North-Holland ISBN 0–7204–0700–1

Publishers:

NORTH-HOLLAND PUBLISHING COMPANY
AMSTERDAM · NEW YORK · OXFORD

Sole distributors for the U.S.A. and Canada:

Elsevier North-Holland, Inc.
52 VANDERBILT AVENUE, NEW YORK, N.Y. 10017

Library of Congress Cataloging in Publication Data

Murphy, Earl Finbar, 1928–
    Nature, bureaucracy and the rules of property.

    Bibliography
    Includes index.
    1. Environmental law--United States. 2. Natural
resources--Law and legislation--United States. 3. Right
of property--United States. I. Title.
KF3775.M8   344'.73'046   77-15455

PRINTED IN THE NETHERLANDS

For Miss J. W.,
with respect and devotion

Acknowledgment

Because of what he learned through the experience, the author wishes to thank the staffs and members of the American Bar Association Special Committee on Environmental Law, the Advisory Committee on Industrial Siting, and the Special Committee on Energy Law. For the same reason, the author thanks the staffs and members of the Governor of Ohio's Task Force on Environmental Protection, the Ohio Environmental Board of Review as well as his colleagues at The Ohio State University. He is also grateful for the learning offered through association with the Athens Center of Ekistics and the World Society for Ekistics. Library assistance is invaluable and gratitude for assistance is due the staffs of the law libraries at The Ohio State University and Case Western Reserve University, as well as to the successive Heads of Reference at the Main Library at The Ohio State University, Miss Eleanore Devlin and Miss Ann Seyboth. And, finally, the author expresses his thanks for the invaluable clerical assistance of Miss Karen Olson and Miss Barbara Sauer of the College of Law at The Ohio State University, whose skill and patience were essential. An author's gratitude to others can truly never be adequately expressed.

E. F. M.

Contents

CHAPTER III.   REGULATION AND ENVIRONMENTAL
LIMITATIONS   72

CHAPTER IV.   A BUREAUCRACY FOR THE RENEWING
ENVIRONMENT   100

CHAPTER V.   SHIFTING THE ENVIRONMENTAL
BUREAUCRACY   134

Regulation and the Environment

What Discovering the Environment has Meant for Regulation

Re-making old words is an important process. One of the most significantly re-worked words in recent times has been "environment." Not until after 1965 was it heard on both a global and a common scale. Since then it has summarized everything in nature surrounding human activity. The word "environment" has proved a means of focusing attention upon the relationship between human demand and the ability of living and renewing systems to respond to that demand.[1]

Concentrating so much attention upon one word might seem a trivial matter. Such has not been the case, however. From the beginning of the Industrial Revolution in the late 18th century, there had been people who had worried about the impact upon what they called Nature or, at a much later date, Conservation of Natural Resources. Those people accomplished important work, none more so than what they did to educate the public mind about the effect human demand made upon the individual living and renewing aspects of the world.

Yet, valuable as these efforts still are and worthy of historical recollection, there had been lacking that comprehensiveness of view which the re-made word "environment" supplied. No longer could attention be concentrated upon saving a single forest, a single species, one river, an isolated air shed. Henceforward, the interrelatedness of air, water, wild-life, and the biomass would have to be the object stressed. The renewal of this one word has signaled this important shift.

By bringing into public consciousness the interconnectedness of everything in nature, the word environment has also broken away from the earlier practice of judging nature as purely an economic resource. To speak only of natural resources, even though one talks of conserving them, is to be bound by a constricting vision. Trees exist for other purposes than lumber and wild animals have a worth other than their pelts. The world of man is an anthropocentric one, but that world needs still more from the environment than market commodities.

Human beings themselves are a part of nature in ways not entirely expressible in financial terms. The health of human tissue can be disturbed by the content of the atmosphere and there is no easy means to put a value upon either that disturbed tissue, or the polluted atmosphere, or the activity which polluted it, or the effort to change the effect of that activity. To talk of mankind and their environment places a particular emphasis upon these relationships that can only change the way man looks around him. In the past, one might think of Man against Nature, two giants locked in strife. Somehow, one cannot easily conceive of humanity and their environment in the same dramatic terms of conflicting duality.

Re-molding the word environment into a different usage in only a few years has been no small accomplishment. Three results stem from that action in the public mind in consequence: just about everything in nature is seen as interconnected with everything else; nature has become more than either discovered or as yet undiscovered opportunities for a cash return; and humanity know themselves as interconnected with natural systems in the way other living organisms are. To reach so many purposes by altering a single word is not a social achievement to be brushed aside.

To be sure, this has been no more than a summarizing action. The transformation had to have been prepared through decades of experience, capital accumulation, resource allocation, and institutional change, even when these were events no one believed would be avenues to the discovery of the environment. As a process, it has been far more than the conferring of a name.

Accompanying the new use of the word environment has been the richness of changed occurrence that has indicated truly different views from those prevailing in the past. In most of the major industrial nations of the world, there have been extensive efforts in environmental protection. Regulations, investments, and mandated conduct have been the increasing pattern. Of still greater significance, there has been an increase in simply thinking about how better to prevent harm to the environment from the result of human demand.[2]

Ever since the discovery of the environment, people have given greater attention not only to applying previously known ideas but to devising hitherto unconceived means of achieving environmental betterment. The disorders have proven to be more than the pollution of water, the degradation of air, the extinction of species, or any other directly perceived condition, complex as these have been shown to be for purposes of correction.[3] Instead, as inquiries have been pursued deeper into the root causes of why the environment suffers so greatly under the demands of every urban-industrial economy, the roles played by government and law have come under steadily increasing scrutiny. They have not always borne their examinations well.

The public arena is always a dangerous place within which to focus attention. The side-effects will often be quite different from those anticipated by the initiators. It is not only within the biologic life-systems that all consequences of change cannot be foreseen. Perhaps in the human forum unpredictability is even more true.

Assuredly, the re-working of the word environment, both as to the events it signaled as being summarized and the activity it indicated as being necessarily forthcoming, represents an initiation of this character. Attention having been thereby focused, the changes introduced have been (and will be) more than some alterations in the chemical constituency of air and water receiving basins. The consequences from re-making the word environment are only beginning.

The Environmental Challenge to Law

Once there appeared the concentration of attention upon environmental issues, many previously accepted positions came under challenge. The public had become accustomed to being importuned on a variety of pressing social demands that clearly called for action – but the public previously had not been warned that there were costs attached which offered less than obvious cautions. Regulation seemed an easy option, but there had been few to say that regulation worked best when there were prospects for internal subsidization in which one part of the system could be employed to subsidize other parts of the system.[4]

Perhaps if regulation had been used in this fashion, then regulation could have served as one type of variety of planning. Unfortunately, regulation through most of the 20th century has not worked in this manner. And for that reason, the term regulation has acquired a poor reputation among those who are concerned with accomplishing ends that consist of more than naysaying.[5]

It is no uncommon occurrence for there to be a demand that the public fisc come forward with a subvention for causes that all agree are worthy of the widest support. Yet little concern has been expressed beyond that initial expression. The result has been that some institutions, having low present income but large capital value over the long run, have been given a current consideration that has made a mockery of all equity comparisons which would take into account the relation of investment to return.[6]

This has been particularly unfortunate in the area of pollution abatement. The more attention that has been paid to this issue the more it has been admitted that the best situation would be one in which the social value of any additional clean-up would be equal to the cost of that clean-up. The impediment to such a rational solution – as well as the proffered justification to the gross discrepancy between demanded investment and expected return in so many of the socially mandated programs – is the difficulty of anticipating either the costs of a given program or of society's desire for that particular program.[7]

Because of this uncertainty – and the ambiguities underlying that uncertainty – the result has been a kind of societal marking of time. The fancy name conferred upon this is the iterative process. As defined, this means that one effort or another is accomplished and, then, there is a casting up of accounts as to costs and benefits, with the decision coming later as to whether the right or the wong kind of action had been taken.[8] Naturally, it is impossible to charge that nothing is ever done under such a program. But, equally, no one can assert that the best results have been obtained.

Perhaps the greatest disappointment underlying this experience is the perception that voluntary compliance has been so often lacking. What makes this a matter of concern is that voluntary compliance is necessary if there is to be substantial success in any program of legal command. Merely to insist upon stringency in law enforcement, or to believe a strong position results in law enforcement simply because there is insistence among environmental protection groups, is of less consequence than the existence of an internal conviction within the polluting sources that their conformity with environmental needs is required.

Should the generators of pollution be indifferent or insistent upon making the most minimum effort that the force of the law demands, then there can never be a satisfying of environmental requirements. Theirs is a response that may come from public pressure to minimally account for a pollution damage previously caused, or their reaction may be the result of a desire to avoid controversy by installing a technology that is more efficient from any point of view. Yet the fact remains that the greatest results will generally come from internally generated responses. They usually will exceed those which grudgingly are conceded as the barest minimum the law commands under direct penalty.[9]

It is still often easier to buy out any possible challengers to economic activity than it would be to alter that activity. Technology is the manner in which man utilizes the environment in order to satisfy both his physical and learned demands. The efficient accomplishment of that purpose is easiest when interests likely to object are eliminated.[10] Changing either the demand or the way it is satisfied can be far more troublesome to the style of technology when it is processing the environment into the stuff that responds to human demand.

A study of the land ownership patterns along the Wisconsin River supports this view. Here is a major river, heavily used by manufacturing industry and power utilities that runs through well-populated and prosperous agricultural country and is polluted. Yet up to 1971 research indicated that no attorney had ever been consulted about the possibility of suing the numerous, affluent polluters discharging into the river.[11]

Why should this quiescence have been the rule? One definite answer lay in the pattern of property interests relative to the Wisconsin River. The manufacturing mills own most of the land downstream from their waste discharge outfalls, which would be the reaches most affected by the resultant pollution. With ownership in common title, no abatement lawsuits will arise. Where the water in the river is of lowest quality, the stretches of land along the river are most often owned by manufacturers and power companies. Often the bed of the stream has been severed in title from the shoreline so that the owner of the river bank loses all riparian rights. This occurs when, through artificial impoundments, flowage rights have been obtained by expansion of the location of the river. In any event by one lawful means or another, including the loss of once provable rights through prescription, the bulk of the riparian land along the Wisconsin River could not give rise to a suit in nuisance for its pollution.[12] It would be, after all, the polluter suing the polluter – and that is less than likely.

For this, among other reasons, the private law suit in environmental matters has been ineffective because the legal bases upon which it would rest have been engrossed by these imposing demands upon the environment. As a consequence, the burden has fallen upon the public sector to be concerned with environmental protection. And the public sector has traditionally fallen short even when there has been an ever-increasing effort to meet the sustenance needs of the environment.

Studies concerning the effect of greater law enforcement in the area of water pollution in the United States during the decade of the 1960's showed a seemingly paradoxical result. Strong enforcement was defined as a situation of strict laws, large water pollution control budgets, and a preponderance of non-polluters on the governing boards of the enforcement agencies. Success was measured by the degree of water quality change during the decade. Using these tests, the conclusion was reached that the greater the law enforcement, the worse the water became during the decade.[13]

Other almost equally puzzling results come from the same study. The greater the supervision of the legislature over the actions of the enforcement agents, the better the latter's performance, even in situations of relatively weak statutory authority. The greater the legislative interest, the strictness of the law, and the amount of resources expended on enforcement, the greater the presence of polluters in the policy levels of the enforcement process. The negative influence of polluters was greatest in the setting of standards, whereas in the enforcement effort their influence tended to be positively exerted in the direction of improved water quality during the decade of the 1960's.[14]

The conclusion from all this is neither that an absence of law enforcement is better or that polluters are nice people with strong altruistic drives for environmental betterment. Instead, it is the recognition that strong law enforcement in water pollution control occurs in jurisdictions with highly polluted waters. The jurisdictions, in which the interest of the polluters is in water pollution control, are those in which the water supply is rapidly deteriorating. And even there, the polluters work to great effect in minimizing the standards which are to be enforced. In short, when the physical and economic conditions of some environmental resource become sufficiently degraded, the attention of both government and those exploiting the environment will be attracted – but they will not be sufficiently attracted to reverse the degradation or even slow down its course.[15]

There is a place for regulation in positively changing the condition of the environment toward a better ability to respond to the demands upon it imposed by human activity.[16] One of the facts that makes difficult the determination of the effectiveness of regulation is the determination of damaged function suffered by the environment. Whether a stream goes up or down one part per million of dissolved oxygen, there is small significance in the event from the viewpoint of human use.[17] The result is, initially, substantial difficulty in physically measuring environmental alterations and in the incurring of high costs in such monitoring.[18] Secondarily, the consequence is the likely public conviction that too little has been happening to make the governmental effort worthwhile in relation to the expenditures invested. And, ultimately, the whole environmental program is imperilled by the very complexities that its character imposes upon government and law.

Few could have foreseen at the beginning the impact of perceived environmental change upon such seemingly remote institutions. But regulation, however maligned or unsuccessful, is the key power for carrying out public purposes relative to the environment whether the public authority seeks to control directly all of the environment, or confines itself to dealing only with areas of critical concern, or seeks to delegate to the market or to local or specialized governmental units the responsibility for coping with environmental problems.[19] But however lacking the powers of prophesy may have been, or how often regulation fails because too narrow an endeavor has been undertaken or too little investment has been allotted to an ambitious endeavor, the impact of the environment upon government and law, upon the bureaucracy and the rules of property, is still a presence.

It is as Justice Holmes wrote to Harold Laski immediately after World War I.

Civilization is the reduction of the infinite to the finite. The realizing that there is so much forest, coal, etc., so much even atmosphere – and no more.[20]

Unless technology and economics can release mankind from that limitation, the heavy burden so lately realized shall remain. It presses upon government and law as the result of environmental conditions. One of the tasks must be to make regulations something other than an ignorantly imposed additional cost to both the human and natural environmental systems.

The Present Sense of Malaise in Environmental Regulation

There is no question that there is a wide spectrum of opinion which believes environmental protection either has failed to protect the environment, or else has harmed the regulatory mechanisms, or both. Irving Kristol, in speaking of planning relative to the environment, has charged that

...a certain oligarchic group of environmentalists, planners, judges, and lawyers imposing certain living patterns on people...[has] a nice cozy thing going on between the environmentalists, the city planners, the lawyers, and judges....[21]

He concludes his charge with the sarcasm that he trusts none of these people have any illusions that what they are doing for the environment is popular.

And perhaps he is right. One of the leading planners for phased urban growth believes that there is such distrust of government, while so much valuable time has been thrown away in the past upon the production of rhetoric, that very little can be accomplished which is not on the most local of levels.[22] Certainly many people, faced with both change and an increased sense of powerlessness in the face of change, want to insert themselves into the decision-making process. They are less concerned with any failures that resulted from a too-narrow understanding of environmental responsibilities than they are with imposing what Holtan Odegard has called "conservative drag" upon the process of change itself.[23] And too often that is all they are interested in accomplishing.

If the perception of regulatory malaise lies solely in a distaste for change, then the fault lies not in the regulatory agencies but in those who are unhappy at living in the 20th century. In many ways, the urban-industrial economies and their supportive technologies have been so productive of material goods that an underlying assumption has arisen that these economies and technologies can do everything, that there is no need to ever be disciplined by such limitations which previously confined other cultures. When choice has to be made, even so, and other potential options foregone, there is often a sense of anger, of frustration, and of rejection of a system that has failed [24] – and the easiest object of attack is any organization for regulation that has been involved, regardless of whether or not it is the cause of the supposed failure.

But the problem probably lies deeper than at the level of petulance over change and unreasonable expectations of what technology and the economy can deliver, important as these are as contributors to the present allegations of regulatory sickness and failure. In any guidance system that concerns itself with the formulation, coordination, and implementation of policies, there must be a capacity for formulating issues to be solved in relation to some set of basic values that shall serve as the judging standard capable of indicating to the regulators whether they have succeeded or failed.[25] Although these agreed values may in themselves comprise extraordinarily complex economic, political and ethical issues, there is a minimum of consensus necessary in order for there to be agreement on how to initiate – much less how to judge – any program.

Some, like Barrington Moore, may say such consensus is as simple as distinguishing between the unity of judgment expected concerning human misery and the diversity of judgment permissible bearing on human fulfillment.[26] Others would insist that such a reduction was intended really to introduce a condition of stasis that must constitute a rare condition in urban-industrial society, however happy mankind might fancy themselves under such circumstances.[27] But whatever the view espoused, what seems to be increasingly clear as the 20th century moves along is that there simply are all kinds of views. What is lacking is much consensus concerning basic values. Without some modicum of that, there are some pessimistic enough to say nothing relative to government and law can succeed, whether it concerns the environment or anything else.

Such persons claim that comprehensive action concerning land and the environment depends upon forces and conditions external to those most concerned with protection of the environment. Planners doing such work, it is charged, can at best have only a fragmentary knowledge relating to the task they are engaged in, so that others feel no compunction in rejecting any claim on the planners' part to "expert" status worthy of special consideration. Any man's intuition becomes as valid under current conditions as the input of anyone claiming special knowledge as the result of training and experience. In the absence of a coherent social agreement of what is good for *civitas*, any forceful group organized around some central set of interests has as much likelihood of committing the public power as any traditional authority figure insisting upon possessing a cohering role in governmental decision making.[28]

At the minimum this means drawing into the decision-making process all groups desirous of expressing an opinion or contemplating exercising a later veto-power without having previously voiced any critical view. The danger now lurking in unexpressed interest-group opinion is so strong that drawing it into the open at least provides those charged with the responsibility of action the opportunity to prepare their responses. With such information they may choose to withdraw, to modify, to refer to a judicial or quasi-judicial body, or to push full-speed ahead. What they may not do in the present unstructured and ambiguous situation is to retire behind a defense of alleged expertise.[29]

Nor have the people having the responsibility for decision been entirely unhappy with this change. It has been asserted that in the current situation of numerous, diffuse, and polymorphously hostile interest-groups that it is futile even to try the initial commitment to bargaining in good faith.[30] A sufficient effort has been made merely to have drawn these people into communication with each other.

Under conditions such as these, the decision-maker acquires an infinite capacity to disperse responsibility. As Edwin Haefele has bitterly observed,

He can then exist on platitudes and good feelings toward all. The political heat is drained off into a kind of infinite sink – a bureaucracy where no one is responsible but all have authority.[31]

The interest-groups involved may enjoy the advantage of an inside deal and insofar as they are outsiders and losers they always may play spoiler by resorting to the courts.

Where the statute commands such a situation, the fact is irrelevant that the decision-maker had considered every conceivable problem relating to the economic, environmental, social or other effects of a project during the period of years in which the project had been under advisement. The policy of such laws, though they may exalt form over substance, "...is to assure that consideration be given not only to expert studies and conclusions but to expressions of fact and opinion by members of the public...concerning the factors listed in [the statute]".[32] Under these circumstances, it is not surprising there are bureaucrats who calculate they cannot lose since, in such a process of carving the turkey ever finer, they serve as the indispensable middleman.[33]

Yet there have always been persons within the bureaucratic structure who have been willing to opt out of their responsibilities and to delegate around the system all the unhappy consequences of the possibly erroneous decision. But right now this has become not only a common practice but one which many seriously seek to justify. The reason lies in the view of many that there is an absence of any accrediting standards to sustain the timid administrator. That severe critic of normative, comprehensive planning, John Friedmann, has charged,

The...multiplicity of societal perspectives cannot by sheer force of logic be integrated into a single normative scheme or...hierarchy of values.... We no longer have validated, traditional standards by which greater legitimacy can be attributed to [any] value perspective....[34]

That being the case, interaction within the bureaucracy becomes a mutual learning process and imbalanced development must be accepted as inevitable.[35]

It may well be so, but if such formlessness should prove inevitable, the public regulation of the environment particularly will be a well-nigh hopeless task. A person in the bureaucracy, after all, shows worth through an ability to explain and to rationalize official conduct. Experience is important only insofar as it can be reflected in meritocratic criteria. A bureaucracy that lacks such measures of judgment because its members are busy passing on the burdens of reasoned decision-making, serving as middlemen to hostile groups in a process never meant to produce an operational result, and considering itself fulfilled as the arena for everyone's mutual learning process is a bureaucracy in serious difficulty. Should this become – or remain – the dominant mode, then Herman Kahn will have prophesied accurately when he said, "...governing may become an uncharismatic, low-morale profession".[36]

One can hope that the malaise of regulation does not lie so deep and that there will be developed some consensus for dealing with the problems of the environment. Given the gravity of the condition of self-renewing systems in the human environment, there must be dissatisfaction with the law, the bureaucracy, and all those in public authority who can be charged with having let it happen or with having done too little to correct it. Those who make the charge may be themselves confused or even dishonest but the regulatory mechanisms cannot hope to avoid indictments and the need both to be defended and to be changed. If it is true that saving the environment puts the present against the future and the individual against society, then any mechanism that must be concerned with the maintenance of long-term use can expect the hostility both of short-term users and those who believe too many concessions have been made to those same short-term interests.[37]

The stress, of course, may prove still greater. Ecologic considerations may require a change in the costing of industry, the habits of consumption, the patterns of human fertility, and the world-wide thrust in favor of growth economies and technologies highly demandant upon the environment.[38] If there should be a need to avert some ecocatastrophe and to safeguard the life-prospects of subsequent generations by sustaining an ecological balance, the work of maintaining that balance and conserving resources would be of the most radical, fundamental quality.[39] Even if all were to agree upon this as a universal ethic, the burden upon the regulatory mechanisms would still be huge in carrying through the necessary public education and the servicing of the necessary credit mechanisms.[40]

But, of course, there will not be any such agreement – if there seems any evidence that one is forming. Instead, possibilities such as the above are held up to mockery. They are called "infantile feelings of dependency" and "petulant demands" for "Father Government to stop interference with Mother Nature's bounteous flow".[41] And, cutting as such humor is, it may have the greater long-run truth about the seriousness of the present environmental situation.

What is the prevailing truth, however, for the regulatory mechanism is the absence of agreement on goals, on risks, on standards, on all judgmental means. The result can only be an over-all reputation for malaise in relation to the regulatory mechanisms. After all, by somebody's measure the mechanisms are continually failing; and the talk of such failure, coming from so many compass points, has become the controlling mode.

If there were no serious problems in the environment, then it would be permissible to talk about the "nice, cozy thing" going on in the environmental protection business. If the future of life on this planet hangs in the balance of what happens in the next twenty years, then it must be imperative to seize the regulatory mechanisms by the throat and squeeze their best from them. Since no one knows for a certainty and since no single interest-group can impose an uncompromised will, all that remains is the reputation for malaise of the regulatory mechanisms.

The one certainty is that the contending interest-groups will not cease either their disputes, or their attacks upon how the regulatory mechanisms work, or their attempts to acquire control of those mechanisms. Even those who want change to stop and who talk about a society of stasis want to control the regulatory mechanisms in order to bring about such societal

conditions. For the final irony of all the talk about the malaise of the regulatory mechanisms is that most lamenters of the sickness want absolute control
over the invalid. Perhaps that above all indicates hope in the long-run survival
possibilities of regulating the environment – or of having an environment to
regulate.

The Magnifier Effect of Regulatory
Failure on the Environment

René Dubos has observed that a characteristic of the late 20th century is the
rapidity with which a new orientation can be imposed upon all social and
economic trends. He correctly notes that this is true of every aspect of human
activity in urban-industrial society and that it is the result both of the techniques making it possible and of the public mood that so often facilitates the
smooth operation of those techniques. The public is no more solidly opposed
to change than the official policy-makers are entirely in favor of it. The
consequence is that there exists the means for a rapidity in the rate of change
never previously known even to the most authoritarian regimes of the pre-
industrial ages.[42]

But helpful as quickness of change may often be, the other aspect is that the
very quickness will hurry along and magnify any conceptual mistakes
inherent in the original policy. Policies whose flaws would gradually be revealed in any slowly evolving process, and either therefore dropped or
corrected, are rushed into effect with intense, precipitous, and horrendous
consequences substantially derived from the speedy capabilities of technology
in urban-industrial society. In the regulatory mechanisms there are so many
means for inducing, cajoling, or compelling adoption of a changed program
that resistance is muted, criticism shunted aside, and the way cleared for
greater harm than a more cumbersome bureaucracy could cause.[43]

When public decision-making can be conducted at a local or single-purpose
jurisdictional level some of this is occasionally avoided because the focus of
the attention of all involved is easier to attract when perception of problems
first begin to form themselves. This does not always happen even in these
relatively simple regulatory situations either, because of apathy or the
operation of baffles built into the system that slow both the perception of
problems and doing anything effective to correct them. Yet whatever the
troubles at these less complex levels, they become far greater as one moves up
the hierarchical ladder of the bureaucratic regulatory apparatus. As some wise
political scientists pointed out years ago,

[A] dominant center of decision-making is apt to become a victim of the complexity of its own hierarchical or bureaucratic structure. Its complex channels of communication may make its administration unresponsive.... The costs of maintaining control...may be so great that its production of public goods becomes grossly inefficient.[44]

It is a magnifying effect that is further distorted by what many close observers of governmental operations claim to be the case, namely that, except in the supply of water, sewer, and sewage treatment services which do exhibit economies, there are no significant economies of scale in the entirety of the public services.[45] That ancient critic of bureaucracy, Ludwig von Mises, would insist that this is to be expected since the results of bureaucratic management cannot be assigned a cash value in the market.

"Remember," he said, "we do not say that a successful handling of public affairs has no value, but that it has no price on the market, that its value cannot be realized in a market transaction and consequently cannot be expressed in terms of money."[46]

The consequences are productive of great risk when major regulatory efforts are undertaken, a difficulty in doing any monitoring using cash outlays and returns as indicators of success or failure, and little prospect of accomplishing the sort of economies of scale managers have been accustomed to anticipate in supervising the production function. As long as regulation was peripheral to the major events in urban-industrial society, the risks were infrequent and the inability to measure of small significance. But when the changes in the economy and the technology started to occur at a geometric rate, the successive increments of change relative to the impacted environment had to become steadily larger. The accompaniment to this has been the demand for, and the creation of, regulatory mechanisms to try to control the effect of this change upon the environment. Out of this has emerged the large, centralized, often complacent, insulated agency whose very technical skill makes the risk of its mistakes so very perilous.[47]

This will not be greatly eased if what has been called the Ricardo effect should prove true relative to the increasing cost of factors of production which will cause a diminution in returns from investment. It is alleged that this will be particularly true for fixed factors, of which much of the environment constitutes variant examples. If this should be the case, "...economies from scale, advanced technology, innovation, design and substitution no longer will be able to reduce costs proportionate to the investment made in them."[48] To add to this gloomy possibility a constitutional infirmity in the regulatory mechanisms to aspire to economies of scale or to establish fiscal tests for productivity can only further increase the magnifying effects of regulatory error.

Perhaps governance ought to be less concerned with the process of regulating what goes on and more involved in facilitating certain operations[49] – but that would require a conviction that the positive actions encompassed in facilitation were right and it would increase the risk if they were not. It is far more appealing to the bureaucratic decision-maker to employ the negative tool of regulation and to risk only failure of omission than to launch out on a positive course of action that could lead to indictable disaster. Furthermore, the responsibilities of the facilitating bureaucrat are far greater than those of the regulator.

Many years ago, Ragnar Frisch, one of the early proponents of scientific planning, outlined why this should be so. He stated that,

...in order to apply existing scientific techniques fully...the responsible political authorities [must] maintain control over the whole thing at every stage of the work.... Scientific planning means coordinating everything in one simultaneous (and integrated) piece of analysis and doing it on some optimum basis. It involves solving the whole nexus as one simultaneous problem, where everything determines everything else.[50]

Clearly, despite the generalizing compulsions of such a burden, the bureaucrats themselves cannot be generalists. They must, instead, be specifically trained technicians or even scientists. They will need, in addition to their training, detailed guidelines integrated with their skills. They must be kept in jobs so that they can acquire a deep expertise and not be transferred or even promoted to other tasks. Their experiential knowledge, plus the use of programmed models in their guidelines, will be the justification for their facilitative decisions and the justification for the prestige that must come from such high responsibility.[51] Their attitude would have to change entirely from preventing harm to actively seeking to accomplish good, with all the concomitant perils such a shift heralds.

And let no one doubt that the perils in such a change in bureaucratic strategy would be enormous so far as the environment would be concerned. If everything is treated as the integral part of an administered nexus, the magnification of every task undertaken must be inescapable. Even that foe of normative, comprehensive planning, John Friedmann calls planning for governmental action,

...the study of policy alternatives, the formulation and evaluation of action and investment programs, the organization and preparation of program budgets, the preparation of forecasts, the monitoring and evaluation of urban and regional systems performance, the preparation of proposals for action, project design, and the development of strategies for institutional change.[52]

With obligations such as these, the risk of failure cannot help but be very much present.

As the environmental problems have become more evident, there has been both an increase of public knowledge concerning these problems and an accompanying growth in the interest shown by more significantly powerful units of government. The public has become convinced that the workings of the natural ecological systems can be profoundly affected by economic and political decisions, with the effects not limited to the precise portion of the environment being directly exploited. The idea of external diseconomies, particularly negative ones, was not a common one in the public mind prior to 1970. Since then however, the public has learned that someone's exercise of a property "right" in one spot can impose a heavy cost in another, so that the exerciser of the "right" collects the cash return and the receptor of the costs absorbs them.

Once environmental actions were perceived by the public in this way, the demand for governmental involvement inevitably had to grow. Imposing some kind of equitable spread of costs between those collecting the benefits and those receiving the negative external effects has become a public charge upon government to accomplish through bureaucratic or other legal means.[53] Under that pressure, government has sought to respond.

Local and special jurisdictions have become involved in the public mind with previous failures vis-a-vis the environment as self-renewing systems suffered the impact of economic demand. Municipalities too often subserved the interests of those exploiting the environment and special purpose jurisdictions were from their inception frequently mere creatures to serve those exploiters, so that these units have lost the image of potential guardians of the environment. In the presence of such disenchantment with these smaller governmental units, the public has turned to the larger more centralized bureaucracies.

Unfortunately, when these larger units become involved, they can respond only by creating layers of bureaucratic structure between the problem in the field and their highest decision-makers. Simply to channel information to the top or effective orders to the bottom requires this hierarchical complexity. In addition, when the bureaucratic structure employed is one with wide territorial and institutional responsibilities, it is drawn in more diverse directions by far more numerous and conflicting constituencies than ever contested for favor from municipalities or special purpose jurisdictions.[54] The task of getting a definitive answer to some fairly well-defined question acquires a formidable quality that in itself must alienate many from the role played by bureaucracy, even if the governmental response comes from a widely expressed public demand.

Knowing the potential for harm, the bureaucracy will insist upon detailed models to guide them and to substitute as much as possible for their own adminstrative discretion. Indeed, the very notion of administrative discretion is in ill-repute today in many quarters, perhaps not least among those bureaucrats who would rather not have the responsibility of the exercise of discretion. Certainly, if discretion is to be applied, the decision-maker must be highly experienced with all the subsectors such a judgment will affect and the decision-maker must be ready to accept both the consequence for good or ill that his actions produce.[55]

What makes the assumption of such responsibility an act of courage is the conflicting values impressed upon the administrator by contending interest-groups and the near-impossibility of knowing in advance the consequences of any actions undertaken. While the technology of economics, government, and science can produce a quick result, and thereby magnify in abrupt terms the effect of what is done, the environment often takes time to reveal the full extent of the response. An administrator may not know from any messages the environment can send soon enough to stop the accelerating effect of his technological actions before irremediable damage is done to the indirectly communicating renewal systems in the environment.

It is for this reason that so many bureaucrats would rather regulate the actions of others than to partake in the facilitation of those actions. As administrators, they would rather impose some plan of negative prohibitions than to undertake a positive planning or action program. Some undoubtedly are made lazy and timid by the risks; but others, knowing how grave the risks may be, draw back because they know how hard the information is to come by that would make more positive bureaucratic action a uniformly preferred course.

Still, insofar as the environment is concerned, bureaucrats are in no different position than are those drawing upon that environment to serve production functions: they possess a technology capable of producing rapid change and of magnifying the results of that change. But technology, because it is cumulative and its effects progressive in time and space as the result of that accumulation, interacts with the environment. Out of that interplay comes the conditions of life in urban-industrial society. The environment can limit the effectiveness of technology; but only man can determine when and how to apply that technology.[56]

And once technology is known to exist, its very progressive pressure forces so many incremental changes that, without intending it, some allegedly new grand design emerges describing the relationship between human demand and the environment responding to that demand. Government and law are no more immune to this consequence of technology's existence than is any other part of a society culturally committed to technological innovation. It is a commitment that has marked urban-industrial society since its emergence over two centuries ago.[57]

The very growth in industrial economic organization has created the demand for large governmental authority.[58] If the economy is moving into a quarternary phase, of which the importance of the environment is cited as evidence, the role of bureaucracy will not shrink.[59] Instead, the pressure can only grow upon government to employ all the technology of which it is capable.

The result can only be a further magnification of the effect of technology's application. Even if the economy should move past such primary economic interests as production and go all the way to the quarternary phase of doing things purely for their own sakes, the effect upon the environment will not lessen. It may, indeed, grow greater with the growth of the recreation industry.

Assuredly, however, the technology of the bureaucracy will be drawn upon to service the demands of whatever economic activities exist. And, equally assuredly, there will be many mistakes, some approximating disasters, if the magnifying effect of an accumulating, accelerating, and progressive technology is overlooked. Whether the environment can absorb all the consequences of such failures remains the only doubtful proposition.

The Current Belief in Environmental Instability and Its Effect

There is a common belief that the two centuries of urban-industrial society had been marked by gross instability. It is well-known that from the beginning of this cultural change, poets such as Wordsworth and William Blake were objecting to the effects of the "dark, satanic mills." What is not so commonly perceived is that the instability may have been even greater in that beginning than it has been at any time since those days.

Such a possibility is hard to accept to a generation that has been initially exposed to atomic power and space travel. For a generation so exposed, there has developed a belief that the instability they have known has been the greatest in historical time. In addition, this generation is concerned that the near future promises a degree of instability unknown even to the severely troubled generations of the late 20th century.

It is the presence of a belief such as this which creates the current conviction that the present is the time of history's greatest instability. Believing this, it is not hard to convince those severely troubled by the unstabilizing events they see all about them that the urban-industrial world may be approaching a climax in nature's ability to respond to human demand. Out of this fear, a call has gone up that the government should do something to stop this instability and prevent the irreversible climax. Whether or not this is done by an administrative allocation of resources or by a regulation of the market mechanism through law is a matter of nearly equal indifference on the part of most of those holding these views of unstabilized times.

Government's recourse has been to strengthen, and in some instance to create, a bureaucracy to protect the environment. Perhaps a more fundamental requirement for change is called for, but the reorganization of the bureaucratic structure has been the governmental means of coping with the demands of those fearful of the effects of accelerating instability.

Unfortunately the bureaucracy has been unable to protect the environment. The setting up of a bureaucracy charged with environmental protection has not solved any of the problems of accelerating destabilization in the surviving life-support systems. Neither have any of the omnivorous demands of the urban-industrial system for processing the environment been lessened by their enlargement. Indeed, the main result of bureaucratic reform has been to furnish each newly perceived problem, and its accompanying focal constituency, with its very own bureaucracy.[60]

The consequence has been that each problem has been separately institutionalized. The environment has been dealt with in the same manner that urban-industrial society deals with the claims of its young, its disabled, and its aged. Sadly, if these latter are any guide as to what is likely to happen to the environment, little is to be expected other than institutionalization.[61] The traditional bureaucratic structure serves that function very well. There seems little sign on the horizon of any government institution serving a better purpose for the environment than recognizing problems and then embalming them in a protective regulatory structure.

Perhaps it is cavilling to be critical of this evolution. Popular opinion, and the manner in which such opinion has been made operationally effective in government, may require a conviction of a crisis condition before acting. The people have to believe in an ever-worsening condition in the environment that is occurring as the result of human demand.

Is it not better for the environment that a bureaucracy be set up, or else expanded, in order to protect it? In the past, after all, government was dedicated to furthering the fragmenting and processing practices of urban-industrial society as demand related to the environment. To a modern critic of those practices, is it not better that some part of the government's, hence of society's, resources be given over to modifying the effects of an intensifying conversion of natural systems into cash-expressible terms? However qualified the answer may be, it seems necessary that it be in the affirmative.

Some conditions in the environment undoubtedly were far worse in the past under the impact of contemporary economic demand. For example, prior to the development of pulp paper, the lumber industry found most of a tree waste. The industry's recourse was to dump those wastes in the nearest stream, even if that meant blocking the stream. Legislatures had to intervene with statutes to prevent the saw-mills from destroying the very rivers upon which they depended for floating their log booms. Manufacturing pulp paper has imposed a different burden on receiving waters, but it would be difficult to say that it has been a harder one for the waters to bear.[62]

Other illustrations, indicating how much more destabilizing effect of urban-industrial demands were in relation to environmental conditions in 1900, or 1850, or 1776, would not be hard for any historian to find. When capital is in short supply, the technology for a new industrial process primitive, and the market resistant to the introduction of expensive new products, the environment will always be treated as if it were a free good. The environment never is a free good; but under those conditions it likely will be perceived as such, and treated accordingly.[63]

Perhaps those are right who argue that in the past conditions were actually worse, that today they can only be described as improving, and that any crises which exist are capable of human management.[64] But even if this were true, there would still be present in nature the cumulative effects of past demands that would continue to be added to any demands now being made or to be made in the future by urban-industrial society. Such a combination would in itself pose a requirement for management. The greater problem is, however, that there are many informed persons who do not hold so sanguine a view.

The perception of an environmental crisis, transcending any previous condition in nature, has been passed along to the general public by many who profess to believe something dramatic needs to be done to reverse the trend established at the beginning of the industrial revolution. Maintaining environmental quality and conserving natural resources for these people requires a radical restructuring of the present growth economy to one of equilibrium if an eco-catastrophe is to be averted and the life prospects of future generations are to be sustained in an ecological balance.[65] The public has not come lightly to their view that two centuries of destabilizing nature are coming to some sort of breaking point.

It is under such a belief that the demands are being made on government to act. Perhaps the demands are forcing government to adopt too-high standards. If so, the ominous words of the philosopher Edward Banfield would be sadly applicable.

The effect of too-high standards cannot be to spur us on to reach the prescribed level of performance..., for that level is by definition impossible of attainment. At the same time, these standards may cause us to adopt measures that are wasteful and injurious, and...to conclude from the inevitable failure of these measures that ...our society is...incapable of meetings its obligations.[66]

In that event, all effort would be counter-productive in salvaging the environment and the very measures meant to save would be further burdens sinking the environment past salvation.

There is always a risk to actions taken when there is a conviction of crisis. Certainly it is better to learn the various means of leaving a building before a raging fire has closed the regular ways in and out. At the same time, however, simply because a sense of a crisis may cause rash actions to be taken, there is in this condition of risk no justification for taking no action at all. This is the situation that pertains to the public demands being made upon government and law today concerning the protection of the environment.

The cautionary word certainly must be heeded not to demand the unattainably "too-high" standard, enforcement order, market regulation, or allocative administrative mandate. But the cautionary word is always useful, even if more valuable during times of crisis. Yet in a world that allegedly had less than three weeks supply in the global food reserve in 1975 and where Norman Borlaug, the genitor of the Green Revolution of the 1960's, can urge the creation of world food stockpiles for famines he foresees soon,[67] the public is not wrong to make their demands in the urgent terms of crisis.

Matters may have been worse in the days of Wordsworth and Blake than they are today. Or they may not. Or Wordsworth and Blake may have been pointing out the beginning of a cumulative process whose garnering period is now.

What remains certain is that Wordsworth and Blake, as well as all their generation, are dead. The responsibility of action or inaction rests not upon the past but upon the present. It is out of this condition that the public, once they have been convinced of an impending environmental crisis as they have been in large measure, has demanded a protecting response from government and law.

Bureaucracy's Own Demands Upon the Environment

To the demand that steps be taken for protecting the environment have come many administrative responses. Government has set up or expanded existing agencies at the central, regional, and local levels. Corporations have been required to create new departments to carry out newly enacted or newly enforced laws for environmental protection. Everywhere since 1970 people have been hired and money spent in the cause of preventing or reducing the harmful impact of urban-industrial activities upon the environment.

And, as has now become a common-place, none of this has been served as part of any free lunch. Salaries call for appropriations when government pays them and for accommodation in the profit-and-loss statement when business pays them. When regulation means something more than saying no and calls for positive action, capital has to be obtained to make the necessary investments. Whether or not anything else has been foregone, the gross national product rises further as the result of such efforts to protect the environment. Ironically, the ultimate bearer of this burden has to be the very environment which is the object of so much solicitude.

In terms of direct cash outlay, the sums talked about have not been small, however much reduced in appearance they often appear when compared to other items in the list of the gross national product.[68] To consider only water-related costs in environmental protection, the states in the United States were circulated for their estimates of the cost of attaining the statutorily prescribed 1983 water goals. The amount they returned was $350 billion and, though it was immediately tagged by many as an exaggerated figure, it probably will not prove so.[69]

This sum, which does not include the costs of the same water protection requirements for the private sector by 1983, would not be a trifling amount even if it could be frozen in time. Of course this cannot be in an economy that must continuously contend with the forces of inflation. On the basis of experience with the effect of inflation on just water project construction costs in the years 1969–1974, knowledgeable people predicted costs by 1985 for such projects could quadruple.[70] Nothing happening since those years would be grounds for concluding such a prediction would be very far off the mark – at least on the low side.

When one combines the absolute size of the expenditures called for and the effect upon expenditures that must be made over a long period of time, there can be no conclusion except that there will be severe consequences of one sort or another. A capital demand of this size would have to distort further what some are predicting will be a capital short-fall of over fifteen percent in relation to capital demand – even without including in the demand heavy environmental expenditures.[71] Even should the predicted capital short-fall be adjusted away in the market by its cost, this would only further increase environmental protection costs through the higher interest rates.

The temptation will undoubtedly be great to cut this burden by reducing or eliminating altogether the now-demanded environmental protection projects. This would be a return to a consideration of nature as a free good since it would assume that among all the competing demands being made for capital, the environment is the one with the weakest cause. Once more the environment would be presumed able to continue self-renewal without human assistance, regardless of the still further increased demands of an urban-industrial society that must result from so much felt need for investment.[72]

Yet even if the commitment to the environment remains and is fulfilled in these more fiscally expensive circumstances, the environmental costs will be part of the continuously growing demands on the environment. These are now the pattern established for the remainder of the 20th century. There are those who would alter this pattern and seek a course less demanding upon the environment. These persons would point to even the plans for environmental protection projects as evidence of the impossible demands they see being made upon the environment. As Father Ivan Illich has said,

When overefficient tools are applied to facilitate man's relations with the physical environment, they can destroy the balance between man and nature. Overefficient tools corrupt the environment.[73]

Such persons may be right in what they seek in the way of changing man's relationship with nature. Theirs is not, however, the world pattern and not the direction being taken for environmental protection. Instead, the course of action being pursued calls for major bureaucratic structure and heavy capital investment in order to enable the environment to better handle the present and, more importantly, the growing urban-industrial demands made upon it.

This environmental protection system, like those systems that exploit the environment as simply a series of natural resources, measures the strength of nature in terms of how much human demand the self-renewing natural processes can absorb.[74] This is commonly the case because of the focus upon dissipating industrial waste in the environment and the division of bureaucracies into competitors for money and public attention. The result is that even the hired protectors of the environment see the living and renewing elements within nature – the air, water, and the biomass – as little more than sinks to be assisted in receiving the wastes of an increasingly demandant urban-industrial society.

If the size of the burden on the environment of the environmental protection bureaucracy is to be reduced, a more unified approach will have to be adopted than any that has been adopted up to this point. Perhaps the absolute size of the expenditures projected, the effect of inflation, and the increasing competition for capital will serendipitously enforce this kind of change. It seems unlikely that the only reaction will be to call for more of the same. But traditional patterns and the force of drift and apathy are so strong that a conscious decision for changed behavior will probably be necessary.

When a unified consideration is given to what urban-industrial society demands as a response from nature, environmental protection will be seen as something more than providing an after-the-fact waste treatment or supplying the means to a more certain source of supply for demanded resources. It will become commoner to explore alternative production techniques that reduce the amount of waste and that complement one resource with another in order to reduce the demand upon any particular part of the renewing systems in nature. Some say the market is doing this already and should be encouraged further. Others claim the bureaucracy through allocation of resources is already doing this and should be encouraged further.

Whatever the facts as to what is or is not happening already, the fact remains that the allocative administrative mechanism, like that of the market, imposes costs upon the environment that are not small.[75] They are costs that ought to be reduced as much as possible for that reason alone. But all costs in an inflationary economy that is highly competitive for all resources come under the compulsion to be lowered. The bureaucratic burden of high regulatory costs intended for environmental protection will prove no exception to this rule. However severe the public views the environmental crisis, they will not write the bureaucracy of environmental protection any blank checks, even if that same public should continue their demand for the existence of just such a bureaucracy.

The Hope for the Environment in Self-Executing Regulations

Under the impact of two world wars, a great depression, and the turbulence surrounding these events, conventional wisdom acquired two tenets of belief. The first claimed that the market mechanism was neither perfect nor fully rational. The second alleged that the direct allocation of resources by administrative order was more rational and prompt than the market. Consciously articulated social and economic preplanning by bureaucracy had thereby become a common 20th century experience.

Beginning with the "directed economy" Walther Rathenau developed for Imperial Germany during World War I, and continuing through all the intervening revolutions to the present, the market's ability to regulate events has been consistently downgraded. The power of bureaucratic structures in government has long held a superior place. Only as so much faith has been reposed in bureaucracy, and as bureaucracy has been tested by trial, has there been any revival of interest in depending upon the "imperfect" market mechanism and the rules of property serving that mechanism in order to regulate public affairs.

Indeed, among many, the belief in the useful function of the bureaucracy has fallen very low. These foresee urban-industrial society developing from a tertiary (service-oriented) to a quaternary (doing things for their own sakes) economic situation. They classify government as the quaternary institution *par excellence*. In Herman Kahn's expressive description, government employees

...will simply be receiving disguised subsidies or welfare. That is, the jobs...will be meaningless in terms of product to society,...; the jobs will merely be an accepted way of transferring income to such people. The salaries they receive will be counted as part of the GNP, but it will be increasingly difficult...to associate this portion of the GNP with any kind of increase in benefit to others.[77]

Certainly this is a long way from the initial belief in the utility of bureaucracy to better allocate natural resources than had been done by the market mechanism. Whether or not government ever purely becomes this sort of paid play-school for paper-shufflers, the fact it is seriously suggested as a major means to absorb otherwise unemployable and probably uneducable people becomes part of any reconsideration of regulatory mechanisms in addition to bureaucratic.

This does not necessarily mean a withdrawal of government from any concern with regulation and a return of responsibility to the Invisible Hand entirely. There is more to regulation by legal action than the obtaining of a permit or the receipt of a governmental command. Even one who would radically reduce the bureaucratic presence could conclude that private attitudes toward the future of the environment should not entirely control and that the government has a responsibility not adequately covered by market decisions. Central bureaucrats in comparison with the market have the advantage of quick action, when they wish to exercise that advantage, and can more directly reflect any differential time and risk preferences on behalf of the environment, again should they not be too sclerotic to do so.[78] But because bureaucracy has so often been unable or unwilling to perform the actions it allegedly does well, attention has turned to other forms of legal action.

The value of this kind of action through law has been stated by Milton Friedman, the economist whose name is so intimately associated in the public mind with the advantages of primary dependence upon the free market. As he expresses the relationship between the market and government,

The existence of a free market does not of course eliminate the need for government. On the contrary, government is essential both as a forum for determining the "rules of the game" and as an umpire to interpret and enforce the rules decided on.[79]

It is a qualified endorsement. He follows it with a demand that the government's role in economic decisions be limited in order to remove the political dimension from market activity and lift the restraint of uniformity stressed by bureaucratic needs for equal administrative action. For him, the market is a great free arena in which each consumer has votes to cast as he alone individually determines, without dependence upon the need to consult a majority or to meet the needs of a bureaucracy that is required to treat all persons equally. But even then, the market needs the support and defining constraints of law and its rules by which property can be held and transferred. Without such support in law, the freedom of the market becomes too various for Professor Friedman.

Even some socialist economists, who emphasize the importance of the government as the owner of capital and natural resources, assign an important role to the market. They do not believe that all decisions of government can be entirely political, taken without regard for such traditional market considerations as the individual's expressed preferences for goods, for choice of occupation, for mobility of residence, for services, and for pleasures. Oskar Lange, one of these socialists, argued in the 1930's that socialism need not be a command economy altogether and that the market would act to constrain governmental production action as it had constrained the production actions of private entrepreneurs.[80]

As the free-marketer Friedman sees the law constraining and supporting the market, so the socialist Lange sees the market constraining and supporting a government that controls capital and natural resources. For both of them, there must be the regulatory mechanisms of law, of bureaucracy, and of the market's operations. Their differences in degree are, of course, ultimately differences in kind when they come to mix these elements.

What is important to one seeking to learn, however, is the commonality of the elements to be mixed. In examining what is being done to the environment, and considering what might be done in relation to its response to human demand, working with elements such as these seems unavoidable. Hopes for change that depend upon freedom from bureaucracy, the market, and the rules of law seem to have small chance of fulfilment.

The possibilities exist quite strongly, however, for contriving different mixes of these elements than those which have become traditional in the 20th century. Many of those who are pushing for a greater reliance upon non-bureaucratic regulatory approaches through use of the rules of law to constrain and support the operation of the market claim that this will lower the cost of regulation. To rely upon laws that execute themselves, to dismantle or at least not further increase the bureaucracies that are now shifting paper from desk to desk, are seen as efforts guaranteeing a lower cost to regulation. One of the most seductive prospects for those who place their hope in self-executing regulatory mechanisms is the accomplishment of their ends on the cheap, at a cost comparatively low when placed alongside the expenditures required by the bureaucratic approach to attain the same goal.

They may be right in this regard. But it may never be possible to fully know whether reliance upon either bureaucracy or upon self-executing regulations is the cheaper alternative. Certainly the costs of bureaucracy comprise more than the salaries of the bureaucrats, the rents upon their offices, the bill for their stationery, or the interest paid on any capital projects they generate. In addition, there are the mirror-bureaucracies they stimulate in the production sector to fulfill their regulations, the investments that must be made to be in compliance, and the readjustments that must follow upon a change in policy as enunciated by the official bureaucracy. Public as are many of the charges which are stimulated by regulation through bureaucratic structures, the full cost of this approach for salvaging the environment, as it impacts upon society and the economy, is ultimately not calculable.

But there is at least an equal vagueness in trying to calculate the cost to the economy and society of self-executing regulations, that at first examination would seem to have little or no cost at all. Edward Banfield, using a non-regulatory and non-environmentally related example, has illustrated the scope, complexity, and perhaps final impossibility of the task of measuring the costs of self-executing actions undertaken in the market. In writing of the costs of self-service stores, he accepts the customer preference for them – the consumer casting his vote freely in the market, as praised by Milton Friedman – and the profits the owners draw from them because of lower labor costs and the ability to discount theft losses through insurance premiums and tax write-offs. But having accepted these market advantages, Banfield is much troubled over the costs transported onto society by these preferences of both vendors and vendees. Accepting these preferences as benefits to society, he wants to know if

...they are worth all the billions that they cost in the higher prices that must be charged to cover losses by theft, in the taxes that are required to support police forces, courts, and jails, and in the welfare payments to the dependents of persons who are in jail.... The consumer, it may be argued, has no right to have his convenience served when the serving of it entails, even indirectly, giving people incentives to do things that are against the law.[81]

The questions are not different when asked about the effect of some self-executing rules of law in raising costs to the general economy. Aside from the fact that some minimally sized officialdom is usually present in even self-executory regulations – as, for instance, the judiciary to enforce them if they should be breached – there is the larger problem of any indirect costs dispersed by them throughout the economy. An ironist, who has been sardonically amused by the efforts at energy conservation, has asserted that if conservation meant doing things which saved money as well as natural resources, and which imposed no added inconvenience in time or other intangibles, then everyone would act not only on the principle of conservation but upon all the details requisite to carrying that principle into effect.[82] The difficulty which bars such a peaceful solution is that it would call for a perfect knowledge of cost and effect. Though it is hard enough to reckon the savings environmental conservation can produce, this is simplicity itself in comparison with determining the addition or the diminution of inconveniences to be located by monitors throughout the whole of urban-industrial society.

Just as there is more to the cost of bureaucratic regulation than the wages of the bureaucrats,[83] so there is a good deal more to the cost of self-executing regulations than the paper on which they are printed. It has been said of an environmental standard that its technical bases should be sound, that the monitoring of pollutant levels permitted by the standard easy, and that it should correct existing inequities between those enjoying benefits and those absorbing costs from any particular production activity. If the environmental standard can do this it will find both social acceptability and effective enforcement. The problem of course in a real world that is "stochastic, probabilistic, non-linear, and variable"[84] is that drafting such a perfect standard just about defies human ingenuity. Predicting its costs, however self-executing its social acceptability might make it, seems well-nigh impossible.

Such difficulties should not deter those interested in environmental protection from using regulatory mechanisms other than the bureaucratic mode. The manipulation of the price structure, the institution of effluent charges, and the alteration of forms of production are among the techniques to be tried. What must be kept in mind, however, is that they, like the bureaucracy, have their costs, both hidden and known, and that they too shall have their regulatory failures.

Growth-Costs to the Environment and the Regulatory Response

Growth in production has been the basis of urban-industrial society since the inception of the Industrial Revolution in the middle of the 18th century.

Inevitably this growth in productive activity has impacted powerfully upon the environment. In the primary economic sectors, minerals are extracted, forests cut, and air, water, and the biomass affected as receiving bodies for production effluent. But even in the tertiary, and now quaternary, economic sectors, where consumers receive service and people act for the sake of action, the environment is as severely (if, perhaps, differently) affected. Multiple-terrain-vehicles and ski-runs in some areas may be as severely disturbing as a strip-mine; and masses of paving increase run-off whether part of a factory's unloading yard or the parking lot of a stadium.

The growth seemingly so essential to the survival of urban-industrial society has now entered its third century. Whether or not this growth has been geometric, as some claim, the increments of growth have become larger and larger. To a considerable degree they have been cumulative since, whether or not conditions have gotten steadily better and better, there never has been a return to a previous level of economic demand. The stability of the physical environment has had to be affected by the character of such a pattern of growth and demand made upon the environment and, in consequence, public demands to do something about it have been made with rising political force.[85]

The tendency of urban-industrial society has been to treat the environment as a source for production and profit through the resources supplied and the services rendered as a sink for any effluent the quest for production and profit desires to discharge into the renewing systems of air, water, and the biomass. The ability of these systems has been taken for granted to absorb this effluent and to recycle much of it back into the system as life-supportive. It seems scarcely possible mankind could ever have played down in their social consciousness the inherent worth of these natural systems. Yet, under the apparently superior requirements for urgent growth, this is precisely what has happened. The environment has been treated as if in infinite supply and of subordinate importance to every casual human demand which might be placed upon its interacting systems.[86]

Public opinion today requires that effective decisions be made to conserve the environment because the supply is not infinite and the environment's importance seems to be at least as important as the demands being made upon it by the primary through quaternary economic sectors of urban-industrial society. Parts of the environment may be nationalized or placed in the title of specially organized public authorities. The environment may be left in private or local hands and subjected to zoning or regulation. Each of these steps have been taken and none by their intrinsic institutional merit have served as an assured means to conserve or salvage those parts of the environment from abuse.[87] In the absence of a larger environmental commitment, each of these institutional devices has proven capable of serving as just another vehicle to abuse the environment further.

Some would solve the problem of accommodating human demand with the ability of the environment to respond viably to that demand by diminishing or ceasing that demand. William K. Reilly, president of the Conservation Foundation, has said,

A moment has begun...to curtail costly or stop urban growth, to see to it that planning powers are used not just to distribute and order development, but to turn it off.[88]

That may be the better, or possibly the only, course capable of achieving what needs to be done for the environment. However, when the recession that began in 1973 lowered the world rates of growth, there was scarcely an economy anywhere that thought this an intrinsically good event or that tried to intensify a further lessening in the rate of growth. As Richard Falk observed,

The unifying pursuit of all national economies at the present time, whether grounded in the ideology of the market or the state plan, is to keep the GNP growing as rapidly as possible, without sufficient concern for environmentally harmful forms of growth.[89]

Insofar as any fear of growth has been expressed, it has not come from worry over the environment but rather from anxiety that too rapid growth would reinforce the strength of inflation. The prospect is very slight that deliberately stopping or diminishing the rate of growth will be one response to the perception that the cost of such growth may be more than the environment can bear.

The response of the law, therefore, will be something other than a prohibition of growth in economic demand. It might be a shift to a steady-state economy espoused by many of those concerned with the environment, but even that is unlikely, whether one considers the policies and practices of either the developing or the developed economies of the world.[90] The legal process can hasten action through the procedural operations of legislators, administrators, and judges; but the law must derive the decision to stop, diminish, or redirect the rate of growth in economic demand from the larger culture outside the immediate confines of the legal system.[91]

As long ago as 1960, William Vogt made as a statement the now commonplace charge leveled by the Third World that the United States with only one sixteenth of the world's population was utilizing over half of the world's natural resources – and he called upon the United States to cut back upon that rate of demand.[92] In the interval, the United States has not moderated its demand upon the world's supply of natural resources but has increased that demand. If the ratio remains as claimed in 1960, it is not because the United States has become moderate in its demand but because the rest of the world have relatively increased their own demands upon the environment. In a finite universe this may prove tragic, but it has also certainly proven the common pattern for world behavior.

What has happened in response to public pressure to take action on behalf of the environment has been an effort at accommodation. This is what has been undertaken, at least, in those parts of the world where anything comparatively extensive in relation to past practice has been done for the environment – the United States and Canada, northwestern Europe, Japan, Australia, and, though less is known, possibly the Soviet Union and People's China. As for the rest of the world, many assert an intention to pollute until they are at the economic level of the industrially developed countries, others are indifferent, and others content themselves with serving the environment with rhetoric.

But as for those states who have acted to address the problem of the relationship between the environment and the demand for economic growth, their regulatory response has taken the form of trying to accommodate the environment to that demand. Mostly this has been through the creation of bureaucracies to monitor, to modify behavior in the production sector, and to forbid outright certain consequences, thereby indirectly affecting conduct. To a lesser extent, the response has been to change the rules of law so as to also indirectly change the harmful conduct. Though bureaucratic orders have the appearance of being directly allocative of resources, their effect has normally been as indirect as the influence of self-executing rules of law. But, in any event, there has been more talk about changing the rules of how property should be held in order to protect the environment than there has been any actual change in those rules of property. And in the meanwhile, the creation of the bureaucratic structures has gone on apace, whether or not they are more or less effective than different rules of property would be.

At the 1976 United Nations Conference on Human Settlements a resolution was passed denouncing the use of land as a commodity and demanding that it be managed as a public-resource rather than a profit-generator. Since land was defined there as a part of the environment, what the Conference said about land could apply, *pari passu*, to all of the natural environment upon which human activity rests. Although Barbara Ward described the resolution as recommending the public recovery of increased land values, the language seems broader than that in intent and potential purpose. The Conference, with the United States voting with the majority, resolved:

Land, because of its unique nature and the crucial role it plays in human settlement, cannot be treated as an ordinary asset, controlled by individuals and subject to the pressures and inefficiencies of the market.... Private land ownership...is a principal instrument of accumulation and concentration of wealth and therefore contributes to social injustice; if unchecked it may become a major obstacle in the planning and implementation of development schemes.[93]

If this language means what it says, then it dictates a value for land, and indirectly for the environment, that is very different from the role played traditionally under rules of property. Property is a bundle of rights in things determined by law; and this most certainly rearranges the sticks in the bundle. But it goes even further: it claims that even when title to land is publicly held it is not to be subject to the "pressures and inefficiencies of the market." The market is not to be permitted to be "a major obstacle in the planning and implementation of development schemes."

Given the language used, one might wonder if the environment itself is going to be allowed to be an obstacle to development schemes. But be that as it may, the resolution goes considerably beyond what such socialists as Oskar Lange, mentioned above, thought possible: the complete freedom of whatever is in public title from the pressures of the market. The resolution implicitly assumes that there are only inefficiencies in the market, that only socially evil consequences can flow from treating any part of the environment as a commodity for generating profit, and that private ownership of such resources can only be an obstacle to a publicly planned development scheme. Perhaps all that is true; but there seems considerable evidence the other way – and in any case, the shifting of ownership to public title, without further specificity and commitment, will mean little if anything to the improvement of environmental protection.

Of course, such a resolution may mean something as insignificant for the environment as that all natural resources shall be under an overarching public title which shall lease rights of use to private lessees. The private lessees shall then have the contractual concession of making the investments necessary for exploitation and collecting any profits above the costs of the operation, with the public title-holder charging either a rent or a royalty for extending the concession. There would be no freedom from the market here, though wealth accumulation and concentration could be very closely controlled; but, then, even if all the exploitation is done by public entity itself, complete freedom from some residuum of market influence seems a dream – unless by changing terms one regards one's dreams as having come true.

But attainable or not, such a resolution is the direct result of the impact of growth costs upon the environment. It is one sort of response in law with a self-executing change in the rules of property by a simple transfer to title from private persons to the public. Politically revolutionary though it may be, to the conveyancer it is just another shift in title which may or may not affect possession, depending upon the intentions of those transferring the property rights in the title. Once accomplished by legislative act, the problems still remain of how the subject-matter of the property interest is to be exploited, who is to do the actual work of exploitation, how the proceeds are to be allocated, what further investments of capital are to be made, and to what degree this exploitation is to be put into accommodation with the environment. Shifting title from private to public entities waves no magic wand so far as these matters are concerned.

There is, in fact, a close relationship between cultural values assigned to objects and institutions and the way in which the law organizes the rules of property providing for the legitimate power to exploit them. Concepts about property are cultural artifacts that determine what the law shall do about the rules of property. When the introduction of the growth-curves took place with the expansion of the Industrial Revolution and when they were perceived as impacting as heavily upon the environment as they have been perceived, the concepts of property inevitably altered. The rules of property changed accordingly.

At the very least, the public began to exercise a power to regulate property, which is to say to limit and to channel the activities of those having the property right. Beyond that, the public has increasingly taken over those property rights through eminent domain or controlled their exercise through the police power. Perhaps this is what Carla Hills, United States Secretary of Health, Education, and Welfare meant when she supported the United Nations resolution on curbing private ownership and said this was not inconsistent with established national practices in the United States. Incrementally speaking, it is only a series of small steps from public regulation to outright public ownership, however much it disarranges private fortunes.

There being no cessation in the growth of economic demand, the effect upon the environment will continue. The public no longer wants to take the risks of having its claims denied – or its rights revoked, depending upon how forcefully one views the public's position – by some private engrosser of any part of the environment. What the public has enjoyed from the scenic vista to open farmland they want to continue to enjoy wherever the title may be located. In return as the public makes these demands upon private owners, such private owners react with increasingly exclusive behavior to prevent the successful assertion of a prescriptive right in the public or overuse by a vandalizing public intruder. At the least, private owners want to cut off the rise in any public expectations concerning private rights to any part of the environment.[95] But in any event, out of this contest between public and private assertion concerning the environment, there must emerge changes in the rules of property.

The pounding increase in the demands of growth, the response of the environment to those demands, and the perceptions of the public as to what is happening to the environment will produce these changes in the legal rules. The public has become more sophisticated about the workings of natural ecological systems. It has learned that what occurs at one point in those systems is not limited to that area and may, eventually, have a far greater influence for change elsewhere in the system. There is public knowledge of negative external effects that transcend traditional property divisions.[96] This being the case and such cultural changes in public attitude having occurred, it would be odd indeed if the rules of property were not to change. They must, after all regulate the lawful behavior of the people who assert interests in what is affected by both the growth curves and the environment's response.

Such changes have taken place and further changes will occur. Whether they take the course outlined by the United Nations resolution cannot be certain. But that the changes will be major ones is assured. Why not? After all, the growth demands of urban-industrial society and the environment's response to them have represented massive change themselves. The rules of property will likely do no less.

Environmental Values and the Rules of Property

The value the environment displays to the members of any culture is a function of the role the rules of property play in that culture. Property, as has been said elsewhere, is the bundle of rights that may be applied to anything that the culture considers capable of having one or more of the asserted sticks in the bundle applied to it. Rights in themselves, of course, are intangible. They are modalities admitting or excluding persons from the culturally authorized assertion of power over something which the culture regards as having value.

Objects within the environment may be as uncertain to define as the magic inherent in an amulet or the shamen's medicine bag or a stock share in a mining company. They may also be as tangible as tons of milled flour waiting for customers. In most instances, however, what is called property partakes of both a solid presence and an insubstantial aura. It is the latter which the rules of property comprise since they are how the culture has decided who may do what with or to the thing that is to be measured or exchanged through the employment of the rules of property. However tangible the substances taken from the environment may be, whether minerals, lumber, or grain, or however hard to measure as in the case of the ability of the air or the biomass to serve as sinks for industrial effluents, they will partake of this mixed character when they are denominated property and are subjected to the rules of property imposed by the legal order of any culture.

There is no single part of the environment, however tangible its physical form, that is in every historically known culture capable of being property. Few parts of the physical environment are more tangible than land and what may be taken from it, grown upon it, or done over it. Yet this seemingly powerful and inescapable physical tangibility has not on its own dictated any universal, eternal cultural relationship between land or any of its uses and the rules of property. More than its physical presence has been required to make property out of land. It is, instead, the rules of property which have hit upon and delimited what anyone may do to include, to exclude, to invest, to harvest the products – some of them very intangible, indeed – human ingenuity has been able to extract from land

A tribe's hunting run or hunting territory is a primitive example of such a right in land that arises from a cultural assertion to take the game there as being the tribe's by right and exclude others from engaging in the same enterprise. Such assertions of legitimacy in relation to land can be as complex as the interests of the shareholders in a mortgagee of a California land warehouse. What both have in common, whether primitive or complex, is how cultural values derived from the land are asserted. In both instances, there is an assumption that the value in the land is best assured by asserting a kind of human control over it. What may be done to the land and what others can be prohibited from doing to that same tract during the time that control is asserted make up the rules of property. By this interaction between the environment, cultural determinations of value, and the adjective services of legal process, the rules of property are formed and developed as separate legal institutions.

The use of the term "rights" in any of these contexts does not mean one must subscribe to the existence of some natural order that determines how such "rights" are segregated and made legally substantive. The use of the word "rights" is regarded as culturally and not naturally determined. What is important to remember is that a culture through its legal process has authorized certain usages and allowed or forbidden behavior in relation to something in the environment to which previously the culture was probably indifferent. Once, however, something is called property, proof is offered that the culture is no longer indifferent to that something.

Even in the absence of that process of legal naming, some part of the environment may even so be vital to the culture's survival. Air is such an element in the environment to which even now in the most developed industrial societies it is hard to apply the term property. But once something *is* called property, the culture likely will cease to treat it as a common existence to be taken for granted. Rather, the usage of calling that something property will enable certain economic, social, or political occurrences to take place upon which the culture, through law, has conferred its own value independent of the matrix in the environment from which this right of property has been carved.[97]

This is not to claim that the rules of property are purely passive or reactive agents of the culture. It is to say only that they do not create themselves nor come into existence without purpose. Once created they begin to exert their own pressure upon the environment, to mold cultural expectations, and to elaborate themselves further as the result of their own operations. The rules of property can themselves be as much a cause of environmental harm as any other technological invention and can require change or abolition as absolutely as any method of extracting minerals, farming soil, or accumulating water.[98]

Yet specifying elements in the environment as constituting property, even while they remain in that environment, is ordinarily better for the maintenance of natural renewal systems than treating them as simply objects of potential property to be held as such only after they have been taken from a common pool. Leaving the environment or any of its constituents in a common pool means that the number of claimants for exploitation is difficult to limit and, worse, that no claimant has any incentive to do other than exploit as much as he can. When all is in a common pool, the claimant has no reason to leave anything for the morrow. He seizes all he can even if he exhausts the pool.

While items of potential property are in the common pool, they are in no one's ownership. The culture may concede some vague but effectively meaningless superiority in a divinity or in a public indifferent to the assertion of rights. What lies in the common pool under such conditions will be brought into the bundle of property rights either by an action cutting a single specimen out of a larger living unit or else exploiting the fruits or content of something that is not the subject of removal. The common pool becomes every one's resource and no one's property until individual or corporate action carves a property right from the common pool.

The rules of property undergo an acute alteration when the items in the common pool can be placed under a specific title without at the same time requiring their being severed. It means reducing the superiority of the common pool but it also means that items to be individually owned do not have to be broken out of the common pool and reduced to a segregated dominion. When land was part of the common pool, anyone could carry off booty from it and no one had any incentive in increasing fruitfulness. But when there could be a single ownership – whether clan, temple, individual, corporate, or commune – there was the authority of excluding others from the benefits of the tract owned and the incentive of maintaining what was owned so that the production of this particular tract might indefinitely sustain its owners and their successors in interest to this tract.

The rules of property define what property can do as a concept effecting natural systems. The greatest role of these rules is the specifying of what interests can be asserted by a specific claimant in what before was an item in the common pool open to everyone's claim. Putting these parts of the environment into a particular entitlement makes it possible to specify the resource. And specification means it becomes possible to determine costs and benefits to both human demand and environmental need, to fix what are externalities and what are internal to the use of the particular portion of the environment under the entitlement, and to separate this part of the environment from what remains in the common pool.

This does not mean that everything in the environment is capable of being brought into a particular entitlement or that doing so would be a sufficient action to protect environmental values.[99] Ocean and air are close to impossible to bring under particular entitlements and the examples of brutal resource destruction by those having particular entitlements – cutting timber, overgrazing, soil destruction through wasteful soil practices – prove that particular entitlements are by themselves not enough. There are other incentives operating in a culture, such as prices, credit availability, or even something as insubstantial as belief in a future that will be productive to the individual resource user, which can be more important than the rules of property.[100] Yet, powerful as these are, often as particular entitlements have failed to protect the environment, substantial as the parts of the environment are which cannot be brought into particular entitlements, the environment is better served by the rules of property that recognize particular entitlements and, hence resource specificity, than it would be by any extension of or return to the common pool.

Private property is not the only form which serves this purpose. Any particular entitlement can perform the functions of resource specificity. Only if there is a deliberate merger into an undifferentiated public of the environment will public entitlements not serve the purpose as well as private property. Because it is easy for public ownership to slip into this undifferentiated state, there must be a rigorous concentration on the functions the public ownership is to perform out of the portion of the environment held in public title. When this assertion of an effective public property interest in the fruits or contents of the environment has been made, the danger of slipping back into the undifferentiated common pool is minimized.

Items in the environment, once claimed by particular entitlement from the common pool, have a tendency not to remit to it in any form. Only when the culture has collapsed that had made them specific objects of property in an unsevered condition has there been such a relapse. Barring such a collapse, it is a one-way operation. The title may be shifted from a private person or a religious institution to a social trust, but the object of the title is not allowed to slip back into the common pool.

This is especially true for any benefits to be derived from a property scheme. Benefits are rarely orphans. It is the costs external to the specific use of any portion of the environment that lack claimants. No one wants specific responsibility for them and shunting them aside on other parts of the environment, particularly those still in the common pool, is still sought. Benefits are not often without specific owners. The costs are those the benefit-holders seek orphaned. Compelling them to internalize these costs into the system that produced the benefits is now the greatest task of the rules of property.

The value the environment has to urban-industrial society is the result of the demands that society has put upon nature. So great have they been that now there are few to claim nature provides free goods at human demand. The rules of property have served both to permit the making of those demands and to prevent those demands from wrecking worse damage than they have. It is also the condition of the rules of property that they can be shifted to greatly further the values of environmental protection. How the rules of property are employed depends in part upon their own form and in part on what values their larger culture expects from the environment.[101]

The Values Conferred by Regulation on the Environment

The relation of the activity of law and government to the environment is not one of burden only. Not only do the actions of government go far in determining the value which property will have in the market, they also influence the ability of the environment to support that value. Without the role of law and government, the prospects would be very strong that the burden of human demand upon the environment would be even greater. To concentrate only upon the deficiencies of bureaucracy and law in protecting the environment overlooks the possibility that their absence need not enhance environmental conditions.

The value property has in the market, for instance, is not the consequence of market action alone. Rather, in part, this value depends upon how government assists in absorbing certain costs that property imposes socially onto the general fund, of distributing those costs to others than those benefited by the property, or directing away from nature the costs of turning some item of the environment into a unit of property. Without the operation of the government, the market would have to account for all of these costs. They would then constitute negative spillover effects in their purer form.

The government can, unfortunately, reinforce the desire of a property owner to direct onto the environment the costs imposed by the way he uses his property. But in the absence of government, it would be the odd property owner who did not automatically do so. The government not only serves as a reinforcement for traditional urban-industrial practices when it supplies the infrastructure of facilities required to keep alive the modern system of extended cities and economic growth demand, it can also serve as the means to modify the effect of that demand. By employing the general fund to absorb many of the costs that particular entitlements impose, the government by this single act does much to benefit the environment even though it might better serve the environment by more specific funding for defraying these environmental burdens.

The general fund is often the means by which politicians do magic. It is as important as any other governmental device for conferring economic value upon items converted from the environment into units of property. After all, the government like business is pressured to lose costs. For government, this means the subsidization of some particular activity by paying their charges out of the general fund or else by granting tax exemptions, deductions, or rebates that become revenues never paid into the general fund.[101] In the general fund, reserves are merged and allocations become hard to deny since no focus exists by which their justification can be measured.

All sorts of costs, therefore, that no longer can be satisfied by treating the environment as a free good, are transferred over to the general fund and charged off upon an undifferentiated public fisc. It is an easy exercise in affability by accommodating politicians. The fact that it is skewed in the direction of benefiting certain property uses at the larger expense of everyone else is kindly passed over in the obscurity of what is general rather than specific.

The role of government and law is a major one in determining where environmental costs are to fall in the economy. Whether or not any of the portions of the environment placed under particular entitlements are in private hands, this power of government and law remains. Private property may be as large as a corporate fee simple absolute, or as limited as the emphyteutic leases demised in a socialist society, yet government in either instance is the major determiner of value in what is held. Even in a totally *laissez faire* economic system, it is the legal framework supplied by law and government – set up and maintained at the expense of the public at large – which is the institutional infrastructure fundamental to the working of the whole process of freedom and free choice that are offered as the justification of a market-controlled economy.[102]

The actions of government in furthering the course of some economic demand upon the environment are easy to treat as equivalent to some force in nature. But legal processes are still the product of human intention and as a means of furthering the purposes of the culture's dominant socio-economic structure. Whatever legal process does in connection with the environment, therefore, merely reflects and carries through the culturally agreed upon rules of property relating to the environment.

Traditionally the rules of property have provided a means to conceal the costs to the environment of the demands of the economy. By dividing up uses and interests to serve the economic or political advantages of those who benefit from the property rules, these rules have furnished ideational devices with high utility for those served by them. Many of these devices have avoided in human practice the recognition of the environment's essential unity in energy budgets, in the interrelatedness in nature of ecosystems and their resources, and in the comprehensive response natural systems make to the heavy demands of urban-industrial society. For purposes of rapidly advancing the exploitation of the environment for the society's profit, none could fault the usefulness of many of the existing rules of property.

But it is not enough to stop there. Even as the rules of property have furthered the processing of the environment into both cash flow and the transitory goods and services of a society whose affluence seems independent of any source in nature, the rules of property by their specifying function have served as a moderating drag upon the extent these demands could impact upon the environment. The insistence of urban-industrial society in resorting to high energy acquisitions and manipulations, the hope that ever larger energy cascades could restore all the previous imbalances between these same energy demands and the environment, have produced a wasting and spoilage of items in the environment that far exceeds the costs that can be laid to the operations of the rules of property.[103]

Increasingly, though, people perceive that the rules of property are not static and that they can serve to reach a condition closer to balancing economic demand and the environment's ability to cope with it. Some insist that only a total reconsideration is worthwhile and others are more modest in their suggestion of change.[104] Some see the role of law to be the government's provision of a specialized and centralized bureaucracy "geared to the speed of a mass-production line".[105] Others think the better approach lies in the alteration of the rules of property under which any part of the environment is exploited.

For these last, there is a suspicion of the efficacy of any bureaucratic allocation of resources. They do not have much faith in an administrative discretion responding to the environmental conditions of a particular time and place and issuing orders as to how the users of the environment are to behave at that time and that place. They are even doubtful about how effectively the bureaucrats will administer any plans for dealing with shortages and other environmental emergencies. The bureaucrats will rather use these crises to squeeze out the specific economic users in order to increase the undifferentiated power of the bureaucracy over the environment and the economy alike, as exponents of reliance upon changed property rules see it.[106] They are well aware that values and value reallocations come through the operations of law and government; and they have less trust in direct exercise of administrative discretion than in the indirect procedures of the market and the rules of property to protect the environment over the long run.

What must be remembered is that law and government cannot be neutral in the symbiosis of urban-industrial demand and environmental response. Law and government will effect both, whatever primary emphasis is consciously adopted by the legal system. But the stress can be consciously exerted to either side. Should no conscious decision be taken, the drift of urban-industrial society is such that law and government will be employed to back demand rather than to enhance the environmental response, much less to protect the environment directly. Regulation, under such conditions, will be used, for example, to alter the hydrologic cycle and to ease the human forgetfulness that – whatever alterations should be made in the hydrological balance – it will ultimately balance again, regardless of the catastrophes it may impose upon the human operations which had interrupted it.[107] What is needed, instead, are regulatory processes that will bring into full consciousness how dependent human culture is upon the planet's life-support systems and which will strengthen and not further weaken them.[108]

Law and government increasingly set the constraints determining the cash value of objects of property and they increasingly affect the potential of the environment to support those values. These are inescapable responsibilities however much they may be abused or incompetently served. Far from there being any chance to turn away, law and government must be urged to recognize the role they play in the determination of both environmental and property values. Denial of this responsibility will produce a confused allocation of values, most likely exceedingly harmful to the environment under current demand conditions. If there is to be any balance between the environment and human demand, the conscious articulation of this power of value formation, modification, and allocation through both bureaucratic regulation and the formulations of the rules of property must occur.

Notes

[1] Frank Trelease, *Cases and Materials on Water Law*, 2nd ed., St. Paul: West, 1974, p. XII. "The word 'environment' had not then assumed its present meaning, yet.... 1964 materials contained the seeds of environmental law."

[2] Barbara Ward, "The Triple Crisis," RIBA *Journal*, December 1974, p. 13. "First the natural environment was discussed. Now it is the turn of man's built environment." *Id.*, p. 14.

[3] E.g., Ted Morgan, "Looking for Epoch B," *New York Times Magazine*, February 29, 1976, p. 33.

[4] W. S. Comanor and B. W. Mitchell, "The Costs of Planning: The FCC and Cable Television," 15 *J. of Law and Econ.* (1972) 177, at p. 185.

[5] Murray L. Weidenbaum, "Regulation or Over-Regulation?," *Wall St. Journal*, April 6, 1976.

[6] E.g., R. A. Kessel, "Higher Education and the Nation's Health," 15 *J. of Law and Econ.* (1972) 115, at pp. 118–119.

[7] Marc J. Roberts, "River Basin Authorities: A National Solution to Water Pollution," 83 *Harvard L. R.* (1970) 1527, at p. 1555.

[8] *Ibid.*

[9] L. L. Roos and Noralou Roos, "Pollution, Regulation, and Evaluation," 6 *Law and Society Rev.* (1972) 509, at p. 513, pp. 521–524.

[10] Walter Goldschmidt, *Man's Way: A Preface to the Understanding of Human Society*, (1959), pp. 110–111.

[11] Peter N. Davis, "Theories of Water Pollution Litigation," *Wisconsin L.R.* (1971) 738, at p. 780.

[12] *Ibid.*, at pp. 777–779. On shoreland ownership of the Wisconsin river, *id.*, pp. 810–816. On problems of "comparative convenience" or "balancing the equities" under Wisconsin law, *id.*, pp. 762–768.

[13] Lettie M. Wenner, "Enforcement of Water Pollution Control Law," 6 *Law and Society Rev.* (1972) 481, at p. 490.

[14] *Ibid.*, pp. 493–494.

[15] *Ibid.*, p. 487, p. 495, p. 503.

[16] Comanor and Mitchell, *op. cit.*, 178–179.

[17] Roberts, *op. cit.*, 1542 note.

[18] *Ibid.*, 1551 note and, e.g., Dan Salcedo and Arden Weiss, "Solution of a Water Resources Problem with Economies of Scale." 8 *Water Resources Bull.* (1972) 546.

[19] Sedway/Cooke for the Planning and Conservation Foundation, *Land and the Environment: Planning in California Today*, Los Altos: William Kaufman, Inc., 1975, p. 130.

[20] Letter of O. W. Holmes to H. J. Laski, February 28, 1919, *Holmes–Laski Correspondence*, vol. I, pp. 187–188.

[21] Irving Kristol, "The Future in the Past," in *Future Land Use: Energy, Environmental and Legal Constraints*, Robert W. Burchell and David Listokin, eds., New Brunswick: Center for Urban Policy Research, Rutgers University, 1975, at p. 345.

[22] Robert H. Freilich, "A Reply," in *ibid.*, p. 137. Mr. Freilich was the author of the Ramopo plan.

[23] John Graham, "Reflections of a Planning Failure," in *Managing the Water Environment*, Neil A. Swainson, ed., Vancouver: University of British Columbia Press with the Wastewater Research Center, 1976, at p. 99 and p. 101.

[24] William K. Reilly, "Managed Growth in Concept and Reality," in *Future Land Use, op. cit.*, at p. 118.

[25] Richard A. Falk, *A Study of Future Worlds*, Intro. by Saul Mendlovitz, New York: Free Press, 1975, p. 51.

[26] *Ibid.*, p. 30, note.

[27] E.g., George Sternlieb, "The Future is a Different Unity States," in *Future Land Use, op. cit.*, at p. 355.

[28] John Friedmann, "The Future of Comprehensive Urban Planning: a Critique," in *Public Planning and Control of Urban and Land Development*, Donald G. Hagman, ed., St. Paul: West & Co., 1973, at p. 172 and pp. 174–175.

[29] Graham, *op. cit.*, p. 107.

[30] *Ibid.*, pp. 113–114.

[31] Edwin T. Haefele, "Representative Government and Environmental Management," in *ibid.*, at p. 119.

[32] Ward v. Ackroyd (D.C., Md., 1972) 4 ERC 1209, at p. 1225.

[33] Haefele, *loc. cit.* His recommendation for avoiding this is representative, elected, regional governments made up of general purpose representatives, *id.*, p. 128.

[34] Friedmann, *op. cit.*, at pp. 171–172.

[35] *Ibid.*, at p. 174, p. 176.

[36] Herman Kahn, William Brown, Leon Martel with the Hudson Institute, *The Next 200 years: A Scenario for America and the World*, New York: William Morrow & Co., 1976, pp. 196–197. See also p. 202.

[37] Erik P. Eckholm for the Worldwatch Institute, *Losing Ground: Environmental Stress and World Food Prospects*, New York: W. W. Norton & Co., 1976, p. 175.

[38] Falk, *op. cit.*, pp. 46–47.

[39] *Ibid.*, pp. 268–269.

[40] Eckholm, *op. cit.*, p. 177.

[41] Eugene Bardach, "Save Energy, Save a Soul," *Commentary*, vol. 61, no. 5 (May 1976), p. 54, at p. 57.

[42] René Dubos, "The Despairing Optimist," *The American Scholar*, vol. 45, no. 2 (Spring 1976), p. 168, at p. 171.

[43] Robert G. Healy, *Land Use and the States*, Baltimore: The Johns Hopkins Press for Resources for the Future, 1976, p. ix.

[44] Vincent Ostrom, Charles M. Tiebout, and Robert Warren, "The Organization of Government in Metropolitan Areas: A Theoretical Inquiry," *Am. Pol. Sci. Rev.*, vol. 55, no. 4 (December 1961) 837, quoted in *id.*, p. 13.

[45] D. A. Downey, "The Role of Water and Sewer Extension Financing in Guiding Urban Residential Growth," Report No. 19, Water Resources Research Center, University of Tennessee (1973), quoted in *New Developments in Land and Environmental Controls*, D. M. Mandelker, ed., Indianapolis: Bobbs-Merrill, 1974, at p. 190. Downey qualifies this slightly by asserting "...the validity of this generalization varies from service to service."

[46] Ludwig von Mises, *Bureaucracy*, New Haven: Yale University Press (2nd ed.) 1962, p. 47.

[47] Healy, *op. cit.*, compare p. 25 and p. 191.

[48] Kahn, *et al.*, *op. cit.*, p. 50.

[49] *Ibid.*, p. 137.

[50] Ragnar Frisch, *Planning for India*, London: Asia Publishing House, 1960, pp. 1–2, quoted in John W. Mellor, *The New Economics of Growth: A Strategy for India and the Developing World*, a Twentieth Century Fund Study, Ithaca, Cornell University Press, 1976, p. 275 note.

[51] Mellor, *op. cit.*, pp. 147–150.

[52] Friedmann, *op. cit.*, p. 172.

[53]   Healy, *op. cit.*, pp. 4–5.
[54]   *Ibid.*, p. 6.
[55]   Mellor, *op. cit.*, p. 279.
[56]   Goldschmidt, *op. cit.*, pp. 112–113, p. 149.
[57]   See *id.*, pp. 113–114, p. 146.
[58]   *Ibid.*, p. 175.
[59]   Kahn, *op. cit.*, p. 205.
[60]   See F. L. Lucas, *The Greatest Problem and Other Essays.* New York: The MacMillan Co., 1961, p. 323 for a criticism of modern "conurbanized man" to turn to "specialized and centralized bureaucracy" in a situation "geared to the speed of a mass-production line."
[61]   This seems true despite such optimistic proposals as those of such a noted environmentalist as Jacob H. Beuscher, "An Ideal Natural Resources Law Future 1980," a 1965 address recounted in Fran Thomas, *Law in Action: The Work of Professor Jacob H. Beuscher*, Madison: Law Economics Monograph No. 4, 1972, pp. 80–84.
[62]   Earl Finbar Murphy, *Water Purity, A Study in Legal Control of Natural Resources*, Madison: University of Wisconsin Press, 1961, p. 49.
[63]   Bardach, *op. cit.*, pp. 57–59.
[64]   This is certainly asserted for the humanly constructed environment of urban-industrial society, Edward C. Banfield, *The Unheavenly City: The Nature and the Future of Our Urban Crisis*, Boston: Little, Brown and Co., 1970, "Introduction" and "Prospect."
[65]   Falk, *op. cit.*, pp. 268–269. Of course those means have been severely criticized, see Irving Kristol, "The New Cold War," *Wall Street Journal*, July 17, 1975, p. 18.
[66]   Banfield, *op. cit.*, pp. 21–22.
[67]   See Kristol, *loc. cit.*
[68]   In 1974 less than one half of one per cent of the United States federal tax dollar was spent on the environment and the conservation of natural resources, Sylvia Porter, "How Government Spends its Money," *Columbus Citizens-Journal*, February 5, 1975, quoting Dr. Elsie Watters of the Tax Foundation.
[69]   United States Environmental Protection Administration, Municipal Construction Division, Pub. WH 447 and BNA *Environmental Reporter*, September 6, 1974, p. 649.
[70]   *Potomac Basin Reporter*, vol. 30, no. 10, (October 1974), p. 2, quoting Robert Perry, deputy director, District of Columbia Environmental Services Administration.
[71]   James J. Needham, "No More Exchange – So what?" *Wall Street Journal*, November 27, 1974. In the summary of items he claims will require $3.5 trillion of additional investment by 1985, he does not enumerate environmental protection. Of course, it may be embraced under one of his general headings. Mr. Needham was then president of the New York Stock Exchange.
[72]   See Homer Page, "Environmental Coalitions: Here to Stay?" Conservation Foundation *Letter* (October 1974).
[73]   Ivan Illich, *Tools for Conviviality*, World Perspective Series, Ruth Nanda Anshen, ed., New York: Harper & Row, 1973, p. 51.
[74]   For a measure of how heavy the demands can be, see Hugo Osvald, *The Earth Can Feed Us*, Intro. by Lord Boyd-Orr, tr. by B. Nesfield-Cookson, South Brunswick, N.J., A. G. Barnes & Co., 1966.
[75]   Mellor, *op. cit.*, compare p. 270 with p. 147.
[76]   *Ibid.*, p. 270.
[77]   Kahn *et al.*, *op. cit.*, p. 205.
[78]   Roberts, *op. cit.*, p. 1545.
[79]   Milton Friedman, "Capitalism and Freedom," in *Economic Foundations of Property Law*, Bruce A. Ackerman, ed., Boston: Little, Brown & Co., 1975, 77 at p. 81.
[80]   Oskar Lange and Fred M. Taylor, "On the Economic Theory of Socialism," in *id.*, 69–75.

[81] Banfield, *op. cit.*, pp. 181–182.

[82] Bardach, *op. cit.*, pp, 54–55.

[83] This is not to minimize their cost. In the United States, the increase between 1950–1975 in the income of government employees is impressive in comparison with the increase for persons employed in the private sector, John O'Riley, "The Outlook," *Wall Street Journal*, June 14, 1976.

[84] Robert P. Ouelette, "The Saga of the Environmental Standard," *Chemtech* (September 1974) 529. The basic requirements of an environmental standard are at p. 530.

[85] Healy, *op. cit.*, p. 25.

[86] For example, consider the environmental consequences of "low-cost" low density urban sprawl relative to more compact urban development. *The Costs of Sprawl* (October 1974), Real Estate Research Corp. for the United States Environmental Protection Administration, Council of Environmental Quality, and Department of Housing and Urban Development.

[87] For example, see Horacio Caminos, Reinhard Goethert, and Tara Chana, "The Urban Land Crisis," *Ekistics*, vol. 38, whole no. 227 (October 1974), pp. 291–296.

[88] William K. Reilly, "National Land Use Policy," in *Federal Environmental Law*, Erica Dolgin and T. G. P. Guilbert, eds., St. Paul: West Pub. Co., 1974, at p. 142.

[89] Falk, *op. cit.*, p. 46.

[90] Compare the First Club of Rome Report, Donella and Dennis Meadows, Jorgon Randers, and W. W. Behrens III, *The Limits of Growth*, New York: Universe Books, 1972, with the Second Club of Rome Report, Michajlo Mesarovic and Eduard Postel, *Mankind at the Turning Point*, New York: E. P. Dutton, 1974.

[91] Some see law, however, as playing a much larger role than this, David Loth and Morris L. Ernst, *The Taming of Technology*, New York: Simon and Schuster, 1972.

[92] William Vogt, *People! Challenge to Survival*, New York: William Sloane Associates, 1960, p. 233.

[93] See Gladwin Hill, "U.N. Meeting Urges Curb on Private Land Holding," *New York Times*, June 12, 1976.

[94] *Ibid.*

[95] *Healy, op. cit.*, p. 4, p. 30, p. 34.

[96] *Ibid.*, p. 4.

[97] Myres Smith McDougal, *Municipal Land Policy and Control*, New York: PLI for the AALS, 1946, pp. 12–16.

[98] William Irwin Thompson has said of culture's relationship to the environment, "...our consciousness of nature is a real event in the 'history of nature'.... The 'feedback' of consciousness to nature is called culture; when culture reaches a certain point in the 'negative feedback loop,' it can destroy nature. We can see this effect in the earth's ecosystem, for our culture is changing the earth's atmosphere and weather," *Passages about Earth: An Exploration of the New Planetary Culture*, New York: Harper & Row, 1974, p. 93.

[99] Kenneth E. F. Watts, *Ecology and Resource Management*, New York: McGraw Hill Book Co., 1968, p. 69, illustrates these points.

[100] Eckholm, *op. cit.*, pp. 171–172. "Confidence in the personal benefits from land-improvement investments greatly increases the likelihood of such investments. Where the tenants are insecure,...guardianship of the long-term quality of land can scarcely be expected."

[101] Malcolm Feeley in defining "facilitative" law in comparison with "command" law says: "...increasing the liability of a manufacturer for...safety...may produce...and facilitate claims..., but the general effect may be to alter the price of goods, to stimulate the use of substitutes, to improve quality control in the industry, and perhaps even to cause the collapse of the industry.... [L]aw...[is] an elaborate and subtle pricing mechanism which cannot only flatly prohibit or expressly require, but can also supplement and shape

natural systems of exchange and interaction by slightly adjusting the costs of an activity...
by altering supply, demand, opportunity, alternatives, transactive costs, etc.... Its main
control effects are not to the occasional...challenges..., but rather the great bulk of the
instances when people accept it and alter their behavior accordingly." M. M. Feeley,
"The Concept of Laws," 10 *Law and Society Review* (1976), 497, at p. 518.

[102]   Torstein Eckhoff, *Justice: Its Determinants in Social Interaction*, Rotterdam:
Rotterdam University Press, 1974, pp. 75–76. Thus it is claimed that, "...before the
public can effectively participate in planning, the government must participate," Thomas
Graff, "State Intervention in the Energy Planning Process," in *Energy Conservation and
the Law*, Proceedings of the Annual Nat. Conf. on the Environment, April 30–May 1,
1976, American Bar Association Standing Committee on Environmental Law, p. 86.

[103]   Ivan Illich, *Energy and Equity*, New York: Harper & Row, 1974 interrelates the
environmental impact of both the energy demand and the traditional law dividing property.

[104]   *Legalized Pollution*, The Report of the Brisbane Public Interest Research Group. St.
Lucia: University of Queensland Press, 1973; *The International Law of Pollution*, James
Barros, and D. M. Johnson, eds., New York: The Free Press, 1974.

[105]   F. L. Lucas, *The Greatest Problems and Other Essays*, New York: The MacMillan
Co., 1961, p. 323, who criticizes this approach.

[106]   Frank Trelease, "The Model Water Code, the Wise Administrator, and the Goddam
Bureaucrat," quoted in Trelease, *op. cit.*, p. 434.

[107]   K. Achuthan, "Man on the Hydrologic Cycle," *Water Resources Bulletin*, vol. 10,
no. 4 (August 1974), pp. 756–758.

[108]   Andre Missenard, *In Search of Man*, tr. by Laurence G. Blockman, New York:
Hawthorn Books, 1957, pp. 168–173, summarizing ideas of Alexis Carrel.

The Importance of Environmental Renewability to Regulation

The Relation of Renewability and Non-Renewability in the Environment

The renewing environment cannot be dealt with by law and government in the same way they handle the non-renewing elements. After all, the renewing environment continuously maintains a returning flow easily noted in terms of human time. While it is true that everything in nature is in motion and in the process of formation and reformation, for the non-renewing environment this occurs over time periods that have little meaning in relation to the mortal spans of man. For the non-renewable environment, significance to human action lies in its quality of exhaustibility by and for human exploitation. Incredible quantities of time were required to form the hydrocarbons, for example, and very little time has been required to draw down their stock. While nature is in the same process of renewing them, to some degree, the rate of formation can mean very little to the human beings so rapidly using up what is now available.

The renewable resources, on the other hand, can be perceived to replace themselves in such a way that human beings can anticipate the action. The wind and rain clean the air of pollutants – or displace and deposit them – and produce fresh air in their place. The flowing waters renew water-bodies at longer or shorter intervals, so that considerable human waste can be cast into them without affecting their internal processes. The grass can be grazed; the animals can be hunted; the fish can be caught – all with the possibility that more will come where the harvest has been taken. Regulation ought not to deal with the renewable and non-renewable environment alike.

Man can expect to exhaust many of the stocks of the non-renewable environment. Conversely, he can anticipate that the renewable forces in nature should maintain their powers. Those that renew through the life process will be replaced by birth and germination and other life-reproducing systems. Those that relate to water and air will be replenished through the actions of the hydrologic cycle and the rush of the jet streams. The fixed stores of minerals, fossil fuels, and such non-replenishable materials shall someday likely fail; but – so goes the myth – what is renewing in nature shall go on forever.

That, of course, is the myth. Perhaps the stock resources will soon be drawn down and lost in precipitous exploitation. But perhaps they can be subjected to recycling, so that the mines of the future will be in the stored materials of past exploitations. At any rate, however grave the crisis, it would not be over-optimistic to foresee that there would exist some chance at choice should some stock resources even simultaneously fail under the pressure of human demand. No one would minimize the extinction of the fossil fuels under the conditions of demand imposed by high energy culture, certainly. And, yet, even if such an extinction should occur abruptly, it could be of far less significance than some interruption to the renewing function of the air, the water, the biomass, or the life support systems in nature.

The dependency of all life upon these renewing resources is absolute. Should they be interrupted in any serious and long-term way, life would either be lost upon the planet or profoundly altered in its character. If, for example, something should destroy the globe's quantity of oxygen, it would mean little to oxygen-dependent organisms that entities could still support life on the planet Earth by drawing upon supplies of methane.

The assumption, once so easily made, that the renewing environment could be taken for granted, no longer possesses a sufficient base in fact. Fears began in the 19th century, under the pressure of industrialism's rising material demands, that the greatest menace to urban-industrial society lay in the possible exhaustion of stocks in the non-renewing environment. These fears, more pressingly, must now be joined by the graver fear that the renewing environment is under a threat posing a more serious challenge.

Steadily, as the 20th century has unfolded its demands for and its devotion to growth, the pressure has increased to protect life-support systems and the renewing forces in nature from the effects of these demands. Treaties have been signed to protect migratory birds and fish. Animal preserves have been set up. Forests have been sealed off from exploitation or replanted. A wide range of permit and tax structures have been instituted.

Indeed, the list of actions taken could be continued to a great length. The enforcers of those actions have been the regulatory mechanisms formed for this purpose. The result has been an intimate relationship between regulation by government and law on the one side, and the renewing aspects within nature on the other.

The Burden and the Hope of Environmental Regulations

Regulation has been the means whereby humanity seeks to restrain themselves and to give greater form to what demand does to the renewing resources in prohibiting or modifying urban-industrial exploitation. The regulatory tools bring the past into connection with the future, tying technology to both the servicing of human demand and the preservation of natural systems. They effectuate whatever values social decision-making has rated of sufficient importance to deserve carrying out on a public scale. Regulatory actions may often have been decried; but increasingly, it is the regulatory mechanism which humanity turns to in their felt need to shape what is done to nature.

Technology, like the realm of pure ideation, forgets nothing, once it is widely earned. Ideational and technical knowledge for humanity are as permanent as biology or the physical elements in nature. Such knowledge comprises the base provided by the past with which man builds from one rapid transition to another. The simplest bits of information may be the foundations of far more complex stages of thought and technique. Little is ever forgotten culturally; and this total memory is particularly true for the sophisticated information systems of high energy culture. Out of this memory bank, urban-industrial society both preserves and chooses from among the ideational and technical inheritances which can then be employed for what the managers of that society regard as its best interests.

Every institution, habit, and form of thought is in some way joined with high energy culture today. There may be a transformation present but nothing will have been lost, forgotten, or even in peril of a real disappearance. The ideational and technical inheritance is always present for the use of the future, capable of continuously shortening the time and the complexity of action. Out of this cumulative consciousness comes the rapid evolution of human thought in the transient movements from age to age.

They constitute a highly usable inheritance that has the capacity to mobilize the knowledge within nature concerning biological and physical control for human purposes. Through the ideational and technical knowledge accumulated, high energy culture acquires the power to discriminately select its preferences from both human knowledge and the facts within nature which such knowledge acts to release. The result is a powerful bind between the accumulated knowledge of mankind and the operation of natural systems that provides its own function of homogenizing both society and nature into new units. Such a force for homogenization becomes its own self-isolating, self-strengthening process.

It is, consequently, a process that looks within itself for salvation and perceives the application of ideational and technical knowledge to nature as the means of preserving man's high energy demands upon natural systems.

There are, however, dangers inherent in such an accumulative system. The changes are becoming more rapid, more complex, and more retentive of what has gone before them. Whole cultural eras seem to pass before they can be fully formed. Instead, their unformed parts are broken up and blended into the new history that is being homogenized for remembrance. There is no longer the available leisure for a period having the length of other ages in history for cognitive and emotional consolidation. Even a generation has become too short to cover the activities of each big new era.

There is the distinct possibility that this time, which cannot have its own historic eras last so long as two decades, may be ushering in a protracted new Dark Age capable of lasting up to forever. The collapse which could occur might involve the wiping out of the ideational and technical memory that hitherto has been impossible. The even more significant risk is the loss of the world's biological inheritances. The loss or diminution of these could mean to mankind a defeat far greater than the destruction of human cultural forms. What could be gathering in this interface between human knowledge and natural systems is a reversal of history.

One cannot ignore such a possibility, even as greater and more intrusive regulatory mechanisms are raised to control the consequences of the demands being imposed upon the environment. A prolonged breakdown in the provision of what have become life-support systems for urban-industrial society could bring on a cultural crisis. Many claim to already have seen in the present urban situation the beginnings of such a crisis. They find tendencies toward the dissolution of the existing social order, a rejection of legal forms even as there is demand for government and law to take on still greater burdens, an abandonment of city cores, and a general preference for a release from responsibility as to the consequences flowing from what has been demanded.

For these critics, they see the future emerging clearly all around them and they insist it will not be the bureaucratic, rationalized, urban-industrial society that has become increasingly common in the past several generations. As a vision, their's is not one to be considered impossible of fulfilment.[1]

Indeed, urban-industrial society may be putting humanity into an apocalyptic stance. From that position, there may be no choice except a final struggle with the environment, with the life-support systems, and the force of life itself. The demands of urban-industrial man may have put present culture into an ecological war with the elements. But even if such should be the case, the time may not have passed for drawing back from such a struggle and regrouping for a very different kind of approach to nature by mankind.

Urban-industrial technology has imposed upon most of mankind "the imperative of the machine." Although the tools invented by humanity are extrusions of the human self, the tools that have been organized into high energy technology have taken on a role possessed of a dominating character. Humanity and the life support systems on the planet are connected to a technology capable of destroying them and demanding for its support the imposition of charges weighing heavily upon the nurturing elements in man's renewable sources. Increasingly, the technological extrusions of mankind are acting as determinants of human choice; and this is giving rise to a growing resistance to a continuance of such a development.

Yet, over history, technology, including the regulatory devices of government and law, has operated under a claim of bringing greater rationality into human affairs. So pervasive has been this asserted priority that a greater cultural value has more often been assigned technology than any part of the life-support process. After all, techniques such as the price structures and the rules of property are so clearly rational, whereas so much of the living environment seems irrational to man, that rationality seems to deserve the higher priority.

The life processes of the planet cannot be so subordinated, however. They are dynamic, never static, involved at every moment with the inheritances from all of the past. To exclude them and concentrate upon technology, in the name of rationality, will serve a "rationality proven unreasonable, pure reason become irrational."[2] The frames in time and space within which such a rationality is justified are simply too narrow to serve the purpose adequately.

The perception of this past narrowness of view, however, is becoming steadily clearer under the pressures of the environment's response to urban-industrial demands. As a result, more regulatory mechanisms, capable of functioning over longer periods of time and areas of space than previously had been thought necessary, are continuously being developed. This compels working with the life processes themselves, in a manner encouraging and preservative of the natural systems.

For the future success of regulations, vested interests of the narrowest kind must be subordinated among the regulatory mechanisms. So often regulation has been the servant of the most fragmenting elements within urban-industrial society. The result is that the potential role of the technology of regulations in the continuance of the life process cannot be sufficiently appreciated by critics. Like other technologies regulation is cumulative. Improvement as well as decay is possible; and its very rationality makes it subject to change.

Modern bureaucrats delight in quoting the famous observation of Marshall

McLuhan that "the medium is the message." They go beyond that and paraphrase it with the statement that "the process is the policy."[3] If by this they mean that the internal operations of regulatory mechanisms are a sufficient justification for the regulative existence, the time may well be running out on them. Persons who would find such justification for existence in the present world are likely to bring about the other prediction of McLuhan, namely the return to tribalism. To turn high energy culture, with its massive demands upon natural systems, into nothing more than the support for regulatory games would be a symptom of advanced decay and a means to only a negative solution for the world's problems.

But the man who said "the process is the policy" was Maurice Strong, the organizer of the Stockholm Conference on the Environment in 1972 and the head of the United Nations Environmental Program. His career has not shown him to be someone who hears and believes only what he wishes to hear and believe or to act as if man were without biophysical restraints on this planet. In borrowing a phrase from a fellow Canadian for paraphrase, Maurice Strong undoubtedly meant to justify regulation in terms of its own internal games plan. He meant that the mechanisms of government and law are now a necessary part of the natural environment. The demands imposed upon natural systems have reached such a degree that only a policy of responsibility can enable urban-industrial society to carry on its course of growth. Regulation is now part of the process of the world's life support systems. Henceforward, the policy for the regulatory mechanisms must be to mediate between human demand and nature's response.

Human Biological Preference, Regulation, and the Environment

As a part of the natural process for life-support, regulatory mechanisms inevitably carry the burden of human cultural bias. The social and natural implications of this must have the broadest consequences for both man and nature. Man has a biological inheritance; but he has for so long subordinated it to his cultural heritage that he perceives his biology only through his culture. René Dubos expresses this by saying,

Cultural forms imply creative acts through which the community as a whole, or individual persons, impose esthetic and social design on men, surroundings, and events.[4]

It is his contention, summarized by this statement, that man remains even under conditions of high energy cascades still a paleolithic hunter. His biological needs, emotional urges, and aspirations have the overlay of culture but beneath the overlay is biology which culture suppresses and, by that suppression, distorts.

It is the view of Dubos that one example of this interrelation between biology and culture is man's treatment of temperature. Man prefers a certain temperature, although human culture has done well at other degrees on the thermometer. Still, whatever the human capacity to accommodate, man has continuously sought, whenever possessed of the material means, the duplication of the climatic conditions of the semitropical savannahs in east Africa where the human species presumably emerged. The effort at simulation traditionally has been made in portions of the human dwelling units; but, as human abilities to heat and cool the air have increased through the growth of high energy cascades, the effort has been extended to far greater scales than a few square feet in a dwelling unit.

Culturally the preference contained within this biological inheritance could mean little until mankind had the technology and the energy cascades to heat or cool air to the biologically desired temperature. It was necessary to create the production-consumption patterns of urban-industrial society in order to provide the cultural ambience for serving a biological preference. Generally, the pressure has increased throughout the world to provide temperatures in buildings, winter and summer, that conform to the human biological determination of what is a comfortable temperature.

It is true that primitive man experienced in his naked state seasonal and diurnal fluctuations in temperature throughout his evolutionary development. The migrations brought human beings into climates of extreme contrast and severity, thereby often putting great stress on humanity's ability to survive. It would be ignorance to deny that man is capable of surviving in any climate the planet has to offer and adapting culturally to that climate. Mankind has the ability to compel their biological inheritance to an accommodation with the climate. Yet it would be equal ignorance to deny that mankind seems to prefer a year-round temperature of about 72 degrees Fahrenheit; and whenever possible, technical ingenuity and cultural decision will be exercised to duplicate that temperature for some space, some of the time, for some of the people.

The urbane sophisticate of ancient Rome had his hypocausts and ventilation tunnels. Modern man has his central heating and air-conditioning. In both the ancient Roman and the modern resident of high energy culture there survived the paleolithic animal who was most comfortable ranging over his environment at the equivalent of the modern "standard" setting of 72 degrees Fahrenheit.[5] Statesmen can urge that the "standard" be lowered to

68 degrees. English aristocrats may have once considered a room "warm" at 60 degrees.[6] But these represent either political decisions or acculturations to which history offers ample evidence that man has always had the power to adjust.

Man can learn to not only bear almost any climatic condition. He can do even more: he can exalt everything from goosebumps to chilblains as his preference and moral justification. But when culture or politics fail to block the biological choice, the human option for temperature lies in the low 70's on the Fahrenheit thermometer.

High energy supplies made it possible to indulge one item chosen from the biologic inheritance of humanity. A technology and an ordering of the economy were encouraged that made such an indulgence a possibility. Previously to high energy culture, this biologic preference was of little significance to either the human economy or the natural environment. Aside from a few wealthy Romans, most of mankind shivered in the winter and sweated in the summer. But with the arrival of both a technical ability and a social decision to act, a biological preference could be triggered in the psyche and economic activities would become possible under climatic conditions that had such actions previously rendered undoable. First, central heat made winter a sometime plaything, with a whole industry built around the heated ski lodge with its roaring fires and never-failing hot showers. Instead of being a fearsome season, it became a toy for lyricists of popular tunes. Then, air-conditioning followed. The heat waves of summer were exchanged for autumn's chill with the swing of a revolving door.

Since the 1920's the energy of urban-industrial society has increasingly made it possible for masses of mankind, even though still a minority of the total, to choose the eolithic low 70's Fahrenheit the year round. Having been offered the option, more and more have elected it. The revolution in technology and the existence of a culture aimed at production and consumption have let mankind choose the atmospheric temperature of human ease.

The resulting problem has an ironic aspect. Using energy for this purpose has put a far greater demand upon the fossil fuel resources and upon natural systems to receive the emissions from the burning of that fossil fuel. Man may be serving a biologic inheritance by preferring a consistent year-round temperature. But it is a service that is destroying much of the life support systems that are the broader base of his biologic environment.

There has been up to this point no interleaving of biology, technology and culture in the social decisions of high energy uses. The condition of the living environment has been subordinated to ever higher energy demands. René

Dubos has addressed himself with equal intensity to this aspect of urban-industrial human conduct as well.

We could not long remain true human beings, [he says,] if we were to settle on the moon or Mars, and we shall progressively lose our humanness if we continue to destroy the unique qualities of the earth by pouring filth into the atmosphere, befouling the soil, lakes, and rivers, disfiguring the landscape with junkpiles.[7]

Maybe it is the supremest of ironies that this imposition of energy costs upon nature is the partial result of man's insistence on serving a biological inheritance that desires year-round temperatures of 72 degrees Fahrenheit in office blocks, apartment projects, the covered malls of shopping centers, and the domes of sports' arenas. Of course, maybe it is the result, too, of another biological inheritance not stressed by René Dubos: the wish to conserve the expenditure of purely human energy. Perhaps nature is compelled to both supply the energy and the means of dissipating the emissions of energy transfer because man wishes to take as little exercise as possible. The mass choice, certainly, seems to be for every technological innovation for cutting down the human need to move whether those innovations are something as slight as the electric toothbrush or as substantial as the moving stair. The comfort of not exerting oneself would seem as biological an inheritance as a preferred temperature of 72 degrees Fahrenheit.

Under the impact of the high energy costs of the mid-1970's, the United States proposes to save energy costs by lowering temperatures in the winter and raising them in the summer in the atmospherically controlled microclimates of modern buildings. There is no doubt, however, that this will make people less comfortable in terms of their presumably biologic preference for 72 degrees Fahrenheit. As one builder said about the proposed federal proposals,

People will have to adjust to being several degrees warmer in the summer and several degrees cooler in winter. Suppose we're designing currently for 100% comfort, we might have to reduce that to 85%.[8]

Further recognition now must also be given to the fact that modern urban settlements were encouraged in climatically hostile areas insofar as the comfortable temperatures desired by human beings are concerned. The chronic air pollution in Fairbanks, Alaska, due to the winter cold that must be counteracted and the use of air-conditioning as a life support process for the economy of Houston, Texas, are only two of the extreme examples. The direction may once more be in favor of greater settlement in the climatically hospitable areas, now that energy costs are no longer cheap enough to be inconsequential in relation to making such a place as Houston a major urban center. Even opening windows may become ⌐ rediscovered air-control technology. Gyo Obata, an architect, says about this,

In certain climates such as California we'll depend a great deal on opening windows. California isn't like Houston where buildings will always need to be air-conditioned.... Differences between regions will have a profound effect on the types of buildings and approach to energy savings possible.[9]

Should the United States' energy conservation standards be effective, and should the growth rate in construction be between 3 and 4 percent, by 1985 some 30 percent of the residential buildings and 40 percent of the commercial structures in the United States would have been constructed so as to be energy conserving.[10] If it works out as expected by some, and despite the considerable opposition of some suppliers of building materials, the future will have begun to re-establish what was true in the past: though man may have a biologic preference for 72 degrees Fahrenheit the year round, he can be price resistant should the cost go high enough. What is also comfortable and saving of his own personal effort has its appeal; but, when the cost of serving that appeal rises, other uses for his means tend to command their own priorities.

Most certainly man can live a full life without a technology which spares him the necessity of movement or a means of temperature control that guarantees him constant comfort. But with equal certainty, these are not the preferences if the conditions are present for their easy selection. Urban-industrial society, however, cannot provide such choices costlessly. Only recently, though, have some of the costs partially incident to these preferences been coming to the forefront. After enjoying the amenities of these preferred choices for two generations, one can predict the residents of urban-industrial society will not sacrifice them easily.

After all, the dream of Utopia anticipates command over temperature and motion. As for the French science-fiction heroine Barbarella, the future is seen by many as effortless, impulsive motion in a temperature allowing the skantiest of alluring costumes. While this may be only a dream, there has been great social force in the human dream of a power over nature capable of commanding temperature and the human need to move only upon human impulse. Relatively minor though the dream may have been in comparison with its ultimate potential, man's brief experience with what high energy cascades have allowed will not be quickly forgotten or dismissed in favor of environmental protection.

The Growth of Developing Economies and Their Environment

Energy costs have been heavy impositions upon the environment, as are human biological preferences for certain temperatures or for certain means of locomotion. What mankind's choice may be about reallocating them remains as yet to be determined. What remains certain is that the dreams for the future, insofar as they pre-exist in the present, continue to be ones that call for human command over such matters as temperature-control and locomotion. There is not yet in the common human consciousness a belief that humanity must provide the artificial regimes within nature that can make such dreams a continuing reality. Instead, there continues to flourish the idea that there is in the natural systems an absorptive capacity in relation to human demand that will render human responsibility for nature unnecessary.

Everywhere in the world, there is the demand for urban-industrial artifacts. The result is that nowhere on the planet are the people free of the problems of population growth, soil erosion, loss of soil fertility, the exhaustion of the richer and more accessible mineral deposits, and the expansion of urbanization over both land and humanity.[11] The poorer, less industrially developed countries suffer the consequences of these problems at least as much as do the richer, more industrially developed. What is hard for the managers at both levels of development to comprehend is that the growth in gross national product will not cure the environmental problems in itself and more often acts to exacerbate them.

Salvation does not alone lie in the growth of gross national product. Yet in countries trying to increase income to provide the means of meeting their people's rising expectation of the environment, the belief flourishes that it does. Under such an attitude, nature is a series of resources to be quickly processed into goods and income. Very little, if anything, is allowed to divert such investments and the creation of that wealth. Somehow, at a distant date never really settled in anyone's mind, the fiscal affluence all this investment will produce can automatically restore any harm that has been done. Once the restoration occurs, a benign future will be ushered in, conferring reciprocal benefits to man and nature from the largesse earned by nature's exploitation. In the meantime, even minimal investments in basic environmental protection are begrudged.

In developing countries, even more than in those who approach maturity in their urban-industrial development, the emphasis is upon production and on fiscal returns. To develop in this context means to create the bases of urban-industrial society. Such a social decision compresses and intensifies the impact upon the environment of urban-industrial demands much more in a country pressing for prompt "development" than was the case in the older urban-industrial states whose change to that condition occurred over a longer period of time. The dialectic relationships between elements in the renewing environment are most often ignored; and the results of such ignorance become more severely disturbing because the time frames have been so reduced. Countries are now doing to the environment in a few years what generally was done over a century in the older urban-industrial states. The results of such a shortened transition are not likely to be less dire.

Ireland can serve as one example in this regard. There can be no doubt that Ireland has wooed industry vigorously despite the heavy dependence of her economy upon tourism and recreation. The Irish have preferred industry and the use of air and water as sinks for the waste of that industry even though this imperils fishing and tourist income. There seems to be a greater pride in securing income from exploiting nature through processing her into units of production and consumption than there is in using nature as a source of income for industries that leave her comparatively whole.

The Chairman of the Kerry Fishery Board of Conservators could say to an Irish audience, "We will have to accept that as far as conservation and the avoidance of pollution is concerned in this country, we are back in the stone age."[12] When one considers what he was asking for and the trouble he was having in getting it, his description seems apt. The gross increase of wastes coming into the lakes of Killarney had been steadily increasing and the waste treatment system had only primary treatment facilities. His proposal was to provide secondary treatment which, in itself, is a far cry from the more sophisticated waste handling that the lakes probably need. Evidence had been steadily accumulating, he claimed, that "Killarney's lakes were slowly being poisoned." He thought this a serious matter considering what a substantial earner of foreign currency the lakes were because of their lure to the tourist industry.

And a serious matter it undoubtedly was, and not only for the ability of Killarney to earn foreign currency. The lakes doubtless could use the tertiary treatment that has been devised for such threatened lakes like Tahoe. Yet secondary treatment could be regarded as teetering over the brink into extravagance. At the same time, it would not be unjust to describe the Irish program to seduce industry to settle in the country as a generous one to the investors in such industry.

Somehow an investment to earn income from production is more desirable than an investment to save a natural resource which is income-producing. One can imagine that if the resource should not be even an indirect income earner, but only something like clean air or a sluggishly moving river, even the discussion of a saving investment would be lacking. What lies behind every environmental issue is the social decision concerning what the society wants; and what developing countries see themselves as wanting is rising gross national product and income.

Nor are the developing countries in any way apologetic about this decision. It is the insistence of Joao Augusto de Araugo Castro that,

There is a pollution of affluence and a pollution of poverty...[T]he assertion that less income means less pollution is nonsense. It is obvious, or should be, that the so-called pollution for poverty can only be corrected through higher incomes, or more precisely, through economic development.[13]

Such societies do not see themselves as free to opt for a retention of their traditional economies. If they are to make any decision in favor of environmental protection, then in their view they must intervene in nature even more vigorously in order to acquire the capital to make environmentally protective investments.

Simply put, developing countries want what urban-industrial civilization has to offer them and which they have possessed in meager quantity up to this point. The ecology issue, therefore, is for them not just a matter of technologic adjustment, as is so often asserted by self-proclaimed realists in the more developed urban-industrial states. Claims on behalf of the environment relate instead to the most significant political and cultural decisions which those developing countries have to make concerning the kind of future each is to have. At the very least it means, if they are to make some decision in favor of protecting existing ecologic structures, that reliance upon the unconstrained market will have to be muted and the role of regulatory mechanisms in setting environmental criteria will become much more prominent.

The developing countries believe themselves compelled to develop as rapidly as possible the urban-industrial forms which may supply the hoped for affluence from whence could come the capital for protecting the environment. The present global economy of urban-industrial process leaves them as little choice as it leaves the mature urban-industrial states. They are competitors and complements for each other in this single worldwide economic structure; and none are free to pursue autarchy. In speaking of this symbiotic relationship between the developed and the aspiring urban-industrial economies, Raymond Aron has said there must be cooperation between them. "This of course will require a dialogue between the two camps – both consultation and confrontation – but eventually could prove beneficial to all, provided that neither party denies the other its trumps."[14] The "trumps," being the capital of the one and the natural resources of the other, are precisely what is most probably to be denied in a world that stresses growth in preference to the essential unity between growth curves and the environment's ability to respond with sustained vigor to them.

The developing countries may choose to internalize the social costs of environmental protection generated by the urban-industrial sector. This would require a preliminary social decision determining that environmental protection was of grave national concern and to be preferred to a go-for-broke, all-stops-out growth in the urban-industrial sector. Such social costs, of course, would include far more than the charges for protecting nature; and this competition for what is to be internalized would not work to the advantage of nature under conditions of capital shortage and a pressing desire for growth.

Insofar as the internalization of any social cost in the production process is concerned, the matter will stand as de Araugo Castro says it will stand: a matter of "...special treatment accorded to genuine national production concerns."[15] In the light of such comparisons, the environmentally concerned cannot be sanguine. One can only hope that the developing countries choose their "genuine concerns" with a greater care than in the past has marked the decisions of the older, more developed urban-industrial states.

Encouraging Economic Incentives for Environmental Protection

Even now, many urban-industrial states think that nature can absorb the costs of the different demands made upon natural systems and that there will be sufficient conditions in nature for cancelling out the effects that otherwise would be imposed. More than a century of experience does not dull this hope in those countries. The environment is seen either as absorbing industrial demands or providing the situation in which the demands will benignly cancel each other. Or else different demands are viewed as cancelling out each others's environmentally harmful effects. And, sometimes, they do.

Many examples could be brought forward, and some of the best can be drawn from English experience. One case involves an English state-owned mine dumping into a Yorkshire beck ochery water from mine drainage, and illustrates one demand muting the effect of another on a resource. If anything should be a learned experience, the effect of acid mine drainage water should be among the clearest as to what it does to streams and adjacent land. But there can be absorptive, cancelling powers capable of rendering such waste less harmful without further human intervention.

The mine water was at the head of the beck...but there was quite serious pollution from sewer lower downstream.... Ochery water has the effect of precipitating organic matter from sewage and the beck would probably have been in worse condition and certainly unfit for fish if the ochre had not been present. In these circumstances no action was possible or even desirable.[16]

This is the hope in serendipitous salvation that occasionally, as here, finds proof in experience. Far more important though for environmental protection has been the conflict between claimants to portions of the environment. Where they cannot be reconciled, and where one cannot buy out or overawe the other, the result – occasionally – is the saving from destruction of some part of the renewing environment.

In England, some streams evidence this possibility. Until the mid-1960's, "the burden of repressing river pollution and publicizing its evils rested mainly upon a few wealthy riparian proprietors."[17] Since 1963, River Authorities have been set up, and they have been operating under an opinion favorable to clean streams and under a 1961 statute that permits the imposition of stream sanctions.[18] But prior to this time, the old River Boards, created under an 1876 statute, were either indifferent or hostile to any interests other than the industrial or municipal; and their prejudice rendered peculiarly ineffective the oldest comprehensive water pollution control statute in the world.[19] The result was that the effective action for clean streams came largely through the courts and through the private initiative of such organizations as the Anglers' Cooperative Association and individual, wealthy riparian proprietors.

The problem lay, of course, in the co-optation of the regulators by those whom they had been deputed to regulate. Very promptly the River Boards had been brought to the position of "balancing" interests so that industrial wastes and municipal sewage would not be dealt with in "unrealistic" harshness. The anglers and the individual riparian proprietors who had a personal stake in clean streams had no such need to "balance" and were without inhibition in pushing their interests. The bureaucracy set up by the parliamentary legislation had no such vested reasons for pushing as hard as possible against pollution; and, in consequence, they were far easier to bring to early "reason" and to cooperate in a "balance" that produced for England a number of grossly polluted streams.

Despite the improvement in legislation, in public opinion, in enforcement, and in vested bureaucratic interest in pushing clean-up of streams, the tendency remains for administrators to come more easily to "balance" than might private interests having a conflicting right in the cleanness of a stream others wish to pollute. An instance of this is the report of the 1970 Working Group on Sewage Disposal. It was surprised at

...learning of the comparatively large number of cases where the provisions of legislation have either been ignored altogether...or discharges permitted for which the available treatment facilities were or have become inadequate....[20]

It was evident that the most effective force protecting the quality of streams in the United Kingdom was often still the landed proprietors who held fishing rights in streams. It was still not the bureaucratic structure provided for that purpose. The desire of the landed proprietor was very simple: a stream clean enough to support the fish for which he sold a fishing privilege, the modern right of piscary. The concerns of the bureaucrats were far more complex. So complex, indeed, that maintaining or improving the quality of the streams was sometimes lost.

The members of the Working Group, interestingly enough, were angered to discover that the civil remedy of private riparian suit remained "by far the most reliable protection." Public administration and publicly prosecuted criminal sanction were not in the same class for effectiveness.[21] The reaction of the Working Group was to call for an investigation of this anomaly, "leading to the elimination of the private suit as something giving an undeserved advantage to private wealth over public good." It was a reaction not unexpected from a humorless and not very self-critical civil servant mentality reflected in the report.

There can be no doubt, of course, that private litigation can confer upon the successful private litigator an advantage that is not available to those too poor or too lacking in juridical standing to bring such an action. To that extent, the Working Group on Sewage is right in seeing it as a product of an unequal social system. Under the same legal and administrative mechanisms, the existence of private litigation does permit sharply different stream conditions to exist.

In Stream A, which lacks a private proprietor interested or financially capable of bringing a suit, the demands of urban-industrial growth induce the administrators to permit a degraded stream quality. They have acted to "balance" matters. In Stream B, where the administrators have responded in the same way to the same pressures for "balance," the presence of an interested riparian capable of litigating produces a court decision that makes Stream B a higher quality water body than Stream A. Both are under the same law; but because of the private – and admittedly unequal – intervention by a private person, the consequences to nature are widely different.

But what the egalitarianism of the Working Group misses is that the publicly supported bureaucrats must always be under great pressure in urban-industrial society to maintain a posture that will be regarded as "reasonable" by industrial producers and the municipalities running treatment facilities. The private litigant with private motives to assert cares nothing for how "reasonable" these other special interests may think him to be in his own special demands. To the administrator under pressure, the pollution of a stream may be regarded as of far less seriousness than a cost to be borne by some product price or municipal rate. After all, he may comfort himself from the example given above, varying pollutants may cancel each other out. In that event, change would have been "neither possible or desirable." Why, therefore, act, when natural forces may remedy the whole situation so much more cheaply and without disturbing any local industries or politicians?

It is the private litigant who is substantially immune to this kind of "reasonable" argument. He sees no reason why the stream should not be of high quality, especially when it may have had that higher quality very recently and he has profited from that quality. If he has the resources, or can marshall them, he sees no reason not to pursue his remedy until the stream is clean.

Interestingly enough, while the cost of cleaning up the stream may be external to his operations, the benefits obtained cannot be entirely internalized by him either. Nature and natural systems relative to the cleaned stream are benefited, even if this may to him be incidental to his own profit. It is, however, no more incidental than the pollution of the stream in the first place by the discharge of wastes from processes that were passing their costs onto the environment and the public.

The pressure for open-ended, undifferentiated growth in urban-industrial society makes it difficult for bureaucracy to act adequately to protect nature. Somehow, when the "balance" gets struck, the renewing elements in nature – fish, water, plant life, the biomass – have less weight than the demands of the production-consumption function. Private persons, with their narrow views, have no such burden of "balancing" thrust upon them; and they can pursue ends without limitation, conferring in the process both external costs and benefits. The bureaucrat is not often given such an insulated interest to administer; and even when he is, the pressure is always intense to be "reasonable."

So much has worked to nature's charge in urban-industrial society, that the action by private litigators in English streams to protect their fishing rights seems the object of a cruel, Kafkaesque joke when a government report proposes to wipe it out in the name of equality. This is particularly true when regulatory equality so often turns out to be of the lowest common denominator.

The law generally purports to be equal. Still, a private litigant may have to make the personal investment to enforce the law fully on behalf of a stream or a class that the regulatory mechanism has barre 1 itself from enforcing for reasons of "balance." A personal profit may result; but personal profits regularly result from private action in any event. It scarcely seems an act of wisdom to argue that private action will be allowed in the name of "balance" that contributes to stream degradation, but that private litigation providing better stream quality in one stream in comparison with others will not be. To ban the private remedy might produce a kind of equality, but not the kind having anything within it favorable to the environment.

What is far preferable is to reduce the need for the private action. The regulatory mechanisms need to be jacked up so that they would seek at least an approximation on all streams of what can be brought into being for only a few streams simply because those few streams have been advantaged by purely selfish litigation. Any other recourse is more dog-in-the-manger regulatory self-pity than an indicia of public spiritedness.

There can be no denial that the forces are strong that generate pressure upon the regulatory mechanisms to "balance" demand at the expense of nature. It can never be easy to raise the effective level of public improvement in the area of environmental protection. Organizing the regulatory apparatus capable of dealing with a general alteration of behavior toward nature is admittedly difficult. But it is not impossible.

There are strengths in both man and the environment that can be mobilized in this cause. Within the systems of nature, there is a resilience and degree of response it would be folly to deny. What is needed are legal and administrative mechanisms that take advantage of the process of human demand and that utilize, or even create, vested interests who profit indefinitely from prolonging their interaction with the environment. Man must increasingly assume the costs of accommodating within his regulatory mechanisms the costs his demands impose upon the living and renewing environment. The failure to see the advantages in encouraging such economic-environmental interactions can only intensify the existing crisis between urban-industrial society and the environment.

Urban-Industrial Measurements of Environmental Strength

Current cultural judgments of what constitutes strength in the environment are generally based upon an increase in demand and how completely such demand is satisfied from the environment in terms set by the demandant.

There is a sort of perversity inherent in this kind of definition of strength. Urban-industrial society judges its strength in relation to nature by the size of the demands its growth structure places upon nature. Too little thought is expended in seeking other means of judging strength. One is strong because one can impose a demand structure and weak when one cannot. The environment is strong when it can either resist totally or completely satisfy such a demand structure and weak only when it cannot. The definition of what is strength and weakness for either nature or man, therefore, is skewed around the core of human demand upon nature.

It has been the production of energy, manufactures, and urban growth in urban-industrial society that have particularly composed the demand structure around which strength or weakness have been measured. Neither the quality of human relationships nor whether conditions in the environment can be renewed have provided the standard of judgment for what is or is not environmental strength. The technology, which has accompanied urban-industrial society's development, has been only a partial application of man's cognitive powers to the material arrangements of the living and renewing environment.

Urban-industrial demand, through its organization of culture and provision of technology, has given certain forces an attention productive of great change. These may have been forces always present in nature but the previous low energy cultures had caused man to give them little heed. Under the impact of high energy machines and of the networks to facilitate the movement of the production from those machines, all this changed. A perpetual agitation and an agglomerated abundance were needed to keep the networks in a condition of expanding growth. Only the forces were encouraged that were productive of the demand for cascades of energy, goods, technical service, and urban expansion. In all this the environment was given a low priority. Increasingly, man measured his strength on the speed with which his demands for consumption could reduce resistance in nature. Little regard has been paid to the effects thereby released in renewing and life support systems.

Central to this kind of demand has been urban-industrial society's chronic demand for an increase of available energy. Although in the mid-70's the use of energy in the United States failed to increase for the first time in a generation – actually dropping about two percent in 1974 – there can be no doubt about the intimate correlation subsisting between energy consumption and disposible income within urban-industrial society. From 1949 to 1974, the ratio of energy consumption to gross national product in the United States stood at about 90,000 BTU's per 1958 dollar. Consequently, reduction in energy consumed must indicate that a reduction of income has or soon will occur – unless the reduction in consumption is the result of a more efficient use of the energy being consumed.

H. R. Linden, president of the Institute of Gas Technology, points out that there are new exceptions to the rule that a high standard of living in high energy culture requires a large per capita consumption of energy; and he notes that these so-called exceptions are really fragmentary parts of the larger world economy. While the high value-high technology goods economy of Switzerland seems an exception, this is because it is but part of a global high energy culture. It is in no way comparable to the agricultural-heavy industrial economy of the United States. For these reasons, Dr. Linden insists that in the present state of urban-industrial technology and economic expectations, it would be impossible to reduce energy consumption prior to 1985 without creating a corresponding decrease in the gross national product.[22]

It is because of this correlation between energy consumption and income that the interest in nuclear energy persists despite the known risks. The steady, long-existant demand by urban-industrial society for cheap energy is related to the traditional indifference which it has shown to the needs of natural systems. In order to provide an abundant supply of cheap energy, there has been a predominant willingness to sacrifice much of the terrestrial environment to severe insults from pollution of which the accumulation of radio-active elements will be more. Perhaps in comparison to the ultimate horror of nuclear war, the risks of nuclear energy are what Khruschev called a "bagatelle." But the danger of the peaceful use of nuclear energy for power generation ought not to be minimized – particularly when it is cast as a crash program needed to immediately relieve the problems of pressing energy costs.

At a time when many were happily engaging in rhetoric about the utility of atomic energy, Jules Romains was clairvoyant in his warnings. On the pacific utilization of atomic energy in comparison with the use of atomic weapons, he said,

...it is still more difficult to combat because of its multiform and dispersed character – and particularly because of the deceptive aspect by which it is masked.[23]

Nothing has changed in this regard since Romains wrote those words – except that the pressure has greatly increased from the side of those who want to draw what they claim will be cheap power from nuclear fission. No one should be surprised at this. By now, everyone should fully grasp the growing dependence upon cheap energy and growth in the gross national product which urban-industrial society requires. Any other kind of pressure than that for allegedly cheap and abundant energy would be surprising in the historical perspective of how this society has developed its potential.

There is no limit to the potential of the human energy demand; nor, once one perceives the ultimate possible sources of energy over a sufficient time span, is there an absolute limit on the sources of energy. The crisis in supply is important for this time and place, of course, but the long run limitation is quite different. The long-run problem for which solutions do not seem to be in the offing is the earth's capacity to handle energy transfers. It is not the ability to transfer enough energy to meet human demand, therefore, that may pose the limitations. Rather it will likely be the biophysical limits of the earth that will be unable to respond in a way favorable to the renewing systems under the pressure of so much intensified energy transfer.

This is the basis of the opinion of those who think that an energy "plateau" will be reached in the not-too-distant future. The reason for that flattening out in the energy growth curve would be the inability of the biophysical environment to handle the transfer of so much energy. Pumping energy into the natural systems inevitably disturbs the operations of those systems. If comparative biological experience is any guide, such disturbances must lead to ecological disaster if continued long enough upon a large enough scale.[24]

Man himself is not exempt from this biological limitation. Man is vulnerable to his own energy demands in this respect because his body relates directly to the living environment. In urban-industrial society, man's soma has been made another part of the environment for his mind, to be treated no differently than the more external natural environment; the soma will be processed into the units of production and consumption called for by growth-dependent demand structure. The body is no more than a depreciable artifact of the mind under those conditions.

The human physiology, and perhaps psychology as well, derive from a biological history going back to the beginning of life on earth. Man, until just a handful of recent years, has not lived an urban existence even at a low energy level. The whole history of the human species has been vastly more involved in natural environments than anything the current high energy culture normally lets most of its inhabitants experience.[25] Man's biological heritage is far closer to natural ecologic systems than to the cultural artifacts which urban-industrial society has so casually employed to impose those demands which that society persists in viewing as its strengths. The wise man might well inquire how much pressure any natural system, including the human body, can take from the demand structure whose chief by-product seems to be the productions of instability and flux.

Ecological systems all require equilibrium and seek homeostasis. But the demand structure dominating urban-industrial society views destabilization as one of its strengths. The conflict of mankind with natural systems seems to have been imposed by that cultural attitude. René Dubos, the biologist, claims,

all ecological systems, whether man-made or natural, must in the long run achieve a state of equilibrium and be self-regenerating with regard to both energy and materials.[26]

Assuming this is a scientifically supportable statement for biology, the problem with it culturally is that urban-industrial society has been in a self-induced state of disequilibrium with the environment for decades. This ecological instability, far from showing any indication of reaching an equilibrium, is showing every evidence of increasing at an accelerating rate – because to many within urban-industrial society it has produced what appear to be freely extracted profits.

It is not that the ecumene of which man is a part requires stasis. Stagnation, too, is not supportive of natural systems. A healthy relation between humanity and their natural environment must have continuous qualitative changes. Such a relation offers an intellectual challenge as serious as any offered by the alleged utility of undifferentiated, unlimited growth which has for so long been the great legitimizer of social conduct. There cannot be a continuous turning away from stability as a major social goal unless both human activity, as well as the natural systems of the ecumene, are to suffer the consequences of chronic disequilibria.

Biophysical conditions, despite a human insistence on cultural determinism, are still beyond human manipulation. They are not, however, beyond the power of change by human activity. Human beings would prefer to deny that they are conditioned as much by physical and biological forces as they are by social ones. Perhaps at some future date, the social regimes at humanity's disposal will enable mankind to manipulate the biophysical environment at human will. When that day comes, human beings may be able to duplicate photosynthesis, inject oxygen into the atmosphere, control diatoms in a biological water purification program, modify weather or the make-up of micro-climates for urban zones, provide negative ionization, create air reservoirs to relieve pollution inversions, guaranty sufficient space to keep on-going the ecological inheritance that preceded the arrival of high energy culture, and regenerate soil.

Ian McHarg, the planner who stresses the natural elements in all urban planning, lists all of these as possibilities for the next century and predicts,

We will then be able to quantify the necessities of a minimum environment to support physiological man. Perhaps we may also learn what forms of nature are necessary to satisfy the psychological memory of a biological ancestry.[27]

The day is not yet, however, in which human technology can do all the multivarious tasks McHarg claims the 21st century will see accomplished. Even should all these events come about on the schedule which he forecasts, it will still not be known how much biological inheritance dominates human decision. Maybe there is encapsulated in man some sort of Jungian arche-typal structure.[28] Or perhaps man has none of this inheritance within his psyche and each generation starts with a blank psychic slate. Not even the biologically committed can overlook the power of cultural choice. Any claim of predeterminism, whether biophysical or cultural, must seek its proof in nature. However, the freedom which may be man's through his cultural parameter, is not available for the biophysical parts of nature, ranging from the ecumene of the plankton in the ocean to the cell structure within each human being.

Perhaps Ian McHarg is right in thinking that within a few generations humanity can massively intervene in a confidently manipulative manner. This would be entirely different from the presently arrogantly or unconcerned destructive style so common to the way human incursions have taken effect upon natural systems. Should McHarg be right, mankind will have taken over direct responsibility for the kind of life maintenance upon this planet that is presently being handled by slowly evolved ecologies. The degree of responsi-bility would then be awesome. But humanity is seemingly not very close to reaching an ability to set up and maintain such artificial life-support regimes.

Instead of such a condition of humanly constructed life-support systems, humanity still depends upon the natural life-support systems within the renewing environment. The latter are accepted as a free good from nature and investments are withheld from the potential of artificial regimes that might better enable nature to respond to urban-industrial demand. It is part of an attribute that is willing to see nature strong, and to measure that strength by the gravity of the human demands made upon it. From the angle of competi-tion for capital, the view seems to be cheaper that way.

The conclusions seem inescapable that this in no way either tests the strength inherent in natural systems or assists them to be strengthened in order to sustain the demands made upon them. Instead, this becomes rather a means of accomplishing irreversible ecologic breaks. Such breaks would then prove the final measurement. Simply imposing exploitative demands upon the operations of natural systems measures their renewability in the environment by terminating its possibility – and that is truly a peculiar measure in its finality.

Notes

1   Among others, see John Lukacs, *The Passing of the Modern Age*, New York: Harper & Row, 1970; and Roberto Vacca, *The Coming Dark Age*, Tr., J. S. Whale, New York: Doubleday, 1973.
2   Lester Mazor, "The Crisis of Liberal Legalism," 81 *Yale L.J.* (1972) 1032, at pp. 1051–1052.
3   Richard N. Gardner, "The Role of the UN in Environmental Problems," in Kay and Skolnikoff, eds., *op. cit.*, see note 13, *infra*, p. 73, quoting Maurice Strong.
4   René Jules Dubos, "Civilizing Technology," in *Essays in Honor of David Lyall Patrick*, Tucson: Univ. of Arizona, 1971, pp. 10–11.
5   *Ibid.*, pp. 12–14.
6   The Marquis of Salisbury required his room at Queen Victoria's Balmoral Castle be kept at 60°F., which her Private Secretary, Sir Henry Ponsonby, considered "warm," Barbara Tuchman, *The Proud Tower*, New York: MacMillan & Co., 1966, p. 6.
7   Dubos, *op. cit.*, pp. 10–11.
8   *Wall St. Journal*, April 8, 1975, p. 8, quoting Joseph Newman sr. v-pres. of Tishman Realty and Constr. Co.
9   *Ibid.*
10 *Ibid.*, quoting Gerald Leighton, Chief, Energy and Utilities Div., United States Department of Housing and Urban Development.
11 J. P. Cole, *Geography of World Affairs*, Baltimore: Penguin, 1959, pp. 106–107.
12 Cork (Ireland) *Examiner*, July 13, 1970, quoting Mr. S. Casey, the Chairman.
13 Joao Augusto de Araugo Castro, "Environment and Development," in *World Eco-Crisis: International Organizations in Response*, David A. Kay and Eugene B. Skolnikoff, eds., Madison: Univ. of Wisconsin Press, 1972, p. 245.
14 Raymond Aron, "Taking The Long View," *Atlas World Press Review*, April 1975, vol. 22, no. 4, p. 36.
15 De Araugo Castro, *op. cit.*, p. 251.
16 George Newsom and J. Graham Sherratt, *Water Pollution*, Altrincham: John Sherratt & Son, Ltd., 1972, p. 272.
17 *Ibid.*, p. v.
18 11 Eliz. 2, Water Resources Act (1963), Chapter 38 and 9 & 10 Eliz. 2, Public Health Act (1961), Chapter 64, respectively.
19 39 & 40 Vict., Rivers Pollution Prevention Act (1876), Chapter 75.
20 *Taken for Granted*, report of a Working Party on Sewage Disposal, H.M.S.O. 1970, quoting Par. 319, p. 39, in Newsom and Sherratt, *op. cit.*
21 *Ibid.*, pp. v–vi.
22 *Oil and Gas Journal*, January 6, 1975, p. 25. This also is the source on the ratio of energy consumption to income.
23 Jules Romains, *As It Is On Earth*, Tr., Richard Howard, New York: MacMillan Co., 1962, p. 100.
24 René Jules Dubos, "Civilizing Technology," in *Essays in Honor of David Lyall Patrick*, Tucson: Univ. of Arizona, 1971, pp. 4–7.
25 Ian McHarg, "The Place of Nature in the City of Man," in Ian Barbour, ed., *Western Man and Environmental Ethics*, Reading, Mass.: Addison-Wesley Pub. Co. (1973), p. 178.

[26] Dubos, *op. cit.*, p. 7.
[27] McHarg, *loc. cit.*, in Barbour, ed. *op. cit.*, pp, 185–186.
[28] See Christopher Stone, *Do Trees Have Standing?* Los Angeles: Kaufman, 1974.

III

Regulation and Environmental Limitations

Dominance: Man or Nature?

It has been a traditional view in all cultures that humanity continuously struggles against the awesome powers of nature. It is a commonplace in folk-myth for a hero to venture forth in search of objects of great value, only to be met again and again with various representations of fearful natural opposition. The fact that the foes are often cast in the form of apparitions does not deny them a natural origin. In overcoming each of them, the mythic protagonist proves his heroism and his difference from ordinary mortals. After all, not every man can be a hero – or so runs the myth.

But myths are valid only as long as they express what a culture regards as truth. Urban-industrial society has not performed in a similar fashion. Instead, this growth-demandant culture has set itself as a task the routine of overcoming nature. No longer is this the work of heroes. It is the purpose of the culture itself; and everything is structured so that the work is done as a regular process, unaccompanied by heroics.

Yet the effect of myth hangs on. Nature is still depicted as awesome. Man still "tames" rivers, "conquers" mountains, "masters" living creatures – just as if these were questions of individual courage, instead of the processing and servicing of a normally anticipated growth curve. A dominance is assigned to nature by the language still commonly employed; and it is this language which masks the shift of power from natural forces to the demands of urban industrial society. Like most deceptions, this masking of the relationship between urban-industrial demand and the limitations upon the environment to respond to that demand serves as the source of considerable danger.

Still, if nature is so weak and mankind is so strong, wherein can there be danger? The risk lies in the overestimation of both the power of human invention and the ability of the renewable qualities within the environment to viably respond to that power. Human artifice is able to monitor, to regulate, and certainly to destroy much – if not all – of what is renewable in nature. But human artifice is not able to control that renewability at the caprice of human will.

The limitation upon mankind lies in having only the power to regulate and in not having the power to control. The limitation in the environment stems from a potential inability within the forces for renewal to maintain themselves beyond a certain – and humanly unpredictable – level of urban-industrial demand. It is in these two conditions that the danger lies for both humanity and the renewing environment.

It is certainly conceivable that at some future time mankind can impose upon nature a series of interlocking artificial regimes which will maintain the forces for renewability within the environment to the same degree now performed by natural systems. When that time comes, mankind can then claim to control nature. But that time is not yet.

Whether the power of control is inaugurated in the 21st or the 25th centuries, presently living generations will not experience such control over nature. And presently living generations of human beings had better learn to cope with an environment suffering in its powers of renewability as the result of urban-industrial demand. If they do not, there never will be an opportunity to discover if mankind can truly control nature through humanly constructed artificial regimes.

Fortunately, there is currently strength not only in the level of urban-industrial demand. The forces for renewability are still powerful, whether one is considering the strength within the human body to withstand insults or of natural systems to undergo interdiction. The ability of science and technology to serve the maintenance of renewable systemic actions is both presently impressive and continuously expanding. The whole story is not one of constant frustration and failure. There remains room for much optimism.

But optimism is justified only if the effort is made to comprehend the potential limitations upon environmental renewability. Once that is done, the next step required is the pacing through regulation of the effect of urban-industrial demand as it impacts upon the environment. This will not represent either a surrender to nature nor yet a control over nature. It will constitute, instead, an accommodation of urban-industrial demand and environmental renewability until such time as a different accommodation can be carried through upon human initiative and under human direction.

Pessimists assert this will not be sufficient. Some say the damage to environmental renewability is already too great to be reversed. More allege that urban-industrial demand cannot be brought into accommodation with renewing environmental systems. In the view of the latter, urban-industrial society would break in the process. The choice lies for many of these critics in either an exhaustion of environmental renewability under the burden of urban-industrial demand or the frustration of urban-industrial society in order to preserve the renewing environment.

Any one of these pessimistic views may be right. No one has a patent on prophesy. But there will assuredly be no basis for optimism if there is pretense. The pretense may be that nature is awesome while man's works are puny, or that urban-industrial demand is not adversely impacting on the renewing environment, or that renewing environmental systems need no assistance from the science and technology of urban-industrial society. But all are false pretenses. Not one of these pretensions reflects reality.

At this stage, to mask reality would be fatal. The limitations upon both environment and human regulatory mechanisms are simply too great for it to be otherwise under present conditions. The sooner this is realized – and acted upon accordingly – the sooner there will be sufficient evidence for a reasonable optimism about the future of both urban-industrial demand and the renewing environment's response to it.

Some Fears and Hopes for the Environment From Human Biology

The fact that the functions and needs of the human body make man a part of the environmental life-support system is a cause for both fear and hope in the possibility of future balance between the demands of man's desires and the environment's ability to cope with them. The strength of man's body in reacting to adversity, as well as his talent for adaptability ensuing from the interaction of mind and body, are bases for great hope.

Yet even these have their limits. The risking of the human body by treating it as just another part of the environment to receive chemical insults is very dangerous. A few even go so far as to claim this risk-taking is a part of man's biologic inheritance. One can only hope such claims have only a very limited truth; or else the human mind can assert dominance over self-destructive biology.

The ecologist, F. R. Fosberg, is one who has developed a metaphor which describes man as a "pioneer species." He describes a pioneer species as one which "exerts a strong effect on its environment and tends to change it relatively rapidly, soon rendering it unsuitable for its own further occupancy." Being an optimist, Fosberg insists that biologically man could be a "climax species." Fosberg does not take the position that man is without cultural choice, for he defines a "climax species" as one "which lives in such adjustment with its environment that it is able to occupy it relatively permanently without serious modifications."[1]

Fosberg's is a poetic means of expression. He borrows from science to furnish philosophy with the example of a moral as old as the first homily: do wrong, and perish miserably – do right, and flourish forever. It is a way of expressing how humanity can either live in balance with nature, establishing a continuing homeostasis; or how the human demand-structure can ignore nature completely. Remaining what Fosberg calls a "pioneer species" would condemn much of the life-support forces on the planet and, in the long run, perhaps all of mankind to extinction. The substance of what Fosberg is saying could not be simpler. But, as is always the case with the easily defined goals of goodness, the process of change and accomplishment is fearfully complex.

To remain loyal to Fosberg's metaphor, being a pioneer species is to have the capacity to produce spectacular results. If urban-industrial society is such a species, one could call what has transpired a spectacular success in building a different culture. But, success or not, the results have been acquired, at the price of imposing deficiencies upon the previously perpetually self renewing quality of the biological limitations of a true pioneer species. It is the ability of humanity to make social choices through their cultural institutions which confers the freedom to break this self-limiting action.

Profit itself may be used to accomplish this change. Profit can act to specify actions and to rank the fiscal values of costs and benefits. When profit does not act in this manner, it is because the social decison has been made to limit the range of profit's service to social organization. If the selection is made to use an individuated definition of profit as the exclusive legitimizer for short-range definitions of utility, then value becomes a matter only of how the cash-flow is directed; and no regard is given to the inherent worth of anything to be found within natural systems. Some quite basic rearrangements in determining and allocating profit will have to be made as to what man thinks can be continuously extracted from nature – if there is any human interest in maintaining the basis for the continuance of the type of accelerating and infinitely expandable demands mankind can make upon nature.

Of course, one must be an optimist concerning the fundamental power of nature to respond to a responsibly managed human-demand structure. Should nature be very limited or fragile in her capacity for renewal, then even a major reduction in the demands of urban-industrial society could be insufficient. But there is a basis for optimism concerning the resilience of nature; and that basis is to be found in the biologic condition of humanity themselves. It is from his own body that man has good reason to be optimistic about the powers of a renewing nature.

The biologic heritage of mankind makes disease the exception and holds as the norm the homeostatic power of the body to maintain health. Disease is an exception. This departure from the norm is caused pathogenicity. It is both infrequent and involved with a very few of the huge population of bacteria and viruses on earth. Statistically, pathogenicity can only be thought of as "freakish." Expressed in cool terms such as these,

Disease usually results from inconclusive negotiations for symbiosis, an overstepping of the line by one side or the other, a biologic misinterpretation of borders.[2]

The human resistance to this "freakish" process is the important operative fact and it is the function of resistance to pathogenic situations that should be the focus of interest.

However, even here the hope of biology is accompanied by fear of biology. It is the postulate of some, in seeking to explain this power of resistance, that there is inherent in man a biologic memory. This memory contains "symbols" from a time when vibrios existed in great numbers and when they posed far more severe threats than any faced by the human race in eons. The memory necessarily is a primitive one. When triggered by an invader, it reacts. Tragically, however, its very primitiveness haunts it with reminiscences of a past of much greater danger. As a result, the defense set off by the trigger of the "symbols" is so much more than is needed that the result is fatal or seriously harmful to man on many occasions.[3]

In this view, the human concern should not be for the pathogenic agents causing illness so much as for natural reactions that the primitive memory summons up to counteract them. Too often it is not the disease which kills, but nature's own cure for the disease. Biologic reaction as part of the cure process becomes the source of serious harm and death. Minimal reactions, therefore, are the ones to be encouraged. Indeed, it is the position of this kind of biologic viewpoint that man should minimize the intensity of intervention in all processess – or, if intervention is necessary, that man should think as seriously of intervening only to moderate the maximum defense mechanisms naturally present.

It is a view that has within it considerable cause for optimism. Pathogens represent an exception. Drastic intervention against pathogens is not biologically wise. The greatest force for human health lies in minimizing the reaction against pathogens and in assisting the primitive memory to acquire symbols capable of triggering less drastic reactions. The argument for *de minimis* seems a strong and cheerful one.

Beyond what such an argument could mean in terms of individual human biologic health, there is the temptation to extend the argument to human society and man's relations with nature. Assuming that biologic health is a matter of minimum intervention, ought not the question of human social health also be one of such minimum action? Or if the most pressing problem in biologic health is one of over-resistance to pathogenic invasion, is not social health also a matter of over-resistance?

It is always very tempting to extrapolate from biologic views to social ones, even before the biologic thesis has been universally accepted. Should such an extrapolation be made in the case of this comparison? Should one concentrate upon change in social structure and in the relationship between man and nature? Or should the concentration be upon resistance all along the line to any sort of alteration in social, economic and political relationships?

These are questions one wants to ask. But, so stated, they are too general to be useful. It is hard, and intellectually dangerous, to borrow directly from postulates in biology in order to engage in social or legal theorizations. The direct translation of biologic into societal conclusions is a practice of which humanity ought to be wary. This much caution ought to have been learned from the sociological analogists of such biologic investigators as Buffon and Darwin. The absence of such caution can be more dangerous than even the refusal to consider the application of any sort of biologic discoveries to social situations.

The biological memory of past pathogenic catastrophes may exist. As a result, the physiologic system may over-react in defense to an invasion of pathogens no longer so strong as those symbolized in the primitive memory. There may be, because of all this, a wisdom in minimal intervention in pathogenic disturbances. Yet, even should all of this be proved, one could never conclude by this fact alone that it would be a reasonable extrapolation of analogy to conclude that socially drastic intervention and change would not still be called for in the way high energy culture deals with nature.

This is not to deny the wisdom of social structure working in accordance with biologic fact as such facts may be known. It is, however, a denial of the possibility of a direct transference of biologic knowledge to the level of social action. What is more immediately available is the use of biology to serve social ends in urban-industrial society. What must be done is to prevent the uses of biology from becoming monstrous intervenors of a kind totally disruptive of the functioning of natural systems. So far from social action about to become an extension of biologic theory, the needs of a demand structure that is still not integrated and comprehensively managed are acting to determine the uses of biology.

Far from biology being as yet the determining factor in human decision-making, it is the demand structure of urban-industrial society which sets goals both for culture and the environment. Whatever the truth that mankind's primitive memory exists in the counteraction of invading pathogens or that man should fear more his powers of resistance than what they are resisting, the time has not come for this image to be a paradigm of man's relationship with nature. The force of human culture is too strong.

What must not be lost to sight in reflection upon any biological base for human action is that pathogens in society are socially created. This means that they are internally formed and do not represent an invasion of vibrios hostile to the social body. Biological concepts when applied to social action can work only by analogy; and the analogies should not be unduly stressed. Social pathogens – assuming that this is a suitable metaphor – are not like the pathogens of disease, coming from organisms independent of the organisms affected by sickness. The defense-mechanisms of society, therefore, may well be rightly at that stage claimed for the primitive memory of man's biologic resistance to disease: the risk is so vast that the powers of resistance must be commensurate.

When the risk of extinction from invading pathogens was present, the massive defense mechanisms of the human organism would have been fully justified. Though the defense posed its dangers, it would then have been less a danger than that with which it contended. Perhaps society is now at a similar stage in relation to its pathogens. There may well be an unavoidable critical condition that results from massive resistance to powerful pathogenic forces. Recovery, as a result, may hang in the balance and a great price may have to be extracted from mankind and nature for ultimate survival.

In biology, there may be cause for both fear and hope relative to striking a balance between contemporary growth curves and the environment. There are models in biologic structure which human planners could profitably study and work with. But biologic and social action are never likely to be in perfect synchronization, whatever mankind's fears and hopes for their biological inheritance.

Once a borrower of an initial biologist's usage starts applying it in social areas never intended by the developer of the concept, it becomes impossible to predict what effect the idea will have socially. There is no bias so fixed as that which claims to be based upon experience. In the long run, the relations between man and nature – that is, between culture and biology in this particular regard – must be of the active-interactive-reactive pattern. In any relationship so complex as that imposed by the demands of high energy culture upon natural systems, human beings are behoved to be cautious in glibly moving from biologic to cultural realms (and then back again, like a weaver at a loom) as guides to the behavior of either man or nature.

The Scientific Responsibility for the Living Environment

The cultural artifact of human scientific knowledge cannot be exonerated from its responsibility to biologic structure in nature. If there is to be any hope in establishing a long-run relationship between man and nature, human economic and political activity cannot be the sole determiner and legitimizer of what science is to do. There is more to such a relationship than chemical invasions of natural systems and the biological accommodation of parts of those systems to what are humanly intended lethal dosages. Science cannot accept the charge of "pest" all the times it is made.

Direct action always has the greatest initial appeal when science is used to single out some object for extermination. The swiftest response for the least investment is what economics and politics expect of science. Also individual results have indeed been as prompt as expected. They have not been unmitigated successes, however. Unfortunately, for simplistic views of what science can do there is so much complexity in the way in which natural systems interact with and react to human invasions that more happens than the destruction of a single "pest."

Taking pest-insect elimination by chemicals as one example, there are entomologists today who denounce the alleged effectiveness of these chemicals. These biocides are meant to directly solve the problems posed by "pests" by simply killing off the individual species that human demand structure has determined to be dispensable. Little regard has traditionally been given the possibility that what is ultimately needed is some change in the human demand structure in order to accommodate to a complex series of natural systems having a larger worth than the fiscal or social value of the human demand for whose protection direct lethal doses have been required. During the 1970's many such biocides have been withdrawn from use under the pressure of the environmental movement but the problem of the damage done natural systems is not solved.

The hazards of pesticides, whether chemical or bio-chemical, may prove more disastrous to both man and the environment than to the creatures eliminated. This may well be too pessimistic a view. Still, the life reactions of target populations have been tending to reduce the effectiveness of campaigns meant to eliminate the insects who limit production of food, fibre, and hide to feed and clothe the world's growing populations and increasing expectations. It once was possible, the way an insomniac switches from sedative to sedative, to change from one chemical to another as the target in nature became resistant to the preceding effort. Now the time-frames for such a change are seven years on the average and involve much larger expenditures than in the past. It is not that either the time or the money involved represent the insuperable. Rather it is what the entomologist Perry Adkinson summarized when he said, "The insects are using guerrilla tactics, and we're using block-busters on them – and it simply isn't working." [4]

The Green Revolution since the late 1960's has exacerbated this particular situation. It has concentrated primarily – some would claim exclusively – upon the increased size of harvests. As a social decision, it is highly consonant with all the emphases that traditionally have been placed upon production and consumption. Under the Green Revolution, plants have been developed more for high yield than for either their resistance to disease or for dealing with the upset to the ecology which delicate mono-culture imposes. Fertilization and irrigation, so very important to the increased production called for, have provided excellent homes for the rapid build-up of populations that are predatory to the new crops being grown by the Green Revolution. It is not that the Green Revolution has been without astounding results: it is only that a single-minded mission was adopted that minimized nature's own systemic complexities.

Few would argue that under the present demand structure for farm products it is possible to dispense with agricultural chemicals. The so-called biological methods of predator control normally rely heavily upon some chemical applications. The biological method is most often a means of integrating both chemical and biological approaches into a single means of predator control. Because of this need for indirection and because the effect tends to be indirect, it is a more complicated operation than the direct application of a chemical intended to knock out the predator targeted. It is also more dependent upon trained personnel than is the case with a system that simply kills off the target population with a few sprayings.

Some see the integrated bio-chemical system as a return to older ways of managing the environment. As a system it depends upon "friendlies" in the insect world to do much of the work. These "friendlies" themselves require sustenance. To the directly-minded, who care only about units of production, it seems a waste of crop-production if any insect hum is heard in the fields at all, however "friendly." The directly-minded are wrong. There is value to "friendlies," in the broader maintenance of the whole ecumene.

What the directly-minded do not care to focus upon is that a lethal dose, one hundred percent effective to the target population, is likely to kill far more than the target population. There is also the strong possibility that the dosage will linger within the renewing environment. If the target population falls anywhere short of a hundred percent in its death throes, these ephemeral populations may develop either a tolerance, or more likely, a genetic mutation productive of a resistant strain. The apparent simplicity of the direct approach, therefore, often turns out to have exceedingly complex results because of the lack of simplicity within the systems of nature.

A procedure that reduced target populations and yet was capable of use over a longer continuance of time would seem far preferable. The quick false victory over a target under high peripheral costs can only be mocked if there is a subsequent resurgence of a mutated target population. What tends to mute the clarity of the preference is that the integrated bio-chemical approach imposes initially higher costs and offers a greater complexity in its operations than the apparently simple method of a few sprayings. The likelihood that the integrated way will produce better results and hence will be cheaper and productive of less complex problems in the long run tends to be overlooked in a fragmented demand structure.

Even the integrated method can run into natural resistances that serve to defeat its effectiveness in dealing with target populations. This is especially true as to the chemical components of the method. Where there is dependence upon them for some biological control purposes, the target populations may accommodate themselves over their swiftly succeeding generations to the conditions imposed by the chemical.

Just one illustration of this sort of reaction in target populations can be drawn from experiences with the screwworm fly. A bio-chemical integrated control was begun in 1962 to sterilize the screwworm fly so as to take advantage of the female's breeding only once in her lifetime. The program was so successful that incidence of the disease caused by the screwworm fly dropped from 50,000 cases in 1962 to nearly none in 1969. The disease seemed about to become extinct. The screwworm fly was not prepared to accept the same fate.

A wholly new type of screwworm female appeared who was willing to breed more than once in a lifetime. The result of her greater willingness was a jump in Texas from seventeen cases of the disease she carried in 1971 to over fifteen thousand by the middle of 1972. The screwworm female, however, was not alone to blame for the greater havoc wrecked by the disease in that year. The human cultural adaptation that had followed the apparent extinction of the disease after 1962 had at least as great a responsibility.

The ranchers had changed their methods of operations during their years of freedom from the disease. They had moved to year-round breeding of cows. Calving by 1972 was occurring in the dangerous months of summer when screwworm infestation would be at its worst. Ranchers had ceased herding cattle. Instead, all they were doing by the 1970's was fencing them off. Cattle might not be seen for weeks at a time. The cowboy of the 1970's rides herd from cars running along trails paralleling the fences. Observation and diagnosis of the disease could not occur with cowboys like these until the disease was so advanced that it would be fatal. The ranchers complaint was,

We just can't find the cowboys to ride those pastures like we use to.

Cowboys could not be found, it was asserted, to straddle a saddle in order to force cattle out of "a jungle of horse-high spiny Mesquite." The ranchers, however, were silent about their own willingness to maintain a bunkhouse full of cowpokes or a stable of cowponies. Was it not cheaper to let the cattle fend for themselves when a couple of men could cruise the fence from a car and know that all was well?

Science was so much cheaper and simpler than the traditional methods, it seemed. The screwworm turned out to have vagrant ideas, however, upsetting to all this cheapness and simplicity. Sadly, as one entomologist had to say,

When you start dealing with an adaptable organism like this, you've got to realize they don't read the textbooks.[5]

This did not mean that the entire effort had been a failure or that all effort to control the breeding of the screwworm fly should be scrapped. It meant, instead, that a whole new program had to be employed based upon increasing the number of sterilized males. Working with nature does not produce permanent, man-preferred changes. A socioeconomic pattern that assumes any such permanency has been attained is likely to reveal itself as a folly.

What technological improvement has caused to become an "extra" cost often was initially a "normal" cost of doing business under natural conditions. The public ought not to forget that a reaction in complex natural systems may undo the basis of any technological change. Should this undoing occur, the costs will return; and nature will be disregardful as to whether or not man regards them as "normal" or "extra."

When the screwworm fly made her mutated return after a decade of biochemical control, the proof was plain the pest had not been extinguished, whatever expectations science had roused. Instead, "It was just like the old times."[6] The ranchers had to accommodate their operations to what the old times had been even though their labor costs had to shoot up. It was a situation in which the imposition of costs had crossed: nature's on the one hand, the human economic system on the other. After a decade of freedom from the old costs, the public had come to think of them as abnormal because their freedom from such costs had come to seem the normal relationship between man and nature in this regard. But with the failure of the basis of that freedom, the costs became regular costs once more – and regular costs they would remain if science did not restore the conditions of the freedom which it had once established.

There is great power in the integrated bio-chemical approach to life control in nature for the satisfaction of the human demand structure. But there is no magic in it. The systems of nature are continuously interacting and reacting to whatever man does; and in these systemic processes lies nature's capacity to overcome whatever man may have planned for her. Nature is not mindful in what she does; but the life-support forces have a continuum without end. Man should curse it only at his peril.

It is very easy for humanity to speedily adapt to new freedoms provided by technology and culture's demands upon nature. What comes hard to remember is that they have been recent dispensations. Should they disappear, there is more likely to be confusion and resentment than acceptance of the fact that they were fairly recent artificial conditioners of natural systems. Man must never forget that every one of his artificial regimes that are based upon the operation of natural systems are subject to dramatic change. What is often referred to as the "harmony" in nature is a process of homeostasis that often includes catastrophes within its continuance.

Mankind finds it very hard to understand, apparently, that their own economic expectations and social institutions are not the reason why natural systems exist. True, man may have found it useful for his purposes to rest these expectations and institutions upon delicate balances within nature; but there is no permanency because man has done this and made all of his plans accordingly. When that balance is upset, the human structures built upon it will break open; and all the human anger and frustration over such a break mean nothing to nature.

Perhaps it would be well if man could have gratitude for the time his institutions had a benefit conferred upon them by nature's support. Since he might reasonably have had a fair expectedness that a break could occur in the natural systems upon which his demands drew, he ought to see it all as a kind of discount operation. What obscures from man such a view as this, is all the rhetoric of man's mastery over nature. A master need not plan for only a brief benefit from what he commands nor discount its future for a present enjoyment.

Unfortunately, the mastery of man over nature works better as rhetoric than it does in actual fact. Humanity takes the word for the deed and is only surprised and annoyed when the word stands revealed as an illusion. Mankind has no "mastery" over nature and is a very long way from approximating a positive, manipulative control. True mastery means the power to act benignly as well as destructively toward nature, in accordance with the human will. This sort of power for responsibility is not within human institutions in the late 20th century. Perhaps the 21st century will see it come to pass, if the present arrogant and ignorant rhetoricians of man's "mastery" over nature do not impose so much damage upon nature that the response of the living and renewing environment is forever broken.

As a contemporary part of this rhetoric, references are continuously being casually made about how some act of human intervention has "enhanced" nature. The idea has caught on among many that the "enhancement" of nature is an act easily within man's capacity. Rarely has the full content, much less the impact, of the alleged enhancing of the environment been fully thought out.

If enhancement projects had been confined to cosmetic performances, this might have mattered little. In truth, however, the language speaking of "enhancing" nature generally accompanies some project of great economic value that calls for nature to make many basic readjustments in the way her systems operate. For that reason, there should be as much concern among those charged with the protection of nature when someone proposes "enhancement" of nature as when a self-proclaimed "exploitation" is under consideration. It is the "enhancements" that so often turn out to provide the new freedoms that are based insecurely upon some delicate balance within nature. In the absence of the ability in humanity presently to control nature, proposing to "enhance" nature is either self-deception or rank hypocrisy.

Humanity too casually assume a power to confer benefits upon nature. The attitude is one conjoint with the opinion that there is within nature a resilience capable of responding to any demand humanity cares to put upon natural systems. Both represent human misjudgements. Just as there is a worth in nature independent of humanly assigned value, so is there strength and weakness independent of the intensity of human demand and expectation.

A science, which is compelled to concentrate on a single effect of scientific intervention, is a science deprived of the opportunity to make responsible decisions for the environment. At some point, just when such one-purpose science is seen as most successful because so much is being demanded and extracted from nature, unexpected breaks will occur. The alleged success will be revealed for what it has always been: the artifact of human demand which has nothing to do with science's full capacity to act responsibly in relation to the environment. At some moment when this occurs, the re-ordering of priorities may have neither time nor space within which to operate for salvaging the living environment.

The Traditional Human Ambition to Control the Environment

Man has always sought to be free from the operations of natural systems. Primitively, he sought that freedom through magic which he hoped would provide a control over nature and a freedom for him. Gradually, as magic became alchemy and alchemy became science, man has turned to science and technology to provide him his freedom. Whether such an imposition of con-trol over nature on the one hand and man's own freedom from nature on the other would be beneficial to either nature or man is rarely asked. Without asking that question man is pursuing the knowledge through which he hopes to assure his freedom from the power and the weakness of nature.

It may be that the revolution in biological knowledge, which has been occurring since 1950, will supply many of the means for acquiring freedom from natural challenges that mankind has wanted for so long. Certainly knowledge which the biological revolution has produced has been converted into yet more units of production and consumption. Scientific discoveries do not emerge into a social vacuum; and this has been especially true of the new discoveries in biology because of their immediate apparent economic value to urban-industrial society.

Along with the alchemist's touchstone, the most traditional goal for the seekers of knowledge has been the commonly referred to "secret of life." If the "secret" in the past was ever a goal to be reached for itself alone, this no longer is the case. A system that views all the elements of nature as the raw material for processing into individuated units in an open-ended growth pattern of production and consumption is going to treat any "secret of life" the same way every other part of the environment has been treated.

In the manner in which this biologic research has been carried on, there has been an increasing interface between the scientific method and the basic cultural decisions of urban-industrial society. There has been an apparent modesty in the way both have acted incrementally to produce change. It is apparent only. Modest as each individual act for change has been, the overall effect has been massive change. This cannot be surprising since the ultimate ambition and intent of scientific investigation and technological change over the past two centuries has never been modest. Tradition, nature, knowledge were always meant to be reprocessed and homogenized into humanly defined units, if for no greater purpose than a better human understanding.

This is not to be condemnatory of what has occurred. Instead, as an objective fact one has to see both scientific investigation and the growth curves of urban-industrial society as human means to freedom from nature. They fragmented environmental unities into units for better human understanding and for better fulfillment of human demands, but still one has to appreciate the objective quality of this change, at least insofar as the investigations of science are concerned. Otherwise the complexity of what has occurred would be lost to view. It is what separates science from alchemy.

In the mythic chambers of Dr. Faustus, where there stood the astrolabe and and the working retort, the seeker of knowledge is seen as attacking problems that compose such unities as the transmutation of base metal into gold or the search for the "secret of life." The investigation was carried on in a Platonic way. The investigator operated under a preconceived notion of what he searched for and he conducted that search without regard for the discrete facts before him. It is no wonder that in the midst of such activity, Faust would have to turn to the Devil since he had no scientific method.

It was the breakthrough of the 16th century that scrapped this myth. The preconceptions of the investigators were abandoned. In lieu thereof, the immediate goals became quite modest; the work became an episode in an ongoing, mutual inquiry; and the search became one for discrete fragments. There was still an underlying concern for the old subjects of inquiry. There still is today in regard to the "secret of life." If humanity should secure the power to produce life upon demand of the quantity and quality that the human will could command at any moment in time, then sickness, decay, and death would shrink in significance in the overall functioning of human affairs. But as a nakedly expressed purpose, post-Renaissance man gave up this quest, along with conjuring up the simulacra of black cats, blossoming roses, and the creatures of the Wonder Working Rabbi of Prague.

What emerged was research that was confined to very particular inquiries. Just as the bright whiteness of the modern laboratory is far removed from Faust's dark study in its interior decoration, so has the course of scientific inquiry become radically different. Without taking away the poetry and the uncertainty possessed by the modern scientist, or denying the quality of exactness to the remoter predecessors of science, the great difference is in the immediate purpose of research. For the modern, it is a particular answer to a particular question. For the ancient, it was a vasty understanding of the whole of knowledge. Yet in the long run, the old ambition remains; and as the discrete knowledge accumulates, the hope is reborn for learning the "secret of life."

The pose of modesty in scientific investigation freed the researcher from the burden of grandiose purpose which could not – if ever – be fulfilled for generations. Instead, there could be concentration upon the narrow work of the moment without the burden of any grand scheme into which every new discovery had to fit. As a course of action, it was not dissimilar to the manner of development of urban-industrial society which emerged in a series of actions that eschewed any single great social scheme. The 18th century produced many thinkers – Rousseau, Kant, Hegel – who talked vastly about the social contract, the categorical imperative, and the freedom of the will in history. But of greater importance than these ideas, Europe had all unnoticed become interested in man as exclusively a unit of production and consumption; and that change had occurred by concentration upon modest single operations that no one felt required to fit into a grand purpose. Only when the environment adversely reacted did anyone wonder what to do about the consequences of viewing man and nature as units for production and consumption. The same is true for the impacting knowledge of scientific inquiry in the late 20th century.

The double helix, for example, may someday help establish an extra-terrestrial or even metaphysical origin for life on the planet earth. If so, the scientific task is a remote one, of interest presently to philosophers alone. The immediate importance of that discovery has been the study of the genetic code and the functioning of cells. The importance and economic value of that has proven so great, so soon, that those who see this discovery solely as providing further units for production can forgive its discoverer his speculations upon its larger philosophical possibilities. Whether or not it brings closer the revelation of the "secret of life," it will carry forward the vaunted Green Revolution; and a purpose such as this establishes the cultural value of such a scientific discovery.

This is not to say that such research had as its initial purpose anything so large as discovering the "secret of life." Purpose is socially assigned, quite often after the event for which purpose is sought. However, once purpose is socially assigned, the public increasingly comes forward with financing programs for scientific investigation. The assigned purpose then grows in importance for the scientific investigation. What initially may have been a matter of fragmentary scientific curiosity, then becomes part of a larger project whose financing it justifies because of the economic value it will have in furthering growth in production and consumption.

No scientific research is immune to the effect of socially assigned purpose.

This is particularly true of any research that holds forth the promise of vesting in man the control of the earth's life processes. Nature may even be benefited by the knowledge. If such knowledge can by-pass a biocidal approach for satisfying human demand in relation to natural systems, then man may not have to concentrate so much on death-delivery in order to better serve his social and economic purposes. If he can command access to life, then perhaps nature will be less interrupted by the demands of high energy culture.

The way apparently has been opened for biologists to come forward with new types of plants through drawing on the millions of plant cells that are available to them as sources of plant characteristics. This method, called parasexual hybridization in order to distinguish it from the now long-known cross-pollination of mature plants, opens up great opportunities within perhaps a score of years. To unite desired traits at the cell level and produce fertile species, having specific inherent abilities, may have the capacity of making all current concern with biocides or even soil qualities the kind of ancient lore that is of interest only to historians of agriculture.[7]

What may be present here as a result of this research is a crop with the capacity for meeting the world need for a food supply that is not only resistant to disease and capable of high yield but which will produce crops of a multiple character. As such, the promises it offers a world desirous for protein is especially very great. To have pulse and rape upon the same plant, both with high yields and both resistant to disease and pests, is only a single example of the many which may ultimately be created by this one method.

This example of crossing plant characteristics at the level of the cell is just one more illustration of how nature is being manipulated in order to produce direct production and consumption values for a growth-demandant culture. If this truly does relate to research concerning the "secret of life," it is a "secret" being pursued for its fiscal value as seen by the managers of that culture. Where production and consumption values are culturally dominant, there has to be a tendency to convert everything found in nature into a sort of touchstone.

It is still in essence the old touchstone of medieval man meant to convert base substances into gold. What is base and what is noble is not a judgment of nature. It is, instead, a judgment of man; and it is man who determined that the nobility lay in gold.

The same is true for the modern touchstone that is laid to nature; it is intended to convert all the forces in nature into cash. Insofar as some fragment of knowledge does not further the basic social decision in high energy culture for urban-industrial growth, that knowledge will be de-emphasized.

But as to knowledge that intensifies that growth and that is productive of immediate return, all the high energy systems will be on "Go" in order to employ that knowledge promptly in so useful a purpose.

The procedures for increasing plant productivity that seem to presently show so much promise are not as yet available for use in relation to animals or humans. Still, as one of the experimenters on parasexual hybridization in plants has said to the mammalian geneticists,

Take heart. It can be done. It's just a matter of working out the techniques of your system.[8]

The research in cloning may be preparing the way. Cloning is an asexual process which allows the using of a single cell for the exact reproduction of the organism from which the cell has been lifted. It is as if the resulting organism had been plated in a kind of three-dimensional photographic process. It is a technique that would avoid the dangers of a breeding season and a gestation. Depending upon the way in which cell development occurred it might even moderate many of the strains in the maturation process itself.

If applicable someday to humans, it would accomplish the dream of St. Augustine, the procreation of human beings without the necessity for sexual intercourse. But this is not the dream the present researchers are seeking to fulfil. They are instead, whether they work on cloning in animal populations or upon cell crossing in plant production, concentrating upon an economically valuable production. More food would be made more cheaply available and more human beings could be supported by the process. Economically in modern agriculture, the production of fowl and animal products for market already has dispensed with direct sexual activity through the employment of artificial insemination. Very little even now is lost through the breeding process. Parasexual reproduction is only the next step in economic terms, however great an advance it requires in scientific knowledge.

Parasexual reproduction would eliminate all the delays, the stresses, and the risks attaching to the natural means of reproduction and many of the natural means of bringing organisms to a state of maturity. In addition, such processes would allow man to draw upon the gene pool in a manner not possible to nature and to assert a direct simplification which is not possible to the rich and ambiguous complexity of nature. But however expansive this growth of knowledge, it will remain subordinated to the economic advantages to be gained from so many options inherent in this greatly opened access to genetic inheritances. The current demand structure wants growth free of environmental constraints. It is interested in artificial selection in preference to natural selection because what man can directly propose meets man's immediate demands more swiftly and more cheaply in human terms than depending upon the actions of nature's systems.

The possible control of life processes by man raises questions similar to any proposed "enhancement" of nature by mankind. At the moment, man serves his demand structure through extracting from nature what is within her stock and renewing resources. These demands tend to interrupt natural systems in a negative way by ripping out necessary links in a food chain, poisoning an ecumene, or otherwise preventing a process of replacement or healing from taking place. But should man discover how to control life processes to the degree contemplated by some, one need not conclude that interruptions will not occur in the capacity of nature to renew herself.

To assume that biologic discoveries that have been taken into the demand structure of high energy culture will prove purely beneficial to man and nature, simply because they are life giving instead of life taking, is naiveté. If they should be fragmented in the way they are used, they too must then contribute to severe dislocation and malaise within the living environment. It has not been the taking of life in pest control programs with chemical biocides that has been in itself so serious a matter. It is that these programs have been prompted by single-missions meant to serve narrow economic demands.

Little regard has been given to the broader impacts upon nature that lie outside the scope of immediate research missions. The lack of integration and comprehensive consideration has been the source of the harm. Without that integration and comprehension, the multiple impact of what happens when life is created may have an even more harmful effect upon nature than is the result of a careless taking of life. Continuously man seeks freedom from environmental constraints. It would be ironic if this quest eventually should deprive humanity of what freedom they have.

Pacing Efforts for Freedom from Environmental Constraints

At the moment, as has been the case for many decades, the demand upon the renewing environment is heavy in relation to the natural mechanisms for renewability. Control of life processes, in the absence of an integrated, comprehensive concern of what consequences such human power would impose, neither lessen human demand nor better empower nature to respond to the demand. What is needed is to pace the rate of human demand into a different pattern that would be permissive of nature's ability to restore her systemic processes rather than to press on until those processes are permanently ruptured.

The social decisions have been made to demand industrialization, energy cascades, and a standard of living that impose upon the environment's ability to respond. Under the guise of a principle of utility, each of these has been made the estimator of the needs of the other, so that more industry has meant more energy and a higher material standard of living has meant more of the other two. The function of legitimizing action acquired a closed and circular character that believed it had no need to look to any worth of strength in nature for justification of what was happening. Serious as this problem has been in the past, it bids to become more severe as the competition for capital and the environment grows more severe.

This is particularly the case since the fiscal costs of energy, the very basic substance upon which the present culture rests, have risen sharply and show strong indication of remaining high for some time. For this reason, the problem is one that shows little sign of being self-solving under the present scheme for the presentation of choices. The relationship between urban-industrial growth, the expansion of energy cascades, and the rise in the material content of the standard of living is so intimate and so excluding of nature that self-salvation seems precluded.

Nazli Choucri has described what is the cultural predicate for action in a high energy culture.

There is a strong positive relationship between industrialization, energy consumption, and the standard of living [which] is so close, one is often used to estimate the other.[9]

In practice it goes even further since each is used to legitimize the demands of the other. The immediate consequence is the hinging of both industrial growth and the increase in the standard of living, at least until after the year 2000 when new technologies may have altered the energy-transfer statistics, upon energy sources which will be up against a severe limit imposed by "dollar costs, real costs, and costs to the environment occasioned by extraction."[10] It is not that these energy sources will be absolutely depleted within that period. It is only that the cost for their use will rise sharply. This, far more than any moral or environmentally protective intent, is what will affect the pace of urban-industrial growth in the world over the next several decades.

The Club of Rome has insisted that a new social decision must be made relative to the growth of demand for the processing of natural resources. They insist that growth must stop. It is their view that a continuation of the present practices will lead to a decrease in cultural and economic options. The nations that are highly developed examples of urban-industrial society must cease to grow and the underdeveloped must grow only to a condition of rough equivalency. New social forms – and they insist the forms will be new ones – "must be characterized by minimal consumption of non-renewable materials and by minimal emissions of non-degradable wastes."[11] As the Club of Rome sees the situation, this would be true even if there should be, by some miracle, an immediate dramatic change in such matters as the purification of wastes emitted under the present production system. The off-fall produced up to this time has been so great that its consequences would still compel serious actions for coping with them.

In terms of the ability of natural systems to respond to demand, it is not practical to try balancing undifferentiated, open-ended growth on the one hand and waste treatment for the emission from that growth on the other. Those who think this is synonymous with environmental protection are wrong. Neither nature nor human capital formation can withstand the costs of such a purported "balance."

In the operation of natural systems, the paying out of the costs imposed by pollution most often take longer than any financial benefit conferred by the polluting activity. It is not uncommon, either, for there to be a delay of a decade or more to ensure that a pollution control policy is implemented and the first benefits from that program begin to be noticed. What is usually meant by benefit-cost ratio are extremely short-term comparisons. They can scarcely be expected to provide the means of dealing with the impact of urban-industrial demand upon nature.

In transferring the resources from nature through human demand back to nature, costs are imposed upon nature while individuated benefits accrue to certain of the urban-industrial users. The complete realization of both costs and benefits require so much time that no intelligent planning can be done on the basis of waiting until the cost-benefit ratio of past actions can be fully perceived. The only process that can produce this is a *post-mortem*.

A fifty-year planning horizon in growth-demandant culture is the minimum requirement. That planning horizon must rely on forecasts of anticipated consequences rather than delaying any corrective action until the choices have been made clear by crisis conditions.[12] Waiting until all the details are clear beyond cavil cannot be planning the fast-moving events of rising demand curves: it is merely preparing the conditions for a burial detail for the renewable within the environment.

There are those who insist that the environment can be protected under the conditions of such demand if planners are only sensitive enough. The World Bank Group bureaucratically asserts,

...that environmental quality, human health, and social well-being need not be sacrificed, or unduly injured, let alone irreversibly altered, as a result of economic developing activities...[so long as] ecologically oriented planning, appropriately combined with sociocultural awareness and sensitivity, is a necessary prerequisite of project identification, design, and implementation.[13]

A researcher, of course, would be hard put to find planning of this degree of sensitivity anywhere in the world – or much prospect that such planning is in the offing. But quite apart from this deficiency, the World Bank does concede that economic growth injures the environment and what may well be needed is not an accommodation by nature but a reordering of objectives and performances by the economic activities of urban-industrial society.

It is very doubtful if what the World Bank calls "a strictly objective assessment of the physical and biological phenomena associated with naturally-occurring and man-made changes within the biosphere" would produce any change in the conduct of the present demand structure of urban-industrial production and consumption. Man-made changes or modifications of the world environment are objectively difficult to ascertain. They are always subject to value judgments relating to possible costs and benefits of alternative actions while they are occurring and before the final reports about them have been turned in. Often, environmental protection cannot produce positive results, whatever options are elected, without an unwanted loss of benefits.[14] The result is paralysis.

No one in command wants to take the responsibility for ordering a change from what has become a customary mode of conduct. This is particularly so when it means giving up some economic benefit or taking on a fiscal cost in order to serve some "non-productive" purpose like environmental protection. Certainly this is true when there is no consensus that such a change must be carried through if dire consequences are to be avoided. Until that moment of possibly fatal certainty, there will always be voices raised insisting that nothing need be changed now, or that change can come soon enough later, or that no change ever will be needed. The courage to act under such conditions cannot be common.

A culture of demandant growth is only willing to support its managers in change when the changes are compelled because of some threat to the flow of energy transfers or the resource base for material growth. Some easily translatable crisis relative to the costs of energy, or the lack of energy compared to the demand for it, will invariably produce a prompt willingness to accommodate for change. One ought not to be surprised by this. Systems will always respond most swiftly, profoundly, and willingly to changes to protect what they most highly value. In the present situation, there can be no doubt that the energy cascades rather than the condition of the environment hold so strategic a place that the cultural estimation must confer a higher value upon the energy flow than upon the quality of the environment.

A culture whose greatest value for over two centuries has been the symbiotic value of growth in production and consumption cannot suddenly opt for environmental worth or shift from an ideal of pleonexy to one of asceticism. There must be a change in focus from production and consumption – increasingly consumption – before anything effective can be done for environmental protection. It is the social decision that is basic.

If a 50 year planning horizon is essential, man must discover if he can regularly think that far ahead. The legend has it that Thais, overnight, went from the life of a courtesan to that of a cenobite in order that she might live eternally. But that concerns a mystic. A materialistic high energy culture is just not going to volunteer for any similarly dramatic shift in values unless convinced the life support systems of the planet are in perilous shape.

What is to be much more anticipated is that crises in the supply of energy and materials for the production and consumption processes will produce the greater pressure for change. Practically, though, how much change will even these kinds of crises produce? Up to this point, they have been slight.

Reports such as those of the Venezuelan Ministry of Mines remain common. In Caracas in 1975 over 88 percent of aerial pollution came from the internal combustion engine. Because of the city's location in a high, narrow valley, the quantity of air is limited and not subject to sufficient natural cleansing. Yet the government has aimed its air pollution control program exclusively toward industry and simply announced that by 1980 the air pollution from automotive sources would increase 24 percent. Although the city is literally headed for death by asphyxiation, no demand is made for a mandatory requirement of anti-pollutant devices on cars, or to the limitation of the number of motor vehicles, or for a non-automotive public transit system.[15]

As matters now stand, the exploitation of the hydrocarbons and the manufacture and use of petrochemicals are creating major crises by their emission into the atmosphere and the oceans. If it were not for the world crisis brought on by politics and a demand that is soaring in relation to a politically controlled supply, the situation would be worse. Perhaps the increase in the price of oil may make oil and such oil products as plastic too precious to waste. Where oil has remained cheap, as in Venezuela, little regard still is paid to its waste emission. Possibly its very expense may redress the harm the use of oil has caused and is causing the environment – a very little bit.

However what is still typical is the sort of report made by the United States National Oceanic and Atmospheric Administration based upon a survey of 700,000 square miles of sea from Cape Cod to the Caribbean for oil and plastic in July and August 1972. The report showed that at that time, oil contamination covered 665,000 square miles of open ocean. This meant that fifty percent of the survey area along the East Coast Continental Shelf was contaminated, eighty percent in the Caribbean to the Gulf of Mexico, and ninety percent north of the Antillean Chain in a belt five hundred miles north and south of the coasts of the Bahamas. There was a twenty percent occurrence in the waters of the Antillean chain and between Cape Cod and Florida. Half the plankton samples from surface waters were contaminated.[16]

The plastic debris, mostly polystyrene, was unexpected in its incidence. It may prove more dangerous than the oil because of its indigestibility by marine life. Hopefully, the expense of oil and its expense per barrel as a result of events in the mid-70's might act to moderate the amount of such waste and act thereby as a salvager of nature. Certainly increases were dramatic, moving from a per barrel price for Iranian oil of $1.90 in 1971 to a startling auction in December 1973 for Iranian oil that brought $17.40.[17] After that, oil seemingly settled down at a world posting of $12.40 a barrel. With market costs such as these, some hope throw-away plastic may become too valuable even to be manufactured. If so, less ought to wend its way to the oceans as the universal sink.

Unfortunately for any optimism that could be gathered from this, the same high energy costs will put great pressure on suppliers to extract oil from the ocean bed and particularly from shallow waters. Perhaps the price of oil will be so high as to discourage the incidence of oil spills, though an absolute elimination of them is not technically feasible. However improved the technology, there will be human error and natural catastrophe. A vigorous search is being conducted for oil under the oceans and estuaries of the world. Leakage and spillage from any successful wells drilled are just about inevitable.

However high the price of oil and however desirable it would be to have a perfect extraction of a substance commanding so high a price, there will be loss to leakage and spills. Market pressure will be in the direction of preventing these losses and perhaps of moderating the use of oil for throw-away manufactures. Yet simultaneously that same market pressure will be offsetting its protective effect by its demand for the bringing in of new fields regardless of where in the ocean floor the oil has been discovered.

Those who continuously demand an ever-greater supply of energy for urban-industrial use cannot help but place the environment low in any list of their priorities. Anything they do on behalf of the environment is done as the result of their viewing the environment as part of a waste-reception process. One can anticipate that it will be the world's demand for energy and material exploitation which will determine the extent to which the high price of oil and petrochemicals will protect nature because the market will not want to waste what it sets a high value on. Conversciy, of course, such price-imposed conservation could be completely offset by the demand for bringing previously unexploited resources into production in places where spills and leakages will do maximum damage to the environment.

If the environment enjoys any benefit out of the dealings with the crises in material exploitation in the mid-1970's, it will be fortuitous to the operations of those trying to keep up the accelerating growth common to the 20th century in its energy cascades and urban-industrial expansion. There is very little evidence as yet that, as between supporting energy cascades and protecting the environment, future behavior will be any different than past conduct. Crises alone, of whatever kind, will compel response.

Continued Growth and Environmental Regulation

A growth-demandant culture, as has been the case with every culture, shall determine the intensity of the demand to be made upon the environment as well as the setting of any self-imposed limits which could affect the making of those demands. There is no autonomy from culture in science, the market, or regulation. These are tools for carrying out social decisions, extensions that may make certain social action possible but which have no function independent of the social decisions to use them. This is certainly true for the application of scientific and technical knowledge and, increasingly, it is true for whether or not social decisions shall be made to invest in the expense of acquiring such knowledge. It is human culture, not nature, which determines the limits of man's freedom.

What if the research upon genetic structure should make it possible for man to eugenically manipulate human beings? Should this occur, the decision to manipulate will depend more upon social decision-making, whether of a moral or a political kind, than it will upon any scientific ability to carry out a draft on gene pools through parasexual reproduction among humans. The purpose under culture stressing encouragement of demand will be economic, intended to serve the demand for growth in units of production and consumption. Demand for growth will have retained the superior value assigned to it by social decision.

A culture intent on increasing production and consumption could find very good reasons to apply any scientific knowledge to mankind of something such as non-sexual breeding. In a culture that increases demand by serving the individuation of units of production and consumption, there would be all sorts of market advantages for manipulating the gene pool to provide such trivia as particular skin colors, facial features, body outlines, and quality of hair. Just as plants, fowls, and animals are biologically manipulated to meet demand purposes – and just as human beings currently are psychologically manipulated to the same end – so would the knowledge of genetics be used.

Those who argue that either men or women are each essentially super-fluous are both going to be proven right. Very soon neither sort of sexual characteristic will be needed to serve demand functions. Perhaps acculturated sexual attributes will continue to be encouraged to provide a market stimulation function or perhaps a unisex approach will be employed for the same reason if it works more efficiently in furthering demand. But in a culture where processing is the reality, there will be no reason not to process sexuality too – once the scientific knowledge is present permitting parasexual manipulation of human beings.

As Octavio Paz has already helped us to see, there is no reality in substance. There is only the reality of a series of actions. Nothing permanent exists in growth-demandant culture. Only the sequential acts demanded to serve growth have reality.[18]

Urban-industrial society, with its processing demands, moves ever further away from the recognition of physical and biological unities in the renewing environment. The need to serve the demands for growth drives toward the processing of everything which is capable of being homogenized into units of production and consumption useful to the demand structure. The social decision first to fragment and then to process the living environment in order to better serve that demand structure seems to have been made. Probably it cannot be reversed. Possibly it can be modified. Hopefully the rate of demand and of environmental response to it can be phased in order to sustain a long-term relationship.

The regulatory mechanisms being provided for the renewing environment must be empowered to do more than merely monitor the stages of this crisis. Otherwise the maintenance of such an investment in regulation will be of little avail. The National Oceanic and Atmospheric Administration, for example, has monitored a perceptible decline in sunshine in the 48 contiguous states of the United States and has attributed this decline to the increase of air pollution in the same area. The survey covered the years from 1950 through 1972. Interestingly enough, the yearly average did not show any significant variation between 1952 and 1964. But between 1964 and 1970, there was a 1.3 percent decrease. The overall decline in the entire 22 years surveyed was 8 percent for the autumn, somewhat counter-effected by a 3 percent increase for the spring.

The decrease, however, was not an even one for the entire area surveyed, being more severe in the industrialized Northeast. It could herald a long-term weather change; but more likely, the increased cloudiness stems from human actions, either air pollution or the "enhancement of natural cirrus clouds from contrails formed by high-flying aircraft." As good monitors should, the scientists at NOAA "at this time...hesitate to specify which of the alternatives is most likely."[19]

But in the long run – and the not very long run, at that – more will have to be done than monitoring the reporting. Determinations will have to be made by the regulatory mechanisms as to pace what is done to the environment. The seriousness of effects on the operation of natural systems of high energy demand and rising growth curves will have to be calculated further. Having done this much, regulation will have to respond to its charge of protecting both man and his environment from his own demand structure. Plans and actions will have to be taken changing the course of conduct previously socially determined. This decision to pace urban-industrial environmental impact will also be a social decision of the culture and not an approach externally imposed by regulation. There is no outside institution that will save humanity from themselves.

Stopping anywhere short of this requirement of pacing cannot represent effective regulatory activity. There has to be more to the protective role of regulation, insofar as the environment is concerned, than that of observer. Observations, however acute, which lead to no change in behavior, when the facts observed cry out for change, have precious little value. Furthermore, under the conditions human demand is imposing upon nature, the renewable qualities in the environment can only decline. In order for regulation to be worth its maintenance under the competitive situations impending, more will have to be done than monitoring. The pulse of demand may be so strong that even pacing may be insufficient to preserve what is renewable in nature. But the unrestrained pressure to increase demand being so destructive to those elements of environmental renewability, the decision must be made and globally implemented to regulate the pace of what demandant growth does to its environment.

Notes

[1] Quoted in John Lewallen, *Ecology of Devastation: Indochina*, Baltimore: Penguin, 1971, p. 136.

[2] Lewis Thomas, "Germs," *Yale Alumni Magazine* (March 1973), Vol. XXXVI, No. 6, p. 8. See also René Dubos, *The Mirage of Health*, New York: Anchor, 1961.

[3] Thomas, *op. cit.*, p. 11.

[4] Ellen Graham, "Bugs vs. Bugs," *Wall St. Journal*, July 21, 1972. Perry L. Adkison was chairman, Department of Entomology, Texas A. & M. University.

[5] Mike Tharp, "The Screwworm Turns," *Wall Street Journal*, August 22, 1972, p. 34. The entomologist is Weldon Newton, Texas A. & M. University; the ranchers are B. K. Johnson and William Donnel, president, Texas and Southwestern Cattle Raisers' Association.

[6] *Ibid.*, "old times" quotation is from Dr. M. E. Meadows, chief, Southwest screwworm eradication program, U.S. Dept. of Agriculture.

[7] Milwaukee *Journal*, August 18, 1972, p. 1, p. 26. Similar research has been conducted in England and Japan.

[8] *Ibid.*, quoting Peter S. Carlson. The other experimenters in this at Brookhaven have been Harold H. Smith and Rosemarie D. Dearing.

[9] Nazli Choucri with J. P. Bennett, "Population, Resources, and Technology," in Kay Skolnikoff, eds., *op. cit.*, p. 25 and p. 25 note.

[10] *Ibid.*, pp. 25–26.

[11] Jorgen Randers and Donella Meadows, "The Carrying Capacity of Our Global Environment," in Ian G. Barbour, eds., *Western Man and Environmental Ethics*, Reading, Mass.: Addison-Wesley Pub. Co. (1973), p. 272 and p. 253, p. 269, p. 271, p. 274, p. 276.

[12] Dennis L. Meadows and Jorgen Randers, "Adding the Time Dimension to Environmental Policy," in Kay and Skolnikoff, eds., *op. cit.*, pp. 64–66.

[13] James A. Lee, "Environmental Considerations in Development Finance," in *ibid.*, p. 179.

[14] J. Eric Smith, "The Role of Special Purpose and Non-governmental Organizations in the Environmental Crisis," in *ibid.*, p. 158. The earlier quote is from his definition of what constitutes an environmentally scientific inquiry.

[15] Columbus *Dispatch*, April 6, 1975, United Press International, quoting from the Caracas *El Universal*.

[16] MARMAP (Marine Resources Monitoring, Assessment and Prediction), NOAA, *Clean Air and Water News*, Vol. 5, No. 9 (March 1, 1973), p. 121.

[17] *Time*, December 23, 1973, p. 27.

[18] Octavio Paz, *Alternating Current*, Tr., Helen R. Lane, New York: Viking Press, 1973, pp. 23–24.

[19] *Wall Street Journal*, March 20, 1975, p. 21, citing the work of James Angell and Julius Kroshover.

A Bureaucracy for the Renewing Environment

Establishing an Environmental Bureaucracy

Increasingly since the end of World War II, there has been a popular demand that the living and renewing environment be protected by a bureaucracy organized for that purpose. The brittle defenses of a bureaucracy operating within a system of undifferentiated, open-ended demand seems an easy choice in comparison with any basic changes in the way growth-curves have traditionally been formed. A problem is seen; there is great reluctance to change the conduct causing the problem; and the solution seems to be the creation of bureaucratic mechanisms that will somehow mediate the problem out of its acute stage into a more benignly functioning situation.

In the 20th century there has been much disillusioning experience with bureaucracy. Despite this experience, the hope remains that there is a power of reprieve from crisis in organizational management and public administration. The demand is made by even sensitive and reflective people for powerful agencies who, hopefully, will be "animated with intentions above suspicion."

This is the conclusion of Jules Romain, after a book filled with painful and ironic insights. The future must be subjected to the strong regulation of central administrative mechanisms. Why? Because the growth and the intensification of demand of the human network impose such chances for disorder and futile conflict that there is no other choice. For anyone who has ever been a bureaucrat, such a predictive necessity is as much chilling as it may be comforting.

Still, whether one is chilled or comforted by the proclaiming of such a necessity, current evidence supports it. Some say this is, however, merely being manipulated in order to increase the personal power of the bureaucrats themselves. As Seymour Melmin has charged,

...the state management shows a propensity in problem-solving to select solutions that also serve to extend its decision-power.[1]

The insight too is objectively provable. But it implies that bureaucratic management is growing because of the drive toward power by the bureaucracy's managers or because there is some inherent drift to power aggrandizement with bureaucratic mechanisms. Either or both may be true. But the possibility is just as strong and at least as provable that the current expansion of the "decision-power" of bureaucracy is not just an internal political pressure but the result of a larger social decision to use bureaucracy for purposes external to it.

The bureaucracy is not extending its power for decision because the bureaucrats alone wish to do so. Indeed, very often it is the bureaucrats who least wish to have more power since with that goes more responsibility. Too frequently what the individual bureaucrat seeks is to be comfortable rather than to be responsible. Manipulative bureaucrats who do wish for power are indeed taking advantage of every aspect of the situation which encourages them to do so. But the pressure for the extension of the administrative mechanisms into additional areas of the operations of the demand-structure of urban-industrial society draws its greatest force from sources not concerned with the power plays of ambitious bureaucrats.

Throughout urban-industrial society there has been popular insistence that all the old relations between each individual and the larger society have so broken down that there may be no way to salvage the Aristotelian values of private ownership, of privacy, and individuality. The language used to describe the change is borrowed from Einstein and the nuclear physicists and is as complicated as the phenomena delineated.

The framework for social interaction...must be subtle and complex enough to communicate in a structure of time which is no longer linear, unidirectional, and evenly measured and in a frame of space which is no longer two-dimensional and bounded.[2]

Social tradition, property concepts, the cohesion of the individual, and nature have all been altered by the demands made upon them. The perception of this forms the basis of the call for a bureaucracy that will create the appearance of unity and permanence which are no more. But even if such an appearance should come into being, it would be an appearance only. The fragmenting condition of urban-industrial society, although scarcely two centuries old and employing late 20th century terminology, plunges late 20th century humanity into a conflict first sketched by Platonist administrative theory.

The mode of social decision-making must be able to render advisory opinions in "polycentric" situations, and render them continuously and instantaneously.... It will be difficult to accommodate to the notion that security does not reside in exclusivity of possession, identity does not find its strongest protection in a wall of privacy.[3]

It is the advantage of Plato's administrative theory that it offers direction under conditions in which the idea of security – indeed the idea of identity itself – has been broken up and processed into some strange homogenized unit of production and consumption. When identity breaks up, there has to be provided in lieu of it some administrative means for getting a handle on the process that has broken up identity. This is what is pushing for the growth in administrative mechanisms. At the moment, some think themselves satisfied to seek "advice" from the bureaucracy – an advice that will somehow be forever on tap, continuous and instantaneous, a surrogate but not commmand-ing parent. But the time must come when more than advice will be required.

The bureaucracy cannot hope to remain wholly polycentric nor willing to give only advice. More centrally exercised power and more direction than that are necessary since the risk of advice misapplied compels a bringing together within the same organization of the planners and the doers, the advisers and the actors. Social decision might like to keep this also fragmen-ted; but the pressure in the opposite direction grows continuously. Those who want to get some sort of control over the processing of man, social structure, and natural systems that is carried on by a culture of demandant growth insist upon a greater role for bureaucratic mechanisms.

Why Bureaucracy Alone Cannot Protect the Environment

Ironically, from the point of view of the history of bureaucracy's interface with human compassion, this demand is producing a rediscovery of the im-portance of such figures as St. Benedict of Nurcia and Brother Elias. The rediscovery is at a secondary level to be sure, but it is real just the same. In an age of destabilization, when everything in nature, society, and the human individual are processed into homogenized units for production and con-sumption, it is easy enough to see why there would be a re-enforced apprecia-tion of such directly compassionate religious personalities as Jesus, Buddha, or St. Francis of Assisi. What may be harder to immediately grasp is the rediscovered importance of the more bureaucratic figures of St. Benedict and Brother Elias. But as the need is increasingly perceived for a bureaucracy to protect the living environment, the contributions of these men can only be more appreciated than was formerly the case.

René Dubos has established the significance of this cultural attitude, as has Arnold Toynbee. As for St. Benedict, Dubos claims that here is

a patron saint of those who believe that true conservation means not only protecting nature against human misbehavior but also developing human activities which favor a creative, harmonious relationship between man and nature.[4]

At the same time, Arnold Toynbee has helped rediscover the significance of Brother Elias. He was the friar who took up the management of the Franciscans, who insisted upon the building of the great friaries, who established the capital funds of the order, and who, in brief, converted the enthusiasms of Brother Sun and Sister Moon into a massive, long-lasting, self-renewing organization.

However, what must be understood about these men, if they are to be more than the proto-types of management specialists, is their total commitment to the purposes for which they created bureaucratic mechanisms. They had first accepted basic decisions concerning the way things were to be done. All that they later did was performed in order to carry out these previously determined purposes. It was their purposes which were basic to their actions and not the bureaucratic institutions they set up. The latter were subordinate enterprises in their eyes.

In the re-discovery and the re-stress upon St. Benedict and Brother Elias, there is a danger of losing sight of this. Too many, who would like to identify in the late 20th century with their earlier success at bureaucratic innovation and management, overlook the motivations of the conduct of these men. Today's bureaucrat, who can see no reason to make any shifts in basic social decisions in the present operation of high energy culture, cannot have any such similar success. His bureaucratic work would be as well buttressed by propping a statue of St. Francis in his desk terrarium.

Too much dependence is being put upon the bureaucratic mechanisms themselves without a sufficient regard to basic redefinitions of social actions which are those of a growth-demandant culture impacting upon natural systems. Since the middle of the 19th century, the world has witnessed the tight final closure of the world ecumene, the living space of the population of the globe. Under the aegis of high energy demand, something has been created which prompted profound social change. Those social changes, many of them of truly revolutionary character, are still occurring and even more are going to be required.

Ecumenes of less than world scope have closed in the past. Whenever this has taken place, there has been deep social change. The change has generated a phenomenon of similarity in cultural forms and especially in the institutional forms of the new conjoint society. This was true when Hellenism extended western Asian civilization to Europe and when Europe in turn extended the descendent of that culture to the New World. The same development had to be anticipated to occur when the world was brought into the single high energy culture that has dominated it in the 20th century.

In this world-wide ecumene, changes have taken place to a degree and with an intensity never known before. It is not only the elite who have been transformed, as was the previous case when smaller ecumenes closed. When those events occurred, much of society could believe itself unaffected. Such an illusion has not been possible with this final world closure of an intensely interlocked ecumene under the pressures of accelerating demand. The mass of mankind, including the peasants in the least industrially disturbed or least urbanized regions, have been changed.

Because such changes have affected human culture in every part, only equally global and deep alterations in bureaucratic mechanisms will suffice. In René Dubos words,

If we limit our efforts to the correction of environmental defects, we shall increasingly behave like hunted beasts taking shelter behind an endless succession of protective devices, each more complex and more costly, less dependable and less comfortable than its predecessors.[5]

If a means is not found under the increasingly demanding conditions for the closed world ecumene, there can be no resolution of the crisis. Human behavior has to be integrated with nature in a way which will not be destructive to both humanity and the bio-physical world. Man is external to nature as a result of the burden of his imagination; but if there is to be human survival, that imagination must come forward with mechanisms capable of creating a viable relationship with nature.

Bureaucracy as a technology is one among several human instruments for regulation. It is an ideational artificial construct developed by human culture to deal with humanly perceived difficulties by directly allocating resources. No one in the late 20th century believes that it has had a uniform success. It often has disappointed most where its achievements have been greatest in the sense of accomplishing initially set goals. Once the goals have been achieved, the achievement has proven to have been a deception for those who set the goals and helped carry them through to success. The satirist Rabelais on this point is very clear.

Do you plead assurance for your hope? The principal point and content for what you do lies in your hope for it. All the remainder is luck and dependent upon the fatal disposition of the Heavens.[6]

The Heavenly disposals have been particularly fate-laden insofar as the human hopes for bureaucracy have been concerned. In a growth-demandant culture, the pressure upon bureaucracy, as for the organization of all technology, is to reflect the basic social decisions of the culture. Up till now, the dominant content of that social decision has been the fragmenting, processing, destabilizing role that is to be played by its undifferentiated, open-ended demands for growth in production and consumption.

Perhaps the popular demand for more bureaucracy and bureaucratic intervention into the conduct of such growth curves is in resistance to that role. More likely it is merely the wish to be relieved of the problems without any accompanying desire to alter the demand structure which constitutes the source of those problems. But the evidence seems strong that the interface being demanded between bureaucracy and the environment is not meant to signal much basic change in growth demands upon the environment. And that being so, there is no chance that a shift to bureaucractic mechanisms can by itself preserve either what is renewable in the environment or the urban-industrial society whose demands are destroying that renewability.

Choices in Structuring the Environmental Bureaucracy

To control the effects of the behavior of high energy culture, it has become increasingly evident that bureaucracies must be created in hierarchical chains of command. At the lower and middle echelons of those chains, there must be some specialization of function that has been predicated upon the existence of an identifiable expertise. There must be a procedure for the formulation of orders and an authority to issue them. The orders then must pass through the varying echelons of the organization. The major force for preventing an arbitrary government through bureaucratic fiat is the existence of specialization within the organizaton which is its reason to be. Indeed, because of the importance of that specialization, it may be the lowest level in the structure which actually formulated the order. It ostensibly has flowed from the top down through the hierarchical levels, but that appearance is a sham.

Specialization is the source of the power and autonomy in many of the lesser levels of the management structure. Through control of needed information, lower echelons assure their own independence and prevent a monolithic response to the orders of the top bureaucrats. The incorporation of technical knowledge by the specialists in function within the bureaucracies greatly increases their autonomy. The assertion of any control over them by nominal administrative superiors becomes correspondingly difficult.

In actuality, the assertion of any control over administrative subordinates who have technical expertise hugely increases administrative costs. The reason for this is that "instability in costs, prices, and profits are not major constraints for the managers of the state machine."[7] The creation of substantial environmental bureaucratic structures has not been at basic issue for many years under the impact of growth demands upon the environment. The need for some control has appeared too pressing to worry about the bureaucratic costs.

What has been and is at issue is what is to be done with the bureaucratic structures themselves. How are they to be controlled? What purpose, other than their own aggrandizement, are they to serve? In answering such questions, it cannot be enough to respond by simply recounting how they function. It is an insufficient answer to point out how specialization provides autonomy for individuals within the structure and acts to prevent monolithic movement by the bureaucrats' mechanisms. When people are not so sure but what they *do* want is massive action of an integrated kind, such answers appear to be more indictments than a defense for the way bureaucracies now are working.

There are, of course, those who would argue that discreteness and lack of overall control by the central administration is a wholly good thing. Indeed, some would go beyond this and would argue that this is inescapable because it is the result of man's biology, so that the way humans act within the administrative mechanisms is predetermined by their psychology. Man may have a biologic memory that limits the effective size of operational units, regardless of how large the overall bureaucratic structure may appear to be. In reality, the biologically oriented assert it will be composed of individually small units.

Perhaps any credence for such a view ought not to be based upon biology at all. Rather it may be a human reaction against allowing the bureaucracy to be used for furthering the processing propensities of a culture stressing only production and consumption. At least the bureaucrats will not let themselves be processed. Thus it would become a matter for the protection of individual identity; and, while clearly a function of psychology, it would need no argument for a biologic basis to support it. Yet, whatever the existence of a non-biologically based argument, Antony Jay for one has argued with great forensic skill that such a base does exist for the way bureaucrats use their expertise as a device for sealing themselves off from the larger bureaucratic structure. From their biologic memory, he says, bureaucrats extract their means to freedom.

It is Antony Jay's strong assertion that group relations for human beings are still the same as they were for a hunting tribe. Whether one is talking about a governmental bureaucracy or a modern business corporation, he insists that there is proof man works best in groups of well under a thousand persons. Acting personally, the human being finds it difficult to deal directly with more than about a dozen people.[8] Some relate this to man having evolved from an intimate hunting group of about fifty people.[9] Until the arrival of urban-industrial society, it was still exceedingly rare for people to live upon a scale much exceeding the breeding community of five hundred to one thousand persons. During this protracted time, it is claimed that man formed his biologic memory and his preferences which must then be beyond the power of any culture to break up, process, and homogenize into new units — or so assert the advocates of human biologic limitation.

The demand structure today, of course, pays no regard to any such biologic limitation, if it should exist. Instead in its pressure for growth, it pushes harder and harder for agglomeration and sprawl. If man has a biological or genetic past that makes his adjustment difficult or ultimately impossible, nothing is done except to violate that past. The trend has been toward larger grouping of people and absolutely against the existence of self-contained groups small enough to develop their own social identity as a group or a spirit of place to be associated with the group.[10]

It is true, of course, that there concurrently exists a pressure that is very strongly against this agglomerating. It resists the monolith as an ideal and pushes toward a polycentric dispersal of power in order to effectuate decision-making.[11] So dangerous does the consequence of the present growth demands appear to these resisters, that they despair of any sort of wholistic approach on anything larger than a very small scale, not much different from the sizes that Antony Jay insists are biologically preordained. In setting up units of a size to which they believe man can relate, they ask no more of the larger bureaucracies than that they monitor what is happening and pass on the information to those who can better use it.[12] The fear and distrust for the surveillance and policing functions of these larger bureaucracies and their effectiveness in enforcing their own regulations and standards are simply too great to allow any greater reliance upon them.

What is disheartening about all this is that it may be acting to reinforce the already powerful forces that are moving in the direction of the final fragmentation and processing of the environment. If man is biologically blocked from operating in the sort of large organizations that ought to be of a size with the humanly created environmental problems, then obviously man ought not to attempt to form such organizations. If bureaucracies cannot succeed, and their existence is only a reasonable cause of fear, then the bureaucratic mechanisms are not the means for the solution of the problems being generated by the demands imposed upon the environment.

Perhaps there can be no effective response to the processing demands of a culture convinced of the need for open-ended accelerating growth. Perhaps man's biological ancestry does limit his effective conduct to small groups and perhaps poly-centric decision-making is a defense mechanism produced by this biologic memory to counteract the sense of being overwhelmed by ever larger problems. In that case, dealing with the size of the demands and their environmental responses will prove very difficult, if not impossible.

On the other hand, if the options for man are not foreclosed in this biologic or psychological manner, it would have been a shame to have missed any of the chances for redemption. Assuredly, until more evidence has been garnered, man ought to follow the advice of Rabelais and live in the hope that his will can accomplish something to counteract a culture which – when all is said and done – man himself created, whatever his biologic heritage in a hunting group. It may even be that man may devise bureaucratic and other regulatory ways to deal with – to go so far as to cut back upon – the processes and products of his own creation. When that decision is made, the regulatory mechanism will be neither slighter nor less empowered for action than the forces with which they contend.

The actions of this growth-demandant culture have had a continuously destabilizing effect upon each tendency toward balance between renewing environmental systems and the social structure. The principle of undifferentiated, open-ended growth has been received as the predominant utility. The result now is in the direction of a struggle between those who want still more rapid change, thereby furthering the forces for disequilibrium, and those who would resist or channel change differently. Bureaucracy is often an ambiguous response, intended to satisfy both without antagonizing either point of view. Bureaucratic action, therefore, often serves as much to obscure the perception of any need for basic change as to help bring into focus man's relationship with the renewing environment.

In a juridically organized society, the disequilibrium and the conflict over whether it would be furthered or resisted produces litigation and statutory amendment. In more authoritarian structures brought under the disequilibrating influence, change comes from decree, either of a revolutionary kind or one meant to conserve the established authority through dramatic responses under the pressure of change. In either political structure, juristic acts and regulations must be formed to express the emergent point of view.

Before such acts can appear, there will be an accumulation of experience indicative of the need to modify or alter either the form or the content of the demand structure. Initially in the predominant number of instances, the change prompted by experience will best seem to be merely prohibitory. Established authority will only want to restrict the effect of the shock of change and to minimize costs without sacrificing any of the benefits. Even in societies accustomed to massive governmental control, action will rarely be carried on by which any affirmative policy would require that massive change in the growth demands of urban-industrial society be continued in those demands along specified lines for preselected purposes. The glad acceptance of future change in all its complexities is a rare occurrence. A single prohibition here and there, a bit of tinkering, is always a first preference.

Action will generally be modest, though timid might better describe most legal and administrative responses to the ill environmental effects of the imposed demands. Comprehensive action is fended off on the basis that the "facts" are not and cannot be known until there has been an accumulation of even more experience. The argument is put forward that acting on the basis of hypothetical knowledge assumes responsibility for the channeling of technology. This is downgraded as a possible option because of the fear that deterring a technological change might bar mankind from some benefit; and no one is quick to run the risk of the opprobrium for such responsibility.

Unfortunately for any wisdom that might inure in such a wait-and-see attitude is the way in which the demand for growth has been operating. With its fragmenting, processing, and homogenizing practices, there is a poor prospect for even experience to provide sufficient "facts." These elusive points of information will tend to remain forever segregated in the individuated units that generated them. Pulling them together becomes the task of no institution unless a centrally coordinated institution is created for the purpose of putting all the fragments of "fact" together into a mosaic of conclusory opinion. This is one of the tasks that the bureaucratic mechanisms can provide; and it is one of the reasons why mankind should be most reluctant to come to any conclusions about man's inherent inability to compose such mosaics or to set up and operate the institutions for carrying out such a task and acting on the knowledge generated.

The choices in structuring the environmental bureaucracy are likely far more open than many fear. Some may regard any degree of local control as a return to feudalism. Others may reject central planning as unmanageable. But, like those who assert man is biologically or psychologically limited in the bureaucratic structure he can choose, they should be extremely careful in what is categorically rejected as having any chance at helping set up a balance between demand and environmental response.

Since no central office, whether for planning or for implementing decisions, can know everything, there ought to be a role for local control. And whatever degree of power should be determined, it ought to be control and not an advisory capacity or some participation with a larger authority in which local knowledge and opinion are smothered. But there is invincible ignorance and incapacity at the local level, too. A central power to monitor the larger effects upon the environment and to force action beyond local strength is necessary. The mix will never be a comfortable one. But the environment will be lost as effectively as if nothing had been done if the cultural choice should opt totally either for central bureaucratic planning and management or else for local control of the parochial variety. The fear of the shortcomings of one ought not drive mankind totally to reliance upon the other.

The Environmental Need for Control over the Impact of Knowledge

Rightly or wrongly, science and technology in the late 20th century are under a social commitment to implement knowledge. Just as social peace may be bought by *not* enforcing laws, so may it be purchased in exchange for *not* fully implementing the knowledge available to science and technology. In either event, it will be a social decision reached in part outside of the inner workings of the scientific and technological communities. This possible option in regulatory control is what is pushing in the direction of a technological assessment previous to the inauguration of additional technological change. Until late, urban-industrial society saw few costs in the discoveries of science and the implementation of those discoveries by technology. But a wedge is now being driven between these two cultural instruments of man, seeking to control implementation without losing the chance of discovery. The wedge being employed is bureaucracy.

What is the source of that wedge? Perhaps it lies in the fear that those who are the knowledge seekers want to implement that knowledge regardless of consequences to man and nature. Perhaps it is because those who seek and implement knowledge find only positive good in a society of permanently unstable relationships whereas others oppose such an attribute. Certainly legal restraints upon science and technology are not regarded as tolerable by most in either the scientific or the technological communities; nor, granted the closeness of their relationships, is it scarcely possible to subject the technologist to social control while saying the scientist may continue functioning outside of such jurisdiction.

Whatever the explanation or the source of the pressure for the wedge, however, bureaucracy is being compelled to disengage itself from purely a service function for the scientific and technological communities. The administrative mechanism, necessarily with the assistance of scientists and technologists, is being compelled increasingly to move into the judgmental role of assessor. More than juristic acts are required, but it is within a bureaucratic frame that the scientists and technologists will operate in protecting the environment from the impact of new knowledge and its application.

It can be logically argued that it is the scientist who is more unsettling to nature, social structure, and the human individual than the technologist. He has made possible the existence of technologies which would never have been called into being without the scientific knowledge that served both as their base and their reason to exist. Social institutions may conclude that it is these technologies which have become intolerable because of the risks imposed upon nature or man. Yet behind those technologies there has been the work of many scientists who pursued their quest without any intention to impose costs arising from what they regarded as the pure benefit of knowledge. Not even knowledge, however, is cost free in either its acquisition or in the consequence of its possession. Simply putting the application of knowledge into some brief timespan may itself be so drastic an action that any sensible social institution for assessing impacts would want to stretch it out over a longer term.

As the 20th century has advanced, one of the contributors to instability within society has been the decreasing time lag between the scientific discovery, the technological interpretation, the introduction into the market, and the environmental impact. The accordian of these events over time has been compressed into a very brief interval between the initial discovery and the ultimate consequential social crisis resulting from it. Because knowledge and technique are cumulative, almost instant effects, most never intended, are now being produced with few means for imposing any sort of anticipatory control. So much is now known, that even the Draconic action of cutting off all government expenditures for research would be insufficient.

The increasingly brief time lag between discovery and its implementation is a powerful source of imbalance and of fear in urban-industrial society. It is from this same source that the demands for legal restraints on technology and perhaps science too have been originating. It is the same source as the pressure for increased bureaucratic structure. It is those who perceive that the demands upon the environment may be intolerable and who want to regulate them who push for bureaucracy and technological assessment. They do not necessarily want to change the demands being made by that culture. As a result, they fail to realize that the reason science is so distractingly unsettling in its effect is because that effect falls upon a culture in which fragmentation and in-dividuated processing are basic to its course. If a culture having a recognition of the interrelatedness of natural systems could be socially acceptable, science need not be environmentally unsettling. If the consequences of science upon the environment could be mostly anticipated, then the shock and fear of change would be lessened.

Legal systems, however, look to the past for guidance. Exceptions to this have been rare and for the most part fleeting. The law primarily attempts to plan for the future by references to past experiences. This makes it very difficult for law to deal with change, even when changes occur with relative slowness. It is nearly impossible for law to cope under conditions of rapid and shocking change, even when the bureaucratic mechanisms have been developed for this very purpose. Because the law-maker cannot anticipate all the permutations of future actions in the language of his statute, he creates a bureaucracy which can flexibly deal with problems as they arise within the limits of some broad policy declaration. But, when the culture has been given over to ends which are exclusively meant to unsettle the structures, there is little that either law or the bureaucratic mechanisms can do to prevent the con-tinuous disequilibrium being so sedulously sought by the dominant cultural forces.

Yet the compulsion is growing within society to make the attempt for such broad control through bureaucracy and technological assessment. Despite the resistance of the scientific and technological communities, this popular pressure wants a bureaucratic control on at least the implementation of scien-tific discovery, if not upon scientific discovery itself. The pressure predomi-nantly is for a broad control and is not in the direction of either decentralized regulation or small group integrity. Fear is pushing against a belief in the possibility of any generalized small group integrity or of sufficient power in the decentralized units, within a system insistent on expanding production and consumption, to make them believable alternatives for most.

Harold Green, a legal scholar concerned with the law's regulating the inter-face with change, has expressed the problem as science and technology's

impact on the basic, vital relationships between man and nature and between man and his fellow-men...[It] is so substantial that the type and scope of even the wisest regulation may be especially regimental and freedom-destroying.[13]

What is disturbing about this possibility is the preference for the power inherent within central bureaucracies. Despite expressions of preference for a decentralization of power, for polycentric decision-making, for participatory democracy and the better ability of small groups to reach wholistic positions, and for limitations upon centralized government, the social pressure is not in those directions. The fear is that they are too much of a part with the existing fragmenting, isolating, processing operations of growth-demandant culture. Approaches such as these would lack the ability to compel the necessary changes – or so it is feared.

The arguments are very potent for a central, comprehensive, encompassing authority. The present relatonship between growth demand and the renewing environment is so brittle that across-the-board action is needed to restore viability to it. Despite the popular calls for simplicity, the complexities of the times show no sign of simplification. Instead, everywhere the citizen turns he sees grave risks being almost routinely imposed by the present culture which is so hesitant to judge any one of its growth demands on any general scale of externally imposed costs. The citizen sees this and thinks that what is needed is a bureaucracy sufficiently large enough, informed enough, and powerful enough to make the hard choices and take the actions necessary for survival. The small polycentric groups, in which otherwise the individual human being feels most comfortable, are seen more as veto units, acting for self-serving reasons, and not as the way to an integrated, comprehensive solution for the pressing, complex problems posed by the perceived demands and the response of environmental systems to those demands.

Politically, the choice seems to be heading toward a conflict in choice between large central structures and a series of polycentric structures. It is not that the conflict has been consciously arranged. Rather there is a drifting to it and no one seems to perceive that both are needed because each serves different purposes. Insofar as the living and renewing environment is concerned, each has something different to contribute for the establishment and maintenance of viability in man's relationship with nature.

Yet increasing processing of the renewing environment to meet demand growth is having an unfortunate effect on human attitudes concerning bureaucratic mechanisms. The condition of natural systems is seen as so severely depressed that people feel compelled to opt for means of bureaucratic control for which they have no personal preference but which they believe offer environmental salvation. In a choice so stark, the risks are very great.

If the choice is made with which the individual feels comfortable but which he believes to be inadequate in meeting the problem, then the present agglutinations will go completely out of control. Should a strong central authority be chosen instead, then great dependence must be put upon its managers or there is little value in a central authority. Should these managers – as managers have been known to do – make catastrophic mistakes of judgment, the consequences may be irretrievable. Man's last wish would then be that he had opted for decentralized islands of power.

This apparent conflict in what bureaucratic mechanisms to choose epitomizes a far wider range of social problems. Questions of institutional arrangements are really acting only as masks for the more basic decisions needing to be made. There is, however, an accelerating drift in the area of governance that is leading to the time when crucial elections will have to be made. There will need to be both responsible, directing, centralized institutions of government and polycentric, small group venues for decision-making. The two will have to be reconciled.

This hope of reconciliation has for long been a purpose of modern political theory. Popular support has come the way of this hope since the disasters that have overtaken so many of the purportedly monolithic governmental structures in the 20th century. At the same time, however, the popular mind is aware that these governments have had their successes too. In times of crisis the pressure becomes greatest for the doing of some comprehensive act that has a general effect. Any sort of restraint, or deferring to polycentric autonomy, is not preferred in crisis. Despite the preference of a high-growth culture to live forever in an eternal future tense, the experiences of the past will be forming these choices of bureaucratic mechanisms – and the experiences of the past have not as yet been sorted out in such a way as to be capable of giving guidance for the future of bureaucracy.

The reaction to the demand for bureaucratic structures capable of assessing technological innovation is illustrative of this. Science and technology regard this demand for judgmental assessment as part of a neo-romantic, anti-intellectual, mystic criticism that wants to bring back the Papal Inquisition that harrassed Galileo. They see it as of a part with the dialectic authority asserted over scientific inquiry by Marxism. The common demand for technology assessment, which has become prevalent since 1970, they view as a challenge to their freedom. Since they see themselves as the ones capable of moving mankind from stagnation and of saving them from chaos, this they describe as a disastrous loss of freedom.[14]

But a more cogent argument to use against the assessment of new knowledge before it is applied is that the issue of technological assessment is simply a means of avoiding more basic social questions. Social decisions are needed to allocate in better fashion the products of both science and technology. Rather than engage in this important revaluation, attention is diverted to the issue of technology assessment which, in the long run, cannot resolve the problems posed by the operation of unchanged social decisions productive of those problems. Science and technology in their applications may have exacerbated these problems, but they have not been the primary source of them.[15]

After all, in this view, technological innovation is only the result of the limiting factor of capital in economic life. Hence scientists must defend the technological imperatives which they see as being derivatives of technological innovation. It is not scientific discovery or technological innovation which are basic here but the formation of capital which is both a product and a further generation of the demands of urban-industrial society. The scientist and the technologist, regardless of whether or not they should do more, act only to clarify the issues which the limitations of capital have referred to them. The referrals themselves come from the social decisions directing the location of investment capital and from the legal constraints within which the demands for technical innovations must be fulfilled.

Even in private capitalist economies, government controls the location of investment in such areas of public need as the environment. When there is a comparative capital abundance, governments make a larger diversion of capital to environmental programs than they do when there is competition for a shorter capital supply. It is not science and technology which independently determine goals. At most they simply clarify the issues so that the problem involved can be made accessible to judgment by the entire community.

Law and bureaucracy, which are a part of technology, share this limited condition. They have failed to accommodate for the environmental hazards that have been the by-products of the innovations of science and technology. But the law cannot provide a system of damages for redressing harm until there has been a social decision that sees harm as being present. So long as society perceived no harm, or believed benefits could be extracted from nature as free goods, or thought acts costless or that no one needed to absorb any of the costs as they appeared, then there was nothing for the law to do. When no social decision has been made to recognize or internalize environmental costs, law can make no provision for them. Its character is adjectival and not nominative; and like the scientists and technologists, lawyers too can find a defense in Joshua Lederberg's furious attack on "...the legal fiction of causal responsibilty, a theory totally at odds with modern statistics."[16]

Society, under the impact of its shock and fear of what has happened to the environment, is not interested very much in such defenses. Instead, there is an insistence that there must be an identification and study of the consequences of cognitive change. As the international legal specialist Milton Katz has said concerning these developments,

In recent years the values of the society seem to have shifted from an automatic acceptance of new technology for its own sake toward a deepening concern for environmental and other social consequences. The shift in values has begun to permeate the political process....[17]

At a minimum, this is leading to a call for the accumulation of information, for the requirement that data be collected, and that a means of interpreting the complex bodies of fact – and conclusions to be drawn from those facts – be established. What is wanted is some bureaucratic means for the public management of what science and technology are doing or are about to do. It is a response by the legal system to a preliminary stage in the social decision for change.

Justicializing Knowledge to Protect the Environment

What is being demanded is the subjection of the discoveries and implementations of science and technology to judgment prior to application. Instead of allowing these to proceed forward, a justicial process is called for. An attitude such as this represents a proposed change in the way culture now views science and technology.

The change may be as modest as the process of data mediation. This depends upon the initial ability to be open about the source of prospective conflict and the recognition that in environmental disputes there are likely going to be several angles of confrontation. It then requires an agreement on what the issues are, a willingness to keep the mediation open to all those affected, and an agreement upon the kinds and categories of facts to be garnered. At various stages of data collection the mediator gets agreement on the validity of the data going into the data bank or, in the absence of such consensus, narrows the range of differences upon the interpretation of facts. A corollary to this is a consensus on the use and interrelationship of the data in the model and the accessibility of all affected persons to the model in order to test out various hypotheses as alternative solutions to the problems that are allegedly adverse to them.[18]

It is an incremental approach, designed to work within the present system; and, if the present system is capable of so much openness, an approach with considerable potential. But it is not the only approach.

Some lawyers have gone so far as to urge that technicians who are not lawyers should be excluded from any quasi-judicial role in the bureaucratic process. The data mediation process outlined above is dependent upon technicians. But there are those who believe that only a basically adversary system can resolve the difficulties. So engrained, they insist, are scientists and non-legal technologists in their biases and so stultifying are these prejudices to any consideration of a wide range of broader significance which they have, that only legal officers who are free of these prejudgments can adequately serve the cause of pushing for the viable relationship needed between man and nature.

It is a dramatic point of view to anyone who is not a lawyer and especially to a scientist or technologist who for so long has enjoyed the approval of society for his work. Insofar as these unabashed lawyers are concerned, they predicted that the environmental impact statements called for under the National Environmental Protection Act of 1969 would create a body of law that would force legal evaluation of the projects coming under the broad sweep of the act. Eventually this body of law would furnish precedents capable of judging all innovative proposals of both scientists and technologists in a manner that would be free of their built-in prejudices.[19] It would serve as a means of carving out of the present a sufficient past experience to serve as a regulatory guide for the future.

Some would say that this has been the equivalent of putting science and technology back into the hands of the Inquisition. After all, many of the functionaries of the Inquisition had been canon lawyers, so the comparison has historical justification. Many scoffed at the time such suggestions were made as being outside the realm of possibility. The scoffing, however, has been replaced by lamentations over the interference of "ignorant" law-men in the areas of science and technology where it is alleged they have no business intruding. One such critic, himself a lawyer, is James Kramon, who insists,

The judicial process is ill-suited to handle sophisticated scientific and technical problems.... The courts do not possess fact gathering machinery with which to acquire the necessary knowledge, and the adversary process of litigation is not ideal for determining what alternative methods are open to the offending polluter.[20]

A caveat such as this one may have substantial support in fact. A sensitive jurist like Judge Bazelon has never been fairly charged with a fear to assume any of the burdens of judicial responsibility. And yet he has been moved to disclaim any justification in the legal process as the proper place to pass judgment upon the rightness or wrongness of scientific and technological positions. As he said,

Socrates said that wisdom is the recognition of how much one does not know... [T]he court...deal[s] with technical intricacies that are beyond our ken. These complex questions should be resolved in the crucible of debate through the class of informed but opposing scientific and technological viewpoints...[O]ur decision...is sure to be tested by analysis and challenge in Congress, in the scientific community, and among the public.[21]

It is a charmingly phrased and modest disclaimer. It has not been representative, however, of the actions in the 1970's of courts, of legally trained
administrators, and of the way the law itself has been phrased. The active
intervention of judges, bureaucrats and lawyers in scientific and technical
matters within the United States has apparently met with wide public approval. What has been called "the process of legal challenge, court ruling, and
agency accommodation" is well under way within the social structure of the
United States as "a powerful engine for change." [22]

This has meant that science and technology have been subjected to justicialization in the same manner as have many other parts of the social structure
within the United States. There has been an enormous growth in comparative
terms in the introjection of the law-trained person into the administrative
process of environmental protection. Despite the scoffers and the lamenters,
there has thereby been created a "promise...toward the goal of better...
decision-making" out of all the legislation, rule-making, litigation, and adjudi-
cation that justicialization has produced. [23]

Justicialization of this kind has been the result of a social decision to use
law and government to limit the effects of what may be demanded from the
environment and from human biology itself. This justicialization is a compromise that falls short of basic social change, though ultimately it may be the
vehicle to carry through such changes. However, justicialization must by its
nature be limited in its effects.

Putting actions under bureaucratic control can slow the doing of any
actions, whether relative to implementing new knowledge or otherwise. It
can make those actions more expensive. It can clarify adversary positions.
But justicialization cannot produce more than a compromise. And the
compromise will be an ineffective one quite soon unless it serves to open up
the means toward the necessary social changes required to produce integrated
and comprehensive actions concerning nature, the human individual, and the
operation of a culture that has been so growth demandant.

In the United States, the emphasis in justicialization during the 1970's has
been more upon the role of the courts than that of administrative agencies,
despite the popular demand for more and stronger bureaucracies. There has
been much disenchantment on the part of the environmentally sensitive to the
administrative process. They have regarded it as too much involved in the
servicing of the growth demands of urban-industrial society and not enough
in limiting the impact of those demands upon the natural environment.

It cannot be denied that the requirements of the environmental impact
statements have activated the need for more administrative mechanisms and
more law-trained persons to work within those mechanisms. The rejoinders,

the rebuttals and the surrejoinders that the requirements of these statements have produced have almost seemed a model borrowed from the extinct formulary pleading of the common law. Perhaps it represents a waste in funds and energy. Perhaps both would have been better invested in improving the administrative expertise that might directly have been applied as a counter-knowledge of science and technology for the protection of the environment. But the distrust of the purely bureaucratic had proven too strong. Instead a process that would permit court intervention was demanded; and this demand has been met very effectively by the requirement of the environmental impact statements.

The disenchantment with bureaucrats, even as demand rises for more bureaucratic action, has derived from the accumulated experience that has seen the regulated being steadily enabled to effectively control their regulators. To prevent this, there has been a drive in the direction of limiting bureaucratic discretion by the adoption of flat legislative commands or by proposals for legislative review of bureaucratic rule-making. Courts have increasingly insisted on compelling administrators to state the reasoned grounds and measured data for their actions. Interstices have been made wherein there can be informed public participation in the alleged administrative expertise that presumably goes into administrative decision-making, whether quasi-legislative, -judicial, or -executive. As an expression of the disenchantment leading to this conduct, it has been said,

When the New Dealers came to power, they saw administrative agencies as a panacea and the courts as the handmaidens of vested interests.... Today's reformers, seeing administrative agencies grow old and conservative, view the courts as their panacea. Panacea they will not find, of course, any more than their predecessors did....[24]

The latter, fortunately or unfortunately, is quite right. Justicialization, whether in the form of court supervision or through quasi-judicial powers within the administrative process, is no more a solution than bureaucratization. The courts can do no more than administer the law themselves. The law that they administer ultimately must serve the functions of the culture of which it is a part. If there is disenchantment with how that culture has affected the renewing environment, then there will be disenchantment with the way the law is administered by either a bureaucrat or a judge. For this kind of disenchantment, there is no escape, except the kind of basic social change that most seek to avoid.

What has not developed as a popular demand, however, has been any return to purely local control. This has been the case even for many of those who would decentralize decision-making among polycentric groups. Matters previously thought to be of exclusively private and local concern are now seen to involve the entire public and to require at least national involvement. Local control is seen as offering no protection. Instead, the pressure has grown constantly to move power to larger and larger units of government in an effort to free governmental decision-making from the special influence of those forces pressing for undifferentiated, open-ended growth.

Those who have exploited the environment in ways that engrossed the benefit to themselves and passed the cost onto others or to nature have effectively undermined the old traditions of decentralized power and their supposed democratic operation. Too often these turned out to be masks behind which occurred manipulation for those privileged to take the profit and pass the cost along. Local hands had only nominal power while at all times the real measure of control lay in others, usually the far-removed managers at a national corporate headquarters. The sense of helplessness and outrage at the local level has established an expanison of horizons that now embraces a far larger and more significant arena than any at a local or often even at a state level.

A concern has come into being at the popular level for the creation of nationwide bureaucratic mechanisms. These mechanisms are intended to regulate diverse constituencies and to have a consequently growing power to act in connection with environmental protection that could not exist at any level less than the national one.[25] In the last analysis, no one has insisted effectively on turning away from the constant aggregation of central administrative power.

Fear and unhappiness has been expressed over the exercise of that power. There has been a desire to find the means to make the mechanisms work more effectively in accomplishing the goals for which they were created. People have wanted more responsiveness and accountability from the bureaucratic managers of these mechanisms than has been the case in the past. But there have been few demands that these central power structures be dismantled and matters turned back to local government or private voluntarism.

But even the seeming decision to justicialize the future action of science and technology, which once were thought incapable of social harm, is still no conclusion to alter the growth-demandant structure that imposes the harm upon the environment. Environmental problems will continue to be met by a few bureaucratic adjustments such as moving the point of origin for decisions to larger governmental units or by judicially assessing new knowledge provided by science and technology. Ironically, the worth of natural systems to man has come to be commonly regarded as "an inalienable social right," even as society simultaneously insists on the equal right to undifferentiated, open-ended growth. It is asserted that the failure of law and bureaucracy to implement man's "right" to a fully renewing environment has deprived them of the kind of legitimization able to insulate society from repeated social conflicts.[26]

Maybe so. But even rights do not come costlessly. Simply demanding that a bureaucratic, or a juridical, or a technology assessment fence be built to separate consequences from causes will prove hopelessly insufficient. These devices will have a brittleness that can only snap under the pressure which will be brought against them when these "rights" to unlimited growth and to an unimpaired environment come together.

A Role for the Bureaucracy under Conflicting Environmental Values

The growth of bureaucracy is, in part, the result of both popular demand and of seeming necessity. It is a seeming necessity because of the constraints imposed by an unchanged growth demand and the false hopes that by its mere existence bureaucracy can solve the problems resulting for the environment without requiring any basic change in the way those demands operate. Furthermore there is a very real necessity in that every function directly related to the demand structure of urban-industrial society requires the existence of elaborate bureaucracies.

In discussing the operations of government, business, and environmental protection one must admit that they function through the media of bureaucratic mechanisms. As social complexities have increased, the bureaucrat has had thrust upon him more, and more important, functions. Gradually his official actions have come to be considered as both social duties and necessities. It has been the successes of urban-industrial society which have provided the financial support, protection, and extensive markets for producers and consumers that constitute the need and the base for modern bureaucracy.

If there is an iron law of social development for our time, it is that the greater size of organizations in modern society makes certain an increase in the extent, scope, and influence or bureaucracy.[27]

Traditional society and low energy culture used other methods for social control. The family, the guild, and status relations were among the means whereby such control was exercised. As long as such emotions as sin, guilt, salvation, reward and punishment, eternity and succession (or their ideological equivalents) dominated social intercourse, then the requirement of an external machinery for compulsion was at a minimum. It is only when tradition fails and belief lapses that an external mechanism for enforcing behavior, which society believes essential for newly developed needs, has to be created. This is the origin for the emphasis the 20th century has placed upon external controls and the allegedly rationalized processes of bureaucracy.

In the 20th century, for the market managers and the bureaucracy, handling both demand and its environmental impact have been beyond any individual's ability. Apparently personal actions have turned out upon analysis to have been institutional decisions. Everything for purposes of bureaucratic, as for market, management has had to be broken up into numerous narrow points. Each of these, in turn, has had to be assigned to a single official's initial responsibility in the manner of a mechanized assembly line. Bureaucracy operates in the same way as the production and consumption functions of urban-industrial society. It chops up whatever it processes, preparatory to the homogenization of new units. The bureaucratic structure grudges to anyone the duty of perceiving the entirety of what is involved in decision-making that affects the environment.

Under such conditions, coordination, comprehensive control, and wholistic planning, have become aspirations nearly incapable of formulation. The tendency of every bureaucrat to subdivide whatever he has responsibility for greatly strengthens this fragmentation. The purpose of bureaucracy has become the operation of "...a multitude of complex, technical, financial, legal, educational, religious, fact-gathering, and policy-making positions." [28] In consequence, the ability of bureaucracy to provide the grounds for the unity needed between man and nature has been reduced to just about nil.

Whatever traditional hierarchies may once have existed of phased and ordered values, they have been replaced by the promotion of a fragmentary growth of institutionally separate and exclusive venues. Separate special bureaucracies have been created to deal with what have been seen as discrete problems not sufficiently connected with any of the other problems in urban-industrial society to require being dealt with in conjunction. The justification for these independent agencies has been that concentration is permitted upon the problems assigned them, while it has been asserted the way has been cleared for some later integration.

Unfortunately, the integration made possible by the working of these autononomously empowered agencies is really the homogenization of particles broken off from natural environmental connections. The new units are meant to serve the growth of production and consumption more often than is otherwise the case. Little regard has been paid to the re-establishment of relationships that once existed for different purposes than these. The environment itself comes to be only another special bureaucratic jurisdiction. As such, it is assigned its own administrative mechanisms and dealt with as just another technical problem to be institutionalized.

In public administration, as in private life, it seems easier to concentrate upon a single duty. By that concentration, knowledge of everything else which might be disturbing can apparently be legitimately excluded. A technique of survival for the bureaucrat is the adoption of a neutral attitude toward all institutions and values. In a culture, whose only unity seems to be that furnished by economic competition and complementation, the bureaucratic mechanisms are often believed to be all that holds together the normative life of the culture. Pecuniary rationality has come to be the universal replacement for earlier forms of social coherence and many resent the judgment of a price indifferently placed on all they do and upon every worth in nature.[29] In order to avoid perpetual conflict and to salvage what are seen as the benefits of urban-industrial society, matters are turned over to bureaucracies created for that purpose. Any reservations about the risks in doing so are suppressed.

Bureaucratic mechanisms have come to be employed as buffers against the costs imposed by cultural values being in conflict. These mechanisms are meant to prevent conflict and, in so doing, bureaucracy itself tends to become a surrogate for the values that are in conflict. Rather than choose which value shall predominate, the social decision has been made to substitute bureaucratic mechanisms in lieu thereof. In this way decision-makers are protected from the consequences of having to make choices, because results are structured so as to appear to emerge automatically through the operation of these mechanisms.

Law and bureaucratic administration act as the external control mechanisms of society. They ought to be the instruments for expressing cultural values in public decision-making. Instead they have been treated as a substitute initially for value-choice and ultimately for value itself. In the process, the possibility of their being able to reflect any inherent worth in natural systems has gotten completely lost within the ensuing bureaucratic maze.

The 20th century is certainly suffering no shortage of cultural value to be in conflict. There is a frantic competition among them. The competition apparently has compelled the creation of ever additional bureaucratic buffers between them. These buffers have a flat and neutral character of their own which absorbs first the conflict and then the values.

A vast plurality of unrelated and conflicting values pours in on the individual.... Confronted with innumerable inducements, blandishments, role expectations, and idealized life styles, the citizen is less and less able to make any choice.... As the unified personality distintegrated, we strove for mastery of external and automatic means to make decisions.[30]

This has been as true concerning the bureaucracy's relation to environmental protection as for any other part of the problems perceived by society. As relationships between demand and the renewing environment were processed into the production and consumption units of rising demand, bureaucracy became the "external and automatic means to make decisions." Increasingly, there has been a turning to the bureaucratic expert, because he seems to have the protective coloration of neutrality. It seems to be his major contribution. As a result, it has been more important than any other need to insert into executive and legislative processes the expert's scientific and technological knowledge on societal problems. Through neutrality or disinterest will emerge automatically salvation from all problems turned over to the bureaucrat. Or so runs the hope.

A growth-demandant culture has been prepared to welcome such bureaucratic structures since they both sustain the present operating stance of the culture and permit the continued avoidance of hard choices for some further time. The expertise alleged to exist within them, and the neutrality alleged to accompany that expertise, are put beyond challenge. A clear demarcation has been drawn between the bureaucratic expert and the citizen amateur, with all the burdens of exposure put upon the latter.[31]

Bureaucratic expertise and neutrality become the seals seemingly holding together an otherwise fragmenting culture. Because of this, there has been a great investment by many in holding together the structures of contemporary bureaucratic institutions even when stress has revealed an often ramshackle structure. Like the seven seals in the Book of Revelation, there has come into being a great reluctance to closely examine, much less to break, these seals.

The aura of expertise and neutrality hangs thickly around all those functioning within the bureaucratic mechanisms. The questions as to what stimulates this expertise and neutrality, and to what are they the best response, just do not get asked. Perhaps the threat is too great to ever allow asking the additional question: do these neutral bureaucratic experts ever need some supplement in the performance of their duties by anyone not included in the lists of the bureaucratically expert and neutral?[32]

Public Participation in the Environmental Bureaucracy

The condition of renewing environmental systems as they respond to growth demands is indifferent alike to human values, institutions, and psychological defenses. These may seek to find surrogates for the need to make decisions or to avoid the pressures for change, but the environment continues to lose renewability. When bureaucratic structures are formed to protect the environment and do not do so, often to the extent of actually contributing to the further destruction of natural systems, the environment is indifferent to the expertise and neutrality involved.

There are those who do perceive that the expert and neutral bureaucratic approach has not succeeded in sufficiently protecting the environment. In order to redress what they consider as a bureaucratic malaise, they want to open up the administrative mechanisms to those who are not regularly a part of them. Useful though this may be, it remains a minor reform, however. Nevertheless, enlarging the participation of the public in the environmental bureaucracy is worth the doing.

Juggling the ways citizens may have access to the bureaucracy, though, is not the sort of reform that relates to any basic social decisions determinative of how human demand should be imposed upon the renewing environment. In any event, the suggested reforms are of many kinds and mostly comprise one-way communication between the citizens and the bureaucrats. On the one hand the citizen advises, on the other the bureaucrat educates. In either case, interaction is minimal in most reform proposals.

These attempts have ranged from the relatively modest informational aspect to a review procedure that includes citizen participation. In a few cases there has even been interactive dialogue that has led to a meaningful part in the final decision by those who previously would have played no role in reaching it. Still, they remain mostly one-way operations, even when they are something as abrasive for the bureaucrats as a procedure modeled on the congregation's talk-back to the minister's sermon. Rarely, though, will they be the kind of true dialogue out of which can grow a mutually satisfactory program or a continuing reciprocal flow of communication on the subjects assigned to the responsible agency.

Hopefully, public participation of any kind would mobilize the interest of those who in the past have been uninvolved with administrative mechanisms except as the receivers of the consequences of those bureaucratic actions. Yet, in order for public involvement to work best, there must be a common attitude shared between the bureaucrats and the people attempting to participate in the operation of the administrative mechanisms. They must mutually agree upon the importance of the particular agency, upon the salience of its work to the public, upon the legitimate encouraged existence of representative associations to be advocates for diverse public positions not likely otherwise to find such expression, and upon the means of making issues understandable so that the public can focus upon the significance of what the agency has had assigned to it.[33]

This, at any rate, is the goal of public participation. Typically, though, when the bureaucrat is asked what sort of public participation he would prefer, his answers are nowhere so inclusive. Informal contacts, some sort of public meetings, perhaps an advisory board are usually their most encouraging suggestions. But the answer as to how to improve citizen participation which always receives the most enthusiastic bureaucratic response is the one that calls for more funds, more staff, and more staff training.[34] The typical bureaucrat seeks to aggrandize his office and confine the intrusion of the non-neutral, non-expert citizen constituencies. It is needless to add that such bureaucratic responses do nothing to cope with the demands for greater participation by the citizens and responsiveness from the bureaucracy.

Whether public participation in environmental decision-making matters much to nature or not is another matter. Even the broadest form of public participation in bureaucratic decision-making is only a vehicle for implementing social decisions. If the culture remains dedicated to fragmenting and processing the environment, no opening up of the bureaucracy to the views of those other than bureaucrats will effectuate an end to fragmentation or processing. Operating at its very best, all that such an opening of the system can do is to provide a forum for the expression of conflicting values concerning the environment and a means for consciously negotiating among those views.

And should public participation operate at its very best in this regard, would this be enough for the environment? The answer is no. In growth-demandant culture, the public tends to be fragmented and segregated into conflicting constituencies. As political observers have delighted in pointing out since the rhetoric of the Enlightenment became the content of the French Revolution, there is no monolithic entity quite like "*the* public." There are instead many constituencies whose memberships shift in accordance with differing interest alignments. Furthermore, within these constituencies, the people speaking up are the leaders and not the members; also, leadership may be of a particularly transitory kind the more volatile the issues are upon which a constituency has been formed.

Environmental Bureaucrats and Their Constituencies

Bureaucratic managers are very much aware of these distinctions among constituencies. Consequently, when they must deal in negotiations with constituencies, they seek to circumscribe them by geographical area, by income level, by the degree of property interest, and by the extent to which the constituencies have felt aggrievement. Such employment of these distinctions, of course, is done for the purpose of controlling special interest advocates indirectly before the negotiations have ever begun. At the very least, this divisive technique extends protection to the bureaucrat from being controlled in turn by these conflicting constituencies. If such devices were not employed, some measure of the bureaucratic managers' power would pass to the leaders of the constituences.

Power so lost might be amalgamated for political purposes by these persons alien to the bureaucracy for reasons quite independent of the reasons for which their constituencies sought it. From a bureaucrat's vantage even worse might happen. Given the volatility of many of the issues upon which the constituencies are formed, it might be dispersed and allowed to eventually float back to another part of the bureaucracy than the office which had lost this bit of power initially.

It is not at all certain that if a constituency seeking to protect the environment should wrest power from the environmental bureaucracy that the social force of that constituency would be heightened by approximately the degree to which the agency's power had been diminished. It might lead to no more than an identification of alternatives for proposed actions or simply elicit an awareness from an informed constituency of what the bureaucracy had been up to.[35] It could represent a change in relationships but it would not likely be a zero-sum game. What is lost by the bureaucratic structure may not enure to any constituency.

The reason for this lies in the urban-industrial demand for undifferentiated, open-ended growth. Under such conditions, there is a trend (most evident in open-societies) of treating all points of view as equally valid for purposes of negotiated compromise. Systems in nature, of course, do not recognize the necessary validity to this kind of negotiation. Nature has her way of making extinct what have become non-viable parts in a changed life system; and in so doing nature is quite indifferent to any complexities in system relationships that get introduced along the way of changing life situations. To the bureaucratic structure of man, with its mission to mediate all points of view as if all were equally viable in nature, this environmental ruthlessness is unacceptable.

Bureaucracies, as a result of their profit from compromise, seek to reduce the complexity of their constituencies. Should the relationship continue long enough, the goal creates symbiotic relationships between the particular bureaucratic mechanisms and the constituencies interested in participating in their operation. On the other hand, the more constituencies whose interests are administered by the bureaucracy, the better able the bureaucrats are to play off one of the multiple constituencies against others. The conflicting constituencies of environmental exploiters and protectors illustrate often how this play operates.

The bureaucracy can offer the multiple constituencies a veritable fan of alternatives. If this game of apparent openness and receptivity can be played long enough, disenchantment will produce a drifting to the single constituency, most often of the environmental exploiters. Thereafter, the symbiosis will again develop between the bureaucracy charged with regulation and what is to be regulated. Complexity in decision-making is thereby continuously pressured toward simplicity, however complex the problems remain calling for decisions to change the conditions that produced them. Any real chance of change is lost. Neither the bureaucracy nor the regulated constituency will want any modification in their sweetheart relationship once it has been established. Even much relative ineffectiveness in serving the constituency's special interests will be tolerated rather than risk the unforeseeable consequences of change.

The drive on the behalf of the bureaucratic managers is for a single constituency purely reflective of the agency mission. The purpose of the leaders of the constituencies is to become the dominant one and eventually subsume or suppress all others. In this way conflict between the agency and its constituent interests is avoided; and both the agency and the abiding single constituent interest avoid a larger opposition to the basic social decisions of growth-demandant culture.

In the case of environmental protection, agencies want friendly constituencies upon whom they can rely to speak as the agency speaks. In some instances this produces an absolute environmental ghetto where change becomes inconceivable. The little ghetto is off to itself, out of the mainstream, concerned with small matters, and serves as a place where everyone is, or can go to, in order to be comfortable. Some state fish and game operations have had this kind of coziness with their constituency. Everyone can be happy when the game is kept restocked for shooting; and no one wants any intrusion of views which might be different.

Where the environment touches more important demand questions, matters cannot be that simple. They will still follow the overall purpose of co-opting the bureaucratic mechanisms for environmental protection into the contradictory one of serving the demand structure for exploitation. The problem of nature's ability – or inability – to respond to those demands will be institutionalized rather than allowed to make any change in the demands themselves. This, at least, will be done until some crisis occurs in the environment's renewing systems.

Why Bureaucracy Institutionalizes Environmental Problems

The bureaucracies charged with protecting the environment from the demands for energy cascades, urban sprawl, and the exploitation of natural systems have proven far more interested in how the level of those demands could be maintained than in changing those demands. Insofar as they have had constituencies who called for more protective change, they have had less significance than those who demanded the bureaucracy conduct affairs so that demand might be continued at its former pace or accelerated to a more intense form. Only when the ability has faltered in maintaining the demand levels that have been common for decades do the constituencies who call for basic change obtain anything approximating a searching administrative hearing.

There are those who feel a sense of urgency about the need for shaking up the bureaucracy. They believe that an alarming situation can be rectified if only the existing bureaucratic structures could be brought into a focus that would perceive how dangerous the situation now is. A very vocal critic of this kind has been William O. Douglas, who went to Washington in the mid-1930's to be a bureaucratic expert and who stayed on to be a member of the Supreme Court. After more than four decades of such experience, he had lost his belief in the capacity for the bureaucracy to be either expert or neutral.

One who sits in Washington, D.C., for long begins to wonder what administrative "expertise" really is – the talismanic quality which is often given great credence.[36]

His own conclusion is that expertise, and neutrality on the part of bureaucratic expertise, are nothing more than the culture's customary mode of behavior. When there is nothing that needs so deep an uprooting and replanting as those accustomed ways of doing things, the expertise and neutrality of the bureaucracy lose their ability to help. Instead, they themselves become a reinforcing menace to everything that is most menacing to any chance for a viable relationship between man and nature.

The solution of Mr. Justice Douglas is a rather simple one: send all administrators and judges regularly to join battalions of workers. Put them to the tasks society regards as the lowest and most degrading. In this way they could be saved from their expertise and neutrality and brought to see how change is desperately needed. Perhaps then they would perceive what crimes they have committed in allowing the renewing environment to be processed in the service of an undifferentiated and open-ended growth. Only in this way can the administrative mechanisms of bureaucracy be salvaged and the bureaucrats personally redeemed.

For a man like William O. Douglas it is morally revolting to see the creeping pollution of a natural gem like Lake Tahoe – for no greater purpose than the growth of the Nevada gambling industry.

The people who gather do not even know the glories of a sunrise on a spit of white sand washed by sparkling water. They come to Nevada only to gamble and defile one of God's most startling sanctuaries...[S]end gambling and the sleazy development it generates out of the basin....[37]

And it is here that William O. Douglas loses his ability to produce effective change. It is not just enough to shake bureaucrats from one frame of mind into another or bring them into contact with other levels of public opinion. Something much more basic is required from culture.

The expertise and neutrality of the bureaucracy may not exist as alleged. It may be nothing other than a pompous restatement of the lowest common denominator of the current views of the culture. But one cannot forget that in so doing, the administrative mechanisms serve the constituent interests that dominate them. Do the bureaucrats act so that their operations intensify the processing of the environment? Mostly they do. But sending them to work battalions will not by itself cause them to see any worth inherent in nature.

The people who destroyed the great pine forests of North America, in order to subsidize cheap frame housing for the sprawling urban growth of the late 19th and early 20th centuries, illustrate this. They saw "the glories of a sunrise on a spit of white sand washed by sparkling water" – many times. But it meant less to them than getting lumber to market at a cheap price. Unless the bureaucrats were to acquire a different view than this, their labor among work battalions in the natural environment need do even as little as enhancing the cause of environmental protection. The fragmented course of high growth demand would continue. Nature would still be broken and homogenized into units determined by the demands of limitlessly conceived production and consumption through bureaucrats made self-righteous by their ·rvice in work battalions.

It is not merely for their own administrative convenience alone that bureaucrats allow the environment to be processed and homogenized. Much of the indignation against bureaucrats in the area of environmental protection is that they permit the loss of portions of natural systems that are fragile, mortally threatened, and irreplaceable simply for their own ease of internal management. But that is only a surface manifestation without deep significance to the relationship between the conflicting demands of their constituencies and the response of the bureaucrats to mediate those demands.[38]

Providing for more public participation in the decisions of the bureaucrats charged with either environmental protection or environmental exploitation ultimately means increasing the number of those able to make effective demands upon the bureaucrats. This will be to the good for environmental renewability insofar as it breaks up simplistic, self-contained, smug, and environmentally destructive relationships between bureaucrats and their favored constituencies. By itself, however, the encouragement of more public participation in bureaucratic decision-making will not save the renewing environment. More basic social decisions than this one are needed in order to prevent bureaucracy from simply institutionalizing environmental problems rather than trying to solve them.

Notes

[1] John Lewallen, *The Ecology of Devastation*, p. 136.
[2] Lester Mazor, "The Crisis of Liberal Legalism," 81 Yale L.J. 1032 (1972), at p. 1052.
[3] *Ibid.*, p. 1053.
[4] Dubos, *A God Within*, New York: Charles Scribner's Sons, 1972.
[5] *Ibid.*, pp. 192–193.
[6] *Ibid.*, p. 288. The apposite quotations from French literature are one of the strengths of Dr. Dubos' work.
[7] Seymour Melmin quoted in Lewallen, *op. cit.*, p. 140. See also *ibid.*, 134 and p. 137 where Lewallen is most pessimistic on bureaucracy and technocracy.
[8] Dubos, *A God Within*, p. 283.
[9] See Antony Jay, *Corporation Man*, New York, Random House, 1971.
[10] Dubos, *A God Within*, p. 282 and p. 286.
[11] Mazor, *op. cit.*, p. 1053.
[12] Brian Johnson, "UN Institutional Response to Stockholm," in David A. Kay and Eugene B. Skolnikoff, eds., *World Eco-Crisis*, p. 110, Note.
[13] Harold P. Green, "Public Policy for Genetic Manipulation: A View from the Law," Program in Policy Studies in Science and Technology, The George Washington Univ., Occasional Paper No. 1 (March 1969) reissued at NTIS, PB 192 457 (August 10, 1972), p. 12. I have been indebted to the thoughtful insights this brief paper contains.
[14] Raymond Aron has been credited with developing many useful insights in this subject area, Paz, *Alternating Current*, p. 151.
[15] Joshua Lederberg, "The Control of Science," 45 *So. Cal. L.R.* (1972), 596, p. 600, Note.
[16] *Ibid.*, p. 609.
[17] Milton Katz, "One's Profession's Finding of Fact Is Not Necessarily Another's," *NRC–NAE News Report*, June–July, 1972, pp. 4–5.
[18] Donald B. Straus and Marshall R. Greenberg, "Data Mediation on Environmental Disputes," a paper for the 141st meeting AAAS and Society for General Systems Research, January 30, 1975.
[19] Irving Like, "The National Environmental Policy Act and Technology Assessment," 1 *Lincoln L.R.* (1970) 23, pp. 44–48. On such a decided shift in the political process in the connection between environmental law and the energy crisis, see the two articles by Barry Newman in the *Wall Street Journal*, January 2–3, 1974, p. 1.
[20] James M. Kramon, "Towards a New Federal Response to Water Pollution," 31 *Fed. Bar J.* (1972) 139, p. 144.
[21] Bazelon, C. J., concurring opinion, International Harvester v. Ruckelshaus (Ct. of Apps., D.C. 1973), 4 ERC 2041, at pp. 2062–2063; 478 F2d 615, at pp. 650–651.
[22] Joseph L. Fisher, Foreword, to Frederick R. Anderson with Robert H. Daniels, *NEPA in the Courts*, Baltimore: Johns Hopkins Univ. Press, 1973, pp. v–vi. Mr. Fisher subsequently was elected to Congress as an outspoken advocate of these views.
[23] *Ibid.*, p. 292.
[24] Donald W. Large, "Is Anybody Listening? The Problem of Access in Environmental Litigation," 1972 *Wisc. L.R.* 62, pp. 112–113.
[25] Grant McConnell, "Environment and the Quality of Political Life," in Richard

Cooley and Geoffrey Wandesford-Smith, eds., *Congress and the Environment*, Seattle: Univ. of Wash. Press, 1970, pp. 10–12.

[26] Robert I. Reis, "Environmental Activism," 18 *Boston College Industrial & Commercial Law R.* (1972) 633, at p. 680.

[27] Joseph Bensman and Bernard Rosenberg, *Mass, Class, and Bureaucracy*, Englewood Cliffs, N.J.: Prentice-Hall, 1963, p. 288 and see pp. 269–270. On their description of bureaucracy, see pp. 262–266, pp. 508–509; on the disadvantages on bureaucracy, Ch. 10; on the advantages, pp. 267–268.

[28] *Ibid.*, pp. 511–512. See also p. 491.

[29] *Ibid.*, p. 185. See also pp. 181–182.

[30] This is a consolidated quotation from *ibid.*, pp. 514–515, p. 522, and p. 534.

[31] Katz, *loc. cit.*

[32] Edmund M. Burke, "Citizen Participation Strategies," *Journal of the Am. Insti. of Planners*, September 1968, p. 293.

[33] Katharine P. Warner, "A State of the Arts Study of Public Participation in the Water Resources Planning Process," National Water Resources Planning Process, National Water Commission (July 1971), NTIS, PB 204/245, pp. 2–7.

[34] *Ibid.*, pp. 13–14.

[35] *Ibid.*, p. 23, p. 25, p. 30, p. 33, pp. 43–44.

[36] William O. Douglas, *The Three Hundred Year War*, New York: Random House, 1972, p. 182.

[37] *Ibid.*, pp. 43–44.

[38] See David Zielenziger, "The Regulatory Agencies: Salvage Job Ahead," *The Nation*, vol. 223 (October 2, 1976), pp. 302–304, who gives five reasons for American bureaucratic failure at the federal level: (1) "key phrases written in Pickwickian language ...in regulatory laws"; (2) hostility to Congressional policy by the President which is "taken into account...by everyone from policymakers in the Office of Management and Budget to the mine inspector in Pikeville"; (3) Advisory Committees "dominated by political hacks and corporation representatives...or...academic 'consultants' with ties to industry"; (4) "by various departments filling the Code of Federal Regulation with existing regulations from industry standards"; and (5) insufficient "Congressional oversight and active monitoring by citizens."

V

Shifting the Environmental Bureaucracy

The Environment's Indifference to Bureaucratic Bargains

It is inescapable for the functioning of bureaucratic structures that they operate on the premise that bargaining within the systems, with whose responsibility they are charged, is valid. Matters could be socially regarded as so vital that they would be legislatively put beyond the reach of such bargaining and compromise. Until that occurs, however, the bureaucrat will operate on the assumption that there is legitimacy in trading off one value for another in order to reach agreement and maintain social peace. Very often, the common view of how claims should be adjusted in essentially economic bargaining is splitting the difference. Unfortunately, it is a judgment of Solomon that is fatal for any living creature. When a part of the living environment is caught in such a splitting of differences, it is in as grave a danger as the infant brought to Solomon. The bureaucrat avoids the recognition of consequences so clear to King Solomon himself.

What must be recognized, however, is that up to this time no social decision has been reached putting any significant part of nature beyond the trade and bargain relationships that go on continuously among bureaucracies and their constituent interests. Only the constituencies have been enlarged. The consequence has been that there is no illegitimacy in compromising any part of the renewability in nature in order to salvage another or in order to prolong some demand being made upon some part of the environment. It has been the undifferentiated, open-ended demands which have set the norm of compromise within which bureaucrats must operate. Until that is changed, there is only a little that even the most well-disposed bureaucrat could do for the renewing environment.

There are those who are insistent on a social decision that would terminate the sort of trade and compromise practices that are still regarded as valid by most of those participating in them. Grant McConnell makes the flat assertion,

The values of natural beauty and wilderness...are really not bargainable.... The bargain...is...immoral if your concern is with scenic beauty and wilderness.[1]

His justification is this: where the subject-matter on both sides of an allegedly bargain situation cannot be expressed with equal precision in units of cash or energy, then there is no basis for compromise.[2] In such a situation, the internalization of the costs of the destruction would be impossible. Such costs are not calculable. Arbitrarily assigning cash values, when cash values are irrelevant, is the bureaucratic equivalent of trusting to the invisible hand of the market for environmental protection. Nor is it any more suitable to argue that such costs are being absorbed by the human social structure.

Neither is it a mistake for society to be the bearer of costs which the demand structure of urban-industrial growth will not internalize. In the absence of legal constraints, it is true that sections of society least able to take up the bulk of those costs often have such costs left to them. Sometimes this transfer occurs by having the general fund of the public fisc assume these costs, thus putting them into competition with expenditures on behalf of the more vulnerable sectors of the economy. More often, however, people in their own bodies and social relationships absorb pollution and, by so doing, make it seem irrational to those profiting from the emission of waste to think they ought to have to internalize such costs.[3]

Yet, important as all this human suffering is, human beings may be better able to absorb urban-industrial demands than is the environing non-human nature. What is done to either society or nature in order for urban-industrial society to appear profitable are both serious matters. The costs the renewing environment has been asked to bear, however, may yet destroy the life support capabilities of the planet. Mankind can equitably readjust the costs they refuse to internalize and not thrust them on the poor. But such readjustments are not so simply done to nature.

Nor is the demand, made by the environmentally concerned that all costs imposed by urban-industrial processes be internalized in those processes, easily conceded. There simply are situations where cost internalization is impossible. The demand being made upon nature, in those instances, can only be absorbed by nature or foregone. The question of how to cover the losses within a human price or energy process cannot be asked because the burden cannot be moved out of the natural system. The only legitimate question in these cases is whether to discontinue the human demand or to recognize that something within nature must be forever sacrificed to meet the demand.

Losses to the environment may or may not be simultaneously costly to the social structure. Individually, even if peculiar to the renewing environment, the burdens may be bearable by the natural systems. But if such burdens are unbearable in themselves, or else accumulate until their sum becomes a condition with which a natural system cannot live, the consequence may be far more ominous than when a social structure reaches the social decision that it is being asked to sustain an unbearable social burden.

What the social structure considers to be an unbearable burden leads to social change. It may be violent and bloody; but, afterward, the reformed social structure is able to exist. When natural systems break under unbearable conditions, this leads to at least some life extinction. If the break is severe enough, the extinction could be on an unprecedently broad scale.

Lake Tahoe to the present demand structure, for instance, is of less significance than helping the gambling and recreation industry. While every effort is being expended to save the lake on behalf of these industries, all action is predicated on the continued operation of the economy as it has developed along the California–Nevada border. Practically speaking, no one proposes dismantling that development in order to save Lake Tahoe. The losses being imposed are of course a social cost, in the discounted sense of what posterity must eventually assume as a burden. But the loss of Lake Tahoe would be immediately a loss to nature; and it is the natural systems which would have to promptly accommodate. No discount operation works on nature's behalf.

Nature has her limitations as to the number of repeated insults to ecological systems which she can sustain. The demand structure continues pushing against these limits without trepidation or acknowledgement that there is a finite character to what in nature has been drawn upon in order to sustain the seeming profitability of the growth-demandant culture. Cavalier action to nature as a source of resources for human demand has been the tradition, though for many doubts about its wisdom have begun to creep into the consciousness.

Environmental Shortages and Predicted Demand

There is a growing consensus that during the remainder of this century there may be inadequate supplies of material resources and energy to satisfy the kind of demand urban-industrial society will want to continue making. The president of the National Association of Manufacturers could say in 1974, "...the approaching raw material shortage is a greater crisis than the energy crisis." The Club of Rome could predict,

We have used lead, copper, zinc, chromium, aluminum as though there were no end to them.... We have wasted our raw materials at a rate which means we're going to run out if we don't slow up.[4]

These are seen as fairly imminent threats to the ability of high growth demand to continue functioning in any but a very limping fashion. It is this fear, in all probability, that has sent so many diverse interests scurrying to the law and government with the call to "do something" to prevent such awful events from transpiring. To do something, that is, except anything that would require a change in the operations of the threatened demand curves.

Of course, many still insist there is no crisis approaching rapidly for the way urban-industrial society relates with natural systems. They are not impressed by the Club of Rome, so why should they be any more convinced by the president of the National Associaton of Manufacturers? For them, there is no crisis between what will be demanded of nature and what the renewing environment can supply. When pressed as to what the real problems may be, they respond with the assurance that the problems are the kind that will respond very well to institutional reform.

Those who find this blandness not in accordance with the evidence put such persons in the "if" category. Thusly, *if* there were no crisis between the demands being made on the environment, *then* only incremental changes would be needed. Incremental changes, of course, are always needed. They must go on forever. It is basic social change which occurs rarely; and the people in the "if" category see no reason to go through anything so painful.

For these "if" people, every scientific investigation of the environment proves there is no impending crisis. For them, there is a consensus among scientists that there is no imminent threat of extinction. There continues to be only the same, long-known experience of risk, uncertainty, and the likelihood that much more can be learned if only there were more study and research. Any problems caused by industrial activity, urban sprawl, or bad agricultural practices are purely local in their effect on the renewability of the environment. Perhaps they might be serious enough to treat upon a regional scale but they scarcely rise any higher in significance.

Clearly for these optimists, there should be no cause for alarm. One should first accumulate the *proof* that there is a threat to the integrity of the biosphere in some fairly short time-frame. In the current absence of such proof, they remain comforted by the conviction the lead times for every kind of corrective action must still remain very long.

Of course they are realists enough to recognize that human demands are made in an environment of finite resources and that mankind must maximize production from this finite stock of resources. It would not be rational nor equitable to fail to do that much, but this scarcely amounts to the need for any crash program or crisis atmosphere. As Abram Chayes, Harvard law professor and former legal advisor to the State Department, has spaciously explained,

...the new awareness of environmental constraints implies a political process extending indefinitely in time. Its characteristic instruments will not be policing and regulation of environmental insults but planning and management of environmental resources.[5]

In such a view, environmental protection is just another cost to be weighed along with other costs of a social or economic or other human interest. There is certainly no need on behalf of the environment to make any changes in the operations of an expanding demand structure. In any event, there is ample time for reflection and study. Environmental protection can never be more than one more surrogate for the ideal of human betterment, after all; and human betterment has never seemed to be a matter calling for urgent action. The possibility that human betterment might be a concept not synonymous or in harmony with guarding renewability is given scant consideration.

The "if" category of people usually regard themselves as the pragmatists. The late 20th century political process functions, as the pragmatists admit, in the crisis of crises. Incommensurable values such as economic efficiency, income distribution, social welfare, and national security struggle for attention. Environmental protection to them is just another competitor for what the proponents of the other values are seeking: capital investment, energy commitment, and popular support.

When environmental protection is seen as just another competitor for such commitments – and a lately arrived one at that, as many claim – policies on behalf of the environment cannot be expected to register in favor of environmental protection as the single, most important choice social decision could make. Before that can happen, scientific knowledge, the awareness of current technology, and the perception of the burdens both impose will all have to come together into a single opinion evidencing the over-riding importance of sustaining the renewability in the environment in comparison to the maintenance of any number of human demands.

About the best that can be hoped for at a public level, pending the basic social decision to act in an integrated and comprehensive manner toward nature, is to protect parts of the environment from the demands of what are seen as the environment's rivals. Economic efficiency, income distribution, social welfare, and national security are not prepared at this time to take any subordination in importance.[6] Perhaps they will be convinced to do so one day. But that day is still seen as long distant. For many there is no reason to hasten the arrival of that day. For them, there will be many future occasions to fully work out the properly applicable means of dealing with what they see as separable and local problems, as such problems emerge. In brief, there is for many no urgency in any prediction of environmental shortage.

Bureaucracy as a Palliative for the Environment

Attitudes of indifference to the renewing environment are common in a growth-demandant culture still incapable of reflecting on the risks it imposes upon nature. Among beneficiaries of the way that culture has functioned only the human condition is worthy of human concern – or some claim.

[C]oncern for the "environment" becomes a surrogate for concern for the preservation, amelioration, and improvement of man's condition.[7]

Someday this may involve major political, economic and social changes. But many other matters of purely human involvement could insist on change of equal extent. All problems become equal, in this view, with the environment's a little less so. And if the environment has problems that are only surrogates for human problems, many can see no reason for not believing the crises will serendipitously extend indefinitely in time. Resolution and equilibrium may never be attained but bureaucracy will contain the crises of both humanity and the environment by institutionalizing them. The bureaucratic proclivity for striking bargains satisfactory to nearly all will thereby be sustained.

Unfortunately for so happy an expectation no one can predict that some apocalypse is not going to foreclose a future course along such lines. A relationship may be worked out in the 21st century and later that will envelop and sustain all human activity within a viable renewing environment for an indefinite future history. There is evidence that this is possible. But humanity must get from here to there.

And there is other evidence humanity may not make it. For example, there is enough evidence now accumulated to indicate that an extrapolation of what has been the accelerating condition of growth curves for about two centuries is not possible. The evidence is also at hand that the rest of the 20th century is going to be a period of crisis between urban-industrial demand and environmental response. What is more, there seems little evidence that any self-generated shift is going to occur among those enjoying the benefits of the way the demand structure has been working. And, still, the evidence is strong that,

...man must start immediate restructuring of societal institutions at all levels to better provide for environmental planning, for technology assessment, for study of environmental impact, and for similar functions.[8]

Yet, despite the public demand for more bureaucratic involvement in current affairs, there is a simultaneous public dismay at the role bureaucracy has been playing and likely shall continue to play. Such a role is unavoidable unless there is a shifting in priorities of fragmenting and processing the environment to an integration of human demand and the ability of natural systems to respond to that demand. This would mean altering priorities so that such matters as urban sprawl and aggrandizement of growth would not be given an automatic first place. Industrial activities would no longer be allowed to be carried on in indifference to nature. The maintenance of ecologic systems and the ecumene would not be regarded as somehow independent of, and inferior to, the human existence.

Shifts of this kind in priorities require as a minimum a change in political decisions. Beyond that, there must eventually be an alteration in values so that legitimacy does not derive from growth alone. They are not changes that can be carried through by persons who regard them as a part of a spare-time avocation to be taken up when nothing else preoccupies them among the problems of the late 20th century nor to be the subject-matter of happy bargains between bureaucrats and their conflicting constituencies.

It does seem to be true that the late 20th century is one where the people of the world live in a crisis of crises. But all crises are not equal in importance. The situation of the renewing environment vis-a-vis the demand structure is likely of another order. Either it is greater than the others or else it is the crisis that is the backdrop and intensifying reflection of those others. Environmental issues cannot be kept at a low level on the list of priorities for the culture or for the bureaucracies within the culture. With rising force, they are compelling themselves ever further up the list.

Innovating a bureaucracy on behalf of nature is not a sufficient change. For too many, there is a fear-provoked flight to bureaucractic mechanisms, without regard for whether there can be enough strength in these by themselves. The evidence grows ever stronger that they cannot possess or be delegated that kind of power. Bureaucrats do not act in a social vacuum nor perform their duties without regard for the basic values of the culture in which they function. The legal system itself will not find an inherent worth in nature if there is no social decision within the culture that first recognizes such worth independently of any value conferred by human activity.

Until that change occurs, bureaucracy at most will be a palliative in relieving nature's burdens. At worst, it will be just another institution pushing nature further along to irretrievable breaks in her life systems. The renewing environment cannot find a source for renewal in bureaucratic mechanisms by themselves. To all bureaucratic bargains to accommodate conflicting demands, the renewing environment will respond with indifference. Behind that indifference, though, will be reactions that ought to be moving social decisions toward the basic changes, in lieu of all temporary bargains, that environmental conditions are in the process of imposing.

Juristic Alternatives to an Environmental Bureaucracy

There is a steadily wider public perception that the environment is not responding well to the impact of urban-industrial demands. This has led to an insistence that regulation create a stability in man's relationship with nature which has never existed. Nor can a balance in that relationship be brought into existence, barring changes in the intensity of demand, when there is still a reluctance to carry through. As a consequence, many bureaucratic mechanisms have been judged as failures; and the suggestions have been brought forward that there are better legal ways than these for protecting the environment.

Many misleadingly think of them as in some way more "radical" than the bureaucratic process. This is ironic when one considers the bureaucratic process was once turned to as itself a "radical" change. In actuality, neither bureaucracy nor the alternatives being offered to it within the legal system are in any sense of the term "radical." They simply represent different kinds of procedures and are probably more complementary than competitive to bureaucracy.

Many of those who have lost faith in the bureaucracy have turned to private civil actions and to the extraordinary injunctive powers of equity. The law suit and equity pleading, once thought hopelessly reactionary and archaic, are now seen by many as the bright and better alternative to the operations of public administration. Damages are seen as the way to grant immediate and tangible relief to private persons. Beyond this, however, they also may serve as a means of compelling some cost internalization of what have thereby become external diseconomies.

Primarily, however, it is not the law side, with its relief in damages, that is seen as the better recourse. It is equity, whose chancellor has so much broader power to do justice than any judge, that is preferred. Equitable relief is seen as providing essentially what can be called a "public good" by the decree itself. The public benefits from stopping certain grievous conduct will presumably have broader social benefits in most instances than they have merely for the individual seeking the prohibition. An order for the payment of damages to an individual is not seen as having imposed so extensive an external cost.

Equity is also perceived as having an attribute not shared by the law court's orders for the payment of money judgments. This is because injunctions are nearly impossible to simply incorporate into an ongoing, basically unchanged method of doing business. Damages or even criminal fines can be paid by the obdurate. They can then make them a part of their costs and pass them along to their customers without making any adjustment on behalf of the environment in their business conduct.[9]

What makes the decree of the chancellor so "radical" lies in his power to frame the decree in a way to absolutely, permanently shut down an offender. In so doing, in order for the offender to reopen, all the dislocating costs up to that time borne by the environment, the social structure, or individual human beings can be made an incurring prerequisite before the plant may reopen. If the enterprise closed should have been sufficiently marginal and imperilled by economic risks, as commonly has been the case with many environmentally harmful activities,[10] then some would argue that the harm of the closing has been compensated by the benefits. So many factors would have therefore combined to prevent reopening that the environmental reasons would have been only a precipitant.[11] But whatever the case in this regard, it is hard to offer anyone a more severe alternative than ordering their enterprise closed down. The ones closed usually consider this a very "radical" action indeed.

The chancellor really has no greater powers capable of permanent effect than has been the case in modern times with administrative mechanisms. Bureaucracy has been delegated power as broad as equity. But because of the often closely symbiotic relationships existing between the regulating agencies and their constituent interests, this power is used most sparingly. In addition, there is the sense of "other-ness" attaching to the law courts and equity which the long-established agency does not possess. The character of the courts as intervenors in the bureaucratic relationship with its constituent interests gives a greater effect to the courts' orders and decrees. If courts were to become a routine part of that relationship, then by that fact alone the power of their actions would be diminished. It is because law and equity come into the bureaucratic process as an intervention that their actions have their apparent "radical" quality.

Some do not regard this intervention by law and equity as being really productive of any positive change. So disenchanted are they with the whole system that they believe this to be an impossibility. However, they believe such intervention is able to prevent action, even though unable to produce positive beneficial change. For them, prevention of action, the way the world is now, is an environmentally salvaging goal. These are the advocates of what has been called the "no-win strategy."

A "no-win strategy" works, if it works at all, only in close relationship with established practices that are capable of being used favorably to it. The law is seen as a theater. It is scarcely judgmental at all and the courts exist as vehicles to influence public opinion. The assumption is implicit that one has done enough if one has kept anything from being done at all. By thrusting the burden of proving benefit upon the proponents of technological change and economic growth, their proposals can be kept from ever coming to fruition. The prospects of any other kind of victory are not relevant in deciding to oppose this or that kind of allegedly environmentally harmful project.[12]

For the "no-winners," a losing fight may in the long run be a victory if it leads to a change in public attitude and if the emotions of the majority can be fully engaged in the anguish of the defeat. To hold to traditional views of "win" or "lose" is to risk defeat at the very beginning of the struggle. To those who may be shocked by the situational ethics involved, the answer is that the advocates of "no-win strategy" are justified by the quality of their opposition. They are in confrontation with

...the military-industrial research and development complex...of dependent trade associations, economic interest groups, public relations media,...congressional protectors...[and] powerful allies among the major corporations, the military services, utilities, universities, and research institutes in the United States and abroad...the well-orchestrated chorus....[13]

In brief, it is the battle of David against Goliath; and it must be so depicted. The best stones for the sling in this drama will be the education of the opinion-formers and the policy-makers. A scenario has to be acted that makes out of raw events a melodrama of suspense. The climax in the public's view must be the slaying of a giant. The humiliation of a final defeat must be avoided and so the struggle must be cast as guerrilla theater. The legal process has to be turned into the stuff of political drama since the ultimate power is not in any particular court or bureaucracy. The final power for social change lies with a public who have been enlightened through the use of law as an audio-visual teaching tool.

The legalist can say it will have a dissolving effect upon all institutions and asserts it is doom to the legal process. But the "no-win strategist" is indifferent to the charge. He does not really believe the institutions will dissolve; and, if they should, then their dissolution will scarcely have come too soon. His purpose is not with institutions. It is with preventing further impact upon the environment. In such a cause, there may be costs suffered by human institutions; but they are of not so great a magnitude as the costs the urban-industrial demand structure has for so long been imposing upon the environment.

The "no-win strategy" is related to a similar theatrical technique, the "eco-commando." For "no-win strategists," it is the law and its institutions that provide the scene for mummery. For the "eco-commando" it is the political arena where the dramatic action takes place that is to instruct the public and thereby produce basic social change. Although on its face a non-juristic approach, it is meant ultimately to affect the actions of both courts and bureaucracies.

Because the legal system and the bureaucratic mechanisms have done so very much to serve the causes of undifferentiated growth in high energy culture, the "eco-commandos" charge that their authority and legitimacy have been fatally undermined. Judges and bureaucrats can now best be used by persons deliberately violating existing legal and bureaucratic prescripts. Realistically, the present court and bureaucratic forms can only push along the kinds of growth demands now known. If the social demands are to be changed, the public must be educated to make the changes and to force different courses of action upon the courts and the bureaucracies. For this purpose, violence is to be carefully scripted and the established values brought to a condition preparatory to change by the "eco-commandos."

The favorite examples for people with this viewpoint that is drawn from American experience are the riots by blacks that torched parts of Detroit, Los Angeles, and Newark. As Professor Donald Large, one of the advocates for the "eco-commando," has argued,

Violent tactics are contradictory to the spirit of the ecological movement, but...the contrast in efforts to assist the urban poor before and after Watts indicates that a few factories may be blown up and a few executives kidnapped for ecological ransom before legislators, administrators, and judges begin to get the hint.[14]

The legal system is seen as incapable of action in the face of environmental deterioration because the pressure has not been exerted upon decision-makers sufficiently to bring their attention into focus. The public has been insufficiently educated to make demands preventive of the plundering of nature and the potential destruction of life support systems. Indeed, the present conditions are viewed as so desperate that the public itself remains ignorant that their demands are in the direction of further plundering rather than in its cessation.

To the "eco-commando," it is folly to think there will be any generosity or favorable systemic response from the managers of the present social order, except under pressure. The extralegal means will violate only laws that have already exhausted their legitimacy. In any event such actions, however violent, would be symbolic only. By themselves they could not produce change. All they would be intended to do would be to prepare the public mind of the need for a revolutionary change in the organization of the culture. A new consciousness would emerge, productive of changed laws and a succession to legitimacy for the legal and bureaucratic institutions from their present state of invalidity. Out of symbolic violence would come social peace.

One wonders how revolutionary the effect would be of such dramas. The riots in the 1960's in certain American cities did produce an increase in welfare expenditures but they did not bring closer a redistribution of wealth. The course of history has not ended on that subject, of course, and ultimately they may prove an influence in that direction.

Yet, in bringing about quicker social change, are the scenarios of the "no-win strategists" and the "eco-commandos" enough? Their purpose seems quite different from those who do violence, in any case. Where violence is practiced in the world, it has not been for its educational power alone. Rather there has been a concern for an anticipated turnover of political power. This violence in the world has been more a symptom of change trying to take place than of any effort to educate the public of a need for change.

But the change that is called for in how demands are formulated and how the environment is to be assisted in responding to them transcend the usual distinctions to which political attention is directed. As a result, to accomplish the change needed in social consensus there must be broad support. Without broad public support, the work of the "no-win strategist" and the "eco-commando" will extract the grant of just enough concessions to isolate their position and to render their melodramas into sentimental comedies. If the purpose is not to use these tactics in order to make the present system unworkable, so that there can be a swift movement for the transfer of power, then they will be tactics difficult to orchestrate over any very long interval.

Given the sort of basic alterations needed in social attitudes concerning growth and the environment's capacity to absorb it, one can understand why the proponents of "no-win strategy" and "eco-commandos" do not believe a shift among the holders of power to be a goal equal in importance to that of changing social attitudes. At the same time, however, one may well wonder if the scenarios of "no-win" and "eco-commando" will produce any more drastic shift than changing the personnel who use the legal and administrative processes in conventional ways.

One may doubt the long-run success of "no-win strategy" and "eco-commando." But one cannot examine the actions of the American federal judiciary in the 1970's without perceiving the value for the environment of their exercise of juristic authority. Obligated to enforce a series of federal statutes (including, but not limited to, the National Environmental Protection Act of 1969, the Air Quality Act of 1970, and the Water Quality Act of 1972), they have been innovative and action-forcing. Stimulated by environmental organizations, who have used fairly traditional trial techniques, decisions have been handed down that have changed bureaucratic practices, broken up some of the cozier relations between regulators and the regulated, compelled different approaches by environmental exploiters of forest, swamps, and estuaries – and, most to be hoped for above all the above, may even have helped strengthen the renewing powers of the environment.

Yet, active and useful as law and equity are proving for the environment, they are not a substitute for bureaucracy. Courts are themselves a part of the regulatory process, not an institution external to it. Just as judges use rules of property to enforce the larger social decisions, so do they use the bureaucrats to enforce pre-determined policies. Even the chancellor in equity, with all his seeming panoply of power, is not finally independent of legislative policy, bureaucratic functioning, and social decisions. Consequently, law and equity are juristic supplements, not substitutes, for legislative, bureaucratic and public action.

Hierarchical Alternatives in the Environmental Bureaucracy

There are those who insist that institutionally the environment would be best served by moving all bureaucratic action to almost the precinct level. At that extremely local level, they would concentrate authority, fiscal responsibility, and final decision-making. Instead of invoking experts from central bureaucratic structures, or the powers of law and equity, or the dramas of "no-win" and "eco-command-ing," they would take matters back to the parish pump. Others would try out some intermediate forms of regional authority at stages somewhere between the precinct and the national power. Still others would have a national preemption of certain responsibilities, either because they believe these could be best handled nationally or because they think what has not been pre-empted can then be better served at the local and/or regional level.

Each one of these is more fiddling with incremental change rather than moving on to actions of deeper significance. The hope remains strong that some one of these reforms will solve all problems between man and nature.

A cynic might wonder if the proponents of "no-win strategy" were not the spinners of bureaucratic reform rather than those who talk of "no-win" only in terms of litigation.

The public has shown little interest in the precinct approach. But it would be one way to produce integrated decisions on a very narrow horizon. Historically, this has been where the responsibility for the environment has lain in the governmental structure. While the kings fretted over other questions, water was coming from the parish pump, fallowing and crop rotation were being kept up by the manorial courts, and nuisances to air and water within the boroughs were left to the burgage tribunals. Even where the sovereign authority was centrally asserted, as in the laws relating to forests, weirs, and mill privileges, localizing encroachments were continuous.

But the reasons that swept local control away or into ineffectiveness are the same reasons why it cannot be restored. The most important is that the local integrated decision only appears to produce integration. The deciding unit is no longer autonomous merely because it is local. Local units are part of national markets and other conglomerates that make local decisions more segregative than integrative in character. Furthermore, urban-industrial society itself demands a level of governmental service that cannot be supplied at the local level. It has been this need which has led to the creation and assertion of effective power by central bureaucratic apparatus, far more than the pressure of the environmentalists.

Right now the central bureaucratic structures are under attack as imperceptive, indifferent, unresponsive, or simply as captured by the constituent interests they are charged with managing or regulating. There is no swift solution for the bases of these criticisms. And there is strong evidence that the criticisms are well made.

To abolish the central bureaucracies and to transfer all their duties to neighborhood committees is an impossibility. Perhaps the hundred in Anglo-Saxon England could handle its responsibilities under the demands of a low energy culture. An equivalent number of households formed into a local unit today could not begin to cope with all the consequences of the demands the present culture now imposes. In the long-past emerging decades of urban-industrial society, the larger units of local government already were overwhelmed. Those units still are overwhelmned and scarcely ready even for federal revenue sharing programs. But to transfer total responsibilities today for the environment to intensely localized institutions eventually would collapse the infrastructure of the governmentally sustained public order upon which the whole of urban-industrial society rests. The failures of a central bureaucracy cannot be solved by substituting local committees of house-holders.

More participation by the governed in administrative mechanisms may be needed. But it should come in the course of working toward integrated action. The present demand system is so fragmenting in its actions that integrative actions simply could not come from the decisions of local units of goverment. Even if a random sample could be found to show some such decisions were possible, their isolated character would only act to serve the pressures for processing every phenomenon into the growth of production and consumption.

There are those who would agree that local government is incapable of sufficiently unifying action, but they would simultaneously charge that the national bureaucracies have not proven responsive to any except their more manipulative constituent interests. These are the people who urge the development of intermediate levels of government somewhere between the locality and the nation. They call them regions and they think these would be more responsive to the needs posed by particular issues.

Unfortunately for such hopes, experiments in regional government have not been a success. In most instances, only additional barriers have been inter-posed between the needs of the environment and the means of perhaps meeting those needs. They have simply become additional fragmented units feeding the growth of the demand structure. It has been some time now since environmentalists had an unalloyed enthusiasm about the energy mission of the Tennessee Valley Authority and the reasons are much slighter to have enthusiasm about the work of the typical regional planning agency.

Many will believe that it is unfair to characterize regional approaches to the structuring of governmental units as a failure. Regionalization can assume so many forms that one wonders if somewhere in the shifting images there may not be hidden some successes that simply need being brought into prominence. If the test of success is limited to the regional authorities' ability to exchange views, perhaps success can occasionally be found. They do that fairly well. It is only when operational work assignments come along that they languish into the apparent failures their critics see.

Regional units can be permanent or they can be temporary *ad hoc* coordina-ting committees. They may be formed under an interstate compact, through reciprocal federal-state legislation, or by a simple exchange of letters between the heads of involved departments. Whatever the origin of their formation or their degree of permanency, the multiple sources that generated them commonly cause them to be headed by committees whose members sit in a representative capacity for the governmental units that have been drawn into the regional jurisdiction. There is almost an organic growth quality about the way regional governmental organizations have come into being, growth, and function.

As Gary Hart has said,

One gets the feeling...of witnessing a brief span in a long evolutionary spectrum, of reporting on interim agencies created from the bits and pieces of predecessor institutions and themselves giving way in future years to some elaborate, more sophisticated, and perhaps, even more effective institutions.[15]

The hope is always constant that there will be a more "effective" future, if only some later reorganization can be successfully carried through. Unfortunately, what has not been very often obtained is "the kind of stability generally suggesting permanence." Instead, "a consensus exists that those institutions are inadequate."[16]

The regional approach, even when some might conclude it has resulted in success, has not been particularly integrative. It may be the beginning of integration insofar as there has been success in exchanging views and forming solid fields of information where only bits of expert opinion had previously existed. But insofar as the missions of regional units have had an effect, it has been in the direction of further fragmentation rather than toward comprehensive, integrating action. The welter of regional units, from joint sewer districts to basin authorities, have had their potential integrative effect destroyed by the larger emphasis of the culture upon production and consumption in order to produce the conditions for open-ended growth. They have not even succeeded in often extinguishing the lesser units whose functions they have subsumed as their integrative regional missions. Gary Hart, otherwise a man optimistic about the prospects of regionalization, speaks dourly about this.

Much like a State does not lose its separate and identifiable interest when becoming a member of the Union, neither would the Federal, State or other commission members entirely shed their respective special concerns.... The very process...automatically involves balkanization of interests and perpetuation of narrow protective points of view.[17]

The attempt to avoid this "balkanization" by insulating the management of the regional unit from all influence by the jurisdictions which are the source of power and authority for the regional unit have not been particularly successful. Perhaps the managers acquire a "regional mentality," but even that is not very likely. What has happened most often, as in the case of the New York Port Authority, has been the exchange of political bias for agency bias. The resulting condition can scarcely be described as one of integration, since such regional agencies themselves become additional forces for segregation and the increase in undifferentiated growth.

Regional units have been continuously forced into competition for their financial support with the very jurisdictions which compose them. Revenue sharing between the federal, the state, and local governments has intensified this competition. The struggle for both money and authority between governmental levels in the vertical hierarchy, who confessedly have never been friends, has not eased the situation. What they often have done to paper over the conflict is to create a regional unit which, like already existing regional units, becomes another competitor for money and authority. The agency that establishes the firmest conduits to the reservoirs of money and authority is the bureaucracy that will prevail – and there are very few regional units that are likely to prevail in that struggle.

The situation which compels this struggle among bureaucratic structures can only strengthen fragmentation within a growth-demandant culture. When there is a refusal to reach a social decision in the direction of integration, the bureaucratic mechanisms most vulnerable in the struggle for wealth and power will be those most useful to any effort which might be made in the direction of controlling growth. Control over funds establishes the power, and often the authority, of an agency. Without a change in the way priorities have been ordered, any governmental unit is more vulnerable in direct relation to whether it is seen as helping or hindering the production and consumption demand structure. At the present time, regional units meant to protect the environment are among the more vulnerable.

Regional units of government, of course, will not disappear from the table of organization. Aside from the inertia which protects even the moribund among bureaucrats, the regional units were not created out of some perverse urge to counteract reality. They were brought into existence as the result of situations which fell in the interstices of the current division of governmental responsibility. There is no evidence that the older governmental forms, or revenue sharing, or citizen participation are going to be the means of filling those gaps. A national pre-emption and subsequent reorganization of authority and power could do so. But until there is some desire for a comprehensive, integrated kind of action on a national scale that is socially committed to counteracting the forces for open-ended, undifferentiated growth, there is no point in talking about a national pre-emption.

Environmental Bureaucratic Failures – Some External Causes

Without the basic social decision for change, neither regionalism, nor revenue sharing, nor citizen participation, nor national pre-emption can accomplish the task of resolving the conflict between urban-industrial demand and the response of the renewing environmental systems. There is not even the governmental equivalent in most states today to the national, year-round markets which have come into existence in the more developed economies, acting to tie them in closely to even larger global market systems. Government, however, does not operate in the same way; and, consequently, government cannot be judged by the same tests as to what constitutes efficient performance that are used to judge market operations.

Government in its bureaucratic functioning has no measure of profit or loss, no test for services offered that either few or many take up, and even less for testing whether or not what government has done has offered anyone any advantages apart from the salaries paid the bureaucrats. Benefit, practical effect, sensitivity, and responsiveness have all become common expressions used to express popular discontent because it has been so very difficult to decide if governmental mechanisms have performed well or ill. The crises for the bureaucracy come at a faster pace than ever before and they present the administrative agencies with more complex forms of those crises. Every level of government – national, regional, or local – has to accommodate operations to the constraints these complex crises impose.

The bureaucratic accommodation, therefore, must come sooner or later. If the decision is long postponed, the result can only be at a minimum the cause of the suffering that need never have been. Minimal or not, however, the bureaucratic delay will make its contribution to the suffering malaise.

Under the weight and complexity of current demand, most sectors of government stand indicted in the public mind as failures. Regional government, for many, has been the most severely attacked as most remote from public control, most lacking in accountability to any other units in the governmental hierarchy, and most involved with their own internal bureaucratic governance. However, regional governmental units have not been isolated failures among the general inability of government to cope. The burdens thrust upon the bureaucratic mechanisms by those perceiving the need to do something, other than merely accept the presently existing situation between man and nature, have produced for government in the public eye the appearance of fumbling and incompetence.

Truly the failure of government is not the failure at any level of the bureaucratic structure. It is more the executive and legislative branches who have been unable to meet the demands thrust forward by events. Repeatedly, they have delegated their power to any level of bureaucratic agency that seemed available politically. Wherever there has been conflict, it has seemed simplest to refer the matter to the allegedly neutral experts.

And quite often the bureaucrats at any assigned level have been as successful, within narrow mission ranges, as any could have anticipated. Indeed, it
has often been their mission successes which have produced the popular
opinion of failure. The bureaucracies may have produced in the public mind
a sense of fumbling, incompetence, arrogance, and ultimate failure through
misapplied successes or by way of a plain inability to resolve the conflicts
assigned them, but the blame ought not fall entirely on the bureaucrats.

It has been so simple for the executive and legislative branches to delegate
responsibility to the bureaucracy – and, then, at a later time to denounce the
bureaucracy for its failures. There is a tendency to overlook the 20th century
ability to bring together legal, economic, and bureaucratic forms so as to
interact and produce previously unknown mechanisms for controlling the
environmental situation. The pessimism about the possibilities of bureaucratic operations is currently overdone.

The Determinative Role of Growth-Demand
on the Environmental Bureaucracy

There are many who insist a socialist bureaucracy will protect a renewing
environment whereas nothing can be expected from bureaucracy under
private capitalism. The latter can only be exploitative while the former will
be essentially protective. They cite some of the sensitivities in Engels' *Dialectic
of Nature* as proof. Friedrich Engels said,

Let us not flatter ourselves over much on account of our human conquest over
nature. For each such conquest takes its revenge on us. Each of them, it is true,
has in its first place the consequences on which we counted, but in the second and
third places, it has quite different unforeseen effects which only too often cancel
out the first.[18]

The basis for this observation was the manner in which private capitalism
in his day had dealt with the environment. In the early stage of the development of urban-industrial society with which Engels was familiar, government
had acted in a manner purely incidental to the purposes of private capital in
meeting demand. Insofar as a few governmental actions were taken toward the
environment allegedly meant to protect it from the emerging demand structure, they were more for the purpose of helping in the processes of industrialization by spacing out the resources to be used than saving the environment.
Engels and the early Marxists, instead, were quick in perceiving advantages in
establishing interrelated relationships between this urban-industrial society's
demand structure and nature. To this extent, those are right who claim a

socialist bureaucracy theoretically could assume an effective operating position toward the environment.

In the event, the pressures of a culture having a thrust toward energy cascades and increasing demands for the material exploitation of nature have prevented this from being the case. The Marxists, like most socialists, have had a firm commitment to the expansion of urban-industrial demand and to increasing the amount of energy available to make that a possibility. Lenin's actions in government, for example, may show a dedication to environmental protection stronger than the attitude which was to prevail for many decades following his death, but it was of less impact than his stronger demand for industrialization, for an increase in material resources, and for growth in energy supplies. Insofar as socialism would protect the environment, it would have to do it through serving the demands for growth.

Losses would be eliminated from the process itself by "the rational distribution of industry...from the standpoint of proximity to raw materials," and a generally responsible attitude toward socialist property, compliance with technical rules, and utilization of the by-products of one industry by another.[19]

Although Lenin's remarks express an interest in protecting the renewing environment, it is plain that he foresaw that socialist societies, as had been the case with private capitalist ones, would be pushing for the growth of energy and of the urban-industrial growth. Growth has no more served the environment under socialism than was the case under the old capitalism first denounced by Engels. At a later period, what had been cautionary in his words concerning the drive for this kind of growth, was lost to sight.

The rush to industrialize has impacted heavily upon the natural environment in socialist economies too. As the *Literaturnaia Gazeta* said in 1967, "black streams flow down black slopes," with few effective voices raised in any degree of alarm over the deterioration of the natural environment.[20] Industrialization, as among non-socialists, has been seen as the goal and pollution as the price to be paid for it.

The socialist bureaucracy has seemed to be no different than any other in refusing to obtrude themselves between what is seen as an essential cultural purpose – the increase in energy and industrialization – and something like the renewing environment which is viewed still as an incidental amenity by most. Pollution of the renewing environment is simply not seen as an irreversible processing of essential systemic parts. The benefits obtained through urban-industrial growth have obscured the deterioration of nature which has been progressing steadily. Despite the insights offered so presciently by Engels, socialist bureaucracies show by their actions that the basic social decision has not been made for them to subordinate open-ended, undifferentiated growth for a viable relationship with nature. How soon they might receive such a mandate is difficult to predict, but one may doubt if it will come sooner for them than it will for bureaucrats in other types of economies.

The result of placing burdens upon any bureaucratic mechanism which it cannot support, regardless of the bureaucrats' politics, has to be a growing sense among people of an inherent lack of ability in government. Bureaucracy among socialists and non-socialists alike eventually will be seen as unable to cope with the crises present between the human demand structure and the renewing systems in the environment. Putting aside the limitations that must always be present in any human instrument, this would be a most unfortunate popular attitude to have cultivated.

Law, the courts, and/or bureaucracy cannot do the whole task. If societies believe they can have undifferentiated, openended growth, *plus* a stability and equilibrium between individual human beings, social structure, and the natural environment, they are going to be disabused ultimately of this notion. No combination of law, rule of property, juristic institution, and bureaucracy can provide such a happy state under conditions that would be exactly like those of the present. To insist these structures can succeed under these conditions is to see them all fail and to lead to the conclusion they must always fail. A conclusion like that one would be unjustified and quickly productive of further intensifying the disorder between the renewing environment and the demand structure.

The popular view that stability and equilibrium are values that are needed and that they should have a high priority is not unfounded. The rapidity with which the environment is being processed into production and consumption units of high energy culture, not to speak of humanity's own sense of "future shock" at what is taking place within human social structure, provides the evidence for this view. To those who have known only the relatively static character of pre-urban-industrial society the advantages of change can be very seductive. But to those who have been immersed in the energy cascades and demands of that society, knowing only swift change and disequilibrium, the desire for stability produces its own seductiveness as well.[21]

Nevertheless, stability is not to be obtained by an administrative order. The bureaucracy cannot be commanded to bring about equilibrium between man and nature, or within the social structure, or within each individual human being. If this is insisted upon, without accompanying basic social change, the bureaucracy will break under the strain and its fragments will be cast aside in the general fragmentizing of a by then highly disequilibrating growth-demandant culture. To encourage this by indifference, hypocrisy, or cynicism would be productive of no good.

There is a genuine perceived value for the institution of a state of stability between the environment and the growth demands of urban-industrial society. But to think it can be brought about by bureaucracy alone is an unwise notion. What makes it unwise is the unwillingness to make any other social change in the way urban-industrial society has been functioning. In the absence of that, abstract demands for stability will contribute more to intensifying all crises than in resolving any of them.

The High Costs of an Environmental Bureaucracy

Because the demand structure imposes a condition of instability upon the environment, this inescapably charges costs as well as conferring whatever benefits are extracted by the process. This is what makes it so difficult to effectively shift priorities. A nod is given periodically by everyone in the direction of man and nature being all one world and concluding that bio-physically the unity is an uncompromising one. After the rhetorical flourish, however, effective steps toward the programmatic methods to accomplish a meaningful acceptance of the significance of that unity are not taken.

Instead people discuss how difficult it is to do anything in the political, legal, and bureaucratic world on behalf of the environment. They say scientific assessment and political decision-making, after all, are quite different processes. In an age dominated by a scientific ethos, perhaps one should accept that scientific and technical criteria should shape all social decisions rather than the other way round.

But science can be rigorous and everyone knows that politics is compromise. The pragmatists know trade-offs come in sets. Thus, while environmental assessment is a cognitive process, environmental regulation is a political one. Compromise is, therefore, basic; and this is hard for the scientist and technologist to understand, since bargaining is not part of their cognitive process. What is important to the bureaucrat concerned with the burden of decision-making on a public level is excluded by the scientist and technologist from their value assessments. Hence, to everyone involved, it is all terribly difficult.[22]

And indeed it is. Terribly, terribly difficult. And expensive. Everywhere one turns there are high costs, whether there is to be bargaining or no bargaining. The political process is expensive. Law, government, and bureaucracy do not come cheaply. And there are always those to say there is no agreement as a social consensus, that social decisions do not exist, that problems of a growth-demandant culture are a myth, and the crises between the demands of high energy and open urban-industrial growth and nature are non-existent.

Despite any evidence to the contrary, this will continue to be said and it will justify the avoidance of incurring all the costs that any sort of political action requires. There will never be universal agreement that any problem exists between human culture and nature until the sort of break occurs that is irreparable. But, still, those who believe that a crisis exists and the time is at hand for action must never forget that even the minimum burdens of action will be enormously costly in comparison with anything done previously for the environment by mankind for any purpose.

In the early 1950's such shrewd observers as Robert Dahl and Charles Lindblom were already insisting that the major obstacles to large-scale decision-making were the:

(a) extreme analytical difficulty, and perhaps impossibility, of identifying for policy purposes the complex and dynamic linkages between multiple phenomena and of envisioning the possible consequences of the decisions being made, (b) the problem of forecasting rapid technological change, and (c) the rigidity with which complex institutions meet innovative tasks of major dimensions.[23]

When burdens increase, costs go up; and the greatest burden to a political system is identifying interrelationships at some point in time to do anything about the consequences of those interrelationships upon the institutions of the political system charged with forecasting change and dealing with it. Politics serves nothing but the advantages of the moment when it goes along with something akin to the fragmenting and processing of the renewing environment. But politics is a vehicle whereby changed social decisions can be implemented through the legal and bureaucratic mechanisms. Without such assistance from politics, making legal and bureaucratic changes will prove of little or no use. By themselves, such changes will merely inflate the costs of what political decision-making does produce, no matter how little effect those decisions may have in the direction of environmental protection.

This is probably the source of the disillusionment that lies at the base of the critical views of so sharp an observer as Aaron Wildavsky. Despite the accumulated experience with such devices as information systems, program budgeting, and computer simulation in administrative process, it is his opinion that such devices have all failed without so much as the exception of one single successful demonstration, despite having been widely applied.

All claim to enhance social learning, but none contain operative mechanisms for benefiting from their own mistakes.... The lesson to be learned...is not that computer simulation cannot work but that it is not yet useful for policy purposes. Today no government official should expect to make practical use of computer simulation.[24]

Despite the broadness of the language, it remains basically an instrumental criticism and does not necessarily call for any change in the basic attitudes the managers of growth may hold toward nature. What it does underscore is that technology in the job of political decision-making is no cheap short-cut. It will substantially inflate costs and will offer few benefits capable of outweighing them.[25]

The conclusion ought not to be that there should not be experiment in the techniques of decision-making. It is only that hard, preliminary questions should be asked. And there should be no expectation that technology will offer the miracle of crisis solution without the necessity for hard choice.

Differing Bureaucratic Costs of Environmental Protection

Certainly no mistaken views ought any longer be held concerning the costs of the decision-making process in urban-industrial society. This is especially true at those levels where many of the important environmental decisions have to be made. This stems from the fragmentation of the demand structure in contemporary culture which must result in cost repetitions. There is an inability to transfer savings from one production or consumption unit to another. It is the accompaniment of the refusal of those profiting from the present isolation of their units to agree to any cost internalization.

In advanced conditions of growth demand, the constituent groups tend to be numerous and segregated from each other in a fundamental pluralism which makes the formation of unified opinion quite difficult. This works for the dispersal of pressure groups. At the local or regional level, therefore, they share the attitude of being isolated, with each group being alone to itself. This causes them to move in the direction of a national consolidation. Putting together all their disparate and scattered parts will give them a national influence which was not theirs at the local and regional level. It does not produce an integrated, comprehensive national action; but it does allow the introduction of points of view in an effective political arena that otherwise would be excluded by their dispersed character.

Unfortunately, the cost of moving to a national level may work against integrated decision-making on occasion. It is often true that the distant national officials, who these consolidated constituent interest groups seek to influence, are ignorant of local needs and wishes. They may be bureaucratic prisoners of their own requirements. The advocate for national constituencies may have to admit that, on a locale by locale approach, he has to sacrifice flexibility, the fruits of the wisdom that comes from knowledge of the place, and the relative economies intimate local information can sometimes provide.[26] In so doing, however much such advocates of national action may not want to do so, they themselves are contributing to fragmentation and the homogenizing of the environment, and to the costs of an unchanged demand structure.

But the choice for action is limited. The scattered nature of pluralist, polycentric opinion groups compels them to seek a national consolidation of strength so as to make any impact at all. If environmental groups had remained dispersed across the United States, confining their influence to local issues and seeking no larger forum, their effect could never have been more than locally important. In all probability they would have had no effect. The day for such examples of locally initiated and locally financed *magnificentia* as Fairmont Park in Philadelphia, or Central Park in New York, or Lakeshore Drive in Chicago seems to be over. Only national action is capable of meeting the full spectrum of costs that will be required to accommodate urban-industrial demands and the interrelated systems in the renewing environment.

Throughout the world under the present fragmenting and repetitive system, the cost of maintaining the relationship between man and nature are soaring. Municipal governments, who are generally in the front line of the difficulty with their budgets, are being driven closer and closer to bankruptcy or to delegating their functions (and their costs) to governmental units higher in the hierarchy having greater fiscal resources. In the United States, in Latin America, in Italy, in the United Kingdom, the municipal budgets have found it increasingly impossible to meet the demands that come from every direction under the present uncoordinated situation. Putting aside any comparisons of qualitative success on a city by city basis, the sheer quantity of costs remains.[27]

Those who concentrate only on the problems of municipal finance argue that costly services should simply be withdrawn. Perhaps in the case of services that are mere amenities, this may be so. But the service of the environment is not an amenity. It is a pressing, unavoidable necessity. Simply to back away in the presence of high costs neither solves the environmental problems nor deals in any way with what is needed to reach a bearable level in the costs of decision-making.

The pressure is great for moving to larger units, believing their size alone guarantees them an ability to resolve crises. These newly homogenized regional and national units have themselves proven very costly and are helping drive up what many argue are the exorbitant costs of the public sector. Whatever benefit they may have done the environment, the greatest advantage these spiraling costs have delivered has been to clarify the extent to which the costs of current decision-making are escalating. Under the present fragmented demand-structure they increase the peril of mankind that humanity cannot cope with the consequences of their own actions.

Moving up the ladder of governmental hierarchies will not alone suffice. The fragments will not be pulled together into any degree of unity by this action. The bureaucrats in the higher echelons will be no more capable of unified action than were those at the lower levels, in the absence of a social decision that unified action has the highest priority over undifferentiated open-ended growth. The escalating costs of government under these conditions will only cause people to wonder if there is any area of government worth the prices currently being set by the governmental budgets.

There is just no safe harborage by moving to more prestigious administrative positions. Prestige in the present situation, anyway, means no more than that the holder of the prestige can command a large budget, a large staff, and a jurisdiction of sufficient flexibility which will permit the ultimate responsibility for failure to be side-slipped to somebody else in the bureaucratic maze. Those who claim to be knowledgeable assert that the federal environmental law is "a hodgepodge of programs, prohibitions and precatory declarations." They insist that such a legal system, despite the costs imposed, is incapable of restoring environmental conditions to even a margin of acceptability for the renewing systems in nature.[28]

The fact is that there is no immediately practical reason for bureaucratic managers at almost any governmental level to conclude that a unified approach to nature and the demands mankind make upon nature is in the vested interest of the bureaucracy. Instead, bureaucracy can profit its bureaucrats' careers by being machicolating, making its own contribution to the breaking up, blending, and homogenizing of everything the present operations of demandant growth attack in the same mode. This being so, there is no indication that the environment will presently find bureaucrats at any governmental level more interested in a behavior responsible for the protection of the environment's renewing systems.

It is as if bureaucrats were intent on proving right the claim of William O. Douglas that "all bureaucracies are paralyzing and suffocating." His description of public administration is scathing.

They are closed societies responding to some special interest or reflecting one prejudice, one point of view. They need to be jolted, aroused, and alerted to a new and different problem. Only the voice of the people, speaking in unrestrained but measured voices can rectify the situation.[29]

But the voice of the people has not chosen as yet to speak for basic change in the framing of growth demands. This is not yet an age when environmental conditions have succeeded in compelling the articulation of claims against the isolated benefits produced by the imposition of externalized costs upon nature.

This is not to say that the costs of ever present environmental efforts have not compelled some accommodation. Some claims of a preventive and conservationist character are being legally recognized. In an abstract way, there is said to be a right to individual health that would be free from any harm inflicted by air and water pollution. There are those who talk about a right to some beauty in nature and to an integrity in nature sufficient to prevent the eroding of the rural and the blighting of the urban land. In the transformation of nature into the property of urban-industrial society, the legal system increasingly is compelled to insist upon a minimum level of preventive performance. Already the jurisdictions of the legal and administrative mechanisms have crept forward, aided as much by those timorous of costs as by those bold to act, to accomplish more within the past generation for the renewing environment than previously had ever been the case.[30]

But, then, the demands being imposed upon nature are so much greater than ever they had been in the past. The costs of environmentally protective measures have increased greatly by previous comparisons. But they have in no way come anywhere near to keeping up with the pace set by the demands upon the environment. All that the increases in the costs of environmental protection have succeeded in doing has been to reveal the growth of the crisis and the pressure coming down hard on the demand structure as a result of these mounting transaction costs.

Before bureaucratic authority can beome meaningful to the environment, there must be a social decision that stability and equilibrium in high energy culture and nature are important enough to construct. Until now everything done as a consequence of urban-industrial demand has been in the direction of instability. Change has been the watchword, without regard for the impact of change as an externalizer of costs. The time is coming when a greater stability than has been experienced for two centuries will be needed by urban-industrial society itself. Pitirim Sorokin, the sociologist, predicted that eventually this had to happen. A shift had to occur, he claimed, to the firmness and relative permanency of a demand structure that would be predictable and whose methods, asserted in the name of measured growth and security, would not require a continual turning-over of human relationships and of ecosystems within the renewing environment.[31]

If the time should be near at hand for such a shift, then the power of the bureaucracy to help carry it through will have to be present and the priorities for which that power is to be exercised must be clear and firm. Such a change will be a crisis in itself. But the crisis will reinforce within the culture the recognition of the costs being imposed by the operation of instability in all the existing forms of order of high energy culture.

This does not mean that a single monolithic global government will be produced. Such a governmental form might itself be nothing more than a disguise for continued fragmentation. But it does mean that, after two centuries of commitment to instability, there must be a recasting of law and administration for another purpose.

Possible Shifts in Environmental Regulation

Under the pounding pressure of urban-industrial demand and the environmental response, the structures of legal rules and bureaucracy have begun to produce deep, spreading fissures. The law must now shift from its accommodation to the instability of uncontrolled growth to an accommodation to something more in equilibrium with nature. The law has permitted a time of anarchy, allowing the whole business of environmental renewability to be taken for granted.

The evidence, however, is accumulating for a coming radical restructuring of legal rules and bureaucratic mechanisms as they relate to the renewing environment and to the environment which in terms of biologic time is non-renewing. But first what is required is a basic social decision for something other than the perpetual flow of increasing energy cascades and demandant growth. Instead, the interrelationships between the burden of the human imagination and the environment's capacity to respond have to be granted the highest priority.

There may be several institutional ways of carrying through such a decision. John Stuart Mill's stationary economy might be one. The dynamic equilibrium of the Club of Rome might be another. The creation of the René Dubos' artificial regimes to help natural forces meet human demand could be an alternative. Or the accommodation of human demand to the way natural systems operate, as urged by Barry Commoner, might be still another.

But, whatever the choice, the institutional consequences will appear dramatic. They will reveal in full the instability and turbulence not clearly seen now in the present situation. But it will be a transient instability, not that of a culture which had made instability a permanent condition. It will be the instability which is temporarily inevitable when any system of legitimation has had the bases of legitimizing knocked out from beneath it. But when a new basis of legitimacy has been determined, one that prefers equilibrium, then the instability shall end. Instead of being a basic cultural preference, instability shall have become a passing phenomenon.

The role of growth in the impact upon the environment has been pointed out by the ZPG growth advocates not only in relation to population increase but also in connection with the expectations for urban-industrial growth which the growing populations have been led to entertain. So basic has been the current social decision for growth that no thought was given for long periods of time to the external costs of a growth that was undifferentiated and open-ended. One ought not to be surprised, therefore, that until very recently there was a failure to correlate the effect of growth in the energy cascades and urban-industrial activity upon the environment.

As late as 1946 it could have been asserted that the rate of growth was "a concept which has been little used in economic theory."[32] This is true no longer. Growth has become a technical subject whose publications have expanded faster than the economies of the world in the same interval.[33]

There has been throughout the world since World War II, an insistence upon growth, upon increasing urban-industrial activity, upon pressing upward the supply of energy and the demand for it, and upon a rise in material expectations. All this has been accompanied with great increases in absolute population figures which as yet show insufficient world-wide signs of leveling off for anyone to be sanguine about them. Under the conditions of the present world, matters are as they have been declared to be by the economist E. S. Phelps:

It seems clear that there is no hope for the optimality of so simple a policy as neutrality in a complex world.[34]

Upon the subject of possible neutrality, he is absolutely right. Future growth decisions must be made in terms of environmental impact on the renewing systems of the globe. Institutions must be developed to make this an operative possibility. The energy budget, upon which urban-industrial sur‑vival is so dependent, must be reorganized, both to use energy more efficiently and to reduce the demands which disregardful growth in the transfer of energy imposes upon the systems in nature which must respond to those demands. There must be a recognition of the costs and natural interrelationships of human demand and natural systems. The continued failure up to this point to work for a permanent viability in the response the renewing environment makes to human demand is what underlies the pessimism of people like Stewart Udall, the former United States Secretary of the Interior, charged with primary federal environmental responsibility during the 1960's:

The irony of our time is that each increment of the Gross National Product has gone hand in hand with a decrease in the livability of our cities and the cleanliness of the overall environment.[35]

"Hand-in-hand" relationships such as these cannot continue indefinitely. All the factors which have been accelerating demand and intensifying its impact upon the environment have shortened the time when such relationships can continue. The vexing environmental problems of the late 20th century cannot be cured by an extrapolation of the growth rises known to this point in history. Indeed, the problems of the environment can only be deeply exacerbated by them.

But the job of terminating the "hand-in-hand" relationships established by urban-industrial society from its inception over two hundred years ago cannot be dumped on the regulatory mechanisms of legal rules or bureaucracy. The institutional changes which regulatory mechanisms can carry through would be profound and dramatic. They will be eventually necessary. But these are subordinate devices, instruments for carrying out policies that originate elsewhere within the culture as to their most significant aspects.

Legal rules and bureaucracy are reflective institutions for social decisions that may come through the political process though, on many important occasions, the flow will be directly into the operation of rules and bureaucracies from the social decisions of the culture. In brief, one may not express the relationship too strongly. The most environmentally significant institutional reform is the changing of legal rules and bureaucracy that are meant to assist in furthering a viable relationship between the burdens of the human imagination and nature. But they likely will come "after the fact."

The "fact," which these profound and dramatic institutional changes will follow, will be the social decision on behalf of a human responsibility for the consequences of human actions upon the renewing environment. Institutional changes must reflect the basic values of the culture in order to have their own viability, much less to help further any viability in nature. Imposed solutions which do not take this into account may have an apparent, short-term strength; but it will prove brittle and the strength will snap when the pressure grows.

Either there will be a shift from the unstabilizing effect of undifferentiated open-ended growth as the highest cultural value – or legal rules and bureaucracy will continue to fail the environment. Their externally imposed task of producing stability out of its opposite is foredoomed. Under conditions such as these, legal rules and bureaucracy – indeed, the political process itself – cannot impose stability upon an inherently unstable cultural situation.

And this will be true no matter how urgently or imperiously legal rules and bureaucracy are ordered by the public to do so. The orders may come from worried people; but their worry will be without ultimately positive effect. In the absence of their willingness to make more basic changes, their imposition of external commands without a base within the culture will only serve to destroy the value of legal rules, bureaucracy, and the political process. To sacrifice these institutions in a manner such as this would ultimately block the chances for saving the benefits of urban-industrial society since public action must primarily occur through these institutions.

Yet the risks would be greater still. The roles to be fulfilled by both legal rules and the bureaucracy appertain very closely to the potential future of the renewing environment. They are part of the interface between the demand structure of urban-industrial society, science and technology, and the total potential of the human imagination. Should they be prematurely lost, because there has been thrust upon these institutions responsibilities they could not discharge, there would be more than the loss of these cultural benefits. Their breakdown and subsequent contumely would make it nearly impossible to carry through at a later date any decisions to change the way a growth-demandant culture impacts upon nature. When an institution loses its credibility for competency or relevancy, however unfair the bases for reaching that judgment may be, the restoration of that institution to any stage at which it can once again function is very difficult, except in exceedingly long time frames.

The renewing environment is hard pressed to continue responding viably to the competitive, repetitive, undifferentiated, and unlimited demands from humanity for more and more growth. Human action of some sort is going to be needed soon – and forever after – to keep those systems viable. Such institutions as legal rules and bureaucracy, like the political process out of which they emerge, are both useful and necessary in carrying through any of the programs needed for this purpose. To throw them away out of feckless-ness, before the social decision has been made that would make their use effective, would be an act close to suicidal.

Whether nature in a metaphysical sense needs man may be a doubtful proposition. But so long as man is present in nature, with the burden of his imagination and the sort of demand structure humanity has imposed, nature will assuredly need man's legal and bureaucratic mechanisms. Bureaucracy in the future will be more than a seeming necessity to the living and renewing environment.

The costs of accommodating culturally to the requirements of a systemati-cally interrelated renewing environment will assuredly be high in terms of what will have to be internalized by the urban-industrial demand structure. Nevertheless, in terms of the charges that will be imposed upon humanity in the event these costs are disregarded, the changes required are relatively small indeed. Simply to keep pressing down on renewing nature will only mean the eventual cessation of that renewal.

Notes

1   Grant McConnell, "Environment and the Quality of Political Life," in *Conquest and the Environment*, Richard Cooley and Geoffrey Wandesford-Smith, eds., Seattle: Univ. of Washington Press, 1970, pp. 12–13.
2   See, however, Joe Dean and C. S. Shih "Decision Analysis for the River Wall expansion," 11 *Water Resources Bulletin*, April 1975, p. 237.
3   Jeffrey P. Zucker, "Environmental Right to Action," 7 *Harvard Civil Rights – Civil Liberties L.R.* (1972), 520, at 521, Note.
4   Frank Macomber, Copley News Service, "Raw Materials Supply Gravest Problem," Columbus *Dispatch*, January 6, 1974, p. 13D, quoting Burt F. Raynes of the NAM.
5   Abram Chayes, "International Institutions for the Environment," in John Lawrence Hargrave, ed., *Law, Institutions, and the Global Environment*, Dobbs Ferry, N.Y.: Oceana, 1972, being a Joint Conference of the American Society of International Law and the Carnegie Endowment, September 1971, p. 4.
6   *Ibid.*, p. 9.
7   Eugene B. Skolnikoff, "Comments," in *ibid.*, p. 28.
8   Nicholas A. Robinson, "Problems of Definition and Scope," in *Ibid.*, p. 86.
9   Zucker, *op. cit.*, p. 542 and p. 542, Note.
10 On all that enters into specific adjustment problems of particular industries to environmental protection costs, see the Second Annual Report, Council on Environmental Quality (August 1971), pp. 127–129.
11 Zucker, *op. cit.*, p. 550.
12 Irving Like, "Multi-Media Confrontation – The Environmentalists' Strategy for a 'No-Win Agency' Proceedings," 1 *Ecology Law Quarterly* (1971), 495, pp. 495–496, p.498.
13 *Ibid.*, pp. 499–501, speaking specifically of confrontations with the Atomic Energy Commission. See also pp. 505–508.
14 Donald W. Large, "Is Anybody Listening? The Problem of Access in Environmental Litigation," 1972 *Wisc. L.R.* 62, at p. 111.
15 Gary Warren Hart, "Institutions for Water Planning-Institutional Arrangements: River Basin Commissions, Inter-Agency Committees, and Ad Hoc Coordinating Committees," National Water Commission, part of Legal Study 13 (September 1971), NTIS PB 204/244, p. 2.
16 *Ibid.*
17 *Ibid.*, p. 27 and p. 104. His history, *ibid.*, p. 10, of the antecedents of the present Water Resources Council is very instructive. The quotation is a composite.
18 Friedrich Engels, *Dialectics of Nature* (New York: International Publishers, 1940), pp. 291–292.
19 Zigurds L. Zile, "Lenin's Contribution to Law: The Case of Protection and Preservation of the Natural Environment," in *Lenin and Leninism; State, Law and Society*, B. W. Eissenstat, ed., Lexington, Mass.: D. C. Heath & Co., 1971, p. 109. On the work of Lenin on behalf of the environment, see *ibid.*, pp. 84–85.
20 *Literaturnaia Gazeta*, August 9, 1967, quoted at *ibid.*, p. 96. Professor Zile says some persons became publicly concerned over worsening environmental conditions as early as the late 1950's, *ibid.*, p. 83.
21 Gallup Institute with 32 international affiliates for the Charles F. Kettering Founda-

tion, *Global Survey on Human Needs and Satisfactions* (September 1976): "In general the poorer nations view industrialization as a panacea while the richer nations focus more on its evils," see *The National Observer*, October 2, 1976, p. 3.

[22] Zdenek J. Slouka, "International Environmental Controls in the Scientific Age," in Hargrave, ed., *op. cit.*, pp. 216–217, and 229.

[23] *Ibid.*, pp. 224–225, quoting Robert Dahl and Charles Lindbolm.

[24] Aaron Wildavsky, Book Review, *Science*, December 28, 1973, Vol. 182, p. 1335, p. 1337. It is a composite quote.

[25] Wildavsky says that, because costs will always hugely exceed the estimates in information systems to aid public decisions, the hypothetical benefits should be at least ten to one in relation to the estimated costs, *ibid.*, p. 1338.

[26] See, *CF* [Conservation Foundation] *Newsletter*, No. 3-72 (March 1972), pp. 5–6, quoting Mr. Dwight F. Rettie, executive director, National Recreation and Parks Association, discussing these points in relation to the advantages of categorical grants.

[27] See Robert G. Wilmers and William F. Reilley, "Decay in New York's Civil Service," *The New Republic*, November 10, 1973, Vol. 169, No. 19, p. 18, for the situation especially in New York City.

[28] James M. Kramon, "Towards a New Federal Response to Water Pollution," 31 *Fed. Bar J.* (1972) 139, at p. 141.

[29] William O. Douglas, *The Three Hundred Year War*, New York: Random House, 1972, p. 183.

[30] L. F. E. Goldie, "Development of an International Environmental Law: An Appraisal," in Hargrave, ed., *op. cit.*, p. 116 and p. 147.

[31] Pitirim A. Sorokin, *The Crisis of Our Age*, New York: E. F. Dutton, 1941. This is a popularization of ideas expressed as early as 1926.

[32] Evsey Domar, "Capital Expansion and Growth," in Amartya Sen, ed., *Growth Economics*, Baltimore: Penguin, 1970, p. 77.

[33] Amartya Sen, Introduction, *ibid.*, p. 33.

[34] E. S. Phelps, "Growth and Government Intervention," in *ibid.*, p. 532.

[35] Stewart L. Udall, "Limits: The Environmental Imperative of the 1970's" in H. W. Helfrich, Jr., ed., *Agenda for Survival*, New Haven: Yale Univ. Press, 1970, p. 229.

The Relation to the Environment of the Rules of Property

Rules of Property as Another Regulation of the Environment

Much thought has been given in the 20th century to the development of bureaucratic means to directly allocate resources. It has become a standard reaction, whenever a problem has been perceived, to create a new bureaucracy to deal with that problem. Under such a common attitude, there has been a dependence upon the issuance of regulations and of orders to accomplish desired change. The problems perceived in the relationship between urban-industrial demand and the renewing environment have proven no exception to this resort to bureaucracy.

As the deterioration of air and water, the over-exploitation of forest and grazing lands, the extirpation of wildlife, or other environmental difficulties have come into the public consciousness as constituting intolerable conditions, bureaucracies have been set up or existing bureaucracies have been reorganized to carry through the changes called for. It has not been regarded as sufficient merely to prohibit certain actions and to subsequently leave the enforcement of the prohibitions to the enforcement machinery of prosecution through the courts. Neither has it been thought sufficient to create new environmental rights for private enforcement in civil suits, despite the expansion of litigation by non-governmental environmental organizations. Instead, the major thrust has been in reliance upon bureaucratic regulations through the setting of standards, the imposition of limitations, the institution of permits, and the formation of minima for air and water conditions.

It is probable that this dependence upon bureaucracy as the guardian of environmental renewability will remain the dominant mode of regulatory conduct. Yet bureaucratic actions do not exhaust the scope of regulations. They are not the only – and, in many instances, certainly not the best – means of changing conduct from behavior hurtful to environmental renewability to a beneficial or environmentally neutral performance.

It is increasingly contended that the bureaucratic response is often cumbersome, responsible for increasing transaction costs in a way that only serves the personal advantages of bureaucrats, and even destructive of the environment which the bureaucracy has been deputed to save. In place of this regulatory technique, the proposal has been made to shift the rules of property in such a way as to direct the unadministered forces of the market toward protecting rather than indifferently exploiting environmental renewability. It is not that bureaucracy is never to be used but rather, as Ronald Coase expresses it, that, "In devising and choosing between social arrangements, we should have regard for the total effect."[1]

Twentieth-century opinion is being reminded that options relative to the environment are not bounded by either bureaucratic structure on the one side or court litigation on the other, whether the litigation be of a public or private sort. These can each be a useful mechanism and no chance should be thrown away to improve the technologies of both bureaucratic and juridical process. However, what is once more being brought into prominence for these purposes is the utility of the rules by which property is held. The rules of property also have value, also can be improved, and also ought not to be ignored as to their importance to the environment.

For too long, rules of property have been taken for granted, without scrutiny as to the services they perform or how they might better serve those purposes. Of course, since some think property itself is an obsolete notion (a "radical" view now over a century old), then they would have no interest in rules concerning how it is held, transferred, or put up as security. Others regard the natural law as the source of property; and they too have little felt need to re-examine either property's definition or the operation of that definition upon either society or the environment.

Still there are others who neither condemn the concept of property nor believe that the content of that concept has been fixed by natural law beyond the reach of human improvement. It is these, often summarily treated under the label of the Chicago School though the ferment of opinion has not been confined to them, who are exploring the ways of using private property arrangements for protecting environmental renewability. Their work has pushed evaluators of the rules of property to return to the reconsideration of basic definitions of such terms as property, ownership, title, and vested right. As the ancient terms have been examined, it has been seen they need not be anachronisms further burdening the environment. Rather, they can be additional means for strengthening the capacity of the renewing environment to respond to the demands made upon it by a growth-demandant urban-industrial society.

The market operates in both market-oriented and market-command economies. To ignore the market is at best to increase transaction costs, whereas to be subservient to every market demand will likely strengthen the pressure to thrust all of nature out of the price structure into the realm of the seeming free goods. It is now a commonplace that nothing is freely extracted from the environment, for even intangibles have costs.[2] But there are still those who hope for trifling transaction costs under bureaucratic and juridical systems that either ignore or deny the operation of market mechanisms. It is a vain hope, and the structure of how the rules of property can operate have tried to show why it is vain. Instead, the market advocates urge a better understanding of how the rules of property and of the pricing mechanism can accomplish ends either otherwise unaccomplishable or else to be accomplished only at far higher costs.

As the economist M. Bruce Johnson has noted, it has only been since 1955 that economists themselves have recognized the link between prices and property rights. It may be that there are still lawyers, planners, and bureaucrats who deny or are simply ignorant of such a linkage; but they are scarcely more free of market constraints than are individual consumers. Using the term "property rights" to broadly mean any assignment to an entitlement over resources drawn from the environment, this means there is a symbiosis between how those rights are defined, their scarcity in the environment, and the functioning of prices which is treated contemptuously only at great cost. As Johnson says.

In academic discourse, the debate has progressed beyond the issue of price systems to the structure of alternative forms of property rights themselves. It is very clear that legal, social, and technological limitations on property rights affect the manner in which both public and private owners of those rights elect to exercise them.[3]

How property rights are defined, who holds them, what costs are imposed upon the holders by both regulation and the costs of enforcing rights, will effect the allocation of resources as much as direct allocative orders issued by a bureaucracy. Property rights express through the law all the human purposes to which the environment can be put. Many believe that the market interaction of these rights can accomplish environmentally protective goals better and more cheaply than can a bureaucratic ordering of private decisions affecting the environment or through the use of the judicial process to force change. The people with this view agree,

If economists are right that pollution, spill-overs, and other externalities are the result of undefined or ill-defined property rights, the wiser course would be to improve and strengthen the system of private property rights where flaws exist, rather than to abandon the system piece by piece in form of an arbitrary, authoritarian system of planning.[4]

It may be doubted that the benefits of such action will accrue only to *private* owners of property or that planners have to accept the appellatives of "arbitrary" and "authoritarian." But it does signify that urgent voices are being raised on behalf of another regulatory approach than that of reliance upon bureaucracy and the courts. The rules of property, under the pressure of systemic responses in the renewing environment that are inadequate to the urban-industrial demand being made upon them, are once again being examined. Perhaps through amendment of the law a self-executing system will emerge of regulating that relationship between demand and environmental response. At any rate, at least at the academic level, the effort is being made. It is certainly worthy of serious attention from anyone interested in salvaging the renewability of the environment.

The Environmental Urgency of Re-examining Basic Property Definitions

The suggestion that the renewable qualities within the environment can be protected by working with the rules of property, through market constraints, requires a re-examination of the basic terms being employed. The rules of property will be under a substantial obligation to change in order to meet changing conditions. But before the requirements for these changes are formulated, the present legal definitions must be understood. The principal, if not the primary, term to be comprehended, is what does the law mean when statutes and decisions refer to "property"?

At a minimum, property is the recognition of a legitimacy in an entity controlling a service or a physical presence. Stated as neutrally as possible, it is an entitlement permitting the holder to exercise a superiority against others over some aspect of what he seeks to control. The subject-matter of property is the consequence of custom, or of a consciously adopted legal rule, or of an interrelationship of both. The entitlements in this subject-matter are specified for the purpose of permitting certain social, political, and economic actions to occur. The resulting superiorities in the title-holders legitimize these actions as to them and exclude others not so entitled from this legitimacy.

When an entitlement can be aliened, another rule of property ensues. That rule sets the terms under which transfers can occur. Entitlements need not be alienable; but in systems of privately asserted superiorities, they normally are capable of conveyance, security pledge, or some lesser form of actual or potential alienation. It is for this reason that persons talk of property as constituting a "bundle of rights," in which each stick in the bundle is included or excluded depending upon how the rule of property reflects particular basic social decisions.

If the "bundle" should include the power of alienation, what the law calls property assumes the primary function of preserving that "right." Corollary with that, the law will try to see to the job, in a commerically calibrated culture, of holding the transaction costs as low as possible relative to the total charge. The legal system performs these tasks by a rule of property which legitimates and enforces what has occurred between private title-holders when they assert and transfer their superiorities. It may be done by predetermined rule or by the allowance of consensual agreement. But without this function being performed by law, the authority of entitlements to command legitimacy is dramatically weakened. And once weakened, transaction costs may become so high as to effectively prevent transfer.

It is obvious to see the value of the rules of property which extend support to superiority transfers between title-holders in private property systems. What is less obvious is that the law performs much the same function if property is held communally. As long as any differentiation is maintained between the superiorities asserted by entitlements, the transfer of those superiorities over objects or services requires the assistance of the legal system to validate transfers and hold down transaction costs.

This sort of service is a purely instrumental or adjectival performance on the part of the legal system. It does not directly affect the judgment of value which society attaches to an object or service that is treated by the legal system as part of the subject-matter of property. The substantive valuation of what is under entitlement or subject to alienation is not for the rules of property to determine.

Legal services are derivative functions of social decision-making and are only meant to provide the procedures for effectuating those more basic decisions. The rules of property in an urban-industrial society are under the constant obligation not to clog the easy flow of transactions. In high growth conditions, costs that stem only from the means of transaction quickly become too heavy a burden to the business being transacted. In consequence, the legal system is under a constant pressure to eliminate or hold down purely transactional costs, even if this means shunting them off onto the renewing environment.

It is from this desire to shunt aside transactional costs, among other costs that seem capable of concealment, that environmental problems so often arise in relation to those areas where property is held in common title. The treatment of property held under a common public title stands out for the random, atomistic way in which the commonality has been handled. Nowhere is there a greater need for the legal sytem to fuse claims together into unified, controllable elements than exists in the case of common public property.

Classically in the law, common property has been composed of the unappropriated. Furthermore, this unappropriated subject-matter has the peculiarity of being capable only of limited appropriation in individual property units. Sometimes the character of the subject-matter determines this. More often it is the social system which shapes what will be capable of appropriation.

In a culture based upon hunting or grazing, the land may be considered matter so difficult to appropriate into separate units that it is left in common title. In a high energy culture, anxious so see the air and water as universal sinks, these become resources difficult to individuate as to title. Hence, in both primitive and complex societies certain subject-matter is left in the common title and it is often of the greatest economic value to the particular society. There is, therefore, nothing predetermined to be forever either in common or in individual title. It is the amalgam of human demand, technology, and resulting social decision which casts a part of nature or a human concept into the subject-matter of property and into common or individuated title.

Common property often has a flowing character to it. Whether it is land in a grazing culture, game in a hunting one, or air, water, and the biomass in one with a high energy demand, the property that is by these respective social determinations held in common title seems to flow through the economy and the social structure. For traditional theories of real property, this poses locational problems. If property – be it game, air and water, the biomass, or open range – is flowing through a jurisdiction, the venue asserted over it becomes effectively a very transient one. It is simple to say that the horde of graziers pouring over the open range "owns" that range. It is just as simple to assert that the state through which water, air, or the biomass moves "owns" them too. But such simplicity in each instance is spurious.

When something is transient and in constant movement, in the manner of the jet stream or the hydrologic cycle, meaningful title is difficult to appropriate even in a state entity. Only by breaking into the pattern of movement with a demand that denies the constant flow are individuated superiorities easily established. An entitlement can be asserted in land and in water for purposes of irrigation or steam power. What had been common property thereby is reduced to an individuated dominion and control.

However, the task of appropriation is more difficult when air and water are used as sinks or the flow of fresh air is used as a reservoir for economic receptors. This is illustrated by the problems states are having in asserting control over the high seas. By a steady encroachment of specific control over the continental shelf, or particular sea species, or defined waters, the coastal states are establishing a claimed superiority and an entitlement. What is left has no state entity asserting title to it at this given moment; but the question remains: How effectively appropriated by these individual entities is the water, the bed, and most especially the moving species of the oceans?[5]

It is self-evident that the mobile, flowing character of what are such resources for humanity as water, air, game, and the biomass make them hard to appropriate to an individuated property concept. It is why so many turn to the state as the holder of title or speak of the state as a trustee for the public. The economist E. J. Mishan has urged that we create, along the lines of a trust *res*, "amenity rights" to clean air and quiet surroundings.[6] The problem, as shown by the examples of the oceans and the jet streams, is that the state or the national public may be entities too small for individuation in appropriating these common interests.

Indeed, even if the nation-state should be an adequately large entity for establishing entitlements to these resources, it can be very difficult to know where traditional law stands on the subject. C. Reinold Noyes, the property specialist, seemed to take a good deal of pleasure in reciting the origins of the confusion in both the civil and the common law systems.

The idea is a confused one. It is compounded of the antique *res communes*, and perhaps *res publicae* and *res nullius*, as well as English "qualified" property; of the theory and fact of the original grants to, and purchases by, the colonies and the federal government from various sources, of the national domain; and of a confusion of the idea of the *state*, taken from political theory, with the federated states, of which the resemblance is largely confined to the name.[7]

In case anyone should think his recital of confusion should apply only to a country such as the United States, his view concluded with an ancient Roman invocation:

...it is the auspices, rather than the purpose to which it is dedicated, which determines the public or private character of property.[8]

This, of course, asserts as of over-arching importance the location of title. One experienced with urban-industrial demands upon the renewing environment may offer a few qualifications to this dismissal of purpose. Indeed, how important is the theory of where title to common property is located, in the absence of an effective individuated appropriation? Whether the state has claimed an outright ownership, or the state has seen itself as appointed trustee for the benefit of the people, the commanding fact has been that the control has been often a nominal one for most purposes important to the environment.

It has not been nominal in the sense that the state has not asserted claim to title. Except for a few theorists clinging to the concept of allodial possession that conceptually denies the state any right to assert control, the state has always had claimed for it the authority to lay down the terms upon which common property might be used. The state has not been indifferent to how the subject-matter of property could be used to return a seeming profit to its users and a revenue to the state. In this manner, there has been a very lively interest by states in such items as game, air movement, and the ocean "riches."

States, until very recently, were therefore not especially interested in placing restrictions upon how individuated entities appropriated the subject-matter of property by reducing items within the common zone to their own private dominion. The result has been either that individuated entities could establish such private rights or they could use the resources of the common interest without bothering with the expenses of a private appropriation.[9] In the past, and to some degree even at the present time, items within the common zone are practically difficult to protect from such usage by individuated entities. But whether or not the desire to resist that usage exists in a larger governmental unit depends upon whether or not social policy sees a value in so doing. Once such a value has been determined and the resource specified by social decision from the full potential of the common zone of interest, then a superiority over it can be established for some entitlement.

The holder of that entitlement can be a human being, a private-share corporation, a commune or a state agency; and if the value of the entitlement is sufficient, the practical ways of asserting it are likely to prove doable. As long as resources are unspecified, a part of an undifferentiated commonality, and of no interest to any particular entity except an undefined "public," then so long will there be little possibility of establishing control. However, once an entitlement is established and the value of the item specified as a resource, then practical action becomes far more likely.

The holder of an entitlement has a monopoly in the item to which he has been assigned a superiority. Legitimately the holder of the entitlement can claim as against all others the power of occupancy and use. The holder has the massive power of exclusion. These lie at the base of the concept of property. They are related to the function of resource specification in the way an adjective acts as a modifier of a noun.

The role of specification is to separate from the common mass in nature a definable item which thereafter becomes a natural resource. It is also the function of specification to assist in establishing its value in terms of price, cost, or foregone opportunities. Once this substantive action of resource specification has occurred, then the legal system is able to set up superiorities in particular holders of entitlements that legitimate their power to monopolize possession and to exclude others from the enjoyments of use.

The monopoly is just as real whether it is held by a private holder of entitlements or by some public entity. It is an inescapable aspect of the rule of property and not inherently obnoxious. Indeed, the argument is well made that it serves a valuable purpose when it is asserted, particularly in controlling human demand upon the stores of specified natural resources.[10] When such a monopoly is in practice lacking, trouble arises for the long-term survival of the items under common title, should there be a high demand for them.

At a time when atomic field theory was relatively new, C. Reinold Noyes used an atomic simile to explain the resultant situation. Without an effective monopoly, there is no single point of incidence, nor single point of inherence, so as to create a solid field upon which a unit of property could be, first, aggregated as to interests and, then, consolidated in a polarized unit.[11] Where there is no monopoly, or where monopoly has been asserted very weakly, common property exists. Should the demand for the subject-matter of that property be high, trouble will appear in most disturbing forms.

The False Appearance of the Environment as a Free Good

Certainly urban-industrial society has established demand for items in the renewing environment which in the past were scarcely considered resources for human exploitation. The growth in population, in industrial production, in consumer demand, and in urban sprawl has each been dramatic. The effect has been to create a huge imbalance in any attempt to calculate some benefit-cost ratio under the traditional policy of treating self-renewing flow resources like air, water, and the biomass as free goods.[12] The insistence that such goods are "free" has proven one which those benefiting from exploiting common property have been loath to surrender.

The Canadian economist J. H. Dales has argued that the results of such an insistence, where demand is high, will be "crystal clear." In relation to the subject-matter of property which has been brought under individuated entitlements and for which a monopoly has been made effective, the subject-matter of property remaining in common title will be over-used. It is not just a matter of private *versus* public property, since publicly held property may be just as capable of asserting its monopolistic superiority as any privately held. What is important in public or private title alike is that the subject-matter be under rules of property capable of excluding all those refusing to pay charges for its use. These others must be required by law to submit to rules concerning use laid down by the holder of the entitlement. It is the vulnerability of the subject-matter of property in common title that there is no entity existent – or, if existent, willing – to effectively assert such a monopolistic superiority.

Since what lies in common title is most often subject to depletability or to interruption in its powers of self-renewal, over-use tends in the not-very-long-run to lead to the destructon of the subject matter of the property so held.[13] When the ownership of property is lodged in a remote and aloof level, such as the sovereign or the people or God, there is a lack of resource specificity. The property will often lack its own separate identity from what else lies in common title. The entity holding the entitlement will have lacked the ability to focus its interest sufficiently so as to determine the property's value.

This produces in fact – whatever theory may proclaim – an ineffective or an unasserted monopoly. There is under these conditions no regular accountability for what has become a natural resource in high human demand. This absence of accountability under a rule of property incapable of regulating the use of the resource creates an attitude of "anything goes." The result is that the profits of exploitation accrue to those most assertive of demand, while the resource held in common title is steadily reduced in its stock or in its renewability by these demands.

Here is what constitutes the over-use of common property: (1) the imposition of demand, (2) the absence of any regulation in the use of the subject-matter of the common property, and (3) a continuing disregard as to the long-term survival of this subject-matter. Such over-use imposes high costs upon the renewing environment, upon the social structure, and upon those individuals whose activity is dependent upon the stability and renewability of both. When estuaries are polluted, the polluter profits but the shellfish industry suffers. When acid rain falls upon the forest, the emitter profits but the forest industry suffers. When biocides are massively sprayed, the agrochemical industry profits but the honey-gatherer suffers. The common profit is as non-existent as the common cost. Profits and losses go to segregated sectors of the economy, the society, and the environment. They are profits and costs isolated from each other in every sense, except the ecological. And none of the benefits come free.

The law backs away from trying to define value. It is the asserted function of the law to set up the rules of property which determine the bases of particular entitlements and what superiorities their holders can assert in the subject-matter of property. The law is there to identify and to enforce the entitlement on behalf of its holder. The law, however, denies that it has played a determinative role in setting the value of that entitlement for its holder or for any potential transferee by the holder.[14] The determination of value has been left by the law to private consensual arrangement, to the market, or to the administrative manipulators of production and consumption in urban-industrial society.

The great social determiner of value has been the idea of utility to the individual, to the market, and to the managers of production and consumption in the highly administered systems of urban-industrial society. Occasionally, the law-makers have taken up this idea of utility directly and by means of statutory declarations have set value in the form of rates, wages, and prices. But the law, when so employed, remains a matter of procedure and not of substance in the making of these determinations. The law-makers in such cases have simply put into statutory language the sort of decisions that otherwise would be contained in the language of the market-place or the exchanges among the economy's managers of production and consumption.

What the law finds nearly impossible to do through rules of property is to make a place for an insistence that values exist not expressible in terms of utility, or efficiency, or the motive forces for distribution. The law-makers, like the market forces and the managers when they turn to the determination of value, must seek a compatible means of expression or else lack one means for compromising differences. If all participating values are not part of a compatible system, how are mutually satisfactory trade-offs possible?[15]

The answer is that they cannot be so traded. In the currently fragmented situation, all trade-offs cannot be known. Furthermore, just as the legal system really does confer value, despite a professed neutrality, it also provides, at the general cost of the social system, great value for the individuated units within the system. Their personal benefits are derivative of the services provided by the legal system at the general cost of the whole social decision-making process. This lack of perfect knowledge makes the trade-offs recommended by the professedly bargain-minded an illusion on many occasions. There is lacking a sufficient general knowledge to enable the rules of property to operate with the efficiency desired for them by those who prefer a market to a command economy.

Particularly in the dream-world of Pareto optimality, so favored today, is this perfection unattainable. In that system, the optimum has been attained when the divisions of resources cannot be improved upon because additional changes could not so improve the situation of those benefited as to compensate those losing from the change and still leave matters better off than they were before change was instituted.[16] As a system, it is one quite favorable to the options of individuals. But in practice it is for the environment often an illusionist's box of mirrors.

Pareto optimality requires perfect knowledge in order to reach any final conclusions concerning what is or is not an optimum condition. The knowledge required has a need to be perfect that is almost Manichaean in its purity. Even if that kind of perfect knowledge should be attainable, there would still remain good reasons for wondering if the cost of reaching such perfection might have been better invested.

Is the task of keeping open individual options in the market worth such an effort, given the existing sharp competition for capital? Those say no who are most interested in protecting the ability of environmental systems to respond to accelerating human demand. They believe the costs would be too great in terms of foregone environmentally protective options.

But there is an unreality to the call for perfect knowledge. Such perfection cannot exist, if for no other reason than that too many want to continue the present fragmented system upon which they can free-load and from which they can extract individuated profits from a seemingly free environment. The access to perfect knowledge, therefore, is blocked by deliberate prevarications on the part of those who want to make no contribution to the support of the system from which their individuated profits are derived.

There is no reason to believe that profiting freeloaders will ever stand aside in order to let the flow of perfect knowledge gently inundate their fixed positions. They are obdurate foes of the theorists, mostly academics, who urge greater employment of the rules of property and the operations of the market. In consequence, the market, no more than the commands of bureaucracy is ever likely to be conducted subject to perfect knowledge, anymore than either the market or its regulation will ever be carried on without transaction costs.[17]

The concept of something "free" requires the counterpoise of something "unfree." The problem is that nothing is free but only relatively more or less scarce and expensive. Not even the legal system, by which entitlements are established to superiorities over goods and services, is free. Nor do costs evaporate simply because entitlements, through social policy, are transferred to entities having a collective character. There still remain the systemic costs of either collective coercion or persuasion. Like the exercise of individual choice in a market situation, these collective decisions also have costs to the system in which they are exercised.[18] Neither, therefore, the environment nor the legal structures, which determine how it is to be exploited, are free resources available for exploitation, however they are so treated.

The Difficulty of Calculating Benefits and Costs Relative to the Environment

The problem of calculating either benefits or costs is not an easy one, nor is their comparison. The burden of integrating them both into the economy in order to protect the renewing environment requires the initial adoption of some means of comparability. Any means of legitimation for cost-benefit ratios would require methods generally accepted as objective. Traditionally society has been shy of subjective, psychic reactions of individuals.[19] It would seem, therefore, that a society as dependent as a growth-demandant culture is upon speedy and reliable systems of durable and specialized organizations would put no reliance in eccentric individuation.[20]

Of course, a demand structure calling for open-ended undifferentiated growth, when abstractly considering the situation, likely *would* want to avoid being controlled by individuated judgments. It is no different in this regard from any other culture in wanting to avoid idiosyncracy as a social norm. What is peculiar about culture as presently structured is that there exists a need for it to operate at constantly accelerating demand curves. The most durable systems within it are those that process what can be processed within the environment and the social structure into units for production and consumption. In order to increase this demand level, urban-industrial society has adopted a system of operations based upon fragmentation, privatization, and individuation. To better serve demand growth under such a system, there is a willingness to permit a very broad range of idiosyncratic behavior, just as long as it increases demand for the production and consumption of saleable items as goods, services, and land, whatever the environmental cost.

Yet even this social willingness to accept individuated demand patterns cannot escape the socially unifying consequences that make assertedly individualistic systems of title-holding to property only appear to be individualistic. The subject-matter of property can rarely be merged with the person of the title-holder, however close the owner may feel to what the law and the larger culture lets him own. All the title-holder usually holds is some part of a right to use, and to exclude others from the use of, the subject-matter of what is thereby legally demonstrated as his property.[21]

Conceptually, this has very ancient nominalistic antecedents in legal theory which make a different treatment of the rules of property a difficult matter for contemporary high growth culture. The law for a very long time now has maintained a distinction between the legal processes and the material objects about which they deal. As the historian of the concept of property, C. Reinold Noyes has put it, property

...becomes a composite of disembodied rights to do, [or]...those rights associated together as part of the right to have. Analysed...[each] becomes a prohibition against others interfering with or initiating the doing [or having] – a prohibition rather than an authority...[T]hey are...separable from any particular set of material objects. Their only identification is with a process, to which objects may come and from which they may go.[22]

This means that the rule of property has in law an identification only with process, which responds to changing social decisions, rather than to the fixed material qualities of what is its subject-matter. This brings an amorphous quality to the law of property. Rules of property, perhaps for this reason, make claim to great rigidity. They purport to be closed to the kind of private legislation which marks the law of contract. But such rigidity in the present situation, which calls with increasing urgency to correlate environmental benefits and costs, is impossible for rules of property. Property law now exists at the interfaces between several conflicting forces; and, at the point of these interfaces, there is great flux in the law.

Law today not only interfaces with economics and politics. It also interfaces with other significant elements within the structure of urban-industrial society.[23] Rules of property in the law cannot be immutability fixed. This stems from their intimate relationship with the forces for instability that are such important generators of social decision-making under the current demand-structure. The traditional practice whereby the discipline of accounting has dealt with what the law denominates as intangible property supports this need for changeability. Intangibles are treated as "nuclei around which are centered capitalizations of surplus earning power."[24] They comprise the most significant forms of property in a market economy. This means that they must be expected to represent the constant flux in interchangeable relationships in the demand structure with which culturally responsive rules of property must deal.

Where mobility of every sort is demanded, immutable rules of property will not be possible. Physical, social, and economic mobility require rules of property that serve the same needs as such mobility does. When the culture consistently refuses to recognize the interrelationship of human demand to environmental response, so shall the rules of property. Just as Littleton's book on tenures in the late 15th century summarized rules of property for his time in fixed terms reflective of the static relationships of that still low energy culture, so must rules of property today play a similar reflective social function. Should the social decision be reached to internalize costs in demand processes and to establish a comprehensive approach to how demand impinges upon the renewing environment, then rules of property will also be developed which can handle the procedures for comparing unified benefits and costs.

If all costs should be internalized that are needed to protect the environment from the demands made upon its renewability, would the resulting prices destroy the claimed beneficial affluence of urban-industrial society? This is a substantive question that is not to be answered by a few alterations in the rules of property. Enough projections have been made to cause serious doubts that cost internalization alone would bankrupt the present system. Resource specification and cost internalization, on the contrary, would go far to provide the financial means for environmental protection.

It is true that there will be cases in which resource specificity through the employment of new rules of property will show that the price structure cannot simultaneously internalize the true costs and produce a price that allows the maker to survive in the world by passing on the whole increased amount to the consumer. Such a burden that is unassimilable by the consumer would have to be taken up by reducing profits, cutting payrolls, or paying out subsidies from the general fund. More importantly, in the presence of what specificity has revealed the burden of the costs to be, the question might better be asked whether the production was worth any of these costs. The answer, at least occasionally, would be no.

It is the great contribution of specificity to compel humanity to deal with the problems raised by human demand in the environment in financial terms. In the absence of such specificity, human systems of decision-making, whether economic, political, or legal, will choose to avoid the problems. Instead, they will shunt these costs onto humanity's own health or upon the renewing powers of nature.

Cost specificity, coupled with the determination to express in cash those costs, will provide the evidence for a recognition of the unity in renewing systems which the fragmented processing of the environment is engaged in destroying. It will lay to rest the claims that the costs of human benefit drawn from nature are slight or that their consequences are very limited ones. The dynamic of present demand has assured the converse, namely, that the costs to renewing environment will be many and heavy and that their consequences will in no way be limited.

It is not that the world is yet threatened immediately with the exhaustion of all the subject-matter held as common property. At differing rates of acceler-ating severity, there may well be a coming crisis in materials, as predicted by the Club of Rome. What is the problem presently at hand, however, is the burden of the costs so long deflected upon what is renewable in the environ-ment. Resource exhaustion may be much closer than optimists think, but the present need is a cost-accounting system, expressed in fiscal terms, that would try to calculate the true benefits and costs of the demands of urban-industrial demand relative to the environment. Costs could then be consciously borne as a part of the means whereby the benefits of that civilization have been made possible.

True, some of the costs specified may turn out to be so great that a re-appraisal of the alleged benefits from that activity must promptly follow. It is doubtful, though, if many of these sort of discoveries would be revealed by specification. Far more likely would be a broad acceptance of a knowledge firmly gained. Environmental protection, perhaps even better than the costs of high wages, and social welfare, can be borne by urban-industrial society. Indeed, environmentally protective costs might be internalized in such a way that they would enhance rather than diminish the chances for affluence within this culture.

It may seem to some banal to say it, but the costs of protecting the environ-ment are the long-run economic salvation of high growth culture. It is not the absorption of these costs that represents the doom of a civilization which has spread over the globe within the past two centuries. Delays in setting up the means for reaching such specificity as to what human demand means for the environment would purchase, at best, short-term savings at an exorbitant long-run risk. Refusal to internalize the costs of benefits extracted will be, instead, the likely source of any doom.

Perception of Environmental Costs
Can Change Rules of Property

There is no denying that there are definite costs to be imposed. Some of these should be put upon those who emit wastes into the air, the water, and the biomass. Some of these costs should be put upon those who have been assigned some entitlement by the rules of property, whether by grant, permit, or regulation, to exploit resources to exhaustion. Others should be paid by those who are in the receptor-category, needing purer flows of air or water for their enterprises. In these ways the money can be collected to undertake re-dressing some of the heavy damages imposed upon the environment by the sort of growth of population, urbanization, and production and consumption that significantly identify present demand.[25]

This sort of action will require the intervention of the lawmakers and some modification in the rules of property. Legal intervention is not a substitute for the assumption within the economic and political systems of the costs previously put upon the environment as allegedly "free" goods. When the lawmakers step in with regulations and charges, the costs are simply specified. They in no way are made to disappear. The action of the law, instead, would be an intervention in the fragmented practices of growth-demandant culture. A new legal tradition would thereafter show the interrelatedness between human demand and the ability of nature to respond to that demand.

Such action is a means of making these costs increasingly cash-specific and chargeable to the entities enjoying the benefits of resource use, be those beneficiaries emitters, receptors, or mineral extractors. The old manner of just lumping unspecified costs off onto the renewing environment is not to be longer tolerated with impunity. People previously were willing to accept a polluted stream because they thought the consequence of that pollution was cheaper goods and lower taxes for them. But now the costs to the environment are accumulating to the degree that pollution cannot be allowed upon the grand scale, even though controlling pollution may mean higher taxes, lower payrolls, or higher prices. A cash-expressible means for covering these costs must be found rather than simply pushing them off, in secret fashion, upon the environment.

In a system wherein the rules of property would be designed to specify and internalize costs, each concerned resource user would acquire the advantages of certainty. It is an advantage increasingly lacking under conditions of mounting demands upon the environment and increasing inability of the environment to accommodate all of those demands. Once an emitter had done what the law demands, he would receive for his property both a certificate of satisfactory performance and an authorization to act for a relatively fixed tenure in a particular way. Whatever the rules of property may call it, he will have the form of a publicly conferred licensed right that will be the source of potential capital exchange for him, accruing to the emitter in the normal course of over-all market transactions.[26]

Even if a closed-cycle system should be required by the law, the closure can only be relative as compared with other systems. The physical law will still require a draw-down procedure for the disposing of the residual accretion. In that event, there will be the same requirements for performance certificates and licensed disposal rights. As in more open emitter systems, these will operate as a similar form of property right, conferring a certainty upon what the emitter holds far greater than exists under most rules of property today as they are impacted by bureaucratic command.

The costs of using the renewing environment as a series of technically interlocked economic resources are inevitable in any culture. Man's economic systems and technologies cannot operate in any other way. But because the demands in a high energy culture are heavy, their costs cannot be insignificant to the environment. This means that when they are expressed in cash terms they cannot be inconsequential either, insofar as the market and the political structures are concerned.[27] Once the costs are so perceived as unavoidable, changes will follow in the way rules of property affect and are affected by them.

What must never be forgotten, in any event, is that a refusal to state these costs in cash neither removes nor minimizes their environmental consequence. One must understand also that attempts to shunt costs off upon the environment do not always succeed. At the present time, under a fragmented operation that denies a unity between human demand and nature's response, much of this shunted cost falls upon the industries who are receptors of flow resources. The fishing industry, farming, and forestry are only a few of such industries whose financial health depends upon the condition of resources they draw upon for raw material in their processes.

When receptor industries are affected by pollution depreciating the flow of resources to them, the costs must be internalized by their operations. Either their prices must go up, thus passing it on to their consumers. Or their employees must be laid off, thus passing the cost on to their workers. Or their profits must be reduced, thereby affecting their ability to command capital. In short, it is not fish or vegetation in a state of nature that must alone bear the costs of a fragmented demand that tries to isolate benefits from costs. It is, in part, some portions of the economy, as well as the environment, which must bear disproportionate burdens. These are burdens which they may find it difficult to sustain in the long run.

No benefit is free of cost. Somewhere somebody or some system has to pay the costs for those who reap the benefit. To continue the maintenance of such division is scarcely the best role the rules of property can perform under the conditions imposed by high demand. It is the function of a rule of property to identify the subject-matter, to isolate the holder of the title, to define what title will mean to a holder, and to determine the procedures under which the title-holder will receive his benefits and pay out his charges relative to this property. When this does not occur, the full benefit is lost and the rules of property themselves increase the costs to the environment.

Entitlements to property and superiorities assertable over items that have become the subject-matter of property do not comprise the totality of property law. It is important that the subject-matter of property be identified, that what constitutes the scope of an entitlement and a superiority be defined, and that the law knows how any entity becomes a title-holder. But property does not exist in a void, for the rules of property are exercised in the larger functioning of the social structure. It is the social decisions which determine the extent of the recognition the legal system may extend to the relationship between human demand and the renewing environment. Once the basic perceptions have been accepted, the rules of property can be devised for regulating the impact of internalized costs upon the individuated property units. Property law, therefore, covers more than the internal management or the transfer of these individuated units.

The role of property is an important one at the interface between man and nature. There can be no abolition of the concept of property. All that is possible is alteration in the definition of what constitutes property. It is a mold into which can be poured such basic social determinations as whether there will be private, communal, socialist, or some other kind of property right. Having been so formed, property then becomes a more or less useful tool for carrying out the tasks of identifying the subject-matter of property, specifying the costs of using that subject-matter, and providing the legal means for all transactions concerning that subject-matter. All forms of property do not equally well perform those functions; and to that degree, there may be radical changes in the rules of property.

What will remain eternal, however, will be the existence of rules of property. They can be changed, amended, or individually repealed; they cannot be entirely abolished. They have been the means whereby undifferentiated nature becomes a unit of production and consumption. Demands in this regard show no sign of slackening. It may be good that they do not.

But it will be good only if the costs imposed are perceived. To help realize that there is a unity between the operation of the demand structure in drawing benefits and its renewing environment in receiving costs would be an important service by the rules of property. The substance of these rules comes from social decisions which lie outside them. They are, however, no less important. Indeed, they may prove vital, because they could be a process for the accomplishment of accommodating demand and the environment.

What Turns the Environment into Natural Resources

What will be a resource in the environment is a matter to be determined by demands that are the product of technologic and economic changes. The term "natural resources" is a description of an economic kind that is applied to things in nature upon which public demands can be concentrated. These demands may be of a sort capable of individuated expression either in the market place or the political forum. They may also be of a collective sort only capable of assertion through the machinery of government. In either case, however, they are never a "free" provision of nature benignly made available for exploitation.

Demand, however, is a gross factor to be considered in calculating the renewing environment's response to its burden. It is the cultural patterning of choice in relation to gross demand that causes costs within the economy to vary widely. Culture sets the general goals to be achieved. But whatever purposes a growth-demandant culture determines to reach, the costs will first depend upon what resources can be made available. Secondly, costs will be constrained by the particular demands charged against the available resources by those possessing legitimate claims. And thirdly, costs will be the result of how the legal system has defined legitimacy.

The process of patterning choices can be mediated by more than one means. It can be done by the market, or by a central bureaucracy, or by legislatively or court established rules of property or tax. The higher the demands made upon nature the greater the need to invoke the authority of an articulated central choice. But whatever the mediation service utilized, the costs of resources will change as described above and as the relative degree of abundance or of scarcity for the resources is thereby affected. For this reason it is insufficiently descriptive to use only such terms as weight, or volume, or some other physical unit of measurement. The total calculation needed in determining cost factors is larger than such measurements. Deterioration attributable to cost is of more a social than a physical character.

In determining costs, one might be seeking to identify natural resources and raw materials or to specify the labor and equipment required for processing the stuff into units of production and consumption. Resource allocation for these purposes is attained "...when no marginal units of any resource can advantageously be moved to another use, that is to say, when any given kind of resource is equally 'useful,' 'productive,' or 'valuable' at the margin in all the alternative allocations to which it is assigned,"[28] This is the common test for rationality in economic behavior. It is the test for value at the margin and concerns itself with the ability of the resource under scrutiny to satisfy all those who have any claim upon it. The products of this marginal value are to be equal in every one of their uses if the choice the choosers are to have should be a rational one.[29]

But the rationality of marginal costs rests, firstly, upon the establishment of larger social constraints and secondly, upon the amplitude and degree of renewability of the resources being subjected to economic action. Resources drawn from the renewing environment do not enter into this situation "freely." An economist is just not perceiving the totality of the picture who argues that "free resources, such as air, are so abundant that they can be obtained without charge."[30]

The justification for this attitude is that anything which commands a zero price must be free. Indeed, the argument is made that if all resources were "free, there would be no economic problem since all wants could be satisfied."[31] But trying to distinguish between an "economic" resource and a "free" resource, on the basis that the former commands a non-zero price while the latter does not, is to have failed to search far enough into the landscape of reality.

Philosophic Determinants of Environmental Value

There is a tendency, particularly evident among critics of urban-industrial society, to conclude that the poor relationship between that society's demands and the environment is purely the product of the open-ended growth curves imposed by those demands. But urban-industrial society is itself the cultural residuum of earlier events and ideas. Many of them, from the philosophies of ancient Greece through the speculation of such 19th century thinkers as Bentham and Marx, continue to directly influence the ways in which the environment is impacted upon. Often it is not the flaws of a growth-demandant culture that distort the renewing environmental systems but, rather, concepts of the most ancient and respected traditions which accomplish such results. The manner whereby modern society calculates the values or price of any part of the environment – not to speak of whether society believes these objects have intrinsic worth – is among the most significant of inherited concepts.

Indeed, equating worth with an ability to command a price has been a subject of dispute since the time of Plato and Aristotle. The Platonist view, most comprehensively summarized by St. Augustine, claimed that objects in nature had an inherent worth independent of their ability to hold value in terms of human demand. St. Augustine argued that the value an object held for man was not related to its own intrinsic worth. Value varied for human beings in a manner proportionate to their differing abilities to use the object under assessment. As important as human demand, the Platonists argued that the value of resources would depend ultimately upon their relative scarcity at some particular time and place in relation to demand. This human value, however, would be independent of the intrinsic worth of this object in nature.

The opposing views of Aristotle were put forward by St. Thomas Aquinas in a rejection of the Platonist view. Worth and value become entirely a matter of what any object in nature could command in terms of human demand. Thomas argued that "value was determined by suitability or aptitude for the satisfaction of man's needs and by relative scarcity or abundance according to the condition of time and place."[32] It is, in fact, rather surprising how rigorous some scholastic theologians were in insisting on this merger of worth and value as determined solely by the requirements of human demand and the scarcity of the resource in relation to that demand.

St. Antoninus of Florence (1389–1459) could only find two distinctions to make on the value of objects. One he called *virtuositas*. This is the object's ability to satisfy a demand. The other he referred to as *placibilitas*. This is the pleasure given by the satisfaction of that demand. In modern terms, the former meant an objective and the latter subjective utility.[33] For Aristotelians, this has meant that value for an object in nature comes from human demand.

The consequence of such a belief is that, if anything cannot be reflected in price, it means there is a free gift to man from nature. All objects in nature are thereby valued from the narrow human demands for satisfaction and for pleasure at being satisfied. It is an attitude showing a complete lack of interest in the possibility any inherent worth could be present in any non-human entity or object in nature.

But the last word on the subject perhaps ought not to rest with the scholastic Aristotelians and their secular successors to moral philosophy. The Platonists may have been right who thought there is more of worth in nature than the price set by human demand can alone reflect. To think only of what price contains would be to hold valueless anything which is simply part of a natural system for which the pricing structure at the moment may be unable to set, or uninterested in setting, prices.

When Barry Commoner says there is no such thing as a free lunch, he means that nothing comes free of either its worth to the natural systems of which it is a part, nor free of the ecologic costs which its removal from the system imposes. Every item capable of being an object of human demand is also possessed of worth in the natural systems of the environment. In truth, as human demand increases, this inherent worth and the costs of ignoring it can become painfully clear through distant reflections in the pricing structure. But that reflection is seen only long after some profound shift has occurred in the ecosystems of air, water, living creatures, and the biomass.

Where there is an indifference to, or a denial of, the intrinsic worth of items

in the renewing environment that have been transmuted into natural resources by the operation of human demand, there must result a severe
disequilibrium in ecologic systems. Coupling this with an ever-increasing
demand for growth in production and consumption is to make the disequilibrium a highly unstable one. As the modern Spanish commentator Lopez Ibor
has pointed out, much of what is happening in the world today stems from a
simultaneous indifference to any intrinsic worth in nature and a desire to find
value only in an ever-increasing consumption of goods. All belief in the
intrinsic worth of nature has been subordinated by a culture that finds its
greatest value in considering both social structure and nature as commodities
to be processed for a transient consumption. As Lopez Ibor has said,

One does not speak of satisfying human needs, without thinking and patterning
the needs for increasing consumption and, by increasing consumption, thereby
increasing well-being. In such an economic cycle, natural human energy has been
imprisoned so that everything is transformed into goods for consumption.[34]

The world today is dominated by its orientation to accelerating and continuous growth in production and consumption. Given the predicates upon
which this culture is operating, growing production is necessary, incessant
undifferentiated growth is essential to affluence, and the insatiable consumer
represents an ideal. Inevitably, this has to mean increasingly unstable disequilibrium in the ultimately fateful search for satisfaction from production
and consumption patterns which ignore natural systems. It cannot be surprising under conditions such as this that there is a general loss of belief that
any item in the cosmic rhythm of nature has any intrinsic worth. Instead the
belief can only grow stronger that the renewing environment acquires value
only from having value conferred upon it through human demand converting
natural systems to natural resources.

Utility as a Value-Determinant for Both Environment and the Rules of Property

It was the developer of the divine calculus, Jeremy Bentham, who produced
the eventually simplest, most anthropocentric, and demand-oriented test for
settling nature's worth: the test of utility. After all, standing in back of the
scholasticists had always been God; and the Divine Presence compelled even
the most pragmatic of them to confess that for God everything in Creation
had worth. In terms of how their economic systems operated, this might have
little practical significance; but perhaps it tempered the importance of man
vis-a-vis nature. In Bentham's utilitarian system there was no such ultimate

insurer of nature's inherent worth lurking in the wings. Nature was to be appraised by the test of utility alone; and this was very much a matter of human social decisions rather than a part in any divinely written drama.

The concept of utility for Bentham, as for succeeding economists, expresses the quality of being useful to one or more human beings. When applied to anything as a means of describing it, utility means that the thing has the capacity to satisfy some human want. Bentham raised it to an ethical principle as well, so that the greatest utility inheres in whatever has the ability to bring the greatest happiness to the greatest numbers of people.

As a utilitarian, Bentham had to take an instrumental view of the rules of property. He was compelled by his ethics to see them as involving only issues of economic return and governmental interference. In this view, he was not to lack enthusiastic disciples. Particularly in American legal history, the most minimalizing aspects of Bentham's utilitarianism have been uppermost in forming the limits on the operation of the rules of property. In popular American usage anything has utility which has an immediate practical purpose, has been designed for service rather than beauty, and is of more short run than long term significance.

The American legal historian, Willard Hurst, has described the popular American test for Bentham's utility ethic as "begrudging...an investment of resources of mind and energy."[35] The primary interest in the United States has usually been the test of immediacy for whatever is alleged to be useful. Everything which supposedly takes away from that primary interest has been grudged. The social tendency has been to reduce such Benthamite legitimizers as the concepts of utility and rationality to their lowest common denominators in order to serve the purpose of an immediate profitable return upon an investment venture.

Urban-industrial society in the United States has preferred conditions of chronic instability as a chief source of individuated profits. The larger costs and the longer term have, therefore, traditionally been overlooked or minimized. But continuing close attention and an insistence on full accountability at each major stage of action has to be called for, if there is not to be a further scamping of investment where the well-being of the environment is concerned.[36] The multiplication of potential profit-returning ventures and the continued dynamics of market expansion have been all that have mattered; and this single-mindedness about utility as an immediate determination has created the need for a larger definition as to what is "useful."

The service of this minimally defined function was preferred in the United States prior to 1970 over any approximation of central controls capable of environmental protection. Nature in American history was taken for granted as a "free" good. The mustering of capital for the growth of gross national product had the highest preference. It proved a pattern for other growth-demandant cultures.

The existence or non-existence of this growth has been the means of accountability for the success or failure of a culture. The determiner of whether there has been utility and rationality capable of legitimizing social and governmental actions has been the rate of growth. The final effect has been the demand to convert the renewing environment into economic responses. It has been through this means, almost alone, that utility as an ethic has judged the success or failure of the managers of growth-demandant culture.

In so doing, the recurring and intensifying crises of urban-industrial society, and the popular dissatisfaction with what has produced these crises, have not been eased by the utilitarian ethic as it has been applied. Under urban-industrial conditions, as Willard Hurst describes events,

...a wider spread of problems challenged public policy processes – concerning the market as an institution of social control, concerning diffuse public interests in natural resource conservation and in public health and safety, and concerning [other] important interests...[and] affected [them] in more focused ways....[37]

Americans, as did many English critics of Jeremy Bentham, viewed the Father of Utilitarianism as hostile to governmental action. In a reaction against decadent forms of mercantilism, Bentham did regard governmental action as more often than not an interference with the wise use of private property or, in the pejorative sense, of muddling. Governmental action for Benthamism was to occur only in exceptional circumstances in order to deal with conditions of grave and discrete public danger.

Yet this is too simple a view of Bentham's attitude to property. Bentham's own definition of utility was far more complex than the later reductionist usages of the term which were to acquire popularity. He was not entirely responsible for the damage his views caused the renewing environment.

Bentham believed that the rules of property were to set out the limits within which the owner of property could anticipate a freedom of control from government. But Bentham also believed that there were occasions when it was necessary for government to penetrate that free zone. It might be for purposes of guaranteeing credit security, or for tax collection, or for public safety. Yet, in Bentham's own system, there would always be one or more governmental authorities with the power not only to interfere but with the greater power to entirely oust an owner from his property if the occasion required it.[38] All Bentham asked was that the rules of property be clear and that they leave to the property owner sufficient scope to use his property with security.

Bentham illustrated his position with an example of the greatest environmental relevancy. It was that of a probable *common sans nombre*. In this common title, all members of a particular community have a mutual right in certain land. His attitude concerning the role of rules of property in this situation is quite clear:

considering that [the law] might have commanded...all...not to exercise any act upon that land and that such are the commands...it actually does give with respect to by far the greatest part of the land under its dominion, it is on that account frequently spoken of as if it had done something in favor of those whom it has thus left at liberty: it is spoken of as having given them or rather left them a *power over* the land.[39]

It is a most pragmatic view of the role of the rules of property. For that reason, it is extremely difficult to know what Jeremy Bentham might have recommended if presented with a condition in which urban-industrial demand pressed against the ability of the renewing environment to sustain either itself or that demand. Faced with such finite limitations, Bentham might have opted for a profound governmental interference with property and market control.

Bentham saw law as setting the constraints within which the owner of property had to act. He held to the premise that law initially withholds all power for entitlements, only subsequently making specific grants of superiorities to title-holders over particular subject-matter of property. If the environment needed protection, there is nothing in Bentham's utilitarianism that would have caused him to say it should be denied.

What is different between Bentham and so many self-called utilitarians is that his consideration of utility had a longer term, as well as an emphasis upon social decisions. Mankind, for Bentham, had the capacity to alter those social decisions and to extend, or to shrink, the compass for defining utility and rationality. After all, it is the final usefulness that is the test of utilitarianism. The greatest drawbacks to that test under conditions wherein there has been fragmentation of the environment are the very short-terms within which most wish to test the state of utility. The quickness with which the ultimate price would be presented to people, who wanted to live only in the short run, must have been very evident to Bentham, should he have lived when demand was impacting so heavily upon the environment. If ever a man thought in long term views, he was the man.

Bentham would not have expected the market, by its own internal mechanism, to control the disequilibrium in the environment produced by urban-industrial demand. The roles of bureaucracy and of the rules of property in setting constraints would have been important. Doubtless he would have perceived the need to compel the market to take account of more than the costs of individuated units. At any rate, Willard Hurst, who has thought deeply about the role of the utilitarian ethic in the legal history of the United States, believes this to be true.

The sort of controls required to cope with acceleratingly severe public problems will not come through internal adjustments prompted on their own account by the managers of business organizations. Rather, restraints have to be imposed by governmental action acting externally to the institutions of production, distribution, and consumption.[40] These constraining limits are the means of compelling the market to take account of social costs which the market would rather ignore or, in turn, compel other places than price internalization to absorb them. It is Hurst's considered opinion that at least Jeremy Bentham among the utilitarians would have realized this.

Since Bentham wrote, governmental constraints have become the norm. Whatever their other purposes, they have compelled the market structure to internalize larger social costs. Without that governmental action, the market would not have acted to bring within the price structure so large a range of costs. They would have been left where they were.

Just to list these historical cost internalizations makes this evident. Entrepreneurs in the 19th century saw no reason to be liable for industrial accidents. They were quite willing to hide behind the fellow-servant doctrine or the assumption of risk theory. Equally, they saw no reason to be liable to consumers for faulty or inherently dangerous products. They ran for cover behind *caveat emptor* or doctrines of privity. Only government action, whether by court decision or legislative declaration, have compelled these costs to be taken up into the price structure and absorbed along with the other costs being passed along to the consumer.

Labor and consumer actions of this sort by government set constraints that have not operated much differently than the recently imposed environmental constraints have functioned. The problem is that the social costs earlier internalized could take advantage of an apparently cheap expansion in energy cascades, or by urban growth, or by the other means profits were individuated out of a fragmented environment. Right now many of the environmental constraints are also being imposed in the same fragmented way. Law and government may be external to the market, but they are not indifferent to basic social decisions.

Instead of pushing for unified, comprehensive action, the legal system has opted for a policing that parallels the production, distribution, and consumption functions. Environmental regulation is now another police action of an externally constraining kind. Within those constraints, the production managers have absorbed their costs within the final price, except as there has been some subsidization. At the moment, as a result, even the bureaucratically imposed environmental requirements are having a molding effect upon the rules of property. These requirements are externally imposing the constraints that will compel cost absorption, whether through the setting of prices, through tax collections to be deducted against profits, or through a real wage loss.

Environmental protection is not working any differently, as yet, from the way the costs of worker and consumer protection have been absorbed in urban-industrial society's economic functioning. The need for environmental protection to work even more basically than these forces for social change has not been accepted in the fundamental social decisions that set the constraints upon law itself.

The traditions for social decision still run in the direction of fragmented, open-ended growth. Judging worth by the degree of profit extracted from production, distribution, and consumption is of long standing. Willard Hurst has noted that legitimacy and the legitimizing function in America have been almost exclusively associated with this idea which sprang from "the pragmatism bred of our experience in opening up a raw continent, through generations in which we were under pressure to improvise and make do with resources frustratingly short of the opportunities."[42] The imagery in this summarizing statement deprives the non-human and the non-economic of every attribute except the power to resist human demand and to frustrate that human demand through an inability to respond to it.

The description applies to all growth-demandant culture and not just to the emerging urban-industrial society of 19th century America. What such a culture calls natural resources will always be "frustratingly short" of what the managers of that culture will consider to be the opportunities. Certain ends have been made preferable to others merely because there is a technology to achieve them. There will likely be a dominant interest in the possessors of that technology to profit from its use, regardless of any larger social costs.

It is the style of a growth-dedicated culture that the ease of workability establishes the validity of whatever is being socially judged.[42] Under the value-determinant of utility, worth and value become interchangeable terms. The test for validity is a narrow one: high judgment goes to whatever is useful for production, consumption, profit, and the price system.

The items upon which a low judgment have been passed are losers in the contest for legitimacy. They tend to drop out of the cultural outlook, either forever or until some later pragmatic test resurrects them for legitimizing through their new (or newly discovered) utility. The maintenance of viability within the environment in these conditions has had every appearance until recently of a very strong bind for what has been assigned a low value culturally.

Utility as an Integrating Determinant
Between Demand and the Environment

Perhaps in a socially heterogeneous democracy, such as the United States, utility may be the only norm upon which there can be general agreement. Bentham's American popularity may have deep roots in that culture. Social decisions for "cheap" energy and for regarding nature as a "free" good have set the base line of agreement for determining what is utile. There has been no adherence to any sacred code or obedience to unfettered bureaucratic discretion. Since the establishment of a hegemonic system is unlikely when the basis of agreement is upon the immediate utility of the demand structure,[43] it is more fitting where utility is the judge of environmental values to make social decisions through the market mechanism, through numerous elections in scattered jurisdictions, or through legal decisions whose makers are hard to identify. The same may be true also for urban-industrial economies other than that of the United States.

Scattered market processes represent a way of amalgamating many individual options into a single social decision. That decision will often contain the paradox of directly competing subdecisions within the cover of the summarizing choice. However, the social means, whereby the test of utility passes final judgment, will paper over the fragments that have gone into the expression of a single choice.[44]

The judgment of utility need not be expressible in cash terms. It is only that cash offers what is commonly judged to be the easiest agreed upon expression of what is utility in any situation requiring validation. But, still, what constitutes utility need not even relate to the individuated units for the production and consumption of natural resources, goods, and services.

Herbert Zassenhaus once suggested provocatively that the economy be planned by allocating units of influence. On this basis, the entirety of the social product might be distributed. It was his contention that such an allocation of interests would result in a market wherein influence could be exchanged for goods and services.[45]

Political influence seems to have been what Zassenhaus had in mind. He would have used it as a means of openly obtaining goods in a manner analogous to a cash exchange. As it stands, political influence has mostly been used indirectly. Persons having political influence have been compelled to first convert it in some manner into cash and only then are they allowed access to goods and services. As a means of breaking away from the cash nexus – should one want to break away – the idea doubtless does not go far enough.

Increasingly, however, the 20th century seems to be showing more interest in means of departing from cash exchanges. Some would substitute, in lieu of money, units of public service. Others, like Dr. Fidel Castro, propose that money be abolished and the public storehouses opened up to supply individuals without charge for the basic "needs" for food, clothing, or health care.

It has been argued that these proposals of substitutions for cash are subject to abuse. A system based on the allocation and exchange of influence, for instance, would give the best advantages to the individual who did *not* directly and openly express what influences he possessed but who instead deliberately misrepresented them.[46] Of course, as Dr. Gallup has repeatedly shown, it is nearly impossible, once you ask a question, to stop individuals from expressing their preferred tastes. Even in a system of influence-exchange, people would probably reveal as much of what they possess as they do in a cash-exchange system. People tend to nakedly express what the culture declares to be the basis of wealth. The advantages of revelation normally outweigh the advantages of concealment.

The greater difficulty for cash-alternative utility proposals is that cash furnishes a nexus which makes the choices actually made harder to misrepresent. In the presence of cash, the constraints of government can more quickly compel investments and expenditures than if it were necessary to talk about exchangeable units of political influence. Cash, under the ethic of utility, is a cultural artifact; and it is an artifact that has proven its ease in use. Cash as the primary medium of exchange, even in economies retaining it, is becoming more attentuated anyway. Computers are talking to computers; and the medium of exchange has increasingly become ribbons of computer paper.

In any system that depends upon consumption, both to stimulate the demand for production and to absorb the production that has been thereby stimulated, it is necessary that there be integrability in the choices exercised by the persons pressing this demand. It will be unfortunate for the renewing environment that this will have an homogenizing effect, because it will work to break down the physical environment into units of consumption and production. But the good and the bad go hand in hand here.

Consequently, standing behind the assumption of comparability for all alternatives available to the ones increasing demand, the concept of utility pushes its claim as the common legitimizing judge. Unless social choices should be so infinitesimally close together as to remove the significance of comparability, there must be in a growth dominated culture an integrability of choice. Otherwise, unpredictable and paradoxical rates of destabilization would follow.[47] Not even a system predicated upon individuated demand and disequilibrium could stand this because the result would be inutile: in a very short time, the demand for growth would be severely and adversely affected.

The deceptively simple way to integrability is by some single test of legitimacy. Such a one is a utility determinant expressed in cash profits on both a short term and in a unit individuated from any larger costs. The Nobel laureate Kenneth Arrow has been highly critical of any such one-dimensional schemes. They may have even an elegant appearance of rationality but their real-world validity he regards as highly questionable. The traditional scholastic thought, after St. Thomas Aquinas rediscovered Aristotle, rejected the broader Platonist view that worth exists independently of any assignment of value by man. Today Arrow regards this as a mistakenly narrow outlook; and he hopes for a broader base for integrability between human demand and the environment.

For him, the environment is a "set of admissible strategies." If there is more than one strategy within that environment, it "automatically contains an infinite number."[48] Kenneth Arrow brings into the modern consciousness the underlying scholastic assumptions behind modern economics. Both St. Thomas and Aristotle once more make the scene when Arrow describes the philosophy of current urban-industrial society thusly:

...to assume the ranking [of alternative social] states does not change with any changes in individual values is to assume, with traditional social philosphy of the Platonic realist variety, that there exists an objective social good defined independently of individual desires.... To the nominalist temperament of the modern period, the assumption of the existence of the social ideal in some Platonic realm of being was meaningless. The utilitarian philosophy...sought instead to ground the social good on the good of individuals...[and] to imply that each individual's good was identical with his desires.[49]

This expresses succinctly why the ethic of utility has acquired a larger and larger legitimizing value as the energy cascades have grown and demand upon the environment has increased. As an ethic, utility lays claim to the ability of making all values fungible. It purports to be the single, simple, quick means of integrability. Its calculus of pleasure offers the most admissible strategy – some would say the *only* legitimate strategy – for converting the otherwise valueless in nature into what would be humanly valuable. The ethic of utility provides the way to justify the imposition of accelerating demand upon the renewing environment. In a time of conflicting values, one can easily understand why many adhere to utility as the sole value-determinant for judging the impact upon the renewing environment of urban-industrial demand.

The Value-Conferring Limitations of the Rules of Property

There has been, is, and probably will forever be a division between those who see a worth inherently present in nature and those who perceive only a nothingness until man's demands confer a value upon it. It is a division which will determine views and actions, depending upon which side of the division one is found. The division cannot be dismissed or glossed over simply because it is as old as Plato and his student Aristotle. The theories on either side of this division necessarily form the views and actions of the participants in decision-making as much today as they did for St. Augustine and St. Thomas Aquinas. To believe that human demand confers value upon nature is a basic presumption that will have different consequences than the belief that there is in nature an inherent worth independent of man.

Conceptually, one can argue fairly convincingly that man invented the idea of nature and that the landscape, once mankind arrived upon the scene, became increasingly a human creation. But this is far from concluding that nature takes her reality from man and is legitimized by his activity. Those who see man as a biophysical part of nature's ecosystems will always disagree with those who find value in nature to be purely something conferred by human technical activity.

Attention can be shifted from the sharpness of this division by stressing how the word environment includes sociocultural activity as well as the work of natural systems. One can look at the world and say that much of it is a product of the culture of human technique and that nature is now part of the human ecumene. But this cannot obscure the question of whether or not the environment surrounding human activity has a worth independent of whatever the sociocultural actions of mankind may or may not have done.

There is a milieu in which man must take part because of his own biophysical organism. It is the natural ecumene in which he is so often reluctant to admit the dependent character of his role. Instead, he wants to see his actions as the sole provider of values and himself as the single purveyor of legitimacy. For the environmentally concerned, there must be denial of this claim of autonomy. Even if the environmentalist is charged with holding Platonist ideals and with being an historicist – terrible charges to plead guilty to when the ethic of utility is in the ascendency – then the broader view must still be asserted as having validity.

It is arrogance to think that the rules of property confer any value upon nature. Concepts are among the tools which compose the technology of man. Technology is the way human demand is made upon nature; but it is not the way nature has her worth. To conclude differently is to deny worth to the human organism itself, as well as to the natural ecumene, and to proclaim as the sole source of value the economic, political, and legal activity of humanity. It cannot be a happy conclusion to think some rule of property has the greater power to confer value than just knowing there are healthy cells within your own body. The living and renewing interactions of the larger biophysical universe are mocked when man says it is his actions which give them value and that without his activity they would be without worth.

The worth of nature requires no legitimizing from the rules of property. Whatever utility any portion of nature may have for the market place, the operations of politics, or the functioning of the rules of property, nature herself has a worth transcending all of these. Values are a human creation, part of man's technology. They are the instruments that help human beings in the continuing processes of living and of managing the different human cultures. They are important; and what mankind accomplishes with them becomes part of humanity's entire environment. But human values are not the source of nature's inherent worth, however strongly mankind should hold to the belief that they are.

Still, it is this insistence that nature is without this inherent worth and that value comes only from human activity which has reduced mankind to the belief that in the rules of property and the bureaucratic mechanisms humanity shall find their salvation. Is nature suffering under the impact of the demands of high growth culture? Does it seem possible that natural systems will be unable to support the human claims made upon them? Very well, clearly there is a problem. Since it is assumed that man's activity conferred value upon nature in the first place, then man's actions will save her from the resulting problems.

Technology, therefore, is the best way; says this wisdom. And among the easiest to apply to human technologies are the rules of property and the bureaucratic mechanism. Hence, let the rules of property and the bureaucratic apparatus solve any crisis caused by treating the universe as a resource for human production and consumption demands. Ironically, as Lopez Ibor has noted, a society without any other form of faith believes the technologies of law and bureaucracy can supply "an organism capable of supplying a final determination and, like the administrative organism in a story by Kafka that grows and grows, even of swallowing up the primary need" of mankind to make their own determinations.[50]

Those seeking a stability they do not perceive around them demand that the rules of property and the bureaucracy supply it. It is as if law and bureaucracy were neutral means to quickly reach a state of equilibrium that is lacking. But bureaucracy and the rules of property are alike tools in man's armamenterium of technology; and technology is never neutral. Bias is imposed by social choice; and the way a tool is formed and chosen expresses that bias. A neutral use, therefore, cannot follow upon the choice of any technology.

The environmentally concerned, like those so criticized by the Spanish commentator Lopez Ibor, have had hopes in the ability of the rules of property and bureaucracy to solve the problems imposed by the demands of high growth culture upon the environment. Conversely, like Lopez Ibor himself, they have in all honesty feared the Kafkaesque qualities that they too see present in those technologies. They have not been a social growth viewed with equanimity. But while they must be viewed instrumentally, as being other forms of human technical accomplishment, the rules of property and bureaucracy ought not to be allowed to fall within the contemporary myth that technology is neutral. As Lopez Ibor says, the technologies of law and the administrative mechanisms can be destructive of all tradition, of accepted social values, and of nature herself.[51] They can also be capable of much that is protective of nature or any human value selected by human choice for protection. What both the rules of property and the bureaucratic mechanisms are *not* is bland and neutral. The bias directing their use will unavoidably be present.

In modern culture, technology has a repetitive quality, meant to serve the stimulation of demand and the multiple encouragements of the production needed to meet the stimulated demand. It is most often monotonous in its repetition because monotony becomes relevant only when its avoidance will itself increase an individuated demand. It is an attitude, as Lopez Ibor has pointed out, that has produced "the skyscrapers or the spreading and geometric suburban house," which are both consumers of great quantities of space. Man has become increasingly concerned to be simply the consumer of the increases which his fragmented system imposes upon him, in indifference to what this type of demand does to the renewing environment.[52]

Man has chosen to make himself a synonym for his economic function only. It is a self-reductionism that is a tragic mistake. Man, like the living nature of which he is a part, is a great deal more than his ability to produce and consume. Because he is so much more, his relationship with nature has to be a highly unstable one. Similarly, there must also be within the human social structure much disequilibrium that neither the law, with its rules of property, nor the administrative mechanisms can paper over.

The isolating actions of high growth culture have permitted humanity to take this stance. The repetitive products of technology, applied upon mass and global bases, have nourished the belief that humanity is autonomous. Impersonality and anonymity have become virtues in urban-industrial society. The mottoes for the age have become "progress, new form, development," without regard for how substance comes into those words.

Yet in all of this, the great cry of Lopez Ibor ought not to be allowed to go unregarded: The existence of humanity is primordial, radically anterior to the function of any technical economic order.[53] Like Plato and St. Augustine before him, he insists that man and nature have intrinsic worth antecedent to the ends of production and consumption in a culture of open-ended, undifferentiated growth.

The worth of both humanity and their environment is independent of the values associated with price and tax revenues. Overlooking this has been seen as the sure course to disaster to a line of thinkers from Plato to the present – and the evidence seems to be accumulating that they have been more perceptive of reality than their philosophic opponents.

Broadening the Environment's Value-Determinants

What man has done has been to confuse nature's worth and the means of expressing human values. The great utility to humanity of the rules of property, of the formation of capital, of the integrability function of cash in human affairs has been damaged by equating such utility with the worth of nature. Human demand alone has been allowed to determine value and to represent all that there can ever be within the definition of value. Growth has been the operative factor in the ethic of utility. Intrinsic worth, insofar as any vestige of the idea remains important to culture, has become an item to be deferred unto eternity.

Increasingly from the time of St. Thomas Aquinas and the scholastics, value has been defined as being limited to whatever had the capacity to meet human demand and to confer pleasure on the human being whose demand had been satisfied. The deferral to the divine plane of any issue of intrinsic worth in what had been used to meet demand and to confer pleasure cleared the philosophical path for those later secular comers who have seen value in nature as something fully expressed by the operation of the pricing system.

Perhaps one ought not to be too hard upon St. Thomas and the scholastics.

After all, they were only restating Aristotle. And they never would have gone so far as the Methodist preacher who enthused that stealing is wrong "because ownership is good and right," who insisted "that there is a certain sanctity to possessions and this commandment ["Thou shalt not steal"] is actually the safeguard of property," and who concluded, "we miss the truth of Christianity if we do not see it as the most materialistic religion in the world."[54] But the kind of attitude summarized by scholastic philosophy did open up the way to the reductionist theories of someone like Edwin Mansfield who can sarcastically say,

Even if some smart Philadelphia lawyer, or some other form of philosopher-king, could tell us which combination of resources is best for the production of each good, this would not be a complete solution to the problem.[55]

Indeed it would not. For Mr. Mansfield the reason that such orders would fail lies in the likelihood that a plan, even if put under the management of a highly disciplined organization, would be "executed improperly, even distorted considerably." But in the long run, bureaucratic distortions are themselves social decisions if they are persisted in. The difficulty does not lie in how well a philosopher-king – or a Philadelphia lawyer – could issue orders or run a bureaucracy. The difficulty inheres in the view that all nature is nothing more than a resource for human production and consumption.

The production-consumption paradigm simply does not express the whole of reality. The purpose of the renewing environment to humanity themselves is broader than that. The worth of what is in nature to the operation of natural systems is far more important than what can be put within a cash ledger book. Viewing the environment solely as natural resources for human demand can never be the solution of the problems humanity may have with the environment. The view is too narrow to plan the way to salvaging nature's continuing ability to respond to human demand.

There must be a way to locate within such human institutions as the rules of property the perception of a worth in nature requiring protection from human demand and having importance independently of any conferral of value by human activity. The means for the identification of this worth need not always be internalized within the operation of the rules of property anymore than in the pricing system. But, wherever in the social structure environmentally protective institutions may be functioning, both the rules of property and the pricing system ought to reflect their operations.

The rules of property and the bureaucratic mechanisms may set the constraints, so that no demand generating activity can act independently of such limits. Yet that is not the same as confining the interest of the rules of property and bureaucracy to whatever can be directly expressed by cash costs, cash flow, or the determination of price. Since the worth of the renewing environment is broader than the values resulting from human activity, the protection of that worth by mankind against man's own demands will require changes in the rules of property and in the manner prices can be commanded in the market. When that happens, urban-industrial society will have reallocated cultural priorities.

Worth and value are not the same. Worth intrinsically within the renewing environment is not synonymous with what can be described by a unit of property or by a market price. As human demand has grown, it has become necessary for humanity to assume certain responsibilities for the consequences of their actions.

This unprecedented growth in demand means the protection of natural systems from mankind's demands has become a necessity for urban-industrial society. Such protection means the development of institutions for accomplishing it. They may be bureaucratic; they may be self-policing base-line rules of property. Or they may take still different forms expressive of the social decision to protect rather than to consume nature. Whatever the protective institutions may be, however, what they cannot do is treat nature as a nothingness waiting to have value conferred by human activity.

Notes

[1] Ronald Coase, "The Problem of Social Cost," as excerpted in Frank Trelease, ed., *Cases and Materials on Water Law*, 2nd ed., St. Paul: West & Co., 1974, p. 119 at p. 122. This article, which first appeared in 1960, is essential reading.

[2] Jerome Milliman, "Can People Be Trusted With Natural Resources?", as excerpted in *ibid.*, p. 154. This article first appeared in 1962.

[3] M. Bruce Johnson, "Some Observations on the Economics of the California Coastal Plan," 49 *So. Cal. Law Rev.* (1976) 749, at p. 751.

[4] *Ibid.*, p. 758.

[5] J. H. Dales, *Pollution, Property and Prices: An Essay in Policy-Making and Economics*, Toronto: Univ. of Toronto Press, 1968, p. 61.

[6] *Ibid.*, p. 110.

[7] C. Reinold Noyes, *The Institution of Property*, New York: Longmans, Green & Co., 1936, p. 389.

[8] *Ibid.*, p. 390.

[9] Dales, *op. cit.*, pp. 62–63.

[10] Noyes, *op. cit.*, p. 442.

[11] *Ibid.*, pp. 454–455, where the simile is carried out in great detail under the influence of then very recent physical theories.

[12] Dales, *op. cit.*, p. 65.

[13] *Ibid.*, pp. 63–64.

[14] Guido Calabresi and A. D. Melamed, "Protecting Entitlement," 85 *Harvard L. R.* (1972) 1089, at p. 1092, p. 1092 note. I am deeply indebted to the ideas in Eric John, *Land Tenure in Early England*, Leicester: Leicester University Press, 1960.

[15] Calabresi and Melamed, *op. cit.*, pp. 1102–1103, Note, where the reference to "religious or transcendental reasons" is made for non-compatible values.

[16] *Ibid.*, p. 1094.

[17] *Ibid.*, p. 1094, note, p. 1096, note.

[18] *Ibid.*, pp. 1099–1100, note, pp. 1111–1114.

[19] *Ibid.*, p. 1117, note.

[20] Robert A. Dahl, *Polyarchy*, New Haven: Yale Univ. Press, 1971, p. 76. Professor Dahl is optimistic concerning this necessity in terms of maintaining polyarchy.

[21] Dales, *op. cit.*, p. v. See also pp. 58–59.

[22] Noyes, *op. cit.*, pp. 440–441. He is speaking of "protected processes" as he defines them, but his references seem applicable to all property.

[23] Dales, *op. cit.*, p. 58 for the image of this "interface."

[24] Noyes *op. cit.*, p. 391. The dichotomy between tangible and intangible property concepts is important, however, to Mr. Noyes.

[25] Dales, *op. cit.*, p. 67, p. 75.

[26] *Ibid.*, p. 71, p. 106.

[27] They are not, however, insupportable. See "The Macro-economic Impacts of Federal Pollution Control Programs," Chase Econometric Associates, Inc., for USEPA and the Council on Environmental Quality, January 1975.

[28] Robert A. Dahl and Charles E. Lindblom, *Politics, Economics, and Welfare*, New York: Harper & Bros., 1953, p. 167.

[29] *Ibid.*, pp. 166–168. The chapter is on "social processes for economizing" and deals

with "high resource output" and "resource development" as well as the "preferred distribution of claims, correct choice and allocation, stability" as necessary conditions.

30   Edwin Mansfield, *Microeconomics: Theory and Applications*, New York: W. W. Norton & Co., 1970, p. 9.

31   *Ibid.*

32   Thomas F. Divine, S.J., "The Catholic Tradition and Economics and Business Ethics" in *Ethics and Standards in American Business*, Joseph W. Towle, ed., Boston: Houghton-Mifflin, 1964, pp. 110–111.

33   *Ibid.*, p. 110.

34   Juan Jose Lopez Ibor, *Rasgos Neuroticos del Mundo Contemporaneo*, 2nd ed., Madrid: Educ. Cultura Hispanica, 1968, p. 24, my translation.

35   Hurst, *The Legitimacy of the Business Corporation in the Law of the United States*, 1780–1970, p. 59.

36   *Ibid.*, p. 156.

37   *Ibid.*, p. 163.

38   H. L. A. Hart, "Bentham on Legal Powers," 81 *Yale L. J.* (1972) 779, at pp. 803–804.

39   Jeremy Bentham, *Of Laws in General* (1790) Appendix B, par. 7, quoted in *ibid.*, p. 804.

40   Hurst, *op. cit.*, p. 164.

41   *Ibid.*, p. 58.

42   *Ibid.*, pp. 58–59.

43   Dahl, *op. cit.*, p. 248, would list the United States as a special case polyarchy. See *ibid.*, pp. 140 ff., discussing authority in hegemonic systems.

44   Kenneth J. Arrow, *Social Choice and Individual Values*, New York: John Wiley & Sons, 1951, pp. 1–2, quoting E. J. Hanson, *Trans., etc., of the Royal Society of Victoria*, Vol. 19, (1882), pp. 197–240, at p. 3, note, for the origin of the concept of the "paradox of voting."

45   Arrow, *op. cit.*, p. 5, quoting Herbert Zassenhaus, *Zeitschrift für Nationalokönomie*, Vol. 5 (1934), pp. 507–532.

46   *Ibid.*, p. 7, citing J. von Neumann.

47   *Ibid.*, p. 13, citing N. St. Georgescu-Roegan, "The Pure Theory of Consumers' Behavior," *Q. Jour. of Economics*, Vol. 50 (1936), pp. 545–569.

48   *Ibid.*, p. 20.

49   *Ibid.*, p. 22.

50   Lopez Ibor, *op. cit.*, pp. 30–31, my translation.

51   *Ibid.*, pp. 38–48.

52   *Ibid.*, pp. 234–235.

53   *Ibid.*, pp. 243–244.

54   Rev. Mr. Wesley H. Hager, "Ethics in Business in the Judeo-Christian Tradition," in Towle, *op. cit.*, pp. 94–96.

55   Mansfield, *op. cit.*, p. 11.

The Meaning of Environmental Costs

Spillover Environmental Effects and the Roles of Law and the Market

Traditionally, it has been the rules of property and the bureaucratic mechanisms which have been regarded as the regulators of spillover effects occurring within the economy. Legal rules and bureaucratic orders have been the means of supervising social choices so as to reconcile conflicting mutual interests. When an economic activity, profitable to the one engaged in it, causes harm to the economic activities of others, law and government normally try to produce a change in constraints so that all may share the least harm. It is an old-fashioned kind of equity, not synonymous with the modern terms of Pareto optimality; but it has been the purpose of the rules of property and the bureaucracy for a very long time. Many now claim the deregulated market can do the job better.

At one time it seemed that the primary function of government was the modest one of maintaining order, resolving social contradictions, and enforcing the making of legal decisions. Perhaps that is the primary function of government in low energy cultures. It can not be the primary function of government once the culture has become a producer of high energy and a demander of open-ended growth. As a result, in a high growth situation, it is ironically the public sector which becomes also another significant generator of spillover effects. The institutions, which are perhaps intended as the means of regulating and modifying the adverse external consequences of an action internally intended only to be beneficial, have themselves often become the source of unintended destabilizing, disequilibrating, and harmful effects that are external to the intent of law and government.

This is plain enough in the case of a socialist economy. In a socialist economy, since the government is the originator of all general economic activity, it is the government which must be the generator of the spillover effects which occur. What is not so clear is that all types of governments in a high growth situation, whatever the manner in which investments are capitalized, are sources of spillover effects.

Government, even in a traditional sense, means coercion at some level of action. It may manifest itself as a sanction no stronger than the establishment of priorities that do no more than allow the complex decisions of urban-industrial society to continue their fragmentation of the environment. But in a growth-demandant culture, government concerns itself with the attainment of a maximum in gross national product. Far more than its own internal management, government today sees itself as having to push the entire economy forward toward the goals of optimum growth in production and consumption that have been set by the basic social decisions of urban-industrial society.

The economists who stress the importance of the market have sought a means of reducing this burden on government. One of them, Robert Mundell, in a series of environmental examples, has sought to bring together the complementaries in the spillover, or neighborhood, effects of economic activities yielding external diseconomies or economies. Since the production of external diseconomies seem to be the most common as well as harmful, they occupy the greatest attention.[1] However, the production of external economies yielding benefits to others, though often thought to be in very short production, are not. The facilities infrastructure which government places under the foundations of the economy are simply taken for granted and not perceived as a massive external economy. From the market viewpoint, this means government already does too much and the environment might be better protected by leaving matters to the market for sorting out.

Firms that produce smoke nuisances as a byproduct will get "punished" in the long run as the cities they are in become less comfortable places to inhabit; this change will eventually make these firms unprofitable.[2]

Even to the believer in the power of the market to solve problems, this reduction of the role of government to observer of private dramas must cause some discomfort. To anyone who holds less than this pure faith, it is not to be taken seriously. To "punish" the polluter, the over-all economic activity of a city has to decline. All the inhabitants and all the holders of capital not invested in the polluter, who are in that city, must suffer as the "penalty" slowly forms itself around the smoke-emitting firm. Although they enjoyed little, if any, of the profits of the emitter, they must share in its "punishment," perhaps out of all proportion to the "penalty" put upon the polluter.

Should government not be quite so quiescent and impose a fine, there still will be a time lag. Time will be lost first because of the necessity to build up the political forces capable of deciding in principle upon a fine. More importantly, time will be lost because the investigation and procedure for conviction of polluters allows them to cause harm for which no fine they will pay could ever be adequate. Theoretically, external diseconomies do punish their source; but, in so doing, others are punished first and often far more severely due to the time lag between the imposition of the diseconomy and its later consequences.

This means that the external diseconomies will spill their costs onto others in far greater quantity than can ever be thrust back upon the firms which have spewed out these effects. In a fragmented situation, the profits to the emitter are worth it to him, even if the costs he puts upon others are enormous. Consider the present conditions of places like the Calumet district on the Indiana–Illinois line, the Cleveland Flats in Ohio, and the cities of northern Jersey. Their status is the result of scores of years of spillover effects, of profits taken by some and costs passed on to the environment and others.

What can now be done to the firms which produced those external diseconomies? Many of them have now removed themselves from those blasted areas or have gone through dissolution. Even if that dissolution was their "punishment," how can there now be any redress? Their total current assets would not be enough to redress the terrible urban and environmental harm they have wrought.

Government has the power to order the internalization of external diseconomies by changing the rules under which property is held or by bureaucratic order. Governments serve as the institution with the capacity to exploit opportunities for profit by coordinating the internalization of externalities, both adverse and beneficial. Laws can provide for a collective consumption through public services, can establish a systematic frame for economic activity through the promulgation of regulations, and can interject changed procedures for holding property into the relationship between urban-industrial society and the renewing environment.

Those who have more confidence than reservations about the capacity of the market to redress harms, often would prefer these actions of government to be performed upon a local level, should they be wanted. Local government, through what it does in the way of fire protection, education, water supply, and waste collection is certainly already engaged in services that are specific to the wants of their inhabitants; and such kinds of services could be extended. Those who have a distrust for governmental action in any event, prefer to

rely upon the local units, if reliance upon government should be at all necessary, since

elaborate hierarchical tiers imply a loss of control; bureaucracy sets in, and big
government can accomplish only rather inefficiently many things that can be done
efficiently by the local community or the individual.[3]

Unfortunately, there are many factors undermining this hope. First of all,
the populations of high growth cultures are highly mobile. This undercuts
the ability of decentralized units of government to guarantee the performance
of duties made heavier by high population mobility. Furthermore, the resources of local governments are capitally inadequate for the demands to which
they are currently compelled to respond. And, thirdly, the very talent of local
government to be flexible and responsive makes such government vulnerable
to control by local industrial interests with a low regard for any limitations
being put upon their activity, however socially beneficial those limits might be.
In fact, should decentralization proceed far enough, this fragmentation can
prevent government from capturing any of the gains accruing from common
social purposes.

Even adverse externalities, after all, are not unmitigated social costs. They
represent an opportunity to render a collective social good. Nothing should be
done at any level of government to freeze the present institutional structures
into a fragmenting grouping of relationships. There are indications that the
homogenizations being increasingly demanded by urban-industrial society,
whatever their adverse effects upon the renewing environment, may have the
consequence of forcing social decisions away from segregative exploitation
and toward integration of economic purpose and environmental effect.[4]

It is just most unlikely, anyway, that any institution by itself, whether the
deregulated market or new rules of property or some level of government, can
stop the spillover effects on the renewing environment of a mobile, growth-
driven, chronically disequilibrating urban industrial economy. There are
advantages in high growth culture, stemming from concentration on production and consumption, that cut against the sufficiency of local control, individual initiative, market autonomy, or any other single power to protect the
environment. Rather, the cut is in favor of combining bureaucratic regulation
and adopting changes in the other constraints of law. The thrust, therefore, is
not in the direction of less public intervention and more reliance on the market.
There will be more, not less, regulation by both bureaucratic command and
altered rules of property; and these will be more of central than local, public
than private origin. One must hope, and seek, that their inevitable externalities
will be beneficial as well as adverse.

The "Debt to Nature" and the Regulatory Change Required

Whether one is talking about continued fragmentation of the environment or about the possibility of integrating human demand and environmental response, all of it is part of what Barry Commoner calls the "debt to nature." A demand for growth, which has been disregardful of the environment, has been running up the size of that debt. Neither the market nor the legal-administrative mechanisms have adjusted for either the growth or its impact. This behavior now threatens urban-industrial society with an action in liquidating bankruptcy.

Allowing pollutants to go unchecked into the natural environment, says Commoner, has been a "mortgaging of the environmental integrity." Like all mortgages, its security depends upon the credit accumulated; and, "we have run out of ecological credit." For Barry Commoner, about the best to be hoped for is a receivership which would require "the sharp curtailment of power consumption, the production of synthetics, and built-in obsolescence."[5]

Whatever integration may mean in the future, the past social decisions for increasing demand have used the renewing environment as discrete natural resources to be processed into individuated units for production and consumption. Every effort has been made in this processing to isolate profits for the individuated units and to pass off on nature all the costs that could possibly be shuffled out of the internal functioning of every economic operation. This is the source of the "debt to nature" of high growth culture that has been accelerating the flow of growth or demands for more than a century.

At the very least, what is demanded is an environmental redress that would provide comprehensive and integrated environmental and social decision-making. Beyond this, it may as well require a further social reordering. The lawyer Henry Caudill believes that this social reordering cannot be avoided. Everywhere about him he sees a jungle that wastes all efforts to redress the environmental costs which have been imposed and that are being imposed by the present system. He sees the rules of property and the bureaucratic mechanisms as at best in a state of paralysis relative to the actions for carrying through this redress. He wants a strong central unitary government, totally unlike anything Americans have ever known, capable of doing and not just regulating. In short, he has a very stark message to the managers of capital:

You claim to live by the motto "produce or perish." Now we demand that you produce a decent environment in the lands you dominate or make way for a new system of economics and new order of values.... Moderation in the cause of survival is no virtue! Extremism in the cause of survival is no vice.[6]

Barry Commoner sees the needs for the future as no different from the views of Henry Caudill. Far from turning to a reliance upon the deregulated market, they both would wrench out the whole system of private capital. For them as for many others, it has only an awesome power for abusing the environment and corrupting government.[7] For them, the environmental crisis is the precipitant for paying "in the ancient coin of social justice" the accumulated costs from the "brutality of racial competition for survival" and "the incompatibility between the economic goals of entrepreneur and worker," as well as the "debt to nature."[8] In short, it will not be the deregulation of the market but only the socialization of capital and the use of strong unitary governments which will suffice to introduce "a new order of values."

To confidence like this, one can only respond with the one word: Maybe. Perhaps the abolition of private capitalism, private property, and private profit constitute all that is needed. But is there strong reason to believe that this would produce a lower energy demand, or radically different and environmentally compatible energy sources, or a view of the environment as something other than resources for processing into production and consumption? Certainly many, on the basis of either theory or experience, believe that the answers to these questions would not be necessarily in the affirmative. For these critics, the more things change the more likely they stay the same.

The first theorist to carefully predict that the socialization of production by itself would not necessarily produce all the good results predicted by such seers as Commoner and Caudill was the Italian economist Enrico Barone. It was his insistence that a state-operated economy need not be a no-growth economy. Furthermore, if such a state-socialist economy should seek maximum growth, then all the attributes of a high energy growth culture would be present, insofar as fragmented use of the environment would be concerned. As he wrote in 1908,

even when some resources are collective property, the State can do no less than fix a price for their services, since there would otherwise be an enormous waste of these, with a consequent destruction of wealth.[9]

Even when property comes to be collectively held, this

still does not upset the technical fact that by once subtracting a part of the disposable productive services from the production of consumption goods, and then to produce new capital (new *means of production*, if that term is preferred) there is secured for always an increase of production greater than the amortization of Capital.[10]

It has been called the most important of Barone's economic ideas as a theorist.[11] For Barone, once a collective economy should exist under state direction, there would be no *necessity* for the development of a stationary, no-growth economy. It might happen, but there would be no intrinsic requirement for the managers of collective capital enterprise to elect a no-growth economy or to undertake any costs in a high-growth situation which would not have been undertaken by their private predecessors. They might be, as their predecessors might have been, put under externally imposed constraints, prompted by basic social decisions to protect the renewing environment. But this would be independent of the manner in which their collective enterprises would internally operate, once left to the devices imposed by a high growth production and consumption process.

Few writers since Barone have expressed this point of view so bluntly. Subsequent experience seems to show his prophesy to have had a high degree of accuracy.

If the Ministry of Production proposes to obtain the collective maximum – which it obviously must, whatever laws of distribution are adopted – all the economic categories of the old regime must reappear, though maybe with other names: prices, salaries, interest, rent, profit, saving, etc. Not only that; but...the same two fundamental conditions which characterize free competition [will] reappear, and the maximum is more nearly attained the more perfectly they are realized. We refer, of course, to the conditions of minimum cost of production and the equalization of price to the cost of production.[13]

These are the two great internal devices of both collective and private enterprise – minimum cost and equalization of price to cost – that impose their will, in the absence of external constraints compelling the internalization of larger social costs. Although Barone had no experience of a socialist state in 1908, the operations of state-owned enterprises since his day would prove him reasonably prescient in this accuracy.

Collective economies need not be more protective of the natural environment than private capitalist systems. In them, there are the same forces at work that press against the internalization of environmental costs in all growth-demandant cultures. Collective economies also seek the apparent profits to be made if costs can only be passed along to nature. The managers of collective enterprise are as anxious to individuate profits from costs in their operations as any manager of a private capitalist enterprise about to make his annual report to the shareholders. The refusal to perceive the unity present between human demand and nature's ability to respond to that demand is equally seductive in the short-run for both sets of managers.

Andrei Sakharov, speaking from the Russian experience rather than the purely theoretical stance of Barone, has not found the collectivist economy disposed to protect the environment. The result is about the same for collective enterprise as the critics of private capitalism have noted the performance of the private entrepreneur to be in his search for a very personal profit. As Sakharov says,

[S]enseless despoliation caused by local, temporary, bureaucratic, and egotistical interests, and sometimes simply by questions of bureaucratic prestige, as in the sad fate of Lake Baikal are common in collectivist economies.[13]

The production managers in a collectivist economy, like their counterparts in a private system, have no wish to recognize the interrelationships in nature or between human demand and environmental response. They too want to turn away from considering the time lag that separates the changes wrought in the renewing environment from the consequences of those changes. They do not want the imposition of constraints that would compel them to absorb in their internal costs the burden of environmental protection. Both private entrepreneurs and collective managers would like to reject the necessity of considering whether the inherently complex and interrelated character of environmental systems could limit their economic operations.

Any environmental limitations are matters that they would just as soon not have brought to their attention. It has been no different, so far as the environment has been concerned, in a collectivist state under conditions of high growth than in similarly situated private capital economy. With a ten percent growth each year in wastes, Sakharov points out that in a century such an increase will be multiplied twenty thousand times with the result that the renewing environment must suffer fatal consequences. If a world-wide effort is made to prevent this, it need not occur. But the act of socialization is not by itself such a sufficient world-wide action.[14]

The form by which the title to property is held will not change attitudes toward the processing – or refusing to process – the environment. Just as he criticized collective economies, for instance, Sakharov does not believe that economies with private capitalist systems are in any way justified in criticizing the conduct of collectivist economies. Emphatically he believes the conduct of both sorts of economies are the same insofar as the renewing environment is concerned.

The United States as an instance of one urban-industrial country having to act for the "salvation" of the environment, must reduce its rate of growth through "a fifteen-year tax equal to 20 percent of national incomes." Sakharov would impose a tax in all industrially developed countries. Unlike Barry Commoner who is so opposed to synthetics, Sakharov would invest this tax revenue in increased food production through a wide application of fertilizers, an improvement of irrigation systems, better farm technology, wider use of the resources of the ocean, and gradual perfection of the production, already technically feasible of synthetic foods, primarily amino acids.[15]

Sakharov does not by these intended uses of his proposed tax on growth admit an intrinsic worth of growth for its own sake. He advocates neither the increase in world populations nor increased exploitation of new natural resources. What he is hoping to do is to balance world growth rates so that humanity and high growth culture can survive the response from nature to the impact being thrust upon the environment. It is a point of view sharply, if obliquely, seen by Barone near the beginning of the 20th century:

If it were so desired, it would be possible to augment consumption, at the expense, however, of the formation of new resources, but of *all* the new resources, even at the expense of the birth rate....[16]

It is this sort of balanced "augmentation" rather than undifferentiated, open-ended growth which Sakharov is advocating. This is the ambition that brings so technocratically committed a thinker into approximate accord with so many who are concerned about the ability of the renewing environment to survive the impact of urban-industrial demand and, perhaps, of the ability of urban-industrial society to survive the collapse of renewing environmental systems. The policies which he sees as necessary require deliberate choice and an allocation of expenditure or sacrifice.

If there is to be a radical change in the way demand upon the environment is regulated, it will not be enough to shift the holding of property from private to collective control or to form a strong central government to direct the total economy, anymore than it would be to turn all responsibility over to a deregulated market or local limits of government. Such procedural changes will not be the "salvation" of either the environment or of urban-industrial society. What Sakharov calls "salvation" will come about only if a conscious, fully-articulated, difficult, and probably fiercely resisted decision can be made to set up a maintainable balance between the renewing environment and human demand.

Every human activity requires the expenditure of energy; and, consequently, there is little in the way of human action that does not make a demand upon the environment. Insofar as these human demands are not compensated by the renewing powers in nature, man must set up artificial regimes to either reduce his demands or increase the environment's compensatory powers. To put the matter succinctly, whatever the way capital is held or government organized, humanity must make a sufficient degree of investment to restore what has been drawn down in the environment below nature's powers of renewal. Otherwise what has been a short run, individuated benefit for certain people will become a long run cost to all of humanity.

Public Investment and Environmental Protection

The anticipated conduit for public investment is government. Unfortunately, government is under pressure in urban-industrial society to emphasize the growth of gross national product without sufficient regard for the impact any part of that growth will have upon various interrelated systems in the environment. Little care has been expended upon learning whether these natural systems can cope with this growth or whether some human assistance might better enable them to handle the impact of human demand. Traditionally, economics have had only a muted interest, when there was any at all, in the environment. Instead, economics has been primarily concerned with real income *per capita* or with growth as expressed by the gross national product. And yet such concentrated thinking has been very welcome under the environmentally fragmenting operations of high demand since knowledge has been thereby obtained capable of a different usage.

In the 19th century, it was essentially John Stuart Mill who was most concerned with the advantages of the stationary state. His contemporaries, on the contrary, were interested in growth. In the 20th century, aside from the lamentators in the 1930's who thought growth had been slain by the Great Depression, very few have been interested in a stationary state. If growth ceased, the problems associated with growth would cease as well. But as for urban-industrial society, as to both its benefits and its costs, there was the fear that it too would be one of those "problems" terminated.

True no-growth would put all quantities at rest with no savings and no investment. Rest, in turn, would avoid the opportunities that inure in every problem. Rest might lead inevitably to a low energy culture capable of functioning under what to all social appearances would be stasis; but, given the benefits and the opportunities that high energy culture possesses, there are few who would opt for such a situation of rest. Certainly, neither John Stuart Mill, J. K. Galbraith, nor the Club of Rome – so often called no-growth advocates – want such rest. What they have called for instead is a better allocation of public and private investment. In late 20th century terms, this means an allocation of investment toward the public sector which, minimally, would direct further investment for environmental protection in the production and consumption sectors of the economy.[17]

Investment to provide balance between human demand and environmental systems is also a form of growth, most likely requiring some form of surplus in the economy. It will fail to produce true no-growth; nor should that be its purpose. But, hopefully, the outcome would be the balance now so absent in the present conditions of disequilibrium. In appearance, such investment will often seem non-productive, simply a series of externally-imposed constraints requiring expenditures by producers and consumers. But if these investments work, the resulting balance would be a highly productive return upon the investment.

Capital investment, of what at first blush is an apparently non-productive kind, is essential in an urban-industrial society. Unfortunately much of the investment in the present demand-structured situation is for immediate consumption rather than long term investment. The economy is focused on production and consumption, concerned with the undifferentiated growth in demand and with plans for obsolescence. Even public expenditures, which ought to be primarily long term capital investments for supporting the system indefinitely, are often of such an essentially non-capital kind. But if there is to be long run growth of a stable variety and if the growth is to be fully employed in the national income, there must be an increase in capital investments, including public investments in further environmental protection.

When this balance is not kept, it means either that the capital goods are not being fully utilized or what purport to be capital goods are goods for immediate consumption. Absolute figures on investment simply become misleading when either such condition exists. Without such balance, the "paradox of production," as the Dutch economist Jan Pen calls it, ensues. In this situation, the true low rates of either utilization or of investment lead to what the economic system must treat as overproduction.

Given an analysis like Pen's, the apparently non-productive, seemingly no-growth intended investments, for which an economist like J. K. Galbraith has been calling, are actually necessary. In high growth culture, infrastructural investments are required. Some may think them unproductive. But they are necessary in order to forestall the "overproduction" which harms both the economy and the environment.[18]

This is reinforced by an observation made as early as 1870 by A. Wagner that the relative size of the public sector increases with the growth of national income. Public sector investment is a necessity in high energy culture since the incentive is missing for the individuated units of production and consumption to make such investments on the scale required. Unit by unit, the incentive exists to try to pass such a burden along; and if the public sector does not make the needed investments, this individuated advantage becomes a social disadvantage of monetary costs and environmental harm.

For example, so much of what is required to train a public with a high consumption demand comes initially through the publicly-provided educational system. The smooth distribution of production is made possible by public investment in research. The public consciousness is assisted by the public sector to form wants and then the public sector helps in converting these wants into demands. Having done so much, the public sector must then begin investment programs able to deal with the consequences of the resulting growth in demand. When the public sector refuses to make these latter investments, a retardation in growth results. But it is a retardation which rarely redounds to the benefit of nature, since the distortion reflected in the social structure causes an instability that is productive of further imbalance.

For the most part, public sector investment is long-term capital investment. Public sector investments in such matters as education and environmental protection are for capital growth, not current demand. Far from producing no growth, or perhaps even less growth, they assist economic growth. To the environmentally concerned, whether pleased or dismayed by this, the growth they produce could introduce balance into the destabilized system.

Even in the 1950's, and relying more upon European and English than American sources, Jan Pen could note the rise in local governmental expenditures to meet the demands of urban-industrial society for the support of infrastructure facilities. One of the reasons local government expenditures then showed such a response lay in their greater vulnerability to the immediate pressure of economic demands. When investments are needed to maintain capital-output ratios that will not encourage overproduction and the resulting economic dislocations, local government is the first mobilized. This mobilization contributes to what Jan Pen has called the "inflationary infection of government," [19] and the inflationary infection has raged on since the 1950's, first in municipal budgets and then in those of central government. The reason is that public sector investment is essential, whatever the inflationary risk. Urban-industrial society needs these public investments for its own survival.

Unfortunately as is the case with so much in a system that refuses to recognize its inherent unity with nature, public sector investment has most often not been protective of the environment. Even when it has been a capital investment, rather than one meant for immediate consumption through prompt obsolescence, such public investment more often has served the growth of undifferentiated, open-ended demand than environmental protection. The fact that the public sector responds to the need to keep the capital-output ratio low and simultaneously maintain economic balance, or makes investments designed to keep up demand levels so as to smooth the distribution to consumers of what has been produced, does not mean any automatic protection for the environment.

Public investments can intensify growth problems and, by their incremental actions, generate the sort of cumulative disturbance of equilibrium within the economy which Lord Keynes predicted would always threaten any state of balance. Profit is regularly made in high growth situations by isolating production and consumption units from their costs. It is a basic social decision to profit from a refusal to recognize the interrelationships between the environment and human social structure.

The decision-makers controlling public investment can rise no higher in decisions to protect the environment than the basic social decisions of the culture whose public affairs they are administering. When the moment is propitious to protect the renewing environment, then law and the administrative mechanisms can provide the interface between society and science. Public investment can have many kinds of spillover effects; but so long as the social values stand highest for the isolated units of production and demand, such investment will do more to further the growth of demand than the protection of the environment.

The United States Interstate Highway System, begun under President Eisenhower but wanted since the first World War, illustrates this. Definitely it is an example of the public sector responding to demand and to the pressure imposed by earlier public investments in highways. Perhaps it was an acculturated response. Certainly there were few to oppose its inception, and opposition grew quite slowly during the first decade of construction. Yet the social, economic, and environmental spillover effects have been massive.

First of all, long-haul rail passenger service was dealt its final blow; and even rail freight transit may have been fatally undermined by a competitor financed by the public sector. The impact upon the environment of so much paving, so much concentrated run-off, and so much accelerated sedimentation has been profound. The social disruption to cities has been so severe that an economist in 1975 predicted, "regardless of efforts at revitalization,...the central cities will die because they have nothing to offer...." [20] A shift to time-travel thinking was accomplished that ran head-on in 1973 into the 55-mile-per-hour travel restriction set by those dealing with gasoline limitations.

The United States Interstate Highway System, in summary, represented an enormous public investment. It was a response to a demand that had been generating throughout the 20th century through the workings of an industry whose importance to the economy waxed consistently throughout that same period of time. It was an accommodation to the automobile, a cultural artifact which the public had accepted fully despite the many dangers appertaining to it. In making this accommodation, an incredible amount of harm was externalized upon the environment and to the chance of coping in the future with the relationships of human demand and environmental response.

Amenities have flowed from these ribbons of concrete. But they are amenities that look their economic best when the absorption of so many of their costs by the public treasury makes them so apparently cheap. In a time of low capital-output ratio, they held a value in helping maintain a balance in the economy so long as such an economic situation prevailed. It has been called the period when an economy with a high energy demand "got fat quick."[21]

In the long run of only twenty years, however, the costs the highways imposed to provide those amenities have become ever clearer. In the still longer run, they may prove themselves a hindrance in balancing man's relationship with his environment, including the employment of more conserving energy sources for human economic purposes. As an investment by the public sector, they are an example of massively supporting the growth in undifferentiated demand and of further undermining the ability of nature to absorb that demand in a way that would permit a renewing response. The Interstate Highway System well illustrates why public sector investment, even when of a capital character, is more often inimical to the environment than protective. There can be no doubt, therefore, that for good or ill public sector investments concerning the environment tend to have a massive effect upon that environment.

It would be folly to call for the cessation of public sector investment. However much the market might be deregulated, the character of urban-industrial society would continue the pressure for such investments. What must be kept in mind, consequently, is not the prohibition of public sector investments but rather the full scope of their environmental and other impacts. Moreover, until basic social decisions favoring environmental protection have become far stronger than they have proven up to this time, public sector investment will be as disequilibrating to the renewing environment as any other investment. But in the meantime, the inevitability and significance for good or ill of public sector investment must be kept uppermost in the minds of those planning those projects. Assuredly, environmental harm ought not to be intensified by the public investments called for by urban-industrial demand.

Tax Incentives and Environmental Value

By themselves, tax incentives represent no inducement by production and consumption units for action to protect the environment. The installation of pollution controls are considered by these units to be no more than the building of non-productive facilities without relationship to the income-inducing aspects of the enterprise. With such a view as this prevailing among the managers of enterprise, one need not be surprised to learn that tax incentive programs make small impact upon the economic consciousness.

Unfortunately from the point of view of governmental revenue, on the other hand, the losses can be quite large from those same tax incentive programs. From 1970 to 1979, the United States had anticipated increasing the direct incremental cost of federal pollution abatement incentives in diverted tax revenues from $15 million to $120 million.[22] The costs to the states were to have run at a lower rate during that same period. But heavy as such a loss would be to the government, it would represent only a slight incentive to enterprise to induce environmentally-protective action.

The maximum return that a company can expect from state and federal sources on such tax-prompted investments varies from 40.4 per cent up to a maximum of 71.2 per cent...with the average being nearer the bottom figure. In most states, therefore, a purchaser will be making a non-productive investment of the order of one half the cost. Common sense and responses to industry questionnaires compel the conclusion that existing tax incentives do not induce investments that would not otherwise be made.[23]

This lack of interest is reinforced by the fact such tax incentive programs to encourage environmental protection are usually administered through tax departments rather than through environmental protection agencies. This means a low level of environmental interest among those accountable for the administration of the incentive program. Such a lack can lead very easily to the smug attitude which blames failure on the problem rather than on the tax incentive program which was meant to be the major solution for the problem. This enforcement of the program through tax agencies reinforces the non-environmental aspects of such programs; and such reinforcement acts to reduce further the minimum chance to make a positive environmental impact which might exist.

It is the "non-productive" appearance of that portion of the enterprise's expenditure, which is not reimbursed by the tax incentives, that makes any effort at all by enterprise under a program of tax incentives unlikely in the absence of compulsions. Furthermore, because tax incentives are so often based upon installation of pollution control devices, they fail to center on their target – if, indeed, their target *is* environmental protection. They aim at the financially non-productive methods of waste treatment facilities rather than at alternative methods of production, fuel use, or land control. Rarely do they anticipate what the special circumstances of many of the individual enterprises will be. Putting it metaphorically,

The tax system democratically gives a plant assembling hi-fi equipment in America's cleanest county, and a steel mill in Pittsburgh, the same incentive to reduce pollution.[24]

The irony is underlined when one realizes that the cost of tax incentives extends far beyond any effectiveness that might be anticipated from such programs. As Henry Aaron explained the effect of tax incentives, prior to their suffering some curtailment by the Tax Reform Act of 1969:

[T]he Treasury Department Tax Expenditures Budget published in 1968 estimated the annual cost to federal revenues of tax incentives at nearly $45 billion which equalled 65 percent of total federal individual income tax collections that year.[25]

The figures are old; but the problem they reveal is still with the United States, insofar as the chance tax incentives may have for protecting the environment. Few of the incentives in these 1968 figures were for protecting the environment and the reform legislation in 1969 was designed to prune many of them. But such a statistic does point out the effect on tax revenues of tax incentives and would strongly indicate that they ought not to be used, unless they really can act to improve substantially the relationship between human demand and environmental systems. The evidence for that relationship, however, is sadly lacking.

Tax incentives are most enthusiastically received when they contribute to increasing the yield from the gross income of the affected enterprise. They are least appreciated by entrepreneurs when they merely allow the writing off of a few costs which the enterprise is under no requirement to undertake in any event. If it is the improvement of enterprise capital that is at issue, industry may take up more enthusiastically the provision of depletion allowances or some other tax incentive contained in a government program. These have an immediately perceived consequence in after-tax yield or the calculation of the gross income from which all prospect of ultimate profit is derived as a result of the activity of the enterprise.

However, these incentives rarely relate to environmental protection. Ordinarily, there is not the same independent motive for enterprise to look with equal delight at being able to write off environmental protection costs. These, after all, are to be incurred for the sole purpose of being able to get a tax break as to part of the expenditures. Indeed, if such write-offs were to be considered absolutely by themselves, where *would* be the incentive even if the costs of environmental protection were to be one hundred percent reimbursable in some form by the government?

To enterprise, these environmentally protective actions must be externally imposed constraints, if enterprise is to act at all. Otherwise, they would be self-imposed burdens on what enterprise regards as its basic function to produce maximum yield. And no enterprise would willingly impose such burdens upon itself.

The consequence of the situation, therefore, is that action for environmental protection is caused by the externally imposed compulsory restraints and not by any tax incentive programs. Of course, if in some way the incentive would produce a larger income after taxes for the enterprise or provide business for the enterprise, there would be greater interest in environmental protection. But in the short run, anyway, both of these are normally remote possibilities.

Tax incentives do not induce environmentally protective action. They may ease the stress of it, of course. By that fact, they may reduce the level of political opposition from enterprise to the constraints compelling such action. However, what induces enterprise to protect the environment is an externally provoked compulsion, enforced by changes in the rules of property and the government's bureaucratic mechanisms. In the absence of such compulsion, the attitude of enterprise under a program of tax incentives alone would at best be one of indifference. Enterprise will persist in its view, under so mild a reward, in seeing environmental protection as representing a set of economically non-productive expenditures.

While the tax structure could be used interstitially to enforce environmental sanctions, its use for that purpose would be awkward. However, if the tax structure were to be used for the purpose of environmental protection in such a manner, it would mean a basic social decision had been previously taken that henceforward would refuse to let costs be passed on to the renewing environment.

However, tax programs are marginal to social programs generally. This marginal character must clearly be understood as the limitation upon their effectiveness, particularly as the sole enforcer of sanctions. If an action is important enough for society to pay for, in whole or in part, then it is important enough for the public to require.

The last outcome of all schemes for tax incentives is to put upon the public some part, or all, of the costs of accomplishing the incentive purpose. If the public is to absorb such costs, constraints should be put upon the production unit so that the managers of that enterprise may know how they should operate and within what limits they must calculate the effect of market forces. While taxes can destroy any enterprise by their imposition or by their manner of collection, tax rebate, deduction, and exemption programs have less significance for business success. They may act to assist in further distortion, although even then they only intensify activity already determined by other factors not concerned with tax deductions. But tax rebates, deductions and exemptions will rarely be the primary motive forces for conduct concerning the fundamental decisions of the managers of investment capital.

Clearly, such fiscal questions as tax incentives should not be employed so as to load the balance further against environmental protection. But, with equal clarity, it must be realized the minimal effect tax programs have upon protecting the environment. Generally, anything that is done solely because of a government subvention or deduction ought not to be done at all. Only the presence of a provable common advantage, far outweighing the gain by the recipients of the subvention, justifies such transfer payments. Even if this common advantage exists, the question ought to be asked whether the same advantage could be as easily gained through change in the rules of property or by an order from the bureaucracy. This would especially be true where there could be a cost absorption by market forces rather than a public subvention.

Nowhere is this more plainly evident than in the way tax programs have been employed to encourage environmental protection through tax deductions. Given their common marginal value, tax incentive programs have had success only where other forces have compelled the manager of the enterprise to make any investment at all. Otherwise, if he need make no outlay, tax write-offs, whatever the size of the deduction allowed, mean nothing to his plans.

The function of such tax incentive programs, therefore, is to serve as an expensive sweetener. They serve a political performance far more than an economic one and deprive the government of more revenue than they confer in benefits upon the renewing environment. It must be simply recognized that they are to induce the controllers of capital to accept more easily the expenditures which the legal mechanisms are compelling them to make.

In the absence of the decision to protect the environment despite the cost, tax incentive programs operate at best as pieties and at worst confer advantages upon those doing precious little for the environment. Rather than hoping the controllers of capital can be brought to act through tax incentives or even through outright grants, the marginal character of these programs ought to be plainly perceived. The basic choice is whether or not the environment is to be protected. After that, the decision should be made as to what are the best mechanisms for carrying through the decision to protect the environment from the consequences of human demand.

Instead of trying to innovate tax incentive programs, public energy would be better spent in setting the requirements that need to be accomplished. Having done this much, the next effort would be working with the market in such a way as to show how environmental protection can be productive economically. Once the larger scope of environmental protection had been spelled out, environmental action would become not solely a matter of cost: it would be revealed as a source of benefit to mankind as well as to the environment.

The financial workings of government, usually summed up by the use of the old Roman term of the "fisc," have a marginal influence in protecting the environment. The margin can be a useful one. But the peripheral effect of tax incentive and similar programs must be recognized in the mind of the political decision-maker in order to understand how government can act most effectively in environmental matters.[26]

The traditional role of the legal system has been to act administratively or through the judicial process whenever some crisis has threatened social peace. In acting even this minimally, government has conferred value upon the property interests which it has protected and it has held value from those property interests to whom it has denied aid. But the legal system today cannot act in so minimal a fashion. Because of this compulsion to act in high growth situations, the action of government has wide spillover effects in setting the rules for property values under conditions of urban-industrial growth.

Although tax incentive or subsidy programs are marginal, the totality of governmental actions is not marginal for the environment. The constraints set upon the activity of enterprise form the limits within which property value is ultimately decided and determine what course production and consumption shall take. However property should be held in any legal system within a high growth culture, the value of what is the subject-matter of property will be substantially governed by public action through changing the rules of property and the limitations of bureaucracy.

Important as the market or technological innovation or individual initiative are, the role of the legal system in high growth situations looms as large, or larger, in the determination of the value to be assigned units of property. It may be a fact which many regret. However, they will ignore this importance of the whole legal system to the value of property only at great peril to the preservation of the property values whose social benefit they have asserted.

Calculating Social Costs Relative to the Environment

Under the present system of production and consumption there is no comprehensive social cost accounting for turning the environment into natural resources. The result is that none can determine all of the components which ought to enter into sale prices of commodities. Many social costs are deliberately excluded from the calculation of price; or else they are so deeply buried in what is charged off to the renewing environment that such costs are not calculable. Even if environmental costs should be undermining the present economies of high growth cultures, there is in consequence no way to either confirm or deny it.

Everyone admits now that there have been costs in the mining, extraction, production and manufacturing processes of urban-industrial society which have not been included in the sales prices of the units offered for consumption. Indeed, there are costs of maintenance and social costs following on the use of products sold which few have considered in relation to the product's price. Only a small number of persons have been willing to even try calculating how these costs, that have been unabsorbed in the sales prices, have affected the need for increasing public expenditure in order to make some provision for the burdens imposed.

High growth culture has been only too anxious to accept the allegation of the total price as equivalent to real cost and to ignore the more expansive method of calculation that would include social cost. The geologist, John P. Patton, has expressed in one way the troublesome character of this gap. He has used as his example the price metals can command in relation to any "real" worth that is independent of contemporary market sales tags.

The blunt fact is that metals sell for much less than they are worth. So long as copper, with its requirements of heavy capital investment and skilled technical personnel for exploration and extracton, and the rigors of the mining and the smelting life, sells for less than [half of the price of] a pound of coffee...,society is destined to pay the difference in real value in other ways than as quoted market price.[27]

There is no way to constitute a single expression of a natural resource's "real" worth. Market value is probably not even an approximation of it since the price there is not necessarily representative of the total cost imposed by what has been processed out of the environment and funneled into the market. It is the absence of any system for determining in a single expression the full costs of production, of maintenance, and of use that lends credence to all fears.

The market value is a spurious single expression. Whatever allegations may be made on its behalf, price is quite a partial calculation. Indeed, because price is fixed in terms of returning an individuated yield in some form to a producer or distributor, price is deliberately partial. The market forces have no reason of their own volition to be impartial or inclusive of costs; and, for reasons of immediate apparent self-interest, they have every reason to seek to exclude costs and to be highly partial.

Only forces external to the market have reasons to seek price impartiality and an inclusion in the price and demand structure of the general social costs being imposed by the individuated units of production and consumption. Politically, the reasons must marshal enough importance for the legal system to be imposed as constraints upon the market. Without such actions stemming from the basic social decisions to maintain an on-going, long-term relationship between human demand and environmental systems, there would be no "practical" reasons inherent in every day life for external constraints upon production and consumption to become in any way operative.

When no external constraints are imposed upon individuated demands, the renewing environment can only suffer and retreat to positions that take on an irreducible character. Nature's recourse is not to assert her power but rather to retreat before the onslaught of man's demands. As just one illustration of how this takes place, Jacques Piccard, the oceanographer, has claimed that every year over ten million tons of petroleum products come into the sea in one way or another. Edible fish in the Baltic, as the result of industrial pollution from the rivers draining into that basin, have become nearly extinct.[28] The situations pointed out by him are becoming more frequent; and the refusal to impose international constraints on the exploitation of the ocean resources can only make nature's further retreat more profound.

The social costs to the environment are always present. They are inherent to the employment by man of what in nature his demands define as natural resources. What will not be current on any balance sheet will be the expression of these costs. Only the creation of constraints external to any individuated unit of exploitation will cause the larger costs to be considered.

Too often, all that the public hears are the cries of pain from those who have had the social costs for environmental protection made evident to them by the imposition of such external constraints. From the complaints, one would conclude that it is the surfacing of the costs in the price structure which is the problem, rather than the existence of the costs themselves. A paper manufacturer, faced with absorbing some of these costs, can only denounce environmental "extremism" and what he regards as the wildly swinging moods of public opinion, jumping from a past indifference to how he had run his enterprise to what he thinks is now an intrusive interest. Environmentally, all he could see before him was,

...that the battle we now face is against the wildfire of emotionalism, fanned by mis-statements, ignorance, half-truths, and sometimes no truths at all.[29]

The compulsion to spend money on "non-productive" pollution control measures, and the costly changes they allegedly would make in the operations of the enterprise, are what is uppermost in this cry. Those who have the greatest access to the various public audiences in high growth culture are normally those having the greatest economic growth interest, especially if that growth be of the open-ended, undifferentiated kind. Environmental crises have a periodic success at counter-effect, because the consequence of such growth recurringly produces crises that must be addressed by the legal system. For this reason, despite the hostility to environmental protection by advocates of undifferentiated growth, the strength of environmental interests has never receded to positions of influence as low as they had before the rise of each succeeding crises. Instead the law memorializes these successes within the bureaucracy and the rules of property as the base line for the next environmental crises.

But those who acclaim growth and decry any environmental restrictions upon it have the most persistent access to a generous public hearing. It is their insistence that all concern with environmental cost is to impose upon the valuable productive forces within the economy "non-productive" burdens which only harm the overall system. One would never know from their repeated arguments that environmental protection has ever had a value to the operations of high growth culture, independently of its worth to the renewing environment.

Partly this is a deliberate obtuseness. But partly it may be due to the repeated failure to try to define what might be either economic or environmental "well-being." In the absence of such definitions, the task of seeking objectively to determine if they are each compatible with the other through a calculation of social costs remains well-nigh impossible.

Facing the Costs of Environmental Protection

There has been considerable agitation over the issue of how costly in financial terms the protection of the environment may be under the demands for high, open-ended growth. If the energy crisis of the mid-1970's made anything at all clear, it was the intimate relationship subsisting between natural resources, technology, and the institutional processes of the market, the rules of property and the bureaucracy. It is these institutional processes that establish the public aspects of the interactions between what man demands and the sources within the environment from which he seeks to satisfy his demands.

The proponents of undifferentiated, open-ended growth purport to see only disvalue in limiting growth in order to seek a balance with environmental response. Somehow or other improvements in technology are expected to correct any crisis which might occur. But technology alone is not sufficient. The problems are too immediate, too large, too complex.

Perhaps by the third or fourth decade of the 21st century, technology will solve at least the energy supply and accommodation problems; but in the meantime, technology cannot do even this much for itself. And what is true for technology's relationship with energy, important as the supplying of energy demand has to be, must prove even more true of technology's relationship with the larger environmental problems. So far as the costs of environmental protection are concerned, it will not be improvements in technology that will alone resolve the problems.

This is reflected in the common belief that there is no compatibility between economic and environmental well-being. As a result, people claim that if individuals are to be affluent, nature must suffer, while if the environment is healthy, people must be poor. The Board of Directors of the Tennessee Valley Authority asserted in 1969,

National progress has been slowed by an inability to view economic growth and quality living as compatible partners...[T]he two are not only compatible, but vital, interrelated parts of the...Nation's hopes for progress.[30]

Yet the lawyer and economist William Baxter has insisted that compatibility requires first defining the means of measurement for the different kinds of human satisfaction yielded by what he persists in seeing as merely different kinds of goods. The renewing environment is nothing if not a commodity for him. On the one hand are human artifacts, on the other a "good" environment. Resolutely, he establishes their compatibility by casting their importance as being clearly upon the same level – and that level is man.

People enjoy watching penguins. They enjoy relatively clean air and smog-free vistas. Their health is improved by relatively clean water and air. Each of these benefits is a type of good or service. As a society we would be well advised to give up one washing machine if the resources that would have gone into that washing machine can yield greater human satisfaction when diverted into pollution control...up to – and no further than – the point at which we value more highly the next washing machine...that we have to do without than we value the next unit of environmental improvement that the diverted resources would create.[31]

For Mr. Baxter, it is all a matter of balancing different individuated units of human demand. What he sees as nature's units have intrinsic worth only as they are assigned values in the human units of production and consumption. There is at least no hypocrisy here in Professor Baxter.

So much hypocrisy has been rampant for so long about the promises concerning environmental protection that such reductionist views as Baxter's almost seem refreshing. Of course he scamps nature. The only question is whether his views are worse than the old hypocrisy. In country after country, nature might regard herself as well treated by many should she ever get so much concern from urban-industrial society as Mr. Baxter would give her. Grudging as he is in conceding a worth to nature – "up to" – and no further than – "the point at which we value more highly the next washing machine" – it would probably be effectively more than the renewing environment will ever receive from the hypocrites.

Italy is a good, but by no means singular, example of this practice of hypocrisy concerning nature. In November 1966, the Italian government announced it would spend one trillion lire in five years on conservation. In four years, only a small fraction of that amount had been spent. At the present rate the Italian reforestation plan would take two hundred years to complete. Carlo Arnaudi, a minister of science and research, had found little resistance to the harnessing of rivers through the building of dams and reservoirs. This was economic growth in an economy demanding energy. But he found resistance nearly absolute to reforestation and soil conservation, even though their absence increased the danger from dam construction in mountain torrents and greatly reduced the utility of the projects.[32]

This is the kind of traditional attitude in high growth cultures that has produced the general belief that there can be nothing except enmity between environmental and economic well-being. In the United States, the national leadership of both labor unions and businessmen's associations routinely passes resolutions, couched in the most general terms, that call for protection – when they do not piously call for enhancement – of the natural environment. But the local labor leaders and corporate managers in the field scarcely give lip service to the expression of the ideals pronounced by their national elites. More often than otherwise, local labor and business leaders find themselves working in unison against both the environmentalists and such legal mechanisms as the environmentalists have managed to get enacted into law.

One Maine labor leader summed up the common attitude. In urging acceptance of a new oil refinery and port in the midst of the state's picturesque coastal zone, he said,

We can't trade off the welfare of human beings for the sake of scenery.[33]

The environment stands accused by such people as being a ruling class hobby and an antiworker movement.

The environmentalists have sought a rapprochement, at least with labor, by calling for mandatory special aid to be paid by employers and the government to workers who might lose their jobs because of pollution close-down orders. It has not been a particularly successful ploy. Other kinds of trade-offs have seemed more popular to both labor and business leadership, who are both committed to growth. The president of the United Auto Workers suggested a very different *modus vivendi*, not so appealing to the usual Good Government elements who usually back up the environmental movement. What does he want?

...[A] waiver of the anti-trust laws to let manufacturers share their technology related to both pollution and auto safety.[34]

With labor proffers of this sort being waved about, one can see rapprochement between labor and the environmentalists cannot come any more easily than rapprochement between the demands of enterprise and the environmentalists. However high sounding the national resolutions may be of the labor unions and the business associations, there still seems little depth of belief behind such public utterances. Hypocrisy is so much cheaper and easier to command than seeking to know how the needs of the environment impinge upon the chances for full employment or profit maximization.

This is not to deny that the market cannot help in the task of facing up to the costs of environmental protection. Integrating competing views and establishing compatibility are jobs the market can do well. Among the multiple participating elements who come to the market, market forces routinely negotiate arrangements. These produce a compatibility in the making of decisions which otherwise would be lost in conflict.

But one must also realize that similar roles are performed not only by the economic forces in the market but also by the operations of politics and law in what Harold Lasswell calls, respectively, the arena and the forum. If it were not for these accommodations, socio-economic conditions might not have developed much beyond the biophysical core of the human being. But, when the fragmenting processes of high growth make their demands upon the renewing environment as they now are doing, these roles become harder to play for either market, arena, or forum. The collective good tends under these conditions to be subordinated to the individuated benefits and the costs to be transferred to the environment.

Yet the normal negotiating roles of market, arena, and forum cannot be relied on to accommodate the costs of environmental needs. Should external diseconomies rise to serious proportions, these externalities supply such high transaction costs that private-bargaining solutions of any kind become barred or aborted. These are the reasons why the law has been compelled to intervene with more collective mechanisms to deal with environmental costs.

Notes

[1] Robert A. Mundell, *Man and Economics*, New York: McGraw-Hill Book Co., 1968, pp. 171–172, 177–179, 182.

[2] *Ibid.*, p. 183.

[3] *Ibid.*, p. 191.

[4] See *ibid.*, p. 198 and p. 191 and pp. 192–193.

[5] Barry Commoner, "The World Environment: A Zero-Sum Game," *The Washington Post*, June 4, 1972, p. B5.

[6] Harry M. Caudill, "Are Conservation and Capitalism Compatible?" in *Agenda for Survival*, H. W. Helfrich, Jr., ed., New Haven: Yale University Press, 1971, p. 183.

[7] Compare Barry Commoner, *The Closing Circle* (1972), Ch. 12, with Caudill, *op. cit.*, p. 179, though three specific proposals are modest in comparison, pp. 180–181.

[8] Commoner, note 61 *supra*.

[9] Enrico Barone, "Ministro della Produzione nello Stato Collettivista," *Giornale degli Economisti*, series 2, vol. XXXVII (1908), pp. 267–293, 391–414, translated in an Appendix to *Collectivist Economic Planning*, F. A. von Hayek, ed. (1938), at 275.

[10] Barone, *op. cit.*, p. 277, his emphasis.

[11] O. Nuccio, entry on Barone, *Dizionario Biografica degli Italiani* Vol. 6 (1964), pp. 449–451, my translation.

[12] Barone, *op. cit.*, p. 289.

[13] Andrei D. Sakharov, *Progress, Coexistence and Intellectual Freedom*, Intro. by Harrison E. Salisbury, New York: W. W. Norton & Co., 1970, p. 49.

[14] *Ibid.*, pp. 48–49, p. 88.

[15] *Ibid.*, pp. 44–55.

[16] Barone, *op. cit.*, p. 290, his emphasis.

[17] See the afterword by Aurelio Peccei and Alexander King in Mihajlo Mesarovic and Eduard Pestel, *Mankind at the Turning Point*, New York: E. F. Dutton, 1974. See also, Lincoln Gordon, "Limits to the Growth Debate," *RFF Resources*, No. 52, Summer 1976, pp. 1–7.

[18] Jan Pen, *Modern Economics*, Tr., Trevor Preston, Baltimore: Penguin, 1965 (first Dutch edition, 1958), p. 191, note and pp. 192–195.

[19] *Ibid.*, p. 235.

[20] Dr. William Bryan, Franklin University, Columbus *Citizen Journal*, March 13, 1975.

[21] *Ibid.*

[22] S. Rep. No. 552, 91st Cong., 1st Sess. (1969) at A-405, quoted in a student paper, February 29, 1972, by Walker B. Lowman, Ohio State University College of Law. I am indebted to Mr. Lowman for his references concerning tax incentives. Mr. Lowman is now a member of the Ohio Bar.

[23] K. R. Reed, "Economic Incentives for Pollution Abatement," 12 *Ariz. L. Rev.* 511 (1970).

[24] This is Mr. Walker Lowman's own description.

[25] Henry Aaron, "Inventory of Existing Tax Incentives-Federal," in *Tax Incentives*, Symposium of the Tax Institute of America, November 20–21, 1969 [Lexington: D. C. Heath & Co., 1971], p. 39, pp. 42–44.

[26] Arnold and Glenn Reitze, "Tax Incentives Don't Stop Pollution," 57 *ABA J.* (1971) 127.

[27]   John P. Patton, "To Open Under New Management," *Indiana Alumni Magazine*, November 1970, p. 8, at p. 9.

[28]   Ray Vicker, "Uniform Rules Urged," *Wall St. Journal*, November 29, 1971.

[29]   Ron Wagers, *Arkansas Gazette*, Little Rock, December 3, 1971, quoting Jack E. Meadows, vice-president and general manager, Crosset Division, Georgia-Pacific Co.

[30]   *36th Annual Report*, TVA Board of Directors (1969), quoted in *Clean Air and Water News*, Vol. 2, No. 2, p. 1 (January 7, 1970).

[31]   William F. Baxter, *People not Penguins*, New York: Columbia Univ. Press, 1973, p. 12.

[32]   Columbus *Dispatch*, October 21, 1970, p. 34B. In 1970 the sum of one trillion lire was worth $1.6 billion.

[33]   Byron E. Calami, "Are Ecologists Antiworker?", *Wall St. Journal*, November 19, 1971.

[34]   *Ibid.*

Environmental Regulation and the Rules of Property

Alternative Regulatory Mechanisms for Environmental Protection

It is seemingly more direct to command a change of conduct in order to protect the environment than, for example, to change the way in which price is calculated or the way title is defined. However, even if this always were true (which it is not) bureaucratic commands may still be less effective protectors of the renewing environment than such modes of regulation as these. Commands of bureaucrats, though, remain the most common approach. Other approaches remain too much in the realm of academic discussion. But other approaches ought to be more often applied in the legal system than has been the case until now.

The financial aspects of government, summarized by the term "fisc" borrowed from the Roman law, contain a number of these approaches. Some have been unused, some misused, some insufficiently used. But taxes, rebates, subsidies, exemptions, deductions, and civil penalties are all ways of using the fisc. Seldom have any of them been much employed in order to protect the environment. But they could be; and there should be greater exploration of how this could be done.

The same lack of application of approaches other than the bureaucratic command holds true for manipulation of the rules of property. The determination of what can constitute property is not a closed subject. Relationships and objects in nature continue to pass in and out of the definition of what constitutes property. Similarly the questions of who holds how much title in whatever is redefined as property, and what the titleholder may do in relation to that property, remain open for expansion and redirection.

The rules of property are most commonly thought of as a means of allocating benefits. The legal system through entitlements legitimates certain

234

possessions and stigmatizes others. Certain interests are created while others are prohibited. Most assuredly this is an important function of the rules of property in assisting the general legal system to provide social peace. These rules thereby constitute an orderly way of defining, transferring, and ensuring both economic and social interests.

What is equally true, however, about the rules of property is their function in allocating costs and legitimating cost imposition. This is of less concern to many observers than the allocation of benefits. But cost allocation is at least as important socially as allocation of benefits.

Of course, those holding privatized benefits have a strong incentive to pass off costs upon the social fabric or upon the renewing environment. The incentive of society to thrust costs back upon those enjoying the benefits they impose may be not quite so strong. But such relative strength does not change the significance of the rules of property as means of allocating both costs and benefits.

Too often, many view as "non-productive" costs incurred on behalf of investments for economic infrastructure. Because of this attitude, such investment is often resisted even when social values are the admitted outcome of such infrastructure. The resistance is intensified, of course, when the concept of "no-growth" is introduced into the argument.

There are many who believe in the social value of growth and who consequently decry no-growth. They are unenthusiastic about what they regard as non-productive infrastructure and/or social investments, whether these have been expended on behalf of the renewing environment or not. As a result, they can only regard as disastrous any suggestions that would increase infrastructure investment on behalf of protecting the renewing environment or that would limit urban-industrial demand as it environmentally impacts. And – God forbid!! – those that would simultaneously do both are anathema to them.

If environmental protection required that urban-industrial demand be drastically reduced or even if no-growth meant absolute stasis, such critics might well be justified in their condition of alarm. But few are calling for either sort of change. What *is* being widely suggested is that urban-industrial demand and the renewability of the environment be maintained in balance.

This will mean growth from the viewpoint of the gross national product. Such balance cannot be instaurated, much less maintained, without infrastructure investment. There would also have to be continued investment in changed industrial processes, waste treatment, and materials management. If urban-industrial society is to keep what it has attained and if it is to get more from the renewing environment, then such investments will have to be made. There can be no escaping this kind of growth, short of the extinction of urban-industrial demand altogether or the destruction of the environment's capacity for renewability.

Bringing about such a balance will also require direct commands from bureaucratic structures. Yet, though bureaucracy cannot be avoided, it need not be the sole reliance for those protecting the environment. Perhaps it need not be the primary reliance. An aggressive employment of the fisc and the manipulation of the rules of property may offer alternatives that are cheaper and more efficacious in protecting environmental renewability. Certainly no one will really know if bureaucracy is automatically turned to as the regulatory resolution of every environmental crisis.

What is needed are mechanisms for internalizing into the benefit-producing processes at least some of the costs those benefits impose. Probably all of those costs cannot be internalized. But all the costs can be identified and many can be internalized.

Those costs which cannot be so absorbed can then be paid for in other ways than by simply assigning them to the so-called "free" zones in nature. And those costs which can be internalized will be taken up more quickly into the production-processes through the employment of the fisc and of rules of property than by the issuance of bureaucratic commands.

There may prove to be the possibility of many ways to regulate urban-industrial demand upon the environment and the renewing environment's responses to that demand. Or only a few regulatory mechanisms may turn out to be really efficacious in assuring the existence of a balance between this demand and the responses to it. But unless there is greater boldness in conceiving and in acting upon different conceptions of regulatory management, the drift of apathy and tradition will foreclose all possible options. And the final foreclosure will assuredly include the options which could help the renewing environment tolerate the coming increases in urban-industrial demand.

Resource Exhaustion, Environmental Protection, and the Role of Law

The cost of internalization, and the ease with which the cost can be sloughed off, compel the legal system to intervene. Without that public action, common resources would be destroyed by human demands productive of depletion or congestion. What man calls natural resources possess exhaustibility, whether one is speaking of depleting a species of marine life or of congesting the radio broadcasting frequency spectrum. It is especially evident in dealing with replenishable resources such as plants and animals. Alan Friedman, who has been interested in the maintenance of common pools under conditions of high demand upon them, has said,

Any economic determination of the optimal yield from such a biologic stock over time must consider the relationship between recruiting costs, recruiting effort, population size, and reproduction rate.[1]

Ignoring any of these, as urban-industrial demand so often does, is to risk rapid destruction of whatever is within the common pool. Because those with the greatest accessibility to the common pool will engross to themselves the greatest individuated benefit, the numbers capable of benefiting will always be smaller than would have been the case if external constraints had controlled both what could be demanded from the common pool as well as how benefits could be spaced out on terms other than accessibility. It is not enough to rely upon the effectiveness of the limits that proximity – or lack of it – might impose.

The market system alone is not able to retard the rapid depletion or congestion of exhaustible natural resources. This is due to the fact that there are compulsions to short-term action that act in favor of resource exhaustion. Participants, particularly rivals, are forced in their exploitation of these resources to overlook the inadequacy of any replacement function in a renewable resource. Sometimes this is due to ignorance. Man is often unaware of the effect that the consequences of his actions have upon the interdependencies in nature. But whether it is ignorance or the force of competition, what are to man mere economic externalities become to environmental systems a terminal force.

The impact of competition upon resource exhaustibility is particularly strong in high growth situations where profits are individuated, costs are shunted off, and total cost accounting is not possible. Society would generally, where the demand growth is high, risk the exhaustion of natural resources instead of going to any alternative course of action. After all, when the ultimate risk to a resource is its exhaustibility, despite its potential of renewability, why *not* refuse to allow renewal to that which *can* be renewed? It always seems so much simpler in lieu of cutting production, reorganizing property relationships, eliminating a consumer surplus, raising prices, lowering employment, shifting the tax burdens, or doing any of the troublesome actions capable of retarding the exhaustion of natural resources.

Because the market system will either delay or seek total avoidance of coming to grips with resource exhaustion, the rules of property and the bureaucratic mechanisms have important functions. They provide the procedures of bringing the market and sociocultural attitudes round to helping control the treatment of exhaustible natural resources. Most of the time, of course, the proposal has been simply that they be used incrementally. Usually, no basic change has been permitted in the way growth demands fragment and process the environment into units of production and consumption that deny their ultimate reliance upon environmental renewability.

Law and politics, like the market, have their place in determining the values humanity assigns what eventually are called natural resources. Neither the market, the law, nor politics operate outside the culture within which they function; and merely calling for the forces of law and politics to be added to the forces of the market will not be enough. Far more important and radically searching actions than rhetoric will be necessary. Social costs must be accreted to individuated benefits in order to obtain a comprehensive kind of social accounting. Until this is done, every ameliorative action will be insufficiently fundamental to stop the drifting course of renewing environmental systems toward collapse under the demands of fragmented, undifferentiated growth.

The rules of property must be redefined in the future in order to set the limits for the individual uses permitted relative to the subject-matter of property. Individuals have dramatically different private definitions of property. They insist vigorously on what cannot be allowed in relation to what they call property rights; and they buttress these claims with assertions that any different behavior would destroy the economy, corrupt morals, injure the social structure, or tear up the environment.

The rules of property in high growth culture have been continuously put at issue. Given the fragmenting way in which that culture has operated, there has been a need continuously to redefine the rules of property and the means of legitimacy that justify particular entitlements to property. The rules of property, like the administrative mechanisms, have become the area of interface where these redefinitions reflect their acute significance. Consequently in an urban-industrial society, law has been the tool whereby the public could participate in what would otherwise be individuated reformulations of the traditional rules of property. The same has been the reason for bureaucratic interventions in the definition of what are assumptions of intrinsic worth in nature and in how the basic social decisions for change can be aggregated. Law has sought to attain a generally accepted vocabulary relating to property; and this process must continue to assign common meanings to concepts over which differences rage.

There has always been in human culture the most intimate relationship between the economic bases of the social structure and the legal terms used to give them expression. The law is an adaptive mechanism; and social decisions will determine the course of its adaption. Because of its adaptive origins, law must alter in order to accord with the shifts, progressions, and collapses occurring within the social, economic, political, or natural milieus. The law under the pressure of events seeks to change the way the subject-matter of property is held, is used, is put under entitlements, and is reformed by the determination of a different set of superiorities as to the limits under which property is held.

With technology being standardized, legal transactions have had to be rationalized, so that the use of standard forms has replaced the old rites of individual bargaining. The way has been cleared for faster, more numerous, and larger economic actions. Mass production and consumption have come along simultaneously with the invention of interchangeable legal forms designed to expedite such mass actions. It has only been later that the forces of law and government have begun to be used for slowing down the rapidity of such action.

Because slowing down the spread of growth is a late arrival, such actions through changed property rules and bureaucratic mechanisms have caused an outcry from those previously enjoying the individuated benefits from production and consumption. There is, however, an intimate relationship between resource exhaustibility, environmental protection, and the rule of law. Any action which so much as merely slows down demand's environmental impacts – much less shows signs representing a social decision for altering how benefits and costs should be calculated – will be denounced as an imposer of unbearable costs.

It has been a common complaint in the United States since the late 1960's that any forced revision of the way enterprise is conducted might benefit the environment but that it would impose costs too enormous to be borne. Somehow the costs have been seen as too onerous for anyone to contemplate who is not an ascetic, prepared to sacrifice everything of a nakedly productive and fiscally profitable character on the altar of environmental purity. But events have not shown the political system prepared to assert such a reorganization in the relations human demand have with nature.

Perhaps so rigorous a change may ultimately be necessary. If so, the American social system is a long way from making it. Yet the evidence is strong that much has been and can be done for the environment through the constraints of law. Risking the destruction of high growth culture through the enforcement of cost internalization has not appeared a high probability compared to the need to protect the environment from exhaustion of its renewable powers.

Urban-Industrial Society and the Costs of Environmental Protection

Much thought has gone into the conclusion that "...the national economy will not be severely impacted by the imposition of pollution abatement standards."[2] This statement was made in a study prepared for the federal United States environmental agencies in March, 1972. Eleven industries were examined in twelve thousand plants in 1971. In the normal course of business in the years from 1972 to 1976, about 800 of these plants would have been expected to have closed for reasons unrelated to the environment. Perhaps this figure could have been increased by environmental controls by as much as 300 additional plant closings. Even this increase, however, would have affected plants so vulnerable on other grounds that the environmental burden would only have accelerated an otherwise inevitable event.[3] In any case, nothing like this occurred.

Yet one cannot deny the pain involved in the process of environmental protection. It is, after all, another cost-push item in inflation. As is the way with all such cost-push items, there is a limit as to how much can be transferred to consumers before the buyers interpose their resistance to rising prices.

If all prices connected directly with environmental exploitation were price-flexible, then there would be no limit as to how much in the way of cost internalization each enterprise could pass on to the consumer. But prices connected with environmental exploitation and protection have no such immunity to buyer resistance. All environmental protection costs cannot be worked comfortably into the sales price. Foreign competitors may offer lower prices; customers may switch to a companion product costing less; or the public may decide to do with less, or with none, of the more expensive product.

When consumers offer this resistance, it often means that they have suffered a loss in real income as a result of the cost-push price rise. To counteract this, the managers of the enterprise may choose to absorb some of the costs within their former profit margins. But if they are compelled to absorb so much as to wipe out these margins, production would either have to be curtailed or the plants would have to be closed.

In 1972 it was predicted that during the years 1972 through 1976, this kind of effect from environmental protection would be felt not alone by management but also by reductions in the work force. Industries, it was thought, would have to lay off up to four per cent of their total 1971 employment. This would have meant about 150,000 job losses or about 0.05 percent of the 1970 national work force. These projected reductions in profits and employment, and these increases in prices, would have translated into a lowering of the standard of living in exchange for an increase in environmental quality.[4] If anything approximating this occurred, it was lost to sight in the general inflation and recession of the mid-1970's.

One could well ask if increasing inflationary pressure is worth the relatively slight impact of pollution control measures that has been experienced and is now projected in the United States. The expenditures for environmental protection are themselves stimulators of economic growth through the investment in pollution control facilities. While this should more than offset any losses in the economy caused by environmental protection, some cost-push inflation will likely occur. More massive efforts than those projected might cause a slowdown in "real" product growth and an elevation of the price of domestically produced goods which could make them uncompetitive in the world market. Should that ever happen then fiscal interventions, however inflationary, would be employed – or environmental protection would be scrapped. But, though environmental protection costs may sometimes affect the economy adversely as to,

...the efficiency of capital, in the aggregate production function...,[in the increase in the] prices of consumer and capital goods...[and an increase in] the cost of capital per unit output...,

the results of those costs also

...generate new output and employment in industries producing abatement facilities...[becoming] a factor boosting aggregate demand in the economy...to augment the productive or capacity-augmenting capital stock of the nation.[5]

However, up to this point in the 1970's the costs of environmental protection in the United States have not been major factors for good or ill. Indeed environmental control costs have been statistically insignificant to the economy. Large though absolute figures may seem, their relative strength, compared to the cost factors unrelated to environmental protection, has been slight.[6]

During the recession of the mid-1970's in the United States, charges were brandished about that environmental control had contributed to cost-push inflation, to a decline in economic growth, to rising unemployment, and to a decline in investment. If these charges had been true, in even small part, the environmental protection program in the United States would have had a more vigorous history than it otherwise had after 1968.

The charges were not true. Furthermore, projections indicate that through 1983 environmental protection in the United States will continue to have very small impact upon inflation, growth, employment, or investment. Insofar as the costs of environmental protection will have any influence, they will be in the direction of an increase in the constant dollar gross national product because of the expenditures needed for pollution control facilities.[7]

It should not be surprising that many bureaucrats in the environmental protection programs should heave their greatest sigh of relief at the news that what they are doing is really good for the constant dollar gross national product. For them as for advocates of growth, the only positive effect they find in pollution control is the cost of the facilities. Enlarging the waste treatment industry tends to become for too many the only perceived good of environmental protection. Surely, there ought to be some questioning of the adequacy of this view.

Too little regard seems to be given natural systems already strained by the accelerating demands for high growth. In the midst of the sigh of relief that environmental control costs are not upsetting established patterns of profit, investment, employment, and growth in the gross national product, there almost seems to be an implicit promise that they never could. But it would not be an act of wisdom to make any such commitment, because changing those established patterns is needed even though the costs may be high.

Certainly this is no time to reduce the commitment to assisting the ability of renewing environmental systems to respond to the human demands being made upon them. Neither public nor private expenditures for protection of the environment should be reduced. Whatever popular opinion may have been conditioned to believe, environmental expenditures in the United States have not been too high. They have been far too low relative to the environment's needs.

In terms of hard cash spent, the acceleration in investment in environmental protection has not been as sharp as popularly believed. More significantly, the acceleration did not occur precisely when the size of budget items for environmental protection might indicate. Consequently, one might well question how substantial the investment increase in environmental protection has really been in the United States. When Pennsylvania, often depicted as one of the most vigorous states favoring environmental protection, assigned only 1.5 percent of its 1973–1974 budget to the expanded mandates of its clean air, clean water, and strip-mine reclamation laws, just how important had the environmental investment become?[8]

An even clearer indication of how relatively little has been done for the environment, despite the rhetoric, is a 1973 study done by the United States Bureau of the Census. Because it uses both current and constant dollars, with the base for the constant dollars being 1957–1959, this study reveals some very different vistas from those so commonly accepted. No grounds for self-congratulation are revealed by it.

Looking at current dollars, it appears that the great leap forward in waste water collection and treatment investments by state and local governments began in 1969. Current dollars would indicate also that per capita calculations began going up in 1967 in decided fashion. The view is not the same, however, when constant dollars are used.

In terms of constant dollars, the steepest advance in both these ways of figuring investment was 1961–1962. From 1964 to 1972 there was a plateau, if constant rather than current dollars should be used. In fact, between 1967 and 1969, when current dollars show the great take-off occurring, the use of constant dollars indicate an actual sag, while in the mid-1970's there was a decrease in real investment in pollution abatement by industries.[9] With inflation and the impoundments of appropriations for these purposes during the Nixon administration, there are no bases for believing the mid-1970's can show any improvement in what these figures reveal.

There is no equivalent study for expenditures in the private sector in the United States. However, a 1973 survey by McGraw-Hill showed a very slight upward incline from 1967 through 1973 of a total industrial plant and equipment investment. Starting in 1967, the rise shows a sharp acceleration in total pollution control investment by private industry.[10] Given the impact of inflation, particularly in the construction industry between 1969–1974, however, one could well doubt how "real" these accelerated expenditures are, particularly on an incline tending to flatten out.

When the figures from the public and private sectors in the United States are put together, the investment for plant and equipment in 1973 meant for pollution control had been only about a twentieth of the whole. When constant dollars reduction is applied to the figures, the result in terms of the environment becomes even more modest. The constant dollar comparison would look better for the private sector as to any recent advances simply because the private sector had held back longer in making such investments. There was even a decided dip in private pollution control expenditures in terms of current dollars in 1968 and for certain industries again in 1973 and 1974.[11]

Without belittling what has been spent in current dollars by both the public and private sectors in the United States since 1967 for environmental protection, the environment knows nothing of human inflation or competition for capital. As a result, nature might be excused if her systems fail to notice as yet any very great relief from man's demands. The expenditures for environmental protection have been relatively modest to the point where one need not be surprised that they have not shocked the urban-industrial economy. The continuing condition of the shock to nature remains, however.

Evaluating Criticisms of the Costs of Environmental Protection

Insofar as there is any "momentum" in environmental protection in the United States, as alleged by Russell Train,[12] it is a fiscally sluggish "momentum" at best. In addition, much of that expenditure has gone into a bureaucratic overhead that has itself put a burden upon the renewing environment. "Momentum" there may have been – in public relations, legal draftsmanship, and bureaucratic expansion. If absolute outlays in the mid-1970's are compared with those in the 1950's, there appears to have been great progress. But if all the current dollars, not to speak of all the political rhetoric and the lamentation by enterprise, were to be passed through a constant dollar converter, too little work has been done on behalf of the renewing environment. Certainly before any kind of cut-back is launched on environmental expenditures, it ought to be realized that there is no "momentum" to cut back.

It is sad to see how much enterprise wants such cut-backs. The managers of enterprise seem able only to lament the growing share of expenditure for new waste-treatment facilities going into non-productive, "in purely economic terms" allegedly, anti-pollution equipment, As one official of a business association put it,

Those expenditures don't improve the quality of the product, the plant's productivity, or a manufacturer's capacity...[T]he point is that those dollars are environmental investments, they're not dollars going to expand and modernize productive capacity.

The consequence of such an outlook could only be for him one of depression and fear.

It makes for a scary situation. You've got [foreign] competitors putting in new stuff [for production] while we're sitting here...[W]e don't feel the need to expand.... Our plants are getting older, meanwhile, and we're coming to the point where the quality of stuff coming off their lines is now better than ours.[13]

All environmental expenditures are seen in this view as pure cost, adding nothing to productivity and causing only the likely loss in growth, profit, and business itself to foreign competition that will forever be free of environmental concern. Absent is any sense of the interrelatedness between human demand and environmental systems. For these people, the compulsion to internalize the costs of environmental protection becomes just a dead weight without any countervailing compensations.

What is especially galling to one who is environmentally concerned is the implication in such a view that it is environmental expenditures which will be to blame for any failure American enterprise may suffer in the future in comparison with its competitors in the world market. As those see it who carp at the costs of environmental protection, the United States will lose its competitive edge because its enterprise will have to spend money for the "nonproductive" purposes of pollution control. The United States will become a nation with an obsolete industry because so much is being demanded for environmental protection. United States' industry will have to locate overseas because only there will it be free of such exorbitant demands upon its capital on behalf of the "unproductive" environment.

Somehow in this screed of discontent, there is very little reflection of other needs and pressures. Industries are located overseas because of cheap labor, nearness to resources, proximity to markets, and for other reasons in no way related to either environmental expenditure or the need to make none of them. If American industry is obsolete compared to industry in Germany and Japan, it is highly doubtful if environmental expenditures required by American law have had anything to do with the matter of comparative American industrial obsolescence. Somehow, putting the blame on the requirements of nature for protection from the impact of the demands of urban-industrial society seems a perversity.

Far from the problem arising out of expenditures to protect the environment, many of the lamented problems of high growth in the late 20th century arise from the demands made upon the environment in the past. Population growth in the world at large and the advent of zero population in the advanced industrial nations, urban sprawl, congestion, and all the negative accompaniments of urban-industrial society are more likely causes. As Joseph Spengler has observed, they have far more accentuated

...the tendency to inflation and financial instability in an economy whose population is concentrated in space and disposed to spend an increasing fraction of its national income upon services....[14]

The cost-push in inflation owes its greatest debt, not to environmental protection, but to the increase in the demand for certain services. These are the services which have become necessary to act as countervaillants to the effects of congestion and other burdens upon natural systems. As a consequence, it is predicted that the future will see production increases as only a "sporadic" occurrence, so that persons in urban-industrial society will

...tend to experience increases in remuneration greatly in excess of increases in their productivity.[15]

As a prediction, this seems far more ominous than complaints about how tough it is to run an enterprise when a waste treatment plant has to be attached.

Seen from an attitude such as Spengler's, the need for service expenditures becomes the product of congestion and pollution that simultaneously compels both a holding pattern on production growth and an expansion of services. Environmental protection would be only one of several such services needed under high growth conditions.

What would have to be spent on environmental protection, therefore, would not be an item stolen from a capital investment foregone in growing production. It would represent, instead, an expenditure compelled by factors related to congestion and pollution that would already have challenged the undifferentiated growth in production and consumption. In fact, the transfer of investment into such services would be induced in the long run for reasons not directly related at all to any desire to protect the environment. The demand-structure of high growth would itself have created the requirements for such a shift.

From such a viewpoint, the ultimate strength of the environmental movement would not stem from altruism or some independently motivated discovery of the worth of nature. Rather, the strength of those concerned in protecting the environment will derive in the future from social and economic forces that will be indifferent or even hostile to the traditional positions taken by those who have wanted to conserve the resources of nature. It should then be the holders of the entitlements to the subject matter of property, previously the enemies of those favoring environmental protection, who would be compelled to act.

Their action under the grim circumstances of rising costs and sluggish productivity would be to protect their property interests and the viability of the system supporting those interests. Yet though they would not be concerned primarily with the natural systems, the effect of their actions would have an environmentally protective consequence. Far from being the imposed, "non-productive" burden upon production that has been claimed, environmental expenditures will become essential. The burdens of congestion and of the pollution caused by undifferentiated, open-ended growth in production and consumption will bring about themselves the need to alter the patterns of capital investment. From causes such as these the environmental expenditures of the future will be compelled.

This is not to say that environmental costs in the long run will be small, however modest they have been up to this point and have been projected to be to the mid-1980's. But one can say that they will become measurable and they will be made capable of absorption within the cost price mechanism. Such absorption will be in a manner similar to such social charges as the minimum wage, workmen's compensation, pensions, and all those other costs which sincere Victorian capitalists thought it quite impossible for the market mechanism to assume. Although such social costs have not been assumed entirely in the price structure and though they have been both costly and inflationary, urban-industrial society has adopted them out of its desire for survival. Environmentally protective costs will likely prove to be accommodated in a similar fashion.

As has been true also of these social improvement costs, many of the environmental expenditures can be expected to stimulate technological improvements capable of reducing the demands made upon environmental systems. Society in its economic decision to turn away from labor-intensive products, once labor could command a larger share of income, set an example. The consumer can elect the product with lower pollution abatement costs, as reflected in the price, over those that have the higher levels of demand upon the environment. Once the constraints have been imposed that would set the terms of such a market decision, the public can exercise its rational options for lower polluting products over those with a high environmental cost.

It might seem, if constraints should be imposed for aiding market function in reaching environmentally protective decisions, that the price of pollution abatement devices would go up far faster than would other prices associated with pollution-producing process. It may be a reasonable expectation, but it is not a likely one.

...[S]ince the macroeconomic analysis employs the conventional national income accounts framework, it overstates the net costs (or understates the net benefits) to society because such accounting fails to include the benefits of a cleaner environment.[16]

It could be this inability or refusal, if the attitude persists, that will be the problem for the future, as it has been for the past and as it is for the present in a high growth production and consumption situation. There is an unwillingness to see the income producing potential in environmental protection, just as the Victorian capitalists could see little benefit to the economy from increasing the incomes of the mass of the population. In both instances, there is too much of the outlook of the moralist: do it because it is right, even though it hurts.

To forever see an activity as a cost, as an imposed burden, as an externally encroaching consumption of everything the urban-industrial process has been organized to accomplish, means there cannot be an acceptance of it, even should such activity be legally required. Only the grudging performance of laws whose value is seen to be exclusively moral will be done. To laws so viewed, every resistance will seem justified, from removing the emission controls on autos to avoiding a burdensome waste treatment system on a beneficent factory. There has to be a change in how environmental protection is perceived.

Maybe the radical critics are right when their criticism would decry this as too small a change. They charge,

[T]he ecologists have taken up the old liberal shuck...[but] profit-seekers and growth-mongers can't co-exist with Mother Nature and her fragile children without doing them irreparable harm...[Ecology] should point the finger not simply at profit-making polluters or greedy consumers, but at the great garbage-creation system itself – the corporate-capitalist economy.[17]

In their view of environmental costs, enterprise must absorb all such costs, either from current profits or out of past capital accumulations. In no event should the managers of production be allowed to pass on the costs to their workers or to consumers. For them, it is the concept of profit that is the menace to the environment because of the unlimited growth in production and consumption which this allegedly requires.

The very productivity of which enterprise is so boastful is seen by these critics as the proof for radical change. The costs to renewing environment are too huge for the system to sustain and still survive in its present form. For them,

A society whose principal ends and incentives are monetary and expansionist inevitably produces material and cultural impoverishment – in part because of the abundance of profitable goods.[18]

Unfortunately, the character of the present means for producing that "abundance of profitable goods" makes it impossible to absorb environmental costs in anything called "profit." Current production is not for capital formation, much less capital accumulation. It is the means, instead, of creating goods to be used up in an instant and flung into the environment. Production is for providing goods that are destined promptly to become waste; and the consumer is the conduit to the waste sink which nature has become. A revision of conduct assuredly is needed. Perhaps it will be more fundamental than socialization seems to a private capitalist. The needs of the environment must force

...a whole view of our natural and social environment – from oxygen cycles, from the jeopardized natural environment to the powerful institutional environment which creates that jeopardy....[19]

Integrally a part of any such revision will be the casting of the social accounts. The costs to nature of the demands made upon her systems by man's demands must be calculated. Common terms for cost accounting need to be at least approximated and the non-quantifiable needs to be determined. This represents the preliminary action.

For that matter, even benefits, whether alleged or actual, produced by urban-industrial society need to be defined, identified, and brought into comparable terms of measurement. Though external benefits are often thought to be rare, they may not prove so, particularly when full consideration would be given to the provision of facilities by public sector investment for the support of urban-industrial society. But rare or not in relation to external costs, what is needed is a social cost accounting system capable of giving at least rough notions of comparability to those needing to take an overview of what human demand in high energy culture means to the renewing environment.

There will be resistance to even this first, important step toward a comprehensive and integrated handling of man's relations with nature. Too many enjoy individual benefits from a fragmented, open-ended, undifferentiated demand structure: Too many believe there really are "free" goods in nature. Too many always prefer drift and inertia. And all these compose an alliance that will be critical of the cost of environmental protection.

But the response of the environment to the demands imposed upon its renewability are offering countervailing pressures that must be of the greatest significance for those imposing the demands. It is a response that the demands for high growth cannot afford to ignore. The result is that nature herself is productive of the force that will require social cost accounting and the assumption by urban-industrial society of the full range of costs for environmental protection. The pressure is coming from nature; and that is the most important fact of all.

The Importance of Present Action for Environmental Protection

The Council on Environmental Quality projected the cost to the United States of a cleaner environment for the decade 1974–1984 at about $274 billion, if only the legislation current in 1973 for clean air, clean water, and the disposal of solid waste should be enforced. Since then, some of the requirements have been increased; but there remains for this decade a schedule with differing emphases at different periods. The major hope for improvement has been concentrated on the years 1975 through 1983.[20]

Whether this projection turns out to be prophetic of what actually transpires is less important than the need to take prompt action. Fundamental revisions of the way urban-industrial demands are imposed upon renewing systems must be taken within the next decade. What is not done within this handful of years will delay greatly the necessary actions that will have to be carried on into the 21st century. One hopes that any delay in these years would not produce an irreversible and fatal damage to the planet's life-support ability, though there should be no sanguine belief such fatal interruption could not happen. What is important, worth keeping uppermost in the mind, is that the present is crucial. Decisions made within the next few years may well decide if high energy culture has a future.

Of course, every age might well argue that the decisions made during its ascendency made the future possible. But the impact of current urban-industrial demands upon the environment is causing such signs of strain in nature that it is not hubris for this age to think its actions more important than much of what has happened in history. Certainly what is not needed is any turning away from the problem. Such a denial means an intensification of the very forces that are productive of the present strains in the environment's capacity for self-renewal.

During the energy crisis of the mid-1970's, strong pressures built up to favor the burning of high-sulphur oil and coal. Some local communities which had adopted higher standards on fuel as to sulphur content were induced to lower those standards, either by special exemptions or by an across-the-board reduction. Many enterprises were pushing for the burning of fuel regardless of its high sulphur content or of the absence of adequate pollution-control devices able to control sulphur-oxide wastes in air emissions. Whatever costs might be present in emitting sulphur-oxide wastes into the atmosphere, there were many willing to impose those costs in order to maintain the energy cascades at relatively low price and relatively high abundance.

The National Institute of Environmental Health Sciences found the proposals for allowing an increase in sulphur-oxide emissions scientifically interesting. They planned research that would not miss the opportunities offered by the occasion:

...advantage should be taken of this situation by initiating a prospective study designed to document...the consequences on the health of the exposed populations of these unplanned experiments.[21]

The Institute, appraised of the likely results by studies already conducted by the Lung Association and others, suspected what would be documented. The remaining uncertainty lay only in the degree of severity. When the amount of sulphur oxides rise, just how bad is the consequence to human beings, animals, plants and the living environment? There will be no conferral of a good to any living tissue; and the bad can be of some severity. As the trade-off for relatively cheap, abundant energy, one can well ask if there is anything present for nature except further disequilibrium.

Furthermore, the point should not be overlooked that the aggregate effect of the dangers of air pollution is far more regressive than the expenditures to control them. It is the poor who will absorb the bulk of those costs, just as it would be the lower-income groups who would have to absorb most of the costs of pollution control if the market mechanisms should alone be employed to accomplish that end.

Government financing of pollution abatement is more progressive than either letting the pollution rise or structuring the market alone to reduce it. Taxes tend to be paid in greater proportion by higher than by lower income groups. Of course the whole burden should not be put upon the fisc. Progressive financing does not relate to either the effectiveness of programs or the efficiency with which goals are reached. The market, too, must be employed. But what must be kept in mind is that the refusal to do anything at all about pollution, or the insistence to rely exclusively upon market absorption of environmental protection costs, will not mean that such costs do not exist or that they are not being regressively imposed.

To do nothing about pollution and leave the matter to Heaven overlooks the generative effect of transaction costs on the economy. Transaction costs are "the costs or research, development, planning, monitoring, and enforcement needed to achieve environmental goals and standards."[22] These costs generate great economic advantages that by themselves become productive in terms of both the economy and the environment. John Elliott has expressed it very well when he claims environmental programs

...hold considerable economic and environmental hope [in] discovering urban environmental issues,...[in] develop[ing] a comprehensive energy policy,...coal liquefaction and gasification programs,...[and in determining how to] act decisively to preserve physical and human resources.[23]

It is just another indication that the costs of protecting the environment from the consequences of human demand are not mere negative burdens to be undertaken in the grudging spirit of the sacrificial offering. They are opportunities allowing urban-industrial society to come to unified terms with the renewing environment.

The advantage in the long run will decidedly lie on the side of mankind if unity with natural systems is the approach rather than processing their fragments into individuated units of production and consumption under high growth conditions. Where there is no perception of the interrelatedness within natural systems, nature can only be processed for prompt discard. Where complete dependence is put upon open-ended, undifferentiated growth, everything in nature becomes an actual or potential conduit from demand to discard.

Environmental Perils of a Common Pool

It has not been the needs of the environment that have produced an increase in the operation of the legal and administrative mechanisms of government. The pace of that increase has been long established. Its acceleration preceded any pressing concern over the environment's ability to sustain the demands being put upon her systems. The reason for the steady, and still rising, demand for changes in the rules of property or additional bureaucratic mechanisms has been the growth of "must" obligations which are absolutely essential to the smooth working of urban-industrial society. The law and bureaucracy still find it hard to be other than a mirror image of the forces for disequilibrium in urban-industrial society. The dominant thrust of that society remains the processing of the renewing environment in order to serve the demand for growth. This has produced an homogenization that has not led to stability. Instead, it has been an homogenization that sought a common fungibility for everything in nature.

In essence, urban-industrial demand has tried to turn everything into an unspecified resource of the common pool. Everything is to be of comparable worth to everything – or everybody – else. In that way, trade-offs would become very simple.

If all is fungible, why not trade off for the cheaper energy obtained by high sulphur-oxide emissions with the higher incidence of disease and death these emissions will cause? If human beings are to be socially valued only for their roles as producer, consumer, or taxpayer in high growth situations, then they too have significance only if each one, in individuated terms, responds to the pressure to generate demand, to produce, and to consume the product of what demand commanded. For human beings so defined, why not trade off their individual lives and health for cheaper, more abundant energy? Why should they not be as discardable as anything they produce or as they perceive everything in nature to be? If they are all in a common pool, they have become natural resources that a fragmented demand structure has more reasons to exploit than to conserve.

Homogenization in this situation has not acted to induce unity between human demand and the renewing environment. Rather, it has served to process the environment's fragments into an ever-expanding consumption. Nothing has been allowed not to serve growth. That which could not be fitted into the demand structure often found itself abolished – and abolition can be very hard on such living organisms. The treatment has been scarcely less dramatic for such cultural artifacts as the rules of property or the structure of the bureaucracy as these relate to the environment. Under the harsh conditions of perpetual flux, when all things become interchangeable, compatibility is acquired like a mix in a blender.

Unfortunately, such a view does not adequately represent to man the importance of nature. The environment, which supports life on this planet, has a worth for that function which puts it beyond simple definitions of compatibility and trade-offs. Man ought to make a place in his definitions of value for the worth inherent in the processes of living, of cell replacement, of viral and bacterial confrontations, and of the ecumene within which the life forces interrelate. Life and living have a worth that ought not to make them fungible as trade offs for urban sprawl, air pollution, or undifferentiated growth in high energy culture.

As urban-industrial demand has moved into accelerating growth curves, there has been a tendency to express all environmentally assigned values in cash terms. Land has had value because its production could be sold. Soil has had value because its regenerative quality could command a price in the market. Water has had value because it could be costed out for industrial or irrigation purposes. The whole of the renewing environment, at first gradually and then with rapid acceleration, has been identified with the cash it can command in terms of humanly assigned values.

What has had a more disturbing effect has been merging these cash expressions with the items in the chain of living, even where humanly assigned value is external to any worth these items have within the natural linkages. Ultimately, the merger becomes so complete in the human mind that any inherent worth in any item in nature is forgotten or denied. Persons exist, thinking of themselves as rational, who can find no value in nature not expressible in cash.

Because of the insistence that nature's worth is expressible in cash and that nature's value is a human creation, distortions occur. Arguments on behalf of environmental protection, as a result, are often carried on like the propaganda of the 19th century public health reformers. They too sought to build public support for their cause by arguing human life should be saved not because life had any worth in itself. On a cash balance, only the wages lost, the money spent for treatment and burial, and the taxes not paid made the death of a working man at thirty an economic loss. One wonders, if the balance had shown an economic gain, what would have been the result of the logic.

What is so often overlooked is that forces for environmental renewability have a worth internal to them. It is not a value that is derived from the operations of the human economy. Man forgets this independent worth in nature at his peril. Whether he is medieval man, piling people into unsanitary ghettoes, or modern man, lavishing his lethal doses of biocides without regard for the organisms killed, the consequences of ignoring this inherent worth can be perilous. When natural forces are distorted enough by human activity, they have a pattern of responding most destructively to the human actions which have distorted them. Everything cannot safely be liquefied into a common pool.

The Value to the Environment of Changed Rules of Property

The way that resources have been extracted, processed, transported, fabricated, consumed, and disposed of has been creating problems since the inception of high levels of growth in production and consumption. But however long the problem has been evolving, only recently has the matter come near the crisis stage – or at least near a crisis stage that does not seem to be offering any safe way out of the crisis for a culture persistent in demanding open-ended growth.

The situation has not been eased by the all too common insistence that all environmental protection costs are purely non-productive. Such critics frequently contend the continuance of the present fragmenting, segregating, unintegrated offer no long run threat to viability of urban-industrial activity. They claim the threat, instead, would come from proposed pollution control costs. Accumulating evidence indicates these critics are wrong. Only when the account books are slammed shut on individuated units in a way that mutilates the whole purpose of comprehensive accounting can even the appearance of a general profit be alleged. And the opportunities are diminishing to be convincing with such biased special pleading.

There needs to be a change in behavior. The rules of property in a system that recognizes the worth of environmental protection must reflect the worth inherent in natural systems rather than expecting nature to take her value from an assignment out of a rule of property. How property is held and used must recognize the existence in the renewing environment of the interrelatedness that exists within environmental systems. Whether the title to the subject-matter of property is held privately or in socialist or communal form is of far less importance than the recognition and reflection of what has independent worth in nature.

The role that rules of property can play may be a modest one compared to the bureaucratic function. The rearrangement of methods for holding entitlements to particular superiorities in the subject-matter of property may not be a sufficient change. Such a change, by itself, could happen without the environment feeling enough of an alteration in how demand affected inter-relating systems. There need not be any change in the level of urban-industrial demand just because there has been a shift in the social location of the title to property. But shifts in the rules of property can produce greater protection than the renewing environment has yet enjoyed.

Law derives its values from outside the legal system and law's rules of property are instruments for carrying through at a public level the intentions of those values. Law, like engineering, is technological and comprises one of the tools of mankind. Like any others of his tools, man cannot turn to law for his salvation; nor can he expect just one of his tools, such as the rules of property, to be the sole means of solving complexly formed problems. The rules of property are simply a single means among many which the demands for unlimited growth have til now employed in order to create the benefits and the costs present in urban-industrial society. When the social decision is made to accommodate to the capacity of nature's response, the rules of property will remain one tool among many for carrying through that purpose as they have been for serving the purpose of unlimited growth.

The concept of property is an important one at every point where man and nature make demands and respond each to the other. To this extent rules of property cannot be ignored in any of the steps taken to establish relationships between the human demand structure and the natural systems upon which the demands are levied. They will require change in order to assist in determining that specificity of nature's use which has been so often missing in a fragmented demand structure. Such change will help in clarifying to what extent nothing in nature can be a "free" good once it is drawn into that human demand structure. And the rules of property can be modified to further any decisions made in favor of an integrated rather than a segregated demand structure. Any tool which can assist in each of these endeavors – and which can yet accomplish still others – is an essential one not to be discarded.

Property law is a means for reaching socially determined ends whose purposes have been decided upon within the larger area of social decision. Just as the rules of property did not create feudalism but gave it one kind of formal, public expression, so do the rules of property today not make the decision as to the socialization of the means of production. Rather they have served as one procedure for carrying out the decision. The rules of property are in every sense instrumental; and while the tools shape the product, they remain only tools.

As tools, the rules of property will carry out new purposes. If no new purposes should be assigned, they will continue to carry out purposes previously assigned them, however worn out those purposes may have become. But they will not independently make new social decisions, even if new decisions should be desperately needed to save what is renewable in the environment.

For that reason, no one concerned with how nature is to sustain the demands of mankind can be indifferent to the rules of property and the role of the bureaucracy. They may be merely instrumental, but the allegorical instrument for law is the sharp sword. As a symbol it wisely summarizes the force of sanction capable of both protection and punishment. It is not the sort of instrument either man or nature can ignore. And there is immediate need for the prompt use of law to achieve a viable accommodation between urban-industrial demand and the ability to respond to that demand by the renewing environment.

Notes

[1]   Alan E. Friedman, "The Economics of the Common Pool," 18 *UCLA Law Review* (1971) 855, at p. 856, note.
[2]   "Economic Impact of Pollution Control: A Summary of Recent Studies," prepared for the Council on Environmental Quality, the U.S. Dept. of Commerce and USEPA (March 1972), p. 11.
[3]   *Ibid.*, p. 10.
[4]   *Ibid.*, p. 11. Passing on costs can also be long delayed, *ibid.*, p. 26.
[5]   *Ibid.*, pp. 19–20. The findings of this study are reiterated in the 6th annual report, USCEQ, (1976), p. 533 *et seq.*
[6]   "The Macroeconomic Impacts of Federal Pollution Control Programs" prepared by Chase Econometric Associates Inc. for U.S. Council on Environmental Quality and USEPA, January, 1975.
[7]   USEPA press release on report 1/24/75.
[8]   John M. Elliott, "Ecology and Environment," *Pennsylvania Bar Assoc. Q.* (1973), 655, at 662.
[9]   Environmental Quality, *4th Annual Report*, United States Council on Environmental Quality (September 1973), Figures 3 and 4, pp. 87–88 and *6th Annual Report* USCEQ (December 1975), p. 521 and summary p. XVIII. Nevertheless, note the cheery optimism in the *7th Annual Report* USCEQ (September 1976).
[10]   *4th Annual Report*, USCEQ p. 88 and Figure 8, p. 92, taken from the 1973 *Annual McGraw-Hill Survey of Pollution Control Expenditures* and see the same McGraw-Hill Survey for 1968–1975 in *6th Annual Report*, pp. 522–523.
[11]   *4th Annual Report*, USCEQ (1973), pp. 88 and 92 and *6th Annual Report*, USCEQ (1976), 522 for petroleum chemicals, and "other" nondurables.
[12]   Columbus *Citizen Journal*, November 7, 1973, p. 15 quoting Russell Train's statement of November 6, 1973.
[13]   *Wall St. Journal*, December 28, 1971, p. 19, quoting Mr. E. F. Andrews, Chairman, Business Security Committee, National Association of Purchasing Management.
[14]   Joseph J. Spengler, "Economic Growth in a Stationary Population," *Ekistics*, Whole No. 200, July 1972, p. 17, pp. 18–19.
[15]   *Ibid.*
[16]   "The Economic Impact of Pollution Control: A Summary of Recent Studies," prepared for the Council on Environmental Quality, the U.S. Department of Commerce and the USEPA (March 1972), p. 5.
[17]   Katharine Barkley and Steve Weissman, "The Eco-Establishment," in *The Devil's Party*, Tim Drescher and Glenn Miller, eds., Waltham, Mass.: Xerox College Publishing, 1971, pp. 88–89.
[18]   Martin Gellen, "The Making of a Pollution-Industrial Complex," in *ibid.*, pp. 77–78.
[19]   Barkley and Weissman, *op. cit.*, p. 88.
[20]   *4th Annual Report*, USCEQ (1973), p. 116 stresses the years 1975 to 1981. The *6th Annual Report*, USCEQ (1976), p. 532, extends the time until 1983 for concentrated activity.
[21]   Dr. David P. Rall, director, National Institute of Environmental Health Sciences, in a report prepared by the United States Department of Health, Education and Welfare for

the Office of Management and Budget, quoted by Stan Benjamin, "Panel Warns," *The Tennessean* (Nashville), October 18, 1973.

[22]   *4th Annual Report*, USCEQ (1973), p. 83.
[23]   Elliott, *op. cit.*, p. 662.

The Future of Environmental Regulation

Why There is Pressure for More Environmental Regulation

People in urban-industrial societies have built up a hope that stability between human demand and the renewing environment can be created through the manipulation of bureaucratic regulation, tax policy, and alteration of the rules by which property can be held. Perhaps they are right, but in the meantime the pressures toward instability among relationships in urban-industrial social structures have severely strained the existing basic regulatory mechanisms. The failure to develop adequate regulatory systems relative to the pressures pushing toward disequilibrium threatens the present growth-demandant situation with entropy.[1]

Among the current regulatory mechanisms, the most popular – even if at the same time the most criticized – has been bureaucratic regulation, with its anticipated powers of mediating conflict or of settling conflict by the issuance of orders. One ought not to be surprised by this. At a time when all technology is required to deal with continuous change, when financial institutions are pressured to produce a maximum return on minimum investment, and when the biophysical environment gives signs of irreversible stress, one could expect there to be a turning to the bureaucracy. Thereafter, it provides all the certainty, predictability and ultimate security that elsewhere is so singularly lacking.[2]

The historian of western culture, William McNeill, insists that the masses in urban-industrial society will always look for a "stalwart immobility" from the bureaucratic structure. Out of bureaucratic action, they would like to extract the chance to define their daily lives in terms other than responding to the demands of constant change.[3] If so, then there is a deep cultural justification for the approach now standard in matters of environmental protection of reliance upon direct controls. What has been called a regime of legal orders, in which each polluter is told precisely what must be done subject to a defined penalty if the order is disobeyed, is certainly the common preference.[4] Whether or not it is as efficacious as other approaches is now very much at issue.

Of course, if what the "masses" are pining for in urban-industrial society is not environmental protection but a cessation in changes being imposed upon the environment, they are not likely to achieve such a cessation merely by turning more matters over to a bureaucracy. It is true that there is some degree of immobility in any bureaucratic operation. But bureaucracies have been described as "output" institutions, compelled to produce decisions at however slow or cumbersome a rate. Imperfect as they may be in responding to the values and demands being fed into them, these governmental operations ultimately do move.[5]

There is far greater pressure today for increased governmental activity, even if this is simultaneously accompanied with a decline in confidence in governmental integrity, than was true prior to 1960. And governmental activity still emphasizes the processing of the environment and the serving of the growth demands of urban-industrial society far more than it does environmental protection. As the French publicist Teissier du Cros informs us,

The State intervenes without cessation as the principal motor of economic and social innovation. It determines the great objectives. It shall be the guardian of a veritable national vocation.... It imposes social justice. It guarantees the security and the elementary dignity of the citizen.[6]

What the state bureaucracy does *not* produce, myths to the contrary notwithstanding, is stasis and immobility.

Nor should this be surprising. The laws and institutions of urban-industrial society have a strong pro-development bias in all their actions. So far from being primarily an intended means to protect the renewing environment, these laws and institutions often imposed their own additional burden upon the environment. For decades, bureaucracies and the legal system generally have been used to pursue a policy of unlimited and undifferentiated growth, with little regard for the biophysical environment. It has been sufficient to have merely invoked such terms as security and affluence in order to justify such actions.[7]

A task force of the Rockefeller Brothers Fund has described such conduct:

...historically, public opinion has favored development almost irrespective of the cost to the environment. Our laws and institutions...reflect a pro-development bias.... Processes that allow for sensitive accommodations and balances...are not yet in effect in most areas.[8]

Despite a good many dire warnings that have earned the ones making them the epithet of "doomsayer," bureaucracy and the law have contributed more to the processing, fragmenting, and eventually the destabilizing of natural systems than they have to their protection. About the best a group of "reasonable growth" advocates could say in this regard in 1975 was,

The control of inflation and the promotion of economic growth, taking into careful consideration the effects of such growth on resource exhaustion and environmental pollution,...must have top priority on the agenda....[9]

Only in this manner, they insisted, could "socioeconomic equity" be achieved.

One perhaps should be pleased that resource exhaustion and environmental pollution were to receive "careful consideration" in accomplishing the top priority of economic growth. In the past, this has not been the case on many occasions. That bitter critic of capitalist growth, Friedrich Engels, focused particularly on that aspect of the exploitation of nature done in order to meet urban-industrial demand. It seemed to him that those who were willing to concentrate on an individuated profit were concerned only with short-term results that excluded later events. Had they taken these later effects into account, he asserted they would often have been compelled to recognize that actions remote from the initial activity had actually eliminated the profit. As he said,

In relation to nature,...the present mode of production is concerned only about the first, tangible success; and then surprise is expressed that the more remote effects of actions directed to this end turn out to be quite an opposite character, that the harmony of demand and supply becomes transformed into their polar opposites....[10]

Maybe this has now changed, though one is justified in doubting that the change is very extensive so far as results in the renewing environment are concerned. The short-range view, the individuated profit, the transferred or postponed cost retain a very strong attraction, as environmentalists know. The manager with the "bottom-line" view is interested in today's profits and losses, as they appear upon his enterprises's balance sheets, and not in the long-run that introduces the possibility of a comprehensive social accounting detrimental to his allegations of sound operations.[11] Even socialist production managers, professing to follow Engels' precepts as to the best use of state property, have not been anxious to cast their accounts in any broader terms.[12]

The demand structure of urban-industrial society has introduced a force for greater disequilibrium into nature; and the response of the interdependent systems in the renewing environment now threatens to counterpose a reciprocal disequilibrium into the demand structure that has imposed these demands. There are still those not troubled by this as a prospect because they see this disequilibrium as adjustable. Indeed they see it as scarcely more than a minor externality if only two or three per cent of gross national product of just the richer countries could be diverted to protect the environment.[13]

Hermann Kahn is one who for many years now has confidently seen the future in such terms of easy adjustment. He is not troubled by the current urban concentration of population, by the demands of energy-requiring life-styles, by the types of both public and private investment being made relative to the environment, or by similar problems that he regards in the process of being resolved. To be sure, even Herman Kahn has occasional tremors about the chance of world famine, the pollution and hence potential shortage of both air and water, and the possible destruction of the biological equilibrium on the planet. But, then, in the Kahn lexicon, technological innovations will treat the polluted air and water, desalinate the ocean, provide chemical agriculture, and make a stable equilibrium between urban-industrial demand and the renewing environment. He – and many others – simply do not believe that the presently "unresolved" problems concerning the environment could prove resistant to the solution of simply increasing the applications of new technology.[14]

The problem with such optimism – or, for that matter, with irredeemable pessimism about the future – is that it is dependent upon extrapolations projected forward from today's accumulated statistics. No matter how such predictions are qualified the commonest fate they are likely to share is being wrong. To take only one example, is there any reason to be worried over a "fixed pie" of either nonrenewable or renewable resources? The optimist Herman Kahn says yes – for nonrenewable resources. But otherwise he foresees present technology able to support a world population of 30 billion at income levels equivalent to $30,000 (in 1974 dollars) per capita per annum.[15] At the same time another critic to the "limits of growth" sees the future in almost reverse terms. Lincoln Gordon at Resources for the Future has said,

In fact, contrary to the popular position..., I am more concerned about shortages of some renewable materials.... The adverse environmental effects of deforestation in many countries, especially through soil erosion and river siltation, make one wish that "depletable"...materials were being used in place of the theoretically replaceable....[16]

Even optimists about the future of the environment can disagree on the basis of present evidence as to exactly how the resource "pie" may be "fixed."

Nor will the further introduction of technology, however successful it should prove for its intended applications, remove the basis for this dispute. From the time of Machiavelli in the 16th century, commentators have delighted in pointing out the unintended and often unrecognized consequences of changed courses of action. Some of the most important results have been the ones never conceived as being a possible outcome of the action initiated. Indeed, they often eventually accumulate to the point of overwhelming the originally intended purpose. The sociologist Robert Merton has summarized this process by observing,

Total commitments to values of every kind – whether these be the value set on rapid economic expansion ("growth"), rapid technologic advance, or rule-free communities or the value set on that full expression of self in which anything goes... – have cumulative consequences which, if not counteracted, in due course undercut the originating values themselves.[17]

Technological innovation is as likely to magnify the problems of the environment's future as it is to shrink them or to produce unforeseen problems to replace any that technology resolves. Technical innovation, on the basis of past experience, is far more likely to further upset any existing equilibrium in the systems of the renewing environment than it is to assist in their stabilizing. The fact that the burdens upon nature have rarely been foreseen does not lighten them. The automobile was planned to provide what it has provided in abundance: speed, door-to-door service, and convenient private transport. And the unintended consequences, which the automobile has also supplied in abundance? These have been air pollution, injuries and death, noise, the dependency of the economy, and the destruction of cities so that cars could be moved and parked. Is there any reason to believe that technological innovation in the future will come without its own similar accompaniment of unforeseen and unwanted costs as well as its fanfare of planned benefits?[18]

It is, therefore, because people both hope and fear for what technology, economic growth, and the other forces of urban-industrial society can do to the renewing environment in the future that they turn to the law. Whether one is talking of the capacities of bureaucratic regulation, the use of the fisc for controlling action, or changes in the rules by which property is held and employed, the law will assist in both furthering environmental exploitation and in protecting the renewing environment. It has been this way in the past and it will be this way in the future.

At no time, even in periods of emphasis upon intense exploitation of nature, has the law been silent as to environmental protection. Someone interested in finding such legal purposes can find them at any age if he searches deeply enough. It may be in manorial custom, municipal ordinances, state statutes, or court decisions concerning nuisance; but the concern of the legal system for the environment, as formally expressed, has always existed. The extent to which the expression has been more than formal, however, has been slight until recent times.[19]

Substantial as the increase has been in legal concern for the environment, it remains less than is needed in order to reverse the trend toward disequilibrium in the natural systems as they are impacted by urban-industrial demand. It is one thing to claim that the salvaging of air and water quality and the careful direction of land use are "problems...manageable within readily affordable costs."[20] It is quite another to get society to meet those costs, however manageable they make the problems. After all, it is very tempting for the law to permit a "policy [wherein] pollution is a necessary evil to be endured whenever it is the by-product of some beneficial activity – a notion still current among many citizens and policy-makers."[21] And those who hold this "notion" have every personally advantageous incentive to seek a continuous re-examination of any commitments the legal system has made toward environmental protection.

The relationships between law, the environment, and the production mechanisms of urban-industrial society are intimate. When pollution regulations on sulphur were adopted, they "were a bonanza for low-sulphur coal suppliers from the Western states versus higher polluting Eastern coal." As a result, the Western coal producers had a highly profitable incentive to favor the strictest pollution control against sulphur and government-enforced conversion of utilities from oil or gas to coal.[22] Nothing exists in isolation that is a product of the effort to protect any part of the environment. Rules harming one producer may help another.

Public action relative to the renewing environment will be not less. It will be more – and it will be regulatory of the demand which urban-industrial society puts upon the environment. The regulations may take the form of bureaucratic regulations, fiscal measures, or altered rules of property. But increased regulations there will be, both because of the likely increase in demand and the difficulty the environment will have in responding to that demand. Ultimately, the only valid question will be to what extent any particular regulatory mechanism mutes the demand or aids the responseability of the environment.

Choices in Environmental Regulation

Regulation always means constraints for some and opportunities for others. At the same time, when regulation affects the production and consumption of goods and services – and how much regulation does not? – costs are imposed.

These costs most often are taken up into the price, although they may also be absorbed through the reduction of profits, the lowering of wages, or changing the quality of the thing being regulated. In the past, costs could also be passed onto the environment on the basis that nature was a "free good" beneficently provided to save cash costs. And at all times there have been – and, doubtless, always will be – proposals that costs be transferred to the burden of the general taxpayer in a final "free-load." What remains constant through all of this allocation of costs, however, is that no regulation can be resorted to that is costless.

It is for this reason that many commentators are now using the language of market relationships to describe the operation of regulation, whether or not the regulations are environmental in character. People, who in the past would have used political terms to describe conditions, say that there now exists a market for regulatory legislation. In this "market" some industries gain more than others from the opportunities that regulation offers. These industries usually have a better ability to mobilize political forces on their behalf in order to obtain the regulations which will maximally benefit them; and, if the benefits to be obtained are high while the costs the regulation imposes are low, the regulations can be expected to play a strong role in constraining behavior, affecting prices, determining costs, and allocating profits.[23]

In democracies the assumption has been made that, in order for them to work over the long run, there must operate within them what have been called "partisan adjustment systems." They are cultural constructs that work well or ill according to the culture framing them. But they are now being analogized to the operation of the market in which economic differences are negotiated in countless bargains.[24] Some have gone so far as to say that the purpose of democracy itself is to act like a market rather than like the sort of command structure in which directives issue from government or from political party instrumentalities.[25] So pervasive is the market metaphor, particularly within the United States, that its use seems a kind of universal intellectual currency to exchange ideas for environmental protection into implemented programs.

As a metaphor, it has a certain usefulness if not pushed too far. However, it must be remembered that the purpose of adopting regulations is often to put a stop to the market negotiation process and to establish a higher minimum for conduct. It is not the function of regulators to continuously engage in a re-determination of the substance of their regulations with those who are to be regulated. When regulators engage in this kind of on-going negotiation, they can be accused of undermining their own purpose. Too often, this occurs when they seek the support of those being regulated, and do so for political purposes not directly a part of the regulators' duties.[26]

Of course, regulation is more than the issuing of orders and the pursuance of enforcement of those orders through the courts. There will be a sense of give-and-take in any discussion between the regulator and the regulated since very often there is a mutually educative process going on in the relationship. But the operation of bureaucratic regulation has caused a distrust of this kind of a relationship and increasingly there is sentiment to either eliminate it altogether or else to much limit the opportunity for engaging in what has to emerge as administrative discretion tailored to meet a particular situation.

Some would eliminate the discretion of the regulators by removing as much as possible the need for direct commands, trusting to essentially market mechanisms. Others would strengthen to a far greater degree than previously known the integrity of the legal command issued to those being regulated. Given the wide differences between the two perspectives, conflict would not be unexpected. Though both agree on the inadequacies of a delegation of discretion to regulators, their solutions are too radically different for there to be an easy consolidation of views.

For example, in the United States in the mid-1970's the Public Land Law Review Commission took the former view of doing away with the need for regulation. It recommended that the publicly owned grazing lands be sold in order to provide an incentive to make the land fully productive and to move the land into the hands of more efficient operators. This would have eliminated the leasing system under which the federal government sets the terms for the lessees, regulates how the lessees use the leasehold, and employs sanctions against lessees for violation of the regulations. Needless to say, this did not receive general approval.

The Sierra Club, a prominent American conservation organization, was for one not happy. This did not mean the Sierra Club was any happier with the existing leasing system and the manner of the regulations it imposed. In their view it had failed almost totally to protect the public domain from raiding. But bad as the system of legal orders had been, the Sierra Club was convinced that resort to market concepts as a means of protecting the western lands was doomed to fail for any purpose relative to environmental protection. Their attack was a word by word dissection of the Commission's recommendation.

Let us make some definitions here. "Disposal" means selling the public domain in great blocks to those who could afford it at prices they would be willing to pay. "Free enterprise economy" means an economy free of the enterprise of any but the corporate cowboys. "Lands fully productive" means lands grazed with no protective restrictions. "Economic efficiency" means bookkeeping efficiency, an efficiency that does not place a dollar value on environmental degradations. And finally, "more efficient operators" means the large operators, the corporate owners, the operators who hire ranch managers to administer lands the owners quite often have never seen.[27]

Many economists, of course, were far more content with the recommendations of the Public Land Law Review Commission than they were with the sort of attack launched by those sharing the views of the Sierra Club. Indeed, many economists profess to being depressed at being ignored in the type of regulation increasingly being resorted to for environmental protection. As they see it, the reliance is of the sort that relies upon direct controls, upon the sort of legal orders' regime the Sierra Club would like to see operating in the management of grazing licenses upon the public domain.

Under such a direct control system, the one regulated is told precisely what steps to take, what modifications to make in his activities, and what the penalties will be for failure to do so. In the case of polluters, an emissions' quota is established by regulation that permits the quantity of pollutant to be so much and no more. Unfortunately for the strict legal orders' regime, it is assailed by the need in each situation to incorporate exceptions for special circumstances or else to run the risk of finding its orders unenforceable. Those who favor reliance upon direct commands would set the limits for exceptions. Those who think it inefficient, ineffective, and inequitous would not rely upon it at all. For the latter,

...its effectiveness depends on the promptness with which the orders are issued, the severity of their provisions, the strength of the regulator's resistance to demands for modifications, his effectiveness in detecting and documenting violations, his vigor and success in prosecuting them, and the severity of the penalties imposed by the judicial mechanisms....[28]

Contrary to those who believe it possible to make the legal orders' system work in just that way, its critics look at the way in which environmental protection bureaucracies have been operating and say: They haven't and they never will, because they can't work.

The critics insist that there should be less reliance on the direct commands of bureaucrats. They want, instead, greater reliance upon the price mechanisms. This means that they would either alter the rules of property by establishing new property rights in permits to be sold at maximum prices to be extracted from a prospective polluter through a bidding process or by the use of the public fisc that would tax emissions. In short, they want to create constraints and then form loopholes through which the environmentally regulated would be invited to step for a price and for a purpose – namely, the reduction of emissions.[29]

The idea is not a new one – hence, probably, the depression alleged to flourish among so many learned economists as they watch continued and even greater reliance placed upon the direct command structure of a regulatory bureaucracy in order to protect the renewing environment. Consider, as one example, the emission charge upon wastes. It was first applied in 1899 in the Ruhr on industrial waste being emitted into receiving waters and, as the American economist Allen Kneese has persistently pointed out for a generation, it has been a continuing success for keeping those waters clean.[30] Yet, notwithstanding their success, emission charges have been little emulated as a means of protecting the environment even in the country of their origin.

Emission charges, though employing the force of the price mechanism, are themselves a product of bureaucratic constraint. They are administered prices to be paid for the use of public waterways for waste disposal – and, for that reason, have often been attacked by environmentalists as a payment for the right to pollute. Certainly they are analogous to payments for the use of public facilities. But what makes them environmentally protective, insofar as they are to so operate, is the manner in which the schedule of charges is drafted. If the schedule is set too low, then the polluter will pay and make no changes in his polluting practices. If too high, he may simply go out of business, however harmful this might be to the larger economy. But if properly determined, they will encourage the polluter to reduce his payments by altering his activities that are producing pollution.[31]

The use of emission charges would not, therefore, be a resort to anything like a free market. Monitoring and continuous redetermination of charges would be required through the operation of a bureaucratic structure. The pollution control agency, through what would have to be a series of approximations, would act either by setting stream standards or determining emission levels of wastes. Thereafter, they would calculate the charges, adjusting the constraints as well as the charges from time to time because of the growth-demandant character of an urban-industrial society. In addition, certain toxic substances would have to be outlawed altogether at any price, since the damage stemming from them would require more than a monetary charge if the renewability of the environment were to be protected.[32]

The proponents of emission charges, like the proponents of auctioned pollution permits, argue that there will be an automatic aspect to their operation not dissimilar to the character of the competitive market. These schemes would tend to put the optimum economic values on the waste carrying capacity of streams. The firm that could not meet its costs for emission charges or auctioned permits would either have to cut its production to reduce costs, increase its earnings from other sources, or cease business.[33] In any event, the bureaucratic costs of the direct command system would be avoided.

This is very much disputed. Both of these systems, like the present system of bureaucratic regulation of polluters through direct orders, depend upon monitoring and subsequent amendment of the charge or fee schedules. This would make the emission charge or auctioned permit approach effective for protecting the environment. In a dynamic growth society, continuing reassessment would be needed if the charges or fees levied were not to become licenses encouraging pollution.

The same defect could undermine these systems as undermines so much of today's bureaucratic regulation: an insufficient commitment to maintaining monitoring procedures and to altering the constraints as the monitors indicate they should be altered. Emission charges and auctioned permits may be very helpful in protecting the environment. They will not, however, be able to function without a substantial bureaucratic infrastructure supporting them.[34]

The Fisc and Environmental Attitudes

But whatever the shortcomings of the alternatives to bureaucratic command, the legal order cannot ignore the problems they are being proposed to solve. An urban-industrial society, if historical precedents mean anything, will remain one in which demand will increase and both economic and population growth are likely to occur.[35] Under such conditions, external diseconomies will increase and become pervasive. Among the inevitable will be the disposal of residuals from the processes of production and consumption. As problems increase and as the ability of the renewing environment to assimilate them decreases, how society deals with them becomes crucial to both the environment's renewability and society's viability.[36] Any belief that the law can shunt them out of the costs of the social system is doomed to frustration.

Some are hoping that if the rules of property cannot be effectively changed through the use of permit fees commensurate with values received by the permittee, or if direct commands of a bureaucrat will not produce positive results, or if an administered price set by emission charges will not protect the environment, then perhaps the tax laws can be used to accomplish such an end. As the economist Otto Eckstein has said, a tax system as pervasive as the one which exists in the United States – and, for that matter, in most of the private or mixed capital economies of urban-industrial society – cannot be neutral as to any activity which it affects.[37] Those who would use the tax system in order to protect the environment admit this and then say that taxes can be made efficient expediters for the protection of environmental renewability.

The critics of tax incentives argue that they produce economic waste and that, if they are useful, the purposes they accomplish would be better served by a direct expenditure program of governmental funds. They claim that tax incentives are themselves really another form of government expenditure in any event since the government is releasing a claim on a portion of the income which otherwise would be subject to taxation. Already as a result of this kind of criticism, the annual budget as presented to the United States Congress must contain a tax expenditure estimate reflecting the amount of federal revenue foregone as a result of the existence of tax incentive programs.

Those who believe tax incentives to be useful (and direct expenditure programs to be less than a perfect substitute for them) justify the tax incentive approach on the basis that it is cheaper, swifter, and easier to channel as to its effects. These, not unexpectedly, are the same arguments the advocates of direct expenditures make for their recommendation. Aside from the difficulties Congress has in setting up any kind of closely organized distributive effect, whether by way of tax incentives or direct grants for subsidy, it is asserted that additional and more complex bureaucratic structures would be required for direct expenditure programs. Given the bureaucratic evidence of the "War on Poverty" efforts of the late President Lyndon Johnson, there is considerable evidence for this assertion. As one commentator has said on behalf of tax incentives,

The speed alone of receiving the benefit under a tax approach may better motivate a taxpayer to act in a desired manner. Also, a taxpayer may be better motivated by a simple change on his tax return because it involves less intrusion into his private life.[38]

The use of the fisc, therefore, is another option declared to be available on behalf of environmental protection. Some would use tax incentives. Some would use direct subsidies. Some would set a tax high enough to discourage particular conduct harmful to the environment and to encourage behavior that would do less damage.[39] Some believe that the proper employment of the fisc would accomplish what the direct command structure of bureaucratic orders either cannot accomplish or can accomplish only at exorbitant costs.[40]

Those who argue strongly for the use of the fisc, those who urge greater reliance upon a change in the rules of property through auctioned pollution permits, may well be right. Unfortunately, they may also be wrong. Even in

Germany, which has had the greatest and supposedly most successful experience with the tax approach for dealing with pollution, there are those who claim that the laws for taxing waste have been useless for the prevention of water pollution.[41] Furthermore, there are those who would apply taxes not only to the emitter of pollution but also to the receptor of resources drawn from the renewing environment who needs purer air and water for goods' production [42] – and this represents a further use of the power of the fisc than many are prepared to go. In any case, the possibility of a wider and different use of the power of the fisc remains as a potential possibility in the future pursuit of protection for the forces of renewability within the environment.

Yet whatever the choice of regulation resorted to by the legal system, one must bear in mind that nothing less than a reversal of long established attitudes of the law toward nature is what is at issue. The Roman law itself traditionally reinforced the necessity of appropriating personal advantages out of the commonality of the environment and calling those advantages thereafter some form of private property. What Roman law referred to as *res nullus* constituted a negative community awaiting capture and justified private title on the basis of having reduced to personal dominion and control what had hitherto been common in nature.[43] American law, and perhaps the English common law as well, greatly expanded the scope of *res nullius*, of things once held in common which would be capable of later reduction to private property, so that the renewing environment was exposed to even greater reductions than theoretically had been true under Roman law.[44]

The Roman law, at least in its later period, justified its stand jurisprudentially on the *naturalis ratio* of Stoic philosophy, whereby nature's existence secured justification through the utility any part of it had for human purposes.[45] It is this sort of attitude that lay behind such American decisions as *Pennsylvania Coal Co. v. Mahon* that employed the balancing test of weighing individual costs against social benefits [46] and which now underpins much of the reasoning calling for benefit-cost ratio analyses on environmental programs.[47] But the attitude may now be changing dramatically with advent of such cases as *Just v. Marinette County*, a recent American state supreme court decision. This opinion specifically rejected the whole balancing act in favor of absolutely favoring one part of nature – wetlands – over any competing human demand. What makes the decision a radical one in relation to two thousand years of legal tradition is the court's position that the location of any part of "nature, the environment, and natural resources as they were created" does not affect that "to which the people have a present right" in preventing change in the natural character of the location.[48] No longer is an alleged greater economic value for human demand going to be allowed always to prevail in the law over the inherent worth of naturally existing renewing systems within the environment.

In the future each environmentally-oriented regulatory mechanism – bureaucratic command, the use of the fisc, the alteration of the rules of property – will be increasingly judged by how it affects the operations of natural systems. The failure or success of any one approach may not condemn or endorse it; but success and failure will be judged in terms of the condition of the environment following application of such a regulatory technique. Theoretical observations to one side, if they can ever be subjected to pragmatic tests, the future performance of environmental systems will have to be the means of judging the benefits and costs of any particular approach to regulation. What most certainly must be avoided are any more costly government programs that act as *dis*incentives to environmentally protective measures that cost less, perform more quickly, and serve to better environmental deterioration.[49] Anything less will be totally insufficient.

The Costs of Environmental Protection

It is becoming increasingly a commonplace that programs for protecting the environment cost money, that there is "no free lunch," and that these costs could very well pose more of a challenge to the urban-industrial demand structure than that structure can absorb.[50] It has also become evident, since the discussion began in the mid-1960's concerning the potential costs of environmental protection, that "the only indisputable fact about the cost estimates so far is that, over time, they all go up."[51] In addition, at any one point in time, the estimates have differed hugely.

To go no further back than 1970, consider the estimates made for the costs of municipal waste treatment. The Federal Water Quality Administration projected that the national municipal treatment needs would require $10 billion. At the same time, a report prepared by the National League of Cities and the United States Conference of Mayors identified the existing water pollution needs at that time as requiring anywhere from $33 billion to $37 billion in order to be solved.[52] It is true that each projection included different contents – e.g., the inclusion or exclusion of the provision of dual sewer systems for municipalities in the United States – but, even taking these differences into consideration, the gross discrepancies stimulated some observers at that time to wonder if anyone had the least idea of what the cost of reducing water pollution would turn out to be in the United States.

In later years there has been no more agreement than was the case in 1970.

Considering all federal pollution-control legislation on the statute-books in the United States in 1975, the Council on Environmental Quality estimated that capital expenditures of $115 billion would be required by 1983, or about 1.5% of the then projected Gross National Product. A private group, the National Economic Research Associates, estimated the capital expenditures for those purposes would be somewhere between $175 billion and $263 billion so that, again by 1983, anywhere between 3% and 6% of the Gross National Product would be required for pollution control. All of these estimates excluded the costs of compliance with state and local environmental protection legislation as well as most of the potential costs that might have to be imposed through having to deal with the wastes of a much-expanded nuclear powered electric utility industry.[53] Lincoln Gordon, an economist with Resources for the Future, at the same time stated, "...there is strong evidence that reasonable protection against major health hazards and impairment of productivity can be achieved at costs not exceeding 2 or 3 percent of the gross national product of the richer countries, including [the United States]....[54] The agreement among the experts seemed as elusive in the mid-1970's as it had at the beginning of the decade.

For a lawyer, interested in calculating the costs of law enforcement, some of these potential costs could be fairly disturbing. For instance, if environmental protection in the United States by 1983 should require 6% of the Gross National Product, this would translate into 10% of the total gross private domestic investment likely to be made in that year. Considering that in 1974 only about 1% of GNP was invested in *all* law enforcement within the United States, so much larger an allocation for environmental protection would be dramatic indeed.[55] One could well believe such a reallocation would not happen on comparative historical data alone. In fiscal 1974, to cite only one instance from the real and not the anticipated world, only 0.47% of the federal taxes collected in the United States were spent on natural resources and the environment.[56] On that basis, even the smaller projections of the United States Council on Environmental Quality seem generous.

As has been pointed out in the case of Lake Erie, little of the water pollution control problems are likely to be met "on the cheap" and, in all probability, the costs of cleaning up the inland waters of urban-industrial societies will be far more expensive and difficult than many expected them to be who were projecting those costs in the 1960's.[57] In the late 1960's, it was thought that the lake could be cleaned up for a little over $1 billion. By 1975 this amount had been spent on municipal treatment facilities on the American side alone – and most scientists were saying conditions were probably worse. They would have been demonstrably worse except for a high water level, water that was colder than usual, and weather unfavorable to the growth of algae. People in 1976 were saying that the amount of money needed would be $2 billion more from industry, $17 billion more for treatment of municipal waste, and a difficult to measure amount needed to deal with storm-water and agricultural run-off. Even then, if population and industrial growth were to continue in the basin after 1985, conditions over the next fifty years would become as bad as they were in 1975.[58]

These cost figures do not surprise Herman Kahn in his forecasts about the future. He is not in disagreement with the 1977 United Nations Conference on Water on the fixed amount of water available and the acceleration of demand for it that must soon produce a situation more serious than any presently existing. Speaking of the future water usages, Kahn has said,

We think that we can no longer use water as a dump or for cooling, or for such other purposes, and that steps must be taken to use water in the sense...[of] "liquid gold."[59]

If Kahn should be correct, the figures for cleaning up such a water body as Lake Erie become nearly incalculable. Until now these costs have been figured in terms of working on emissions coming into the lake. If the lake cannot be employed as a waste receiving body, then extensive changes in production technology and land use, as well as waste management, will be called for. The benefits and the costs of such changes in conduct in urban-industrial society simply could not be calculated at this time. But one fact is certain: whatever the benefits, the costs would be substantial – and some believe the costs would outrun benefits under even current pollution control procedures at the rate of better than thirty-four to one.[60]

Barry Commoner is convinced that the needs for environmental protection will produce a crisis in capital formation because they will present a demand for capital that cannot be met. That is assuming, of course, that other competing uses for capital, which Commoner incautiously describes as "needs," would not receive lesser priorities. Those who are not alarmed at what he predicts, though they may agree it will be one more problem for the late 20th century say,

Business must compete for scarce resources – this is part of the normal process of the economic system, not a sign of crisis.... [C]hanges in investment and consumption, in prices and supply, are all normal, indeed inevitable, and...are necessary components of an equilibrium of economic forces that allow a market system to function.[61]

Yet, even if environmental protection costs should prove merely another challenge provoking an equilibrating response in the market, one must concede that the challenge in terms of costs will be a massive one. And the costs to be incurred will involve more than investment outlays. They will also include activities foregone or terminated. Certain production operations may find it impossible to meet minimum pollution standards and may have no choice other than to cease altogether. Because of distrust that has built up over the past employment of bureaucratic discretion, legislation has increasingly denied to the regulator the power to exempt from or delay the application of such standards. Increasingly, "the classic battle between a cleaner environment and keeping jobs...is likely to be repeated many times over.'[62]

While a few jobs relative to the total in an urban-industrial society will be so threatened, the political repercussions they likely will generate will far exceed their relative economic importance. As the risks of toxic pollutants become better known and the difficulty of handling them does not lessen, no one involved in production that creates toxic by-products can ever be certain of not having his job terminated as the only way to eliminate the dangerous pollution. It will always be necessary to make certain that environmental protection is not being unfairly blamed for such costs; but it is impossible, unless the effort for protecting the environment is to be insufficient, for there not to be *some* disruption of industrial operations.

Calculating Cost-Benefit for Environmental Regulation

The basic role for anyone asserting expertise in the concern of the legal system with environmental protection is to establish the costs and benefits of alternative institutional arrangements.[63] It is no accident that, as the importance of regulation has increased, the public concern with productivity and efficiency of these regulatory mechanisms has also grown. With the greater competition for capital between the economic forces and those called upon to regulate them, the public has demanded budgeting for productivity as a means of justifying capital expenditures in the public sector.[64] The difficulties of calculating these figures may not be capable of being fully worked out to the satisfaction of the critics of the performance of public bureaucracies. The time, though, has passed when there is indifference to the costs imposed by the creation of a new bureaucracy or the enlargement of an existing one. The assumption that only benefits can flow from bureaucracy is not being lightly made these days.

The reason for this, aside from the increase in absolute sums in the public budget, may lie in the realization that all persons in the community perforce share in the costs imposed by regulation as well as in any benefits that are conferred. James Buchanan has explained this compulsory sharing as an inevitable aspect of any legal rule.

> [W]ith the adoption of a general law or rule...that constrains the behavior of all members of the community..., the existence of and adherence to this law introduces...costs...measured in the losses of utility suffered by each person due to the restrictions imposed on his range of options...Each person is subjected to a...tax... not...valued uniformly by all persons.... It is...some arbitrarily determined tax-sharing scheme...independent of the relative evaluations of individuals...that must remain inviolate.[65]

This term "tax," one must realize, is as much a metaphor as the use of the term "expenditure" when the latter is employed by opponents of tax incentives who denounce them as constituting outlays of government.[66] But it is a useful way to describe the consequences as to costs of legal rules and must influence public attitudes toward adoption or extension of such rules.

It is easy enough for the public to see the costs of legal rules when something is purchased for public title or when a tax is levied or a public grant is made. These are costs that must appear somewhere upon a balance sheet. Of much greater difficulty for perception are the costs resulting from the imposition of mandatory regulations on conduct or the alteration of the rules of property to allow the creation of permits in interests that had previously been either in a commonality or else an appurtenance of a larger property interest. The costs of the latter, though hard to pinpoint, may far exceed the sort of cost that public purchase or subsidy lays down upon the public fisc.

Significantly enough, costs that do not appear as public revenues or outlays on a governmental balance-sheet are costs that can be distributed throughout the economy. Everyone has long been aware that if an individual has a personal advantage in polluting, he will do so. Harm is a by-product of his individuated profit and it is economically rational for him to be indifferent to it. Since this is simultaneously true for all persons similarly situated, all of them will have very good reasons to pass onto nature any such costs that would cut into their showing of profits.

The same holds true in the political arena as in the market. It is plainly to the advantage of the politician if he can divert costs off the public account books and distribute them sufficiently widely over the whole spectrum of the economy so that their size is difficult to determine. Perhaps in an ideal polity there would be an effort made to locate and identify the amount of each such cost. In the less than ideal world of current politics, however, such efforts are more likely to be resisted than pursued. The politician is no more anxious to internalize all costs of regulation within the public budget than the entrepreneur of production and consumption operations wants to internalize all the costs his actions generate.

Presently one cannot know what the full scope of either the benefits or the costs of protecting the renewing environment will turn out to be. Despite all the agitation and activity that has taken place since the mid-1960's, with the "monstrously growing accumulation of environmental readings" which has accompanied it,[67] neither the effect upon either the environment or the economy has been determined. Effort is still at the stage best described as trying to make in explicit fashion uncertain estimates about both the costs and the benefits of intended environmentally protective regulatory behavior.[68] Enough has happened, however, to conclude that costs will be far higher than foreseen by most people in the 1960's quite independently of the consequences of the inflation which has occurred since that time. The calculation of benefits, on the other hand, remains as elusive today as it was then.

Perhaps all that can be agreed upon is the size of the costs and the intangibility of the benefits in the area of environmental protection. Hard as the costs may be to reckon, determining the value in equivalent cash terms of enhancing the capability for renewability in environmental systems is and will remain far more difficult. For this reason, many interested in environmental matters reject the calculus of cost-benefit ratios on the basis that their incompleteness will weight them against the environment more often than for it.[69] However, even should the political process be persuaded of the absolute worth of the benefits anticipated from the environment, regardless of the inability to express them in completely objective terms, neither the political, nor market processes can treat lightly the costs to be incurred. Anyone concerned with the cost and the effectiveness of regulatory mechanisms meant to protect the environment's renewability must concentrate on these costs as a major concern to be minimized as much as possible.

The Environment As Another Public Good

Although expenditures on behalf of the environment have been substantial since the mid-1960's and though the costs of environmental protection will have to rise greatly in the future, these have been only a small part of governmental outlays in urban-industrial society. Indeed, even if the most pessimistic estimates of the proportion of those costs to gross national product were to be accepted, the maximum to be spent for environmental protection would still be only six per cent.[70] Most expect that, in the competition with other demands for capital in a growth-demandant culture, this amount will not rise above half this maximum estimate.[71] And these estimates include *all* the costs of environmental protection, not just what appear in govermental budgets.

The growth of governmental expenditures in urban-industrial societies since 1960 has been a much recognized phenomenon. It has taken place in approximate synchronization with the rise in concern for environmental protection. But the expenditures for environmental protection have had insignificant influence on swelling the level of governmental expenditures. The United States since 1960 has been a typical example of the behavior of governmental expenditures in an urban-industrial society. Most of the increase in governmental spending has been in transfer payments rather than in additional governmental contributions to the gross national product.[72] Since environmentally protective costs of the sort incurred since 1965 would contribute to the growth of gross national product, this fact alone shows how little they have added to the increase in governmental spending.

One must keep this fact in mind through all discussions of environmental protection as another public good. Whatever the cost of providing such protection for the forces of renewability in nature – indeed costs which Barry Commoner insists will eventually reach a level threatening to the survival of urban-industrial society – they have been proportionately small items up to this point and they are not projected to go much higher in the fairly near future. Like all public goods that are available to everyone, there is a tendency to understate their demand price. This allows a good many to take a free-ride on the investments of others.[73] It also supplies the good of environmental protection in an inadequate amount. Even when the public authority steps in, imposes a tax or charge to equalize this deficiency, and purports to provide this public good, the pressure remains to understate the amount needed. Politics too knows its free riders, and it is the renewing environment which suffers their shortchanging practices.

Public goods are not unrelated to externalities in their operations. Externalities result from economic decisions that effect others not participating in the making of the decision. They may be benefited or hurt by it. If benefited, they are the same kind of free rider who enjoys the results of public goods without paying for them. If harmed, they are victims who may or may not be in a position to bargain about their hurt either through litigation, purchase, or trade-offs. If the harm is too widely distributed to make bargaining practicable, then the harm is absorbed by the environment or by the general public – or the public resorts to legislation to redress the balance of private benefit and social harm. When externalities are more than trifling producers of either good or ill,

...resources are not used with maximum efficiency unless all the results...of an investment (that is, its marginal social product) accrue to the person making the investment.[74]

The reason all the parties potentially capable of being effected by an economic decision are not made participants in the making of that decision is the cost of such an encompassing transaction. The costs of getting information, of negotiating, and of enforcing agreements loom as too forbidding. Presumably if transaction costs were zero this sort of negotiation would occur; the law could not allocate resources any differently than these negotiations would costlessly provide; and all persons would achieve maximum satisfaction. This, at any rate, has been the view of increasing numbers of economists since Ronald Coase published his influential article on social costs in 1960.[75]

The assumption it makes is that all the significant elements in environmental systems are represented sufficiently in the economic demand structure of urban-industrial society to have a human representative to argue in the negotiating. It is, however, the argument of many that this sort of representation is lacking for portions of the environment which, nevertheless, continue to be important parts in the chain of life-support systems on this planet.[76] Not every aspect of nature is reflected in the economy, at least until it can be minimally expressed in the form of a cost to the operations of some part of that economy. And not even zero-cost economic transactions – some might say particularly zero-cost transactions – can represent the inherent worth of these natural existences in terms of human economic values.

The market approach to the environment is seen by many environmentalists as a means of auctioning off the environment to those who can make the highest cash bid. The money might go to buy out economic activities capable of generating smaller cash flows (e.g., to sports fishermen by industrial waste emitters). Or the money could be paid to public authorities, placed in charge of managing some part of the renewing environment, who might in this manner realize a far higher income to their agency through using that part of the environment as a waste sink than they would from usages protective of environmental renewability. Behind what appears to be an environmentally neutral economic policy, therefore, many fear there would be an effect detrimental to the forces for renewability in the environment.

To take one example, that of offshore drilling, the government auctions leases.... If those interests in society such as shell fishermen and beach owners...can outbid [the oil industry] for the oil rights and then decide to sit on these rights..., that is up to the interests involved. The distribution of resources in our society is such that the outcome of such competitive bidding is, however, a foregone conclusion.

There is no inequity in this, because...society benefits so much from [oil corporations] that it has made oil production sufficiently profitable to allow oil corporations to outbid competitors for the same resources.[77]

The cutting edge of sarcasm is very sharp toward the end of this quote because the writer very strongly believes there is an inequity in talking about the bargaining of environmental interests against the cash-generating powers of such an exploitative interest as the oil industry. In the market there simply do not exist competitors of sufficient economic weight to speak for the environment while pursuing their own economic interest. Whatever the importance of estuaries and shore waters, as well as the shallower waters of the continental shelf, for the maintenance of marine life – and even if one were to make the untrue assertion that all economic interests in the shore line and shore waters shared the same values – the importance of a domestic energy supply, the ability of energy production to command capital investment and generate cash flows, and the importance of the American balance of trade under the impact of foreign oil imports, all bar the success in market negotiations of the non-oil interests. Without the resort to federal legislation and the federal courts, there would be no competition at all, either between these interests and the oil industry or between the exploitation of the ocean and its protection. Insufficient as the protection may be, it would not subsist in even its present form without intervention by the legal system.

However, perhaps too much time has been spent on considering what the situation would be if transaction costs were zero. They are not and, far from approaching zero, they are going to increase greatly in the future. There will be not less regulation relative to the environment. There will be more. And, despite the increase in transaction costs imposed by the use of direct bureaucratic command structures, there will be more reliance on bureaucracy to carry through environmentally protective programs. Hopefully, that will not be all which will be done and alternative efforts using the powers of the fisc and of rules of property will be tried.

Even those who believe in the superior utility of the market when compared to bureaucratic commands agree unconstrained markets may not produce optimal resource allocations. Persons outside the allocative decisions are harmed without the chance of participating in the decisions. Their only way to obtain the power of intervention is to organize politically and to seek an alteration in legal rules so that their interests can be represented. By opening up the number of participants in decisions affecting the environment, it is hoped that at least some of the needs of the renewing systems in nature will receive advocacy and protection.

Perhaps by a scheme of pricing services, public authority can encourage particular kinds of economic activity and discourage others harmful to the environment. When the public treasury is asked to incur added infrastructure costs in order to facilitate certain economic activity, the anticipated income generated by that activity should be marked as subject to later repayment of the publically incurred costs. Increased incremental service costs should not simply be lost in the general fund as if they were a gift from God.[78]

Those who would use means other than the bureaucratic command do so on the basis that their approach would motivate users of the environment to act optimally in favor of the environment in order to avoid the expense of constraints imposed upon their activity. When there are only commands, even the law-abiding citizen is acting rationally if he does no more than what is commanded. And when the legal system offers him any opportunity to lawfully avoid these charges, he will be rational to do so. He would even be economically rational to be less than law-abiding and to evade the law where there is little likelihood of its enforcement or where the enforcement can become an assimilable cost of doing business. Just as the government official who regulates and enforces cannot know everything that is happening,[79] so the person regulated is inclined to do no more than he absolutely must under existing regulations and schemes of enforcement.[80]

Yet, though there are options for the legal system in producing results beneficial to the renewing environment, one must not overlook that law – and hence, all its variety of regulatory mechanisms constraining economic activity affecting the environment – is itself a public good. It is not a consumer good, to be used up in the enjoyment of its benefits. Rather, law can instead be analogized to capital-stock, a capital to back up operations and to be drawn upon with full regard for its potential exhaustibility.[81]

But like capital-stock there is always pressure to draw upon law for purposes that allegedly will strengthen larger operations and return the capital many-fold. Unlike private capital-stock, since the law is a public good, there are the same reasons applicable to law as to any other public good to use it up for personal advantage and not replace it. The economist James Buchanan has succinctly described the process of interaction between motives of personal gain and the survival of law. The incentive to maintain it is not nearly so strong as is the case with the holder of a private capital-stock who sees a very direct connection between his current income and the capital he holds.

By acting so as to maintain the public capital asset...,the individual confers pure external economy on others in the current time-periods. It may be privately rational...to destroy the existing public capital, to convert this asset into privately enjoyed "income"...[T]he term erosion properly applies. An individual's decision may erode the basic structure, reducing the stability of social interaction not only for his fellows but for those who come later.[82]

The consequence for those concerned with environmental protection has been almost a ratchet effect. Since both the renewing environment and any law designed to constrain conduct harmful to it are public goods, the tendency is to underinvest in both to convert as much as possible of them to a personal advantage, and publicly to undervalue them in order to hitch free rides. In short, the thrust is to treat them not as capital-stock but as consumption-items that can easily be replaced or done without once exhausted. Spilling externalities onto the renewing systems of nature, onto the general fund, and onto the overall legal system becomes a highly rational course for private action to take.

Just as the legal system must be used to protect the renewing environment from externalities being dumped upon it from individuated profit operations, so must the legal system understand it must protect itself. And so must the public understand that much of the failure of the law's response to environmental challenges has been due to the dumping onto the legal system, largely through reliance on bureaucratic command regulation, of costs more properly absorbed in the individuated profit systems that have unloaded them. One of the reasons for the ultimate popularity among entrepreneurs of bureaucratic regulation, so puzzling to so many in the Chicago School of economics who think business enterprise would prefer deregulation, lies in this "public good" character of law.

From the beginning of the present century, when Hugo Meyer at the University of Chicago wondered why uniform rates set high by regulators in a rigid mold should be preferred to heterogeneous rates flexibly responding to innumerable market needs, until today, this has been the case.[83] While the law may provide other constraints for a far lower cost, they will not offer the advantages of the sort of regulation that simultaneously assures an enterprise of shuffling costs out of their accounts and being guaranteed an income while doing it.[84] Though not peculiar to the law's relationship to environmental protection, the vulnerable character as public goods of both law and environment makes this particularly true in the regulatory mechanisms to be applied to salvaging the forces of renewability.

In constitutional law, legislative enactments do not have to be economically rational. As Mr. Justice Powell has said, "Nor does the Constitution require that legislation on economic matters be compatible with sound economics or even with normal fairness."[85] Yet whatever the constitution may require, the legislature in matters concerning environmental protection, and the regulatory mechanisms for effectuating such protection cannot be indifferent to costs, the control of externalities, and the long-term maximization of public goods in their utilization. Indifference to these can only be dangerous to both the environment and the legal mechanisms meant to protect the forces for renewability within nature.

Regulation and Environmental Management

In the mid-1970's the United States Citizens' Advisory Committee on Environmental Quality concluded that the environment was faring far better than many had anticipated, although they admitted there were "some inroads" on environmental quality.[86] Others would have reversed the emphasis, saying any improvements were "inroads" on continued environmental deterioration. Henry Caudill, who focused attention on the environmental problems of the Appalachian Mountains in the early 1960's, could only conclude in the late 1970's that environmental conditions there had gotten much worse, despite major federal programs; and that he regarded this as the likely course of events for the Rocky Mountains under the energy exploitation programs projected for the rest of the 20th century.[87]

There is substantial disagreement, therefore, whether or not the efforts made in the legal system on behalf of environmental protection have reversed deterioration, improved conditions in environmental systems, caused a stand-still, or been a matter of irrelevance for whatever has happened relative to the environment. Despite a good deal of sophisticated speculation about alternatives to bureaucratic regulation as a means of protecting the environment, very little experimentation has been carried on. People have said emission charges *could* work in protecting the environment better and more cheaply than bureaucratic commands. People have also said the same thing for fiscal incentives and for introducing permits prices in such a way that the rules of property would self-enforcedly protect the environment. The fact remains that bureaucratic commands remain – and are likely to remain for quite a long time – as the principal means of protecting environmental renewability.[88]

One of the most important action-forcing regulatory mechanisms introduced has been the environmental-impact statement required for major federal programs having a substantial environmental impact.[89] This became effective in the United States January 1, 1970; and it has produced a major impact upon regulation-drafting, bureaucratic activity, and court dockets.[90] How great has been the impact upon the environment is part of that ambiguous ground that describes so much of the legal system's effort to protect renewing systems in the environment. Certainly it has enabled environmentally concerned citizens' organizations to get a litigation handle upon the actions of federal departments and of private exploiters of the environment whose actions require federal action. Certainly it has increased the cost and bureaucratic burden of environmental compliance. This is admitted by its friends who regard these adverse economic effects as mandatory and probably unavoidable.[91] But as to how the environment has been affected one cannot be at all certain.

Two of the United States' federal agencies the proponents of environmental impact statements would most like to have affected were the Corps of Engineers and the Soil Conservation Service, especially as to the latter's stream channelization program. It was suspected that these agencies would be uncooperative with the purposes of the act and recalcitrant in enforcing its purposes. In some ways this proved true. But the reaction of both agencies turned out to be far subtler than blank refusal to cooperate – so much so that, as far as the Corps has been concerned, its reaction had been difficult to characterize.

The National Environmental Policy Act can now be seen in retrospect as part of a general movement toward rationality in governmental decision making and public access to the knowledge of the intentions of government agencies. With loss of belief in the administrative agency as an agent of representative democracy and with a growing conviction these agencies were only additional self-interested political organisms, the pressure could only mount for means of penetrating and challenging their actions. Furthermore, their mission orientation meant that they would more often act in a fragmenting way, scattering complex problems among multiple subunits. This successfully prevented rapid change in how they performed and left reformers little choice except to act after the event, sequentially and incrementally. The environmental policy behind the environmental impact statements was meant to substantially change most of this by posing a direct challenge to agency behavior.[92]

And did it succeed? Again the answer is not easy to come by. In reviewing these two agencies' projects – bearing in mind that these have been agencies both meant to be heavily affected by NEPA and which have had to file larger numbers of EIS than other federal agencies – "some substantive effect" has been reflected in six per cent of the projects of each agency. Of this minority, "substantive effect" has meant delay rather than cancellation or significant change in seventy per cent of the projects affected.[93] Assuredly NEPA did increase the sense each agency felt of having effort wasted and having endured delay. On the other hand, both agencies eventually took these delays as opportunities for a redirection of priorities that would be protective of the agency and its survival in the bureaucratic scene. As the commentator on this experience noted,

The very uncertainty still surrounding both agencies' long-term responses...underscores the central characteristic of NEPA's effects: its procedural requirements were *not* a self-enforcing means to the fulfillment of its environmental policy ends, except when reinforced by an agency's desire to change and by complementary changes in the agency's political environment. The "action-forcing provisions" did not themselves force substantive action, though they did provide new tactical opportunities in the political arena to those who wished to bring about administrative change....[94]

If this is so for a program that has attracted so much popular and scholarly attention, then it could be expected to be so for other forms of bureaucratic regulation. Increasingly critics of the present regulatory system are arguing that it is too difficult to appraise, too gross for the delicate work it must accomplish, and too negative in its approach to environmental problems. They want a more positive, more flexible approach, capable of being judged as to its success or failure after a relatively brief period of time.

Some, of course, believe this can be done through the manipulation of market rules, the operation of the fisc, or alteration in the rules of property. Others deny that these would be effective means since they are predicated upon treating parts of the environment as commodities rather than as resources to be capitally conserved instead of used up in a consumption process.[95] The United Nations 1976 Conference on Human Settlements condemned the legal situation that permitted such a resource as land to be "subject...to the pressures and inefficiencies of the market."[96] Other planners have echoed this attitude when they have said, "...we must have something stronger protecting that resource than a voluntary system...."[97] Resistance even among those who find the present regulatory system too negative is, therefore, likely to be high to any resort to systems relying upon individual initiatives.

In consequence, there is much interest in going over to more positive forms of regulatory intervention by bureaucracy through legal commands. But it would not be by simply setting constraints or sequentially checking performance to determine if there has been compliance. Instead there would be the use of techniques of environmental management employed in the public interest that would more actively mold and direct the course of conduct. Rates and directions of future growth will be influenced by changes in values and in the attitudes taken toward consumption and production. Actual physical constraints will likely continue to be of far less significance, as the studies at the United Nations by Wassily Leontieff indicate.[98] An active management program that would utilize these changes – which might even form them – seems to many far preferable than following along in the wake of action with regulations, monitors, and enforcement litigation. A recent definition of what is meant by "management" illustrates this positive, active role that many want it to play in environmental protection.

Management consists of the rational assessment of a situation and the systematic selection of goals and purposes (what is to be done?); the systematic development of strategies to achieve those goals; the marshalling of the required resources; the rational design, organization, direction, and control of the activities required to attain the selected purposes; and, finally, the motivating and rewarding of people to do the work.[99]

There is nothing new about an emphasis upon management. Lynton Caldwell in his work upon the environment has consistently urged, as part of what he dubbed "action-forcing procedures," that the positive approach of active management be preferred. Like many he does not cherish the more negative, passive, after-the-event method of bureaucratic regulation that simply sets constraints, monitors, and enforces compliance in accordance with those constraints upon the initiative of the regulated.[100] But it is one thing to perceive the value of such an approach and quite another to try to carry it through. Whatever the intention to be "action-forcing," the internal political operations and external rivalries of bureaucratic structures can convert such reforms into additional costly paper-shuffling.

The reason probably lies in a division of function that is unavoidable. The definition of "management" after all has been borrowed from a situation geared to increasing profits from production and service processes. The author of that definition, therefore, can say of good management, "Discretion is the enemy of order, of standardization and...of quality."[101] But environmental protection is intended to emphasize the continuation of the operation of interlocked natural systems that provide life-support and renew parts of the environment regarded as important natural resources in the urban-industrial demand structure. Tying together both the exploitation and protection of the environment under the guise of a comprehensive management that actively sets and achieves environmentally enhancing goals is probably to impose a burden managers cannot carry.

Often the protection of the environment will require courses of action that must come into direct conflict with such worthy managerial purposes as administrative efficiency, higher return on capital investment, and lower costs. One is able to conceive of managers of production and service processes being given as a primary goal the protection of the environment. But one can just barely conceive it on the basis of either past experience or of the values commonly shared by those having responsibility for the operation of such processes. Getting such persons to simply acknowledge the possibility of an ecosystem approach for dealing with their processes as they impact upon the environment has been probably one of the major accomplishments of the environmental movement since 1965.[102]

Not even a socialist economy could be expected to put together within the same management team those intent on maximizing environmental exploitation along with those desirous of protecting the environment. At some point one or the other would have to be given final power of decision, however ideal it might be for the team to internalize all of the appropriate values needed to protect the forces for renewability within the environment. Such ambitious institutional changes as would represent a total alteration in the attitude of managers in urban-industrial society are not yet timely, however much one would wish they were. Occasionally upon a regional or special industrial basis this can be done successfully.[103] More often what will be required will be the continued external application of regulatory constraints upon those whose economic activity effects the renewing environment.

But the formation of those constraints must be done with full consultation with more than lawyers and bureaucrats. The disciplines of economics, engineering, biology, and the earth sciences must be drawn fully into the preparation of all schemes for regulatory mechanisms. As the president of the International Association for Water Law has said, "Lawyers making laws alone are more dangerous than engineers, politicians or economists making laws without lawyers..."[104] The urban-industrial demand structure has known plentiful examples of both kinds of exclusionary practice and most of it has not been good. Failing the ability to bring together into one management consensus both those who exploit and those who protect the environment, the least that must be set up are adequate regulatory mechanisms to constrain the activity of those exploiting or affecting the interlocked environmental systems.

The Environment and Changing Regulatory Mechanisms

Cultural attitudes toward the various regulatory mechanisms capable of affecting the environment have changed over the decades. This should not be surprising since the demand structure of urban-industrial society has so profoundly altered the economic and social bases for those attitudes. But because of these shifts in attitude, anyone concerned with improving regulatory mechanisms so as to enable them to better, more quickly, or more cheaply protect the renewing environment must accept the occurrence of those changes. They must also accept their shaping of the regulatory mechanisms for the future.

Writing in 1938, Peter Drucker pointed out that the traditional western view toward concepts of property had changed completely. The older-view survived only in the teachings of the Christian Church, a fact reinforced by the 1961 encyclical of John XXIII, "Mater et Magistra." This traditional view had two aspects: first, property constituted an inalienable right only because the individual holding that property needed it to discharge social functions required by his commitment to conscience; and secondly, the statement in money terms of the market price of property did not necessarily encompass the total worth of the subject-matter of that property.[105] Beginning with the Enlightenment in the mid-18th century and continuing through the work of the Utilitarians in the early 19th century, this traditional view was first undermined and eventually socially discarded.[106]

But this was not simply a philosophical event, pursued abstractly by writers on the subject of property. The change was the result of the arrival of the urban-industrial revolution with its absolute emphasis upon the superiority of production and consumption. The manner in which property was treated had to be altered to accord with this cultural change. The most significant change is now two centuries old, however much modern commentators may lament it. It altered the entirety of the subject-matter of property. Property was no longer the sort of resource it had constituted under the traditional view. It had become a commodity only under the circumstances of a growth-demandant society. The consequence has been to cause the modern concepts of property to reflect a basic attitude which views the environment as something to be consumed rather than as a public good to be conserved as a capital-stock continuously regenerating itself.

Perhaps those who now seek to alter the rules of property in order to enable those rules to self-execute a protection to the environment are engaged in a philosophical return to some parts of the traditional view of property. If property carries with it only privileges and no duties, then what is privately rational and realistic behavior may well become irrational and an unreal fictive invention as it affects social decisions concerning the environment.[107] The only reason for imposing external regulatory constraints through altering the rules of property, whether those constraints be self-executing or not, arises from the failure of the present rules of property to restrain externalities harmful to the environment. Such changes may well make harmful (or even beneficial) externalities myths which the future will be hard-pressed to recall from its past.[108] But the changes eliminating these externalities will themselves be regulatory mechanisms externally imposed upon the existing rules of property.

The traditional view of property did not believe the cash price it could command at a present moment in the market, even when discounted through credit devices, must necessarily be representative of the worth of the property's subject-matter. Nor did the traditional property concepts view the subject-matter of property to be exclusively a commodity to be exploited, traded, consumed, and discarded. Ideally, it took into account the larger social effect such activity would have upon both the subject-matter itself and other elements in the general environment related to what was economically employed.[109] These cultural beliefs operated as an external constraint, being of a social rather than an overtly legal kind for much of the time. Once they were swept away, however, the subject-matter of property could be considered as isolated from any other than the economic one of individuating profit to the title-holder of any isolated unit having a superiority over any particular subject-matter.

Perhaps the proponents of limited growth, too, are seeking a return to older views of property by insisting that there are natural limits to how much growth is possible.[110] Perhaps the same is true for those critics of limited growth who want to better direct relative to a

...concern at mankind overplaying the Faustian hand: setting in motion forces approaching those of nature in magnitude, risking major environmental crises, permitting the scale of institutions and technologies to grow seemingly beyond control of individuals or even nations, and converting technological advance and economic growth into ends in themselves instead of instrumental means for greater human satisfaction.[111]

Eventually in a growth-demandant culture, once the growth curves had begun their climb at a steep enough rate, a concern over growth, its impact, how it might be contained or directed, and how its impact on the environment could be mediated had to become a major concern. As a developer told a legislative committee in Ohio, with enough anguish to forget his proper English,

I know that across this country now, there is a big legal fight going on as to whether growth for growth's sake is a proposition that can be supported in the law. I don't know about whether it can be supported in law, but I can tell you it's disasterous. [sic][112]

Changed conditions in technology and demand inevitably induce changes in the institutional structures having responsibility for controlling or directing the consequences of those changes. When the direct bureaucratic command produces dissatisfaction over its effectiveness, one can expect alternatives to be suggested using other means. When the rules of property fail to cope with the externalities imposed upon the environment by the actions of the holders of that property, either the rules must change or external constraints must be imposed through regulation. When the fisc has tax incentive programs that do not even marginally produce environmental improvement, then either better tax incentive or direct grant programs must be worked out. If none of this can be done in such a way, then these approaches must be dismissed as unreal alternatives to bureaucratic or other regulation.

Certainly the United States Supreme Court in 1976 has cleared the way constitutionally for extensive legislative experiments in this regard. The due process requirements relative to vested property interests will not be impossible barriers. The constitution will allow efforts to improve environmental conditions through altering the allocation of costs. This may be done either by changing the tax laws or the rules of property in order to accomplish social goals transcending the individuated profits of holders of entitlements to property. Mr. Justice Thurgood Marshall, speaking for the Court, used the broadest language:

We find...that the imposition of liability for the effects of disabilities bred in the past is justified as a rational measure to spread the costs of the...disabilities to those who have profited from the fruits.... We are unwilling to assess the wisdom of Congress' chosen scheme by examining the degree to which the "cost-savings" enjoyed...in the pre-enactment period produced "excess" profits, or the degree to which the retrospective liability imposed on the early operators can now be passed on to the consumer.... [W]hether a broader cost-spreading scheme would have been wise or more practical...is not a question of constitutional dimension.[113]

Of course, one must continue to use the term "rules of property" in the broadest sense, including within it such economic values as choses in action and assertable defenses to causes of action. The United States Supreme Court was reacting to federal legislation that in a particular employment situation created new causes of action, eliminated summary defenses, established presumptions both rebuttable and irrebuttable, and put limitations on what could constitute rebuttal evidence.[111] There can be no doubt that for one class of persons new claims were created for property in the form of cash payments. For another class a diminution and transfer of property was simultaneously required, with some opportunity to pass the costs along to consumers whose property in turn would be affected by the property transfers.

Something not very dissimilar would occur if the recommendation for better environmental enforcement made by the economist George Stigler were adopted. It is his contention, as an advocate of market forms, that there should be "the introduction of competition into the enforcement of regulation."[115] Essentially what he would do is permit *qui tam* actions, private attorney-general suits. They would be brought against alleged violators by persons concerned with what they believed to be happening. These plaintiffs would be rewarded, if successful, by a portion of the fines or by punitive damages.[116] In property terms, it would create, or certainly greatly enlarge, a chose in action that could produce major property transfers.

Using the term "rules of property" in such a way as to encompass these kinds of regulatory mechanisms is necessary if one is to see how flexible and significant the role these rules play in affecting the use of the renewing environment. Indeed, as is true with so many legal concepts, the scope of the rules of property rub against the reach of the taxing power when one discusses the use of price to advance environmental protection. Price can be changed by imposing a tax to internalize costs imposed by use of the environment or by requiring the purchase of a permit whose cost would be equivalent to the costs imposed by the activity.[117] Even bureaucratic regulation is hard to separate from being a part of the rules of property. This is particularly the case where private persons are empowered to enforce regulations administratively or juridically for their own personal property advantage against the private activity of others.

Today regulatory mechanisms must be aimed at assisting the interlocking systems of the renewing environment to better respond to the impact of urban-industrial demand. They must be interactions that will tie together changes occurring in the rules of property, the operations of the fisc both as to taxes and grants, and the employment of bureaucratic direct commands. The very difficulty in precisely knowing in many situations whether one is dealing with a rule of property, a fiscal measure, or a bureaucratic command – or all three simultaneously – underscores this necessity. In carrying through changes as to any type of regulatory mechanism, this potential interaction must be accepted if there is to be sufficient understanding of the available options in regulation.

Regulating in Terms of Environmental Results

It is relatively easy to obtain a consensus that socioeconomic equity requires reasonable rates of economic growth and stable prices and that the attainment of both these must take into "careful" account their effects on resource exhaustion and environmental pollution – as long as one is not insistent on strict definitions for "equity," "reasonable," or "careful."[118] It is also possible to evoke widespread agreement in condemning master planning of scattered resources within the environment because " in the real world...people hold sharply conflicting values,...technological change outstrips the imagination of science-fiction writers, and...civil servants may be uninformed or subject to corruption...."[119] But then once one goes beyond the platitudes, there is no regulatory scheme that is not condemned by some insightful critic whether it is master planning, bureaucratic regulation, tax incentives, subsidy grants, or mobilizing the market through altering the rules of property.

Perhaps what is needed is a willingness to institutionally experiment, to forego a predetermined belief that any one approach by itself will prove sufficient. Most important of all, there must be a willingness to monitor what is happening in the environment under any regulatory mechanism that is in operation. Somehow in the years of increased environmental concern since 1965, there has not been enough attention to what has been happening in the environment.

Maybe this was due to the lack of good base line data against which to make comparisons. Perhaps it was due to false projections of likely results that were made at the beginning of programs for environmental protection. But the problem persists insofar that too little is known about what is happening in the renewing environment. And even less is known as to why it is happening.

Presumably the purpose of all efforts to regulate impacts upon the environment is to better enable the environment to respond to the demands of urban-industrial society being made upon its renewing systems. There could be more ambitious purposes, to be sure. One would assume, however, that this is the minimal one.

Conversely this means that the purpose of environmentally protective programs has not been primarily to add to the number of bureaucrats or lawyers employed, to enlarge the gross national product, to increase prices, taxes, or subsidies, or to enhance political careers through rhetoric. Yet while all of these have happened, one still cannot know if the renewing environment is better able to respond to the demands being made upon it than was the case in 1965. Or, if this should be true, if the reason for the improvement lies in any one – or none – of the regulatory devices employed in that period of time.

The old saw "the operation was a success but the patient died," seems particularly pertinent here. *More* simply has to be done to establish the fact of any changes in environmental conditions, as well as the reasons for those changes. Continuous rhetoric, regulation drafting, and learned discussions are all very well – if they produce some improvement in the response-abilities of the renewing environmental systems. If they do not, they may prove worse than no action at all since they will have disguised their lack of effect until effective action may be too late. They will have contributed to public apathy and disbelief that anything can be done and they will have imposed costs that will make further action even more costly than it had to be.

This is not an accusation that all institutional efforts made since 1965 have failed to improve the condition of the renewing environment. It is to say that a determination of changes up or down in overall environmental conditions are still very hard to reach. And when particular cases can be agreed upon that illustrate improvements, most of these remain ambiguous as to whom to credit.

There is little point in changing regulatory mechanisms in the absence of either such knowledge or of the means of providing it. The concern remains insufficient for monitoring the environment in such a way as to know what is happening and whom to blame or credit for the events. Failing such monitoring, we shall continue to operate in self-administered ignorance that will produce improvement only by happenstance.

Whether continued reliance upon the direct command structure of bureaucratic regulation is to remain the primary focus, or greater reliance is to be placed upon fiscal measures, or manipulation of the rules or property is to be resorted to in order to employ the force of the market, the test of environmental effect for all of them is a necessity. Without this emphasis upon effect and responsibility for effect, none of these regulatory mechanisms are likely to be protectors of the renewability inherent in the environment.

Instead of this certainty, there will be further reports such as those of the United States Council on Environmental Quality made in late 1976. Except for "special problem areas," such as New York and Los Angeles, the United States will have clean air by the early 1980's. The statement was made, in all its optimism, despite the admission that as of the mid-1970's few areas of the country were in full compliance with federal air quality standards. In addition, the Council was almost as cheerful about the likely improvement of water quality by the 1980's, although it apparently was using as its basic indicator the intestinal bacteria counts – and many doubt their pertinency. In short, in its view, environmental controls were productive of jobs and a 2% proportion of the Gross National Product, were providing a level of expenditure in 1976 of $90 million per day for pollution controls, and were going to meet the standards called for within less than a decade.[120]

In the presence of such claims, one can only respond with, "Let's hope so." But one can also be full of doubt. First of all, there is doubt that the facts are present to either prove or disprove these claims. And secondly, one can point to the study by Lynton Caldwell of 68 environmental cases in the United States which concluded that the government in its various manifestations may be the single worst enemy arrayed against the environment.[121] There still seem to be genuine differences as to whether there is cause for optimism or pessimism about the future of the environment. And partially founded opinions either way are no substitute for solid information.

There is certainly nothing new about the view that government programs should be judged by their results. The French sociologist of bureaucracy, Michel Crozier, has been emphatic about the necessity for this. He regards the failure to organize along such lines as irrational and "an *ancien regime* style of thinking." What he finds especially distressful, though, is that it is among such social welfare governmental agencies as those that embrace environmental protection where,

We may expect, and we have already seen, fierce reactions to...lifting of the spell...cast over a new and immense area of social life which until now conformed to pre-industrial forms of reasoning.[122]

It is his conviction that there will be change, if for no other reason than the increasing frustration of repeated failure along the well-trodden regulatory paths. One hopes he is right, though the evidence for such changes is not strong.

Despite all of the talk for increased reliance upon rebates, grants, permits, effluent charges and other means of using changes in the rules of property and the operation of the fisc, the reliance has remained upon the direct bureaucratic command. This has meant that there has been insistence upon uniform conduct and bureaucratic ease which cannot often produce very flexible results on environmental changes conducive to the protection of renewing systems.[123]

Government has had thrust upon it the responsibility of a main contractor in saving the environment. It tries to execute this program but, so far, too many of its methods work against attaining the goal. There has been too little development of different regulatory models that would foster the development of more lasting relations between demand and the renewing environment. The pricing mechanism, the use of rules of property, the employment of the powers of the fisc are all potentially rich alternatives to current regulatory experience. But for all of them, as for the bureaucratic command, the institutions of the state are inescapable external constraints upon conduct. Michel Crozier has summarized this very well:

Institutional investment works directly when the state plays a central role; it may work very indirectly in an economic sphere only marginally linked to the public authorities or when it concerns the internal affairs of a private organization. But in all cases the state's role in society is now crucially important both in financial and regulatory affairs, and in the social and psychological spheres.[124]

Whatever may be true for human psychology in this regard, this statement is quite factual for the matter of environmental protection. Though the bureaucratic mechanism is not the only means to consider for regulation, the general roles of law and government retain their importance. The rules of property, the fisc, and the bureaucracy will continue to provide the means to externally impose constraints. And these constraints upon the formation, operation, and impact of urban-industrial demand will be the means of sustaining the renewing environment – should, indeed, humanity decide to sustain it.

Notes

[1] Michel Crozier, "Western Europe," in Michel Crozier and others. *The Crisis of Democracy*, New York: New York Univ. Press. 1975, p. 12. See also p. 32.

[2] André Teissier du Cros, *L'Innovation pour une morale du changement*, Paris: Robert Laffont, 1971, p. 168.

[3] William H. McNeill, *The Rise of the West*, Chicago: Univ. of Chicago Press, 1963, pp. 804–806.

[4] William Baumol, Book Review, 85 *Yale Law J.* (1976), 441, at p. 445.

[5] Samuel P. Huntington, "North America," in Crozier *et al.*, *op. cit.*, p. 64.

[6] Teissier du Cros, *op. cit.*, p. 237.

[7] Kenneth E. F. Watt, *The Titanic Effect: Planning for the Unthinkable*, Stamford: Sinauer Associates, 1974, pp. 219–220.

[8] *The Use of Land: A Citizens' Policy Guide to Urban Growth*, A Task Force Report Sponsored by The Rockefeller Brothers Fund, William K. Reilley, ed., New York: Thomas Y. Crowell Co., 1973, p. 14.

[9] Crozier *et al.*, *op. cit.*, "Appendix," p. 174, being summaries for the meeting of the Tripartite Commission in Kyoto, Japan, May 30–31, 1975. The Commission is composed of businessmen, bankers, government officials, and academics from western Europe, North America, and Japan meeting as private individuals.

[10] Friedrich Engels, *Dialectics of Nature*, tr. Clemens Dutt, New York: International Publishers 1940, pp. 295–296.

[11] Joseph M. Manke, "Environmental Disclosures – SEC vs NEPA," 31 *The Business Lawyer* (1976), 1907, at p. 1918, note.

[12] On the development of the ideas of Karl Marx and Friedrich Engels on their ideas on the relationship of property, nature, and alienation, see Svetozar Pejovich, "Towards an Economic Theory of the Creation and Specification of Property Rights," in Henry Manne, ed., *The Economics of Legal Relationships*, St. Paul: West Pub. Co., 1975, p. 37, at pp. 44–49.

[13] Lincoln Gordon, "Limits to the Growth Debate," *RFF Resources*, No. 52 (Summer 1976), p. 1, at p. 5.

[14] For earlier Kahn optimism, see the accounts in Teissier du Cros, *op. cit.*, p. 222. For a more recent version, see Herman Kahn and others, *The Next 200 Years*, New York: William Morrow & Co., 1976.

[15] Interview with Herman Kahn by Edward Jay Epstein, *New York*, August 9, 1976, pp. 34–44, at pp. 38–39.

[16] Gordon, *op. cit.*, p. 5.

[17] Robert K. Merton, "Social Knowledge and Public Policy," in Mirra Komarovsky, ed., *Sociology and Public Policy*, New York: Elsevier, 1975, p. 172 and p. 172 note.

[18] See Laurence H. Tribe, "Technology Assessment and the Fourth Discontinuity: The Limits of Instrumental Rationality," 46 *So. Cal. L.R.* (1973), 617.

[19] Lettie McSpadden Wenner, *One Environment Under Law: A Public-Policy Dilemma*, Pacific Palisades: Goodyear Pub. Co., 1976, pp. 11–15.

[20] Gordon, *op. cit.*, p. 5.

[21] Wenner, *op. cit.*, p. 14.

[22] R. T. McNamar, "Regulation versus Competition," *Wall St. Journal*, August 9, 1976. Mr. McNamar was executive director of the Federal Trade Commission.

[23]   George J. Stigler, *The Citizen and the State: Essays on Regulation*, Chicago: Univ. of Chicago Press, 1975, p. xi.

[24]   Crozier, *loc. cit.*, in Crozier *et al.*, *op. cit.*, p. 56 note.

[25]   Ralf Dahrendorf, "Remarks," in *ibid.*, p. 188. The term "partisan adjustment systems" was originated by Robert Lindblom.

[26]   Manke, *op. cit.*, p. 1918.

[27]   T. H. Watkins and Charles S. Watson, Jr., *The Land No One Knows: America and the Public Domain*, San Francisco: Sierra Club Books, 1975, p. 150.

[28]   Baumol, *op. cit.*, p. 445.

[29]   *Ibid.*, pp. 445–446. The imagery is Professor Baumol's.

[30]   Allen V. Kneese, *Water Pollution: Economic Aspects and Research Needs*, Washington, D.C.: Resources for the Future, 1962 is an early work of his touching on the subject.

[31]   Fred A. Clarenbach, "Incentives for Industrial Pollution Control," Industrial Wastes Institute, University of Wisconsin at Madison, March 2, 1966, p. 6.

[32]   *Ibid.*, pp. 6–7.

[33]   *Ibid.*, p. 7.

[34]   Wenner, *op. cit.*, p. 138.

[35]   Allen V. Kneese, Robert U. Ayres, Ralph C. D'Arge, *Economics and the Environment: A Materials Balance Approach*, Washington, D.C.: Resources for the Future, 1970, p. 118.

[36]   *Ibid.*, pp. 4–5.

[37]   Otto Eckstein, *Public Finance*, 2nd ed., Englewood Cliffs, N.J.: Prentice-Hall, Inc., 1967, p. 77.

[38]   James P. Landis, "The Impact of the Income Tax Laws on the Energy Crisis: Oil and Congress Don't Mix," 64 *Cal. L.R.* (1976), 1040, at pp. 1059–1060. See also *ibid.*, pp. 1055–1056.

[39]   Baumol, *op. cit.*, p. 446.

[40]   Allen V. Kneese, "Water Quality Management by Regional Authorities in the Ruhr Area," in Marshall I. Goldman, ed., *Ecology and Economics*, Englewood Cliffs, N.J.: Prentice-Hall, Inc., 1972, pp. 172–190.

[41]   H. Sontheim in 76 *Umschau in Wissenschaft und Technik* (1976), 464.

[42]   See Thomas D. Crocker and A. J. Rogers III, *Environmental Economics*, Hinsdale, Ill.: Dryden Press, 1971.

[43]   A. Dan Tarlock, "Recent Developments in the Recognition of Instream Uses in Western Water Law," 1975 *Utah L.R.* 871, at p. 872. The categories excluded from private ownership were "...*res communes*, which were resources that from their nature could not be owned or were adapted for public use; *res publicae*, which included resources adapted for public purposes by public functionaries; and *res sanctae*...".

[44]   *Ibid.*, p. 875 note, citing Geer v. Connecticut, 161 U.S. 519 (1896). Technology doubtless made possible the conversion of much that had been *res communes* into *res nullius*.

[45]   *Ibid.*, p. 871.

[46]   260 U.S. 373 (1922), opinion by Holmes, J.

[47]   For a criticism of this approach, see Wenner, *op. cit.*, pp. 134–136 and Donald Large, "This Land Is Whose Land? Changing Concepts of Property," 1973 *Wisconsin Law Review* 1039, at pp. 1061–1062.

[48]   56 Wis. 2d 7, 201 N.W.2d 761 (1972) at p. 771 and 768. I am indebted to certain ideas concerning the case to a paper by David Prichard, graduate student in journalism, Ohio State University, July 20, 1976.

[49]   Clarenbach, *op. cit.*, pp. 10–11. One must remember that Professor Clarenbach was writing in the winter of 1965–1966. Since then, how many disincentives have been ended in terms of environmental protection?

[50]   Barry Commoner, *The Poverty of Power*, New York: Alfred Knopf, 1976.

[51]   David Zwick and Marcy Benstock, *Water Wasteland: Ralph Nader's Study Group Report on Water Pollution*, New York: Grossman Publishers, 1971, p. 309.

[52]   *Ibid.*, pp. 309–311.

[53]   Lewis J. Perl, "Ecology's Missing Price Tag," *Wall St. Journal*, August 10, 1976. Dr. Perl was vice-president of the National Economic Research Associates.

[54]   Gordon, *op. cit.*, p. 5.

[55]   Perl, *loc. cit.*

[56]   Elsie Watters of the Tax Foundation quoted by Sylvia Porter, "How Government Spends Its Money," Columbus, Ohio, *Citizen-Journal*, February 5, 1974.

[57]   Though there were some in those days who were pessimistic both about the costs and the possibility of cleaning up lakes, Earl Finbar Murphy, *Governing Nature*, Chicago: Quadrangle Books 1967, p. 131.

[58]   Craig Charney, "Price of Pollution," *Wall St. Journal*, August 31, 1976.

[59]   See the exchange of letters between Herman Kahn and David O. Poindexter, president, The Population Institute, in *New York*, September 20, 1976, pp. 6–8.

[60]   Perl, *loc. cit.*

[61]   Bruce Kovner, Book Review of Commoner's *Poverty of Power* in *Commentary*, vol. 62, no. 3 (September 1976), 114 at p. 116.

[62]   Joan Libman, "Troubled Waters," *Wall St. Journal*, September 8, 1976 recounts the economic consequences to 3rd party economic interests in a town of just the prospects of such a closing.

[63]   Stigler, *op. cit.*, p. 39.

[64]   John W. Kendrick, "Public Capital Expenditures and Budgeting for Productivity Advance," in *Productivity in Public Organizations*, Marz Holzer, ed., Port Washington, N.Y.: Kennikat Press, 1976, pp. 196–214.

[65]   James M. Buchanan, *The Limits of Liberty: Between Anarchy and Leviathan*, Chicago: University of Chicago Press, 1975, pp. 111–112.

[66]   Landis, *op. cit.*, p. 1059.

[67]   *Man and the Environment*, Wes Jackson, ed., Dubuque: William C. Brown Pub., 1971, p. xvii.

[68]   See *Environmental Law and Policy, Supplement*, Eva Hanks, A. Dan Tarlock, John Hanks, eds., St. Paul: West, 1976, pp. 192–193, for material on this sort of estimation.

[69]   Compare Perl, *loc. cit.*, with Wenner, *op. cit.*, pp. 134–136. The former's ratio of costs: 34, benefits: 1 would leave the latter completely unimpressed.

[70]   Perl, *loc. cit.*

[71]   Gordon, *op. cit.*, p. 5.

[72]   Huntington, *loc. cit.*, in Crozier *et al.*, *op. cit.*, p. 68.

[73]   Stigler, *op. cit.*, p. 108.

[74]   *Ibid.*, pp. 104–105. Philosophically Professor Stigler insists, "...people seek to maximize their own utility subject to restraints.... There is, in fact, only one general theory of human behavior, and that is the utility-maximizing theory," *ibid.*, p. 137.

[75]   *Ibid.*, pp. 106–107. "In this regime of zero transaction costs, no monopoly would restrict output below the optimum level because consumers would pay the monopolist not to do so...". The article by R. H. Coase is "The Problem of Social Cost," 3 *Journal of Law and Economics* (1960), 1–44.

[76]   Christopher Stone, *Should Trees Have Standing?* Los Altos: William Kaufman Co. 1974; Earl Finbar Murphy, *A Law for Life*, Law and Society Reprint No. 46 (1970), 1970 *Environment Law Review* 3–20, 1969 *Wisc. L.R.* 773–787; E. F. Murphy, "Has Nature Any Right to Life?", 22 *Hastings L.J.* (1971), 467–484.

[77]   Wenner, *op. cit.*, p. 132.

[78]   Robert C. Ellickson, "A Ticket to Thermidor, A Commentary on the Proposed California Coastal Plan," 49 *So. Cal. L.R.* (1976), 715, at pp. 718–719, p. 725.

[79]   Clarenbach, *op. cit.*, pp. 8–9.

[80]   Baumol, *op. cit.*, p. 446.

[81]   Buchanan, *op. cit.*, p. 123.

[82]   *Ibid.*, pp. 124–125. "...a recognition of the capital or investment aspects of the genuine 'public goods' that are being destroyed makes corrective action much more urgent than any application of a consumption-goods paradigm might suggest." *Ibid.*, p. 126.

[83]   Compare Hugo R. Meyer, *Government Regulation of Railway Rates*, New York: MacMillan Co., 1906, p. 457.

[84]   Compare Meyer, *op. cit.*, p. xx, with Stigler, *op. cit.*, p. xi.

[85]   Concurring opinion, Usery v. Turner Elkhorn Mining Co. (1976), 428 U.S. 1, 44 LW 5181, at p. 5194.

[86]   *Report to the President and to the Council on Environmental Quality*, December 1974 (April 1975). Citizens' Advisory Committee on Environmental Quality, p. 10.

[87]   Compare Henry M. Caudill, *Night Comes to the Cumberlands: A Biography of a Depressed Area*, Boston: Little, Brown & Co., 1963 with *The Watches of the Night*, Boston: Little Brown & Co., 1976. See also the same author's, *My Land Is Dying*, New York: E. F. Dutton Co., 1973, and *A Darkness at Dawn: Appalachian Kentucky and the Future*, Lexington: University Press of Kentucky, 1976.

[88]   Baumol, *op. cit.*, p. 445, who much regrets this.

[89]   Lynton Keith Caldwell, *Environment: A Challenge to Modern Society*, Garden City: Natural History Press, 1970, p. 219. Professor Caldwell as long ago as 1963 was the principal originator of the National Environmental Protection Act of 1969 which he cast as an "action-forcing" piece of legislation.

[90]   Frederick R. Anderson, "The National Environmental Policy Act," in *Federal Environmental Law*, Erica Dolgin and T. G. P. Guilbert, eds., St. Paul: West Pub. Co., 1974, pp. 238–419, and Frederick R. Anderson, with Robert H. Daniels, *NEPA in the Courts: A Legal Analysis of the National Environmental Policy Act*, Washington, D.C.: Resources for the Future, 1973.

[91]   Manke, *op. cit.*, p. 1918.

[92]   Richard N. L. Andrews, *Environmental Policy and Administrative Change*, Lexington, Mass.: D. C. Heath & Co., 1976, pp. 161–162.

[93]   *Ibid.*, p. 138.

[94]   *Ibid.*, p. 130.

[95]   M. Bruce Johnson, "Some Observations on the Economics of the California Coastal Plan," 49 *So. Cal. L.R.* (1976), 749. He is insistent on emphasizing approaches not costing loss of individual liberty, pp. 755–757.

[96]   Gladwin Hill, "UN Meeting Urges Curb on Private Land Holding," New York *Times*, June 12, 1976.

[97]   *The Time for Review*, An Interim Report from the [Ohio] Land Use Review Committee (June 1976), p. 30, quoting a director of a regional planning commission who said, "If...land is a *resource* rather than a *commodity*, then we must have something stronger protecting that resource than a voluntary system which gives local jurisdictions broad powers with few duties or obligations."

[98]   Gordon, *op. cit.*, p. 6.

[99]   Theodore Levitt, "Management and the 'post-industrial' Society," *The Public Interest*, whole no. 44 (Summer 1976) 69, at p. 73 and repeated more tersely at p. 103. He distinguishes management from administration by saying, "Administration merely executes," *ibid.*, p. 84.

[100] Caldwell, *op. cit.*, Pt. III, "Management."

[101] Levitt, *op. cit.*, p. 87.

[102] On the ecosystem approach see Daniel H. Henning, *Environmental Policy and Administration*, New York: American Elsevier Pub. Co., 1974, pp. 161–168. For a basic

work on this approach see H. T. Odum *Environment, Power, and Society*, New York: John Wiley & Co., 1971.

[103] See the description of the work of the Greater Erft Association in Werner Lindner, "Water Resources Management and Strip Mining in the Lower Left Bank Region of the Rhine River," 1 *Water International* (July 1976), no. 3, pp. 11–17.

[104] Guillermo J. Cano, "The IWRA...Output to the...International Conf. on Water Law and Administration," *ibid.*, 6, p. 7.

[105] Peter F. Drucker, *The End of Economic Man*, New York: John Day Co., 1939, p. 107.

[106] For an excellent discussion, see the opinion of Justice Santana Becerra in Commonwealth v. Rosso, 95 Puerto Rico Reports (1967), 488, at pp. 513–518.

[107] Drucker, *op. cit.*, p. 107.

[108] Stigler, *op. cit.*, pp. 104–108.

[109] See Pars. 43, 104–112, and 257. Pope John XXIII, "Mater et Magistra." Insofar as this relates to concepts of property, it restates and summarizes traditional views, Benjamin L. Masse, S.J. "Highlights of the Encyclical" in *Mater et Magistra: Christianity and Social Progress*, D. M. Cameron and E. K. Culhane, eds., New York: The America Press, 1961, 72 at p. 77.

[110] For example, see Jorgen Randers and Donella Meadows, "The Carrying Capacity of Our Global Environment: A Look at the Ethical Alternatives," in *Western Man* and *Environmental Ethics*, Ian G. Barbour, ed., Reading, Mass: Addison-Wesley Pub. Co., 1973, pp. 253–276. However, their expressed mentor is the Utilitarian John Stuart Mill with his idea of the stationary state.

[111] Gordon, *op. cit.*, p. 2.

[112] *A Time to Review, op. cit.*, p. 40, quoting an anonymous developer.

[113] Usery v. Turner Elkhorn Mining Co., 428 U.S. 1, 44 LW 5181 (1976), at pp. 5186–5187. He does preface this, however, by warning: "...we would...hesitate to approve the retrospective imposition of liability on any theory of deterrence...or blameworthiness..." p. 5186.

[114] *Ibid.*, at pp. 5183–5184.

[115] Stigler, *op. cit.*, pp. 176–177.

[116] *Qui tam* actions are described in William Blackstone, *Commentaries on the Laws of England* (James De Witt Andrews, 4th ed., Thomas M. Cooley, ed.) Chicago: Callaghan & Co., 1899, Bk. III, p. 162*. It is plainly described as a "penal action" in *Tidd's Practice* (2nd Am. ed. from 8th Eng. ed., Francis J. Troubatt, ed.), Philadelphia: Towar & Hogan, 1828. See also S. C. McCaffrey, "Private Remedies for Transfrontier Pollution Injuries," in *Environmental Law: International and Comparative Aspects, A Symposium*, Jolanta Nowak, ed., Dobbs Ferry: Oceana Publications, Inc., 1976, pp. 12–22, which argues for the more economic solution of local, private litigation rather than internationalizing the dispute.

[117] See Ellickson, *op. cit.*, p. 725.

[118] Crozier *et al.*, *op. cit.*, appendix, p. 174, which uses all three words without any attempt at definition. See the criticism by Ralf Dahrendorf, *ibid.*, pp. 188–189.

[119] Ellickson, *op. cit.*, p. 735.

[120] *Seventh Annual Report*, United States Council on Environmental Quality (September 30, 1976). See Cleveland *Plain Dealer*, October 1, 1976.

[121] Lynton K. Caldwell, Lynton R. Hayes, and Isabel M. MacWhirter, *Citizens and the Environment: Case Studies in Popular Action*, Bloomington: Indiana University Press, 1976.

[122] Michel Crozier, *The Stalled Society*, New York: The Viking Press, 1973, p. 49. His book *The Bureaucratic Phenomenon*, Chicago: University of Chicago Press, 1964, has been indispensable for my thinking.

[123] The work of Yakov Y. Haimes in the Maumee Basin is illustrative of this. See, e.g.,

Haimes *et al.*, "Hierarchical Modeling for the Planning and Management of a Total Regional Water Resource System: Joint Consideration of the Supply and Quality of Ground and Surface Water Resources," Columbus, Ohio: Ohio Water Resources Center, October, 1976. Although there are many institutional alternatives offered in the academic literature, in reality few of them are operational, remarks of Professor Haimes, Seminar on Non-Point Sources, Columbus, Ohio: Ohio Water Resources Center, September 24, 1976.

[124] Crozier, *The Stalled Society*, p. 175. Some now argue that political and institutional changes alone "will be sufficient to support a growing population and higher living standards, without inevitable environmental damage," Peter Grose, "Report at U.N.," New York *Times*, October 14, 1976, p. 1. See Wassily Leontief *et al.*, *The Future of the World Economy*, United Nations Department of Economic and Social Affairs, 1976.

Bibliography

Following is a list of articles and books the author believes significantly relate to the subject-area of this book, the regulation of the renewing environment. Many of the books are collections of readings; and, in themselves, these selected readings offer a wide-ranging coverage of relevant information impossible to briefly describe. The single asterisk indicates a book or article was especially useful to this author. Double asterisks indicate this author was particularly impressed by these works in the formation of his own ideas. Some sources are under-represented in relation to their importance to the intellectual development of this author, most notably C. A. Doxiadis, J. Willard Hurst, and Myres Smith McDougal; but the contributions of these scholars have been too numerous to be comprehensively included. Undoubtedly, important publications, especially among the periodical literature, have been omitted. The bibliography cannot fully reflect, either, the importance to the author of such newspapers as the *Wall St. Journal*, the *New York Times*, the *Washington Post*, of the various news services, e.g., the Associated Press and Copley, and such legal services as the BNA Environmental Reporter and the CCH Energy Management News. But no list of this sort can ever be complete. Its purposes have been achieved if the reader obtains an insight into the sources of the author's ideas and if the reader also has received assistance in pursuing further research in the subject-area. The author hopes this bibliography fulfils these objectives.

Agenda for Survival, H. W. Helfrich, Jr., ed., New Haven: Yale University Press, 1970.
*Annual Reports, United States Council on Environmental Quality, nos. 1 through 7, 1970–1976.
Challenge for Survival: Land, Air, and Water for Man in Megalopolis, Pierre Dansereau with Virginia A. Weadock, eds., Intro. by William Campbell Steere, New York: Columbia University Press, 1970.

Congress and the Environment, Richard Cooley and Geoffrey Wandesford-Smith, eds., Seattle: University of Washington Press, 1970.

Development and the Environment: Legal Reforms to Facilitate Industrial Site Selection, Chicago: American Bar Association Special Committee on Environmental Law, 1974.

The Devil's Party, Tim Drescher and Glenn Miller, eds., Waltham, Mass.: Xerox College Publishing Co., 1971.

Ecological Crisis: Readings for Survival, Glen A. Love and Rhoda M. Love, eds., New York: Harcourt, Brace, Jovanovich, 1970.

Ecology and Economics, Marshall I. Goldman, ed., Englewood Cliffs, N.J.: Prentice-Hall, Inc., 1972.

*Economic Foundations of Property Law, Bruce Ackerman, ed., Boston: Little, Brown & Co., 1975.

**The Economics of Legal Relationships, Henry Manne, ed., St. Paul: West Publishing, Co., 1975.

Growth Economics, Amartya Sen, ed., Baltimore: Penguin, 1970.

Environment for Man: The Next Fifty Years, based on papers commissioned for the American Institute of Planners' 2-year consultation for a conference on the Optimum Environment with Man as the Measure, August 14–18, 1966, William R. Ewald, Jr., ed., Bloomington: Indiana University Press, 1967.

Environmental Law: International and Comparative Aspects, Jolanta Nowak, ed., Dobbs Ferry: Oceana Publications, 1976.

*Environmental Law and Policy, Eva Hanks, A. Dan Tarlock, John Hanks, eds., St. Paul: West Publishing Co., 1974, Supplement, 1976.

Environmental Protection, Louis L. Jaffe and Laurence H. Tribe, Chicago: The Bracton Press, 1971.

*Selected Legal and Economic Aspects of Environmental Protection, Charles J. Meyers and A. Dan Tarlock, eds., Mineola, N.Y.: Foundation Press, 1971.

Energy Conservation and the Law, Proceedings of the National Conference on the Environment, April 30–May 1, 1976, American Bar Association Committee on Environmental Law.

Ethics and Standards in American Business, Joseph W. Towle, ed., Boston: Houghton-Mifflin Co., 1964.

*Federal Environmental Law, Erica Dolgin and T. G. P. Guilbert, eds., St. Paul: West Publishing Co., 1974.

Industrial Developments and the Environment: Legal Reforms to Improve the Decision-Making Process in Industrial Site Selection, Chicago: American Bar Association Special Committee on Environmental Law, 1973.

*New Developments in Land and Environmental Controls, D. M. Mandelker, ed., Indianapolis: Bobbs-Merrill Publishing Co., 1974.

Future Land Use: Energy, Environmental and Legal Constraints, Robert W. Burchell and David Listokin, eds., New Brunswick: Center for Urban Policy Research, Rutgers University, 1975.

Land Use Planning, Proceedings of the National Conference on Environmental Law, May 2–3, 1975, American Bar Association Standing Committee on Environmental Law,

The Use of Land: A Citizens' Policy Guide to Urban Growth, A Task Force Report Sponsored by the Rockefeller Brothers' Fund, William K. Reilley, ed., New York: Thomas Y. Crowell & Co., 1973.

Law, Institutions, and the Global Environment, A Joint Conference of the American Society of International Law and the Carnegie Endowment, September 1971. John Lawrence Hargrave, ed., Dobbs Ferry, N.Y.: Oceana Publications, 1972.

Legalized Pollution, The Report of the Brisbane Public Interest Research Group, St. Lucia: University of Queensland Press, 1973.

Man: An Endangered Species, Lawrence M. Gress, ed., from material prepared by the United States Department of the Interior, Woodridge, Conn.: Apollo Books, 1972.

Man and the Environment, Wes Jackson, ed., Dubuque: William C. Brown Pub. Co., 1971.

The Fitness of Man's Environment, Smithsonian Institution Annual Symposium, February 16–18, 1967, New York: Harper Colophon, 1970.

Man's Impact on the Global Environment: Assessment and Recommendations for Action, Report of the Study of Critical Environmental Problems, Massachusetts Institute of Technology, Cambridge, Mass.: The MIT Press, 1970.

Management and Control of Growth: Issues, Techniques, Problems, Trends, Randall W. Scott with David J. Brower and Dallas D. Miner, eds., Washington, D.C.: Urban Land Institute, 1975, 3 vols.

Managing the Water Environment, Neil A. Swainson, ed., Vancouver: University of British Columbia Press with the Wastewater Research Center, 1976.

Great Lakes Megalopolis: From Civilization to Ecumenization, Alexander B. Leman and Ingrid A. Leman, eds., based on proceedings of the Great Lakes Megalopolis Symposion, March 24–27, 1975, Ottawa: Ministry of State, Urban Affairs, Canada, 1976.

No Deposit-No Return: Man and His Environment: A View Toward Survival, Anthology of Papers at 13th National Conference, U.S. National Commission for UNESCO, November 1969, Huey D. Johnson, ed., Reading, Mass.: Addison-Wesley Pub. Co., 1970.

Pacem in Maribus, Elisabeth Mann Borgese, ed., New York: Dodd, Mead & Co., 1972.

*Public Planning and Control of Urban and Land Development, Donald G. Hagman, ed., St. Paul: West Publishing Co., 1973.

SMOG, a Report to the People, Pasadena: Environmental Quality Laboratory, California Institute of Technology, 1972.

*Cases and Materials on Water Law, Frank Trelease, editor, 2nd ed., St. Paul: West Publishing Co., 1974.

Western Man and Environmental Ethics, Ian Barbour, ed., Reading, Mass.: Addison-Wesley Publishing Co., 1973.

* World Eco-Crisis: International Organizations in Response, David A. Kay and Eugene B. Skolnikoff, eds. Madison: University of Wisconsin Press, 1972.

Voices for the Wilderness, William Schwarz, ed., from the Sierra Club Wilderness Conferences 1960–1966, New York: Ballantine Books, 1969.

Andrews, Richard N. L., *Environmental Policy and Administrative Change*, Lexington, Mass.: D. C. Heath & Co., 1976.

*Anderson, Frederick R., with Robert H. Daniels, *NEPA in the Courts: A Legal Analysis of the National Environmental Policy Act*, Baltimore: The Johns Hopkins Press for Resources for the Future, 1973.

Aron, Raymond, *The Industrial Society: Three Essays on Ideology and Development*, New York: Frederick Praeger, 1967.

**Arrow, Kenneth J., *Social Choice and Individual Values*, New York: John Wiley & Sons, 1951.

Arvill, Robert, pseud., *Man and Environment: Crisis and the Strategy of Choice*, Baltimore: Penguin, rev. ed., 1969.

Baker, O. E., Ralph Borsodi, M. L. Wilson, *Agriculture in Modern Life*, New York: Harper Bros., 1939.

Banfield, Edward C., *The Unheavenly City: The Nature and the Future of Our Urban Crisis*, Boston: Little, Brown & Co., 1970.

*Barnett, Harold J., and Chandler Morse, *Scarcity and Growth: The Economics of Natural Resource Availability*, Baltimore: Published for Resources for the Future by the Johns Hopkins Press, 1963.

*Barone, Enrico, " Ministro della Produzione nello Stato Collectivista," (1908), reprinted and translated in an Appendix to F. A. von Hayek, *Collectivist Economic Planning*, London: G. Routledge & Sons, 1935; New York: Augustus M. Kelley, 1967.

Bateson, Gregory, *Steps to an Ecology of Mind*, New York: Chandler Publishing Co., 1972.

Baumol, William, Book Review, 85 *Yale Law Journal* (1976), 441–446.

Baxter, William F., *People Not Penguins*, New York: Columbia University Press, 1973.

Bernarde, Melvin A., *Our Precarious Habitat: An Integrated Approach to Understanding Man's Effect on His Environment*, New York: W. W. Norton & Co., Inc., 1970.

**Bensman, Joseph, and Bernard Rosenberg, *Mass, Class, and Bureaucracy*, Englewood Cliffs, N.J.: Prentice-Hall, 1963.

*Borgstrom, Georg, *The Hungry Planet, The Modern World at the Edge of Famine*, rev. ed., New York: Collier Books, 1967.

*Bosselman, Fred P., and David Callies, *The Quiet Revolution in Land Use Control*, Washington, D.C.: GPO, 1972.

*Buchanan, James M., *The Limits of Liberty: Between Anarchy and Leviathan*, Chicago: University of Chicago Press, 1975.

**Calabresi, Guido and A. D. Melamed, "Protecting Entitlement: Property Rules, Liability Rules and Inalienability," 85 *Harvard Law Review* (1972), 1089–1128.

*Caldwell, Lynton Keith, *Environment: A Challenge to Modern Society*, Garden City: Natural History Press, 1970.

Caldwell, Lynton K., Lynton R. Hayes, and Isabel M. MacWhirter, *Citizens and the Environment: Case Studies in Popular Action*, Bloomington: Indiana University Press, 1976.

*Caudill, Henry M., *Night Comes to the Cumberlands: A Biography of a Depressed Area*, Boston: Little, Brown & Co., 1963.

Caudill, Henry M., *My Land Is Dying*, New York: E. F. Dutton Co., 1973.

Caudill, Henry M., *A Darkness at Dawn: Appalachian Kentucky and the Future*, Lexington: University Press of Kentucky, 1976.

Caudill, Henry M., *The Watches of the Night*, Boston: Little, Brown & Co., 1976.

**Coase, Ronald H., "The Problem of Social Cost," 3 *Journal of Law and Economics* (1960), 1–44, widely reprinted.

Cohen, Harry, *The Demonics of Bureaucracy: Problems of Change in a Government Agency*, Ames, Iowa: Iowa State University Press, 1965.

*Colinvaux, Paul, *Introduction to Ecology*, New York: John Wiley & Sons, 1973.

Commoner, Barry, "The World Environment: A Zero-Sum Game," Washington *Post*, June 4, 1972.

Commoner, Barry, *The Closing Circle*, New York: Alfred A. Knopf, 1972.

Commoner, Barry, *The Poverty of Power*, New York: Alfred A. Knopf, 1976.

*Crocker, Thomas D., and A. J. Rogers III, *Environmental Economics*, Hinsdale, Ill.: Dryden Press, 1971.

**Crozier, Michel, *The Bureaucratic Phenomenon*, Chicago: University of Chicago Press, 1964.

Crozier, Michel, *The Stalled Society*, New York: The Viking Press, 1973,

Crozier, Michel, and others, *The Crisis of Democracy*, A Report for the Tripartite Commission, New York: New York University Press, 1975.

Dahl, Robert A., *Polyarchy*, New Haven: Yale University Press, 1971.

*Dahl, Robert A., and Charles E. Lindblom, *Politics, Economics, and Welfare*, New York: Harper & Brothers, 1953.

*Dales, J. H., *Pollution, Property and Prices: An Essay in Policy-Making and Economics*, Toronto: University of Toronto Press, 1968.

*Dasmann, Raymond, *A Different Kind of Country*, New York: Collier Books, 1970.

*Davis, Peter N., "Theories of Water Pollution Litigation," 1971 *Wisconsin Law Review*, 738–816.

Douglas, William O., *The Three Hundred Years War*, New York: Random House, 1972.

**Doxiadis, C. A., *Ekistics: An Introduction to the Science of Human Settlements*, New York: Oxford University Press, 1968.

Doxiadis, C. A., and J. G. Papaioannou, *Ecumenopolis: The Inevitable City of the Future*, New York: W. W. Norton & Co., 1975.

Drucker, Peter F., *The End of Economic Man*, New York: John Day Co., 1939.

**Dubos, René, *The Mirage of Health*, World Perspectives Series, Ruth Nanda Anshen, ed., New York: Harper & Brothers, 1959.

**Dubos, René, *Man Adapting*, New Haven: Yale University Press, 1965.

Dubos, René J., " Civilizing Technology " in *Essays in Honor of David Lyall Patrick*, Tucson: University of Arizona Press, 1971.

Dubos, René, *A God Within*, New York: Charles Scribner's Sons, 1972.

Eckhoff, Torstein, *Justice: Its Determinants in Social Interaction*, Rotterdam: Rotterdam University Press, 1974.

Eckholm, Erik P., for the Worldwatch Institute, *Losing Ground: Environmental Stress and World Food Prospects*, New York: W. W. Norton & Co., 1976.

Ellickson, Robert C., "A Ticket to Thermidor: A Commentary on the Proposed California Coastal Plan," 49 *Southern California Law Review* (1976), 715–736.

**Engels, Friedrich, *Dialectics of Nature*, tr., by Clemens Dutt, New York: International Publishers, 1940.

*Falk, Richard A., *This Endangered Planet: Prospects and Proposals for Human Survival*, New York: Random House, 1971.

Falk, Richard A., *A Study of Future Worlds*, Intro. by Saul Mendlovitz, New York: Free Press, 1975.

Feeley, Malcom M., "The Concept of Laws in Social Science: A Critique and Notes on an Expanded View," 10 *Law and Society Review* (1976), 497–523.

Fiser, Webb S., *Mastery of the Metropolis*, Englewood Cliffs, N.J.: Prentice-Hall, Inc., 1962.

Forbes, R. J., *The Conquest of Nature: Technology and Its Consequences*, New York: Mentor, 1969.

Friedman, Alan E., "The Economics of the Common Pool: Property Rights in Exhaustible Resources," 18 *University of California at Los Angeles Law Review* (1971), 855–887.

Friedmann, Wolfgang, *The Future of the Oceans*, New York: George Braziller, 1971.

Furnas, C. C., *The Next Hundred Years: The Unfinished Business of Science*, New York: Reynal & Hitchcock for Williams & Wilkins, 1936.

Goldschmidt, Walter, *Man's Way: A Preface to the Understanding of Human Society*, Cleveland: World Publishing Co., 1959.

**Goodman, Paul and Percival, *Communitas: Ways of Livelihood and Means of Life*, rev. ed., New York: Random House, 1960.

*Gordon, Lincoln, "Limits to the Growth Debate," *RFF Resources*, No. 52, Summer 1976, 1–7.

Green, Harold P., "Public Policy for Genetic Manipulation: A View from the Law," Program in Policy Studies in Science and Technology, The George Washington University, Occasional Paper No. 1, (March 1969), reissued at NTIS, PB 192 457 (August 10, 1972).

Gulick, Luther Halsey, *The Metropolitan Problem and American Ideas*, New York: Alfred A. Knopf, 1962.

Harris, Marshall, *Legal-Economic Aspects of Waste Law As It Relates to Farming*, Monograph No. 13 with Economic Research Service U.S.D.A., Iowa City: Agricultural Law Center, University of Iowa, December 1974.

*Harris, Marshall, "The Institutional-Legal Face of the Environmental Coin," 54 *Nebraska Law Review* (1975), 299–314.

*Hart, Gary Warren, "Institutions for Water Planning – Institutional Arrangements: River Basin Commissions, Inter-Agency Committees, and Ad Hoc Coordinating Committees," part of Legal Study No. 13 for the United States National Water Commission, September 1971, issued by MTIS PB 204/244.

Hart, H. L. A., "Bentham on Legal Powers," 81 *Yale Law Journal* (1972), 799–822.

Healy, Robert G., *Land Use and the States*, Baltimore: The Johns Hopkins Press for Resources for the Future, 1976.

Henning, Daniel H., *Environmental Policy and Administration*, New York: American Elsevier Publishing Co., 1974.

**Higbee, Edward, *Farms and Farmers in an Urban Age*, New York: The Twentieth Century Fund, 1963.

**Hirshleifer, Jack, James C. De Haven, Jerome W. Milliman, *Water Supply: Economics, Technology, and Policy*, new ed., Chicago: University of Chicago Press, 1969.

Howton, F. William, *Functionaries*, Chicago: Quadrangle Books, 1969.

**Hurst, J. Willard, *The Legitimacy of the Business Corporation in the Law of the United States, 1780–1970*, Charlottesville: The University Press of Virginia, 1970. The author has been especially influenced by the writings of Professor Hurst.

Illich, Ivan, *Tools for Conviviality*, World Perspective Series, Ruth Nanda Anshen, ed., New York: Harper & Row, 1973.

Illich, Ivan, *Energy and Equity*, New York: Harper & Row, 1974.

**John, Eric, *Land Tenure in Early England*, Leicester: Leicester University Press, 1960.

Johnson, M. Bruce, "Some Observations on the Economics of the California Coastal Plan," 49 *Southern California Law Review* (1976), 749–758.

Kahn, Herman, William Brown, Leon Martel, with the Hudson Institute, *The Next 200 Years: A Scenario for America and the World*, New York: William Morrow & Co., 1976.

Kelly, Katie, *Garbage: The History and Future of Garbage in America*, New York: Saturday Review Press, 1973.

*Kneese, Allen V., *Water Pollution: Economic Aspects and Research Needs*, Washington, D.C.: Resources for the Future, 1962.

Kneese, Allen V., Robert U. Ayres, Ralph D'Arge, *Economics and the Environment: A Materials Balance Approach*, Washington, D.C.: Resources for the Future, 1970.

Knight, Frank H., *The Economic Organization*, New York: Harper Torchbook, 1965.

Landis, James P., "The Impact of the Income Tax Laws on the Energy Crisis: Oil and Congress Don't Mix," 64 *California Law Review* (1976), 1040–1084.

Landy, Marc Karnis, *The Politics of Environmental Reform: Controlling Kentucky Strip Mining*, Washington, D.C.: Resources for the Future, Inc., 1976.

Large, Donald W., "Is Anybody Listening? The Problem of Access in Environmental Litigation," 1972 *Wisconsin Law Review*, 62–113.

Large, Donald, "This Land Is Whose Land? Changing Concepts of Property?", 1973 *Wisconsin Law Review*, 1039–1083.

Lederberg, Joshua, "The Freedoms and the Control of Science," 45 *Southern California Law Review* (1972), 596–614.

Leontieff, Wassily, and others, *The Future of the World Economy*, United Nations Department of Economic and Social Affairs, 1976. (Known to this author only through summaries in the New York *Times*.)

Lewallen, John, *Ecology of Devastation: Indochina*, Baltimore: Penguin, 1971.

Like, Irving, "The National Environmental Policy Act and Technology Assessment," 6 *Lincoln Law Review* (1970), 23–49.

Like, Irving, "Multi-Media Confrontation – The Environmentalists' Strategy for a 'No-Win' Agency Proceeding," 1 *Ecology Law Quarterly* (1971), 495–518.

Lillard, Richard G., *Eden in Jeopardy: Man's Prodigal Meddling With His Environment: The Southern California Experience*, New York: Alfred A. Knopf, 1966.

**Lopez Ibor, Juan Jose, *Rasgos Neuroticos del Mundo Contemporaneo*, 2nd ed., Madrid: Educ. Cultura Hispanica, 1968.

Lord, Russell, *The Care of the Earth: A History of Husbandry*, New York: Thomas Nelson & Sons, 1962.

Loth, David, and Morris L. Ernst, *The Taming of Technology*, New York: Simon and Schuster, 1972.

Lucas, F. L., *The Greatest Problem and Other Essays*, New York: The MacMillan Co., 1961.

Lukacs, John, *Historical Consciousness, or the Remembered Past*, New York: Harper & Row, 1968.

Lukacs, John, *The Passing of the Modern Age*, New York: Harper & Row, 1970.

McHale, John, *The Ecological Context*, New York: George Braziller, 1970.

Maddox, John, *The Doomsday Syndrome*, New York: McGraw-Hill Book Co., 1972.

Martin, Roscoe C., Frank J. Munger, and others, *Decisions in Syracuse: A Metropolitan Action Study*, Bloomington: Indiana University Press, 1961.

Marx, Wesley, *The Frail Ocean*, New York: Coward-McCann, 1967.

Mazor, Lester, "The Crisis of Liberal Legalism," 81 *Yale Law Journal* (1972), 1032–1053.

Meadows, Donnella and Dennis, Jørgen Randers, and W. W. Behrens III, *The Limits of Growth*, the 1st Report of the Club of Rome, New York: Universe Books, 1972.

*Mellor, John W., *The New Economics of Growth: A Strategy for India and the Developing World*, A Twentieth Century Fund Study, Ithaca: Cornell University Press, 1976.

Melmin, Seymour, *Our Depleted Society*, New York: Holt, Rinehart & Winston, 1965.

Mesarovic, Michajlo, and Eduard Postel, *Mankind at the Turning Point*, the 2nd Report of the Club of Rome, New York: E. F. Dutton, 1974.

Missenard, André, *In Search of Man*, tr., by Laurence G. Blochman, New York: Hawthorne Books, 1957.

Mundell, Robert A., *Man and Economics*, New York: McGraw-Hill Book Co., 1968.

**Mumford, Lewis, *The City in History: Its Origins, Its Transformations, and Its Prospects*, New York: Harcourt, Brace & World, Inc., 1961.

Murphy, Earl Finbar, *Water Purity, A Study in Legal Control of Natural Resources*, Madison: University of Wisconsin Press, 1961.

Murphy, Earl Finbar, *Governing Nature*, Chicago: Quadrangle Books, 1967.

Murphy, Earl Finbar, "A Law for Life," 1969 *Wisconsin Law Review*, 773–787, reprinted in 1970 *Environment Law Review*, 3–20 and Law and Society Reprint No. 46 (1970).

Murphy, Earl Finbar, "Has Nature Any Right to Life?", 22 *Hastings Law Journal* (1971), 467–484.

Murphy, Earl Finbar, *Man and His Environment: Law*, New York: Harper & Row, 1971.

Newsom, George, and J. Graham Sherratt, *Water Pollution*, Altrincham: John Sherratt & Son, Ltd., 1972.

*Nicholson, Max, *The Environmental Revolution: A Guide for the New Masters of the Earth*, New York: McGraw-Hill Book Co., 1970.

**Noyes, C. Reinold, *The Institution of Property*, New York: Longmans, Green & Co., 1936.

**Odum, Howard, *Environment, Power and Society*, New York: John Wiley & Co., 1971.

Osborn, Fairfield, *The Limits of the Earth*, Boston: Little, Brown & Co., 1953.

Osvald, Hugo, *The Earth Can Feed Us*, Intro. by Lord Boyd-Orr, tr. by B. Nesfield-Cookson, South Brunswick, N.J.: A. G. Barnes & Co., 1966.

Park, Charles F., Jr., with Margaret C. Freeman, *Earthbound: Minerals, Energy, and Man's Future*, San Francisco: Freeman, Cooper & Co., 1975.

*Pen, Jan, *Modern Economics*, tr. by Trevor Preston, Baltimore: Penguin, 1965 (first Dutch edition 1958).

Perls, Lewis J., "Ecology's Missing Price Tag," *Wall St. Journal*, August 10, 1976.

Ramo, Simon, *Cure for Chaos: Fresh Solutions to Social Problems Through the Systems Approach*, New York: David McKay Co., 1969.

Ramsay, William, and Claude Anderson, *Managing the Environment: An Economic Primer*, New York: Basic Books, 1972.

Rienow, Robert, with Leona Train Rienow, *Man Against His Environment*, New York: Sierra Club/Ballantine, 1970.

*Roberts, Marc J., "River Basin Authorities: A National Solution to Water Pollution", 83 *Harvard Law Review* (1970), 1527–1556.

Romains, Jules, *As It Is On Earth*, tr. by Richard Howard, New York: The MacMillan Co., 1962.

*Sakharov, Andrei D., *Progress, Coexistence and Intellectual Freedom*, Intro. by Harrison E. Salisbury, New York: W. W. Norton Co., 1970.

Sakharov, Andrei D., *Sakharov Speaks*, Harrison E. Salisbury, ed., New York: Alfred A. Knopf, 1974.

Schaeffer, Francis A., *Pollution and the Death of Man: The Christian View of Ecology*, Wheaton, Ill.: Tyndale House, 1970.

Schattschneider, E. E., *The Semisovereign People: A Realist's View of Democracy in America*, New York: Holt, Rinehart & Winston, 1960.

Schon, Donald A., *Beyond the Stable State*, New York: W. W. Norton Co., 1971.

Shepard, Paul, *Man in the Landscape: A Historic View of the Esthetics of Nature*, New York: Alfred A. Knopf, 1967.

Smith, Frank E., *The Politics of Conservation*, new ed., New York: Harper Colophon, 1971.

Spengler, Joseph J., "Economic Growth in a Stationary Population," *Ekistics*, whole no. 200, July 1972, 17–20.

*Stigler, George J., *The Citizen and the State: Essays on Regulation*, Chicago: University of Chicago Press, 1975.

*Stone, Christopher, *Do Trees Have Standing?*, Los Angeles: William Kaufman & Co., 1974.

Tarlock, A. Dan, "Recent Developments in the Recognition of Instream Uses in Western Water Law," 1975 *Utah Law Review*, 871–903.

Taylor, Gordon Rattray, *The Doomsday Book: Can the World Survive?*, Greenwich, Conn.: Fawcett Crest, 1970.

**Teissier du Cros, André, *L'Innovation pour une morale du changement*, Paris: Robert Laffont, 1971.

Thomas, Lewis, "Germs," *Yale Alumni Review* (March 1973), vol. XXXVI, no. 6, p. 8.

Thompson, William Irwin, *Passages About Earth: An Exploration of the New Planetary Culture*, New York: Harper & Row, 1974.

Tinbergen, Jan, *RIO, Reshaping the International Order*, the 3rd Report of the Club of Rome, New York: E. F. Dutton Co., 1976.

Tribe, Laurence H., "Technology Assessment and the Fourth Discontinuity: The Limits of Instrumental Rationality," 46 *Southern California Law Review* (1973), 617–660.

Vacca, Roberto, *The Coming Dark Age*, tr. by J. S. Whale, New York: Doubleday & Co., 1973.

Vogt, William, *Road to Survival*, New York: William Sloane Associates, 1948.

Vogt, William, *People! Challenge to Survival*, New York: William Sloane Associates, 1960.

**von Ciriacy-Wantrup, Siegfried, *Resource Conservation: Economics and Policies*, rev. ed., Berkeley: University of California, Division of Agricultural Sciences, Agricultural Experiment Station, 1963.

von Mises, Ludwig, *Planned Chaos*, Irvington-on-Hudson: Foundation for Economic Education, 1947.

von Mises, Ludwig, *Bureaucracy*, 2nd ed., New Haven: Yale University Press, 1962.

**Wagner, Philip, *The Human Use of the Earth*, New York: Free Press, 1960.

Ward, Barbara, and René Dubos, with the Committee of Corresponding Consultants to the United Nations Conference on the Human Environment, *Only One Earth: The Care and Maintenance of a Small Planet*, New York: W. W. Norton & Co., 1972.

Watt, Kenneth E. F., *Ecology and Resource Management*, New York: McGraw-Hill Book Co., 1968.

*Watt, Kenneth E. F., *The Titanic Effect: Planning for the Unthinkable*, Stamford: Sinauer Associates, 1974.

Watt, Kenneth E. F., J. W. Brewer, and others in the Interdisciplinary Systems Group, *Land Use, Energy Flow, and Decision Making in Human Society* (December 1974) and *Land Use, Energy Flow, and Policy Making in Society* (September 1975), Davis, Cal.: Institute of Ecology, University of California, Davis, 1974–1975.

*Wenner, Lettie M., "Enforcement of Water Pollution Control Law," 6 *Law and Society Review* (1972), 481–507.

**Wenner, Lettie McSpadden, *One Environment Under Law: A Public-Policy Dilemma*, Pacific Palisades: Goodyear Publishing Co., 1976.

*White, Lynn, Jr., *Medieval Technology and Social Change*, New York: Oxford University Press, 1962.

**Zimmermann, Erich, *World Resources and Industries: A Functional Appraisal of the Availability of Agricultural and Industrial Materials*, rev. ed., New York: Harper Bros., 1951 abridged as *Introduction to World Resources*, Henry Hunker, ed., New York: Harper & Row, 1964.

Zwick, David, and Marcy Benstock, *Water Wasteland: Ralph Nader's Study Group Report on Water Pollution*, New York: Grossman Publishers, 1971.

Index

311

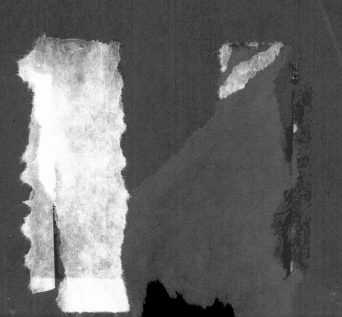

Wendelin Van Draanen

How I Survived Being a Girl

HarperCollins*Publishers*

Special thanks to my husband, Mark Parsons,
for his undying support and enthusiasm,
and to Nancy Siscoe,
who has believed in me from the beginning

How I Survived Being a Girl
Copyright © 1997 by Wendelin Van Draanen Parsons
Printed in the United States of America. For information address
HarperCollins Children's Books, a division of HarperCollins Publishers,
10 East 53rd Street, New York, NY 10022.

Library of Congress Cataloging-in-Publication Data
Draanen, Wendelin Van.
How I survived being a girl / Wendelin Van Draanen.
    p.   cm.
Summary: Twelve-year-old Carolyn, who has always wished she were a boy, begins to see things
in a new light when her sister is born.
    ISBN 0-06-026671-6. — ISBN 0-06-026672-4 (lib. bdg.)
    [1. Self-acceptance—Fiction.   2. Brothers and sisters—Fiction.   3. Family life—Fiction.]
I. Title.
PZ7.D779Ho   1997   96-14565
[Fic]—dc20   CIP
                                                                                        AC

Design by Alison Donalty
8   9   10
❖
First Edition

*Dedicated with love and gratitude
to my parents, Peter and Mieske Van Draanen
and my siblings, Mark, Arlen, and Nanine*

CONTENTS

SCHOOL

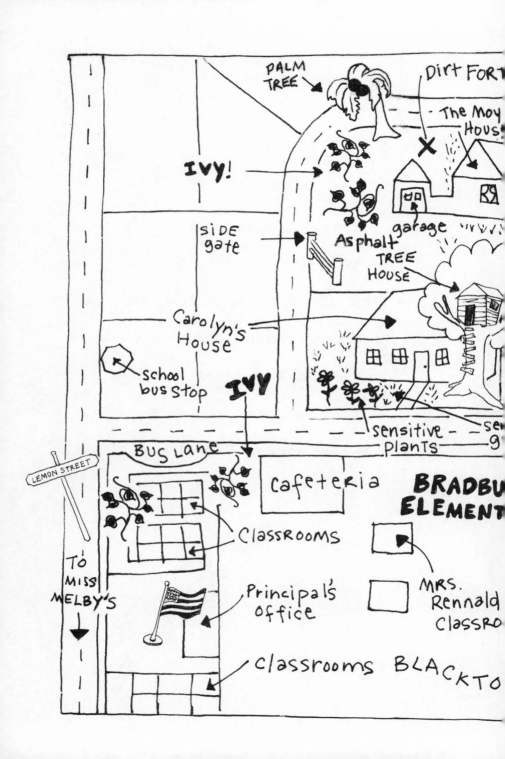

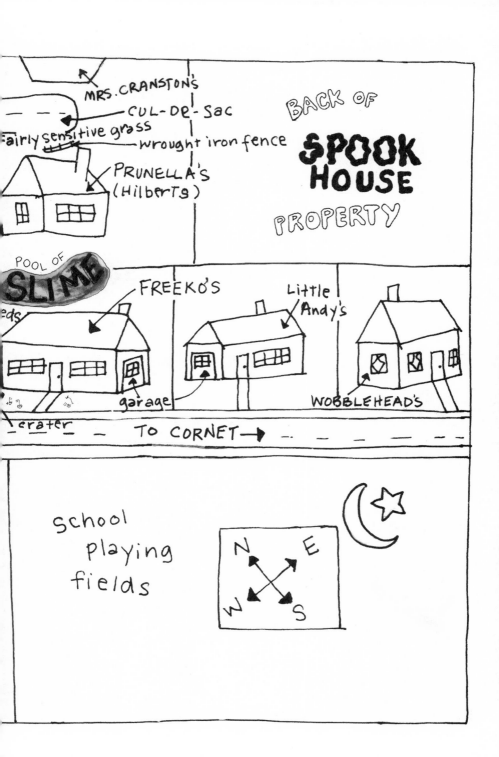

So you See . . .

Things had been a certain way since I could remember and then all of a sudden they were just different. Anybody else would tell you things were the same as they'd always been, but they weren't.

It happened about the time Nancy came along, and there are probably a lot of people who think she should've come sooner. They say she's the one who tamed me a bit—even made me quit wishing I was a boy.

Course, Charlie might've had something to do with that, too. . . .

SUMMER

chapter 1
The Freekos

Jack and Allen didn't help matters much. Picking on me and all. Just something brothers do, I guess. Call you names. Pound on you. And worst of all, ditch you. Now, it's one thing to get ditched because you're whiny or slow or a big-mouth. It's another thing to get ditched because you're a girl.

Things started looking up, though, when Jack decided he'd ditch Allen too. Billy and the boys were always ditching their little brothers, and Billy being Jack's best friend, well, you know how it is.

So Allen and I started hanging around together more, and one of the things we did a lot of was spying. Spying's great fun. It gets the blood pumping, *ba-boom! ba-boom! ba-boom!*, right up in your ears so you almost can't hear anything else.

Everyone knows that when you go spying, you've got to wear dark clothes, and most people think that's because you want to be able to hide, which is true, but dark clothes also put you in the *mood*, and there's nothing better than being in a spying mood.

One night we tossed our beanies out the window and told Mom we were going across the street to the school to play hide-and-seek with some friends. She said that was just fine without even looking up from her knitting, and Dad was busy wrestling with the wiring of a lamp, so it was no problem slipping by him.

Allen wanted to go clear down to the Spook House, but I convinced him we ought to see what was happening over at the Freekos'.

The Freekos were easy to spy on, and we never felt bad about doing it because they weren't very nice people. They hated us way before we ever *thought* about spying on them.

When I say spying on them was easy, I mean *easy*. Normally we spy on people doing stuff in their yards. We don't go looking in just anyone's windows! But the Freekos didn't have drapes, so you could go right up to the window and peek inside. Now, you may think that's not very nice of us, and you're right, but you have to understand that when you've got neighbors like the Freekos, you find yourself doing stuff you know you shouldn't, and pretty soon you just get carried away.

Anyway, Allen and I peeked in the front windows and then in the kitchen window, but we didn't see anybody, and it's not much fun spying on a sink full of dishes. So we looked over the back fence, and boy did that make our eyes pop open! Freeko was lying on his stomach by the pool in a pair of old underwear and he wasn't moving. Not at all.

Allen looked at me and whispered, "Is he dead?"

Well, he sure looked dead to me, and all I wanted to do was get out of there. I whispered back, "I don't know!" and was just about to say we should leave when Allen started to climb over the fence. I grabbed him and said, "What are you *doing?*"

He looked over his shoulder. "Don't you want to find out if he's dead?"

I didn't want my little brother thinking I was a sissy, so before he could start climbing again, I scrambled over the fence and whispered, "Hurry up!"

We went around the pool over to where Freeko was. Well, it's not a pool like you're used to thinking of. It's got water in it, but you wouldn't want to swim in it unless you were a snake or a frog or something that liked slime.

Anyhow, we got up to Freeko and looked at him for a couple minutes trying to figure out if he was breathing or not. That wasn't easy to do, because he was lying facedown on the cement. I tried to get in close to Freeko's face to see if there was any air going in and out, but all I could really see was his stubbly cheek. Everything else was kind of smashed into the cement, which made me think that maybe he *was* dead, because no one could actually sleep like that.

Then Allen poked him with his foot. Freeko groaned and rolled over, which spooked me so bad I almost fell into the pool. Freeko kind of sputtered and started snoring real loud, his stomach going up and down, up and down, with little rocks from the cement kind of stuck to it.

Allen looked at me and said, "Why's he sleeping out *here*?" but before I could come up with an answer, we heard the sliding glass door open and had to scramble and hide behind a trash can.

Well, Fattabutta came swooping out of the house wearing one of her muumuus. She poked Freeko right in the ribs with her foot and cursed at him something fierce. Freeko mumbled but went right back to sleep, so Fattabutta picked up this booze bottle that was bobbing in the pool and used it to scoop slimy water on him.

Just then we heard Dad calling, "Jack, Carolyn, and Al-len!" which made my heart stop. We couldn't go *any*where with Fattabutta right there.

So we were still watching Fattabutta splashing and cursing and waving the bottle around in the air when it came again, "Jack, Carolyn, and Al-len!"

I grabbed Allen in case he was thinking of making a break for it, and we just watched as Freeko got up on his knees and started crawling toward the house like some kind of gigantic snail. Fattabutta walked behind him, cursing and emptying the bottle on his back.

Just as Freeko was getting up on his feet, we heard, "Carolyn! Allen!" and Dad was sounding pretty mad.

The minute Fattabutta was in the house, we climbed over the fence, popped down into our own backyard, and raced for the back door. I tried to catch my breath and act normal, calling, "We're home!"

Dad was on the verge of being mad, but you could tell he wasn't quite there yet. "Where have you two been? Your mother was getting worried," which is what my dad always says when he's the one who's worried.

I smiled and said, "Sorry! We came as fast as we could."

He frowned a little, but all he said was "Well, it's bedtime."

Allen and I said, *"Already?"* so he wouldn't get suspicious, and then moaned and groaned and headed down to the bathroom to brush our teeth.

We were in the middle of brushing when Jack barged in. Jack always barges in. Even when it's locked. He does this little maneuver with the lock, and *snap*, he's in.

And you could tell something was really bugging him. He put some toothpaste on his brush and said, "Where'd you go?"

Now, I wasn't about to say. He was the one who wanted to go off with Billy instead of us, so let it bug him. But Allen blurted out, "Spying!" I just scrubbed my teeth hoping Allen wouldn't say more, but sure enough he piped up with "We went to—"

So I spit my toothpaste out fast and said, "What's it to you? You didn't want to come with us *sissies*, remember?"

Jack just pretended I wasn't in the room and said to Allen, "So who'd you spy on?"

Allen said, "Freeko! We went back there 'cause we thought he was dead!"

That made Jack quit brushing for a minute. "Dead?"

I couldn't help it. "Yeah! He was just lying out there by the pool, so we decided to kick him to see if he was dead or not."

Jack's eyes bugged out. "You *kicked* him?"

Well, that really got Allen going. He told him all about it, adding a little as he went, if you know what I mean.

Jack looked at us for a minute and said, "I don't believe you," and stood there scrubbing his teeth way more than he needed to.

I knew this was just his way of not having to say anything else, so I said, "What did *you* do tonight?"

Jack scrubbed some more but finally decided he couldn't do that all night. He rinsed his mouth and said, "Nothing," and left. Just like that.

Allen gave me a big grin. "You want to go spying again tomorrow?"

I grinned back and said, "Sure," because it feels

nice, having your brother want to go spying with you.

Then he said, "Do you think Jack'll want to come?"

Well of course I thought he would, but I told Allen that if we really wanted him to come, we'd have to be careful and ask him just right so he *didn't* think we wanted him to come.

Brothers can be complicated that way.

chapter 2
The Moyers

The Freekos are our neighbors on one side, and since we live on the corner we don't have neighbors on the other side. What we do have is neighbors right behind us, and that's the Moyers.

The Moyer family is a lot like ours. They have three kids just like we do: Will is Allen's age—they're in fourth grade—and Charlie and I are both in sixth, but their girl, Mary, is a little bit older than Jack. She's in high school and has never been interested in playing with any of us.

What I know about Mary is that she loves her cat and has a best friend named Laura. When I'm over at the Moyers', I see her around, but usually she and Laura lock themselves up in Mary's room and talk about boys or cats or whatever.

So I was pretty surprised when Will and Charlie came over and told us their sister was going to put on a talent show and that we were invited. Well, I was surprised until I found out it was going to cost me fifty cents to watch. I told them to forget it. Then they told me Mary was going to strip. Now, I couldn't quite believe that, but they promised, and I figured I had to see it for myself.

It didn't take long for the whole neighborhood to be talking about it, and the afternoon of the show these benches Will and Charlie put out in front of their garage door were just crammed full of kids.

Finally the garage door swung open and Laura came out from behind these sheets that they'd nailed to the rafters. She was dressed in this weird suit and black hat and announced that the talent show was about to begin. So we all quit squirming and hushed up. Then Laura and Mary started doing really dumb dances and baton twirls to this record that skipped so much that they had to go over and bump the needle every couple seconds.

This went on for a while, and then someone started booing. Pretty soon a lot of people were booing, and I joined in. I mean, I paid fifty cents to see this show. At our house fifty cents is what you get for picking two big bags of weeds, and I didn't stuff two grocery bags with weeds so I could watch some dumb dances and listen to a skipping record.

All that booing made them stop the record and

whisper for a little while before announcing that it was time for Mary to strip. Of course that made everyone quit booing and start clapping. So they turned the lights in the garage off and some different music came on. Laura stood there, still wearing that stupid black hat, and asked us if we were ready. We all hooted and hollered and clapped, so she pulled back the sheets to uncover this big piece of plywood.

No one wanted to boo yet, just in case, and in a few minutes clothes started coming over the top of the plywood. First shoes and socks, and finally a blouse and a skirt. A couple of the older guys whistled, but I thought it was pretty dumb.

Finally Laura made the big announcement that Mary was naked on the other side and did we want to see? Everyone started hooting and hollering, so Laura announced, "One, two . . . three!" and moved the plywood for about as long as it takes to blink.

Well, they tried to make it quick, but it was easy to tell that Mary was wearing a skin-colored bikini. Charlie and Will brought down the garage door, and everyone started booing their heads off, hollering for their money back.

Of course they didn't give us our money back,

and when they finally got everyone to leave, we said we weren't ever coming back.

Trouble was we liked playing at the Moyers' house because there is always something going on. We play kickball and tag in their backyard a lot, and Mrs. Moyer never complains that we make too much noise like other moms would.

At the Moyers' they're always eating snacks— peanut butter and jelly sandwiches or hot dogs and chips—*good* food. If you go over there in the middle of the afternoon, you can usually find them eating something good and watching baseball.

Lots of times they offer us peanut butter sandwiches, but I always say, "No, thanks." It's more fun to watch them eat. They've got this way of eating sandwiches that's kind of gross, but you just can't help watching them, trying to figure out how the food stays in their mouths. See, they eat with their mouths open. I mean *wide* open. Especially Charlie. He'll take a bite of sandwich and then a swig of milk, and chew. And you can see the bread mixing with the peanut butter and squishing into the milk with little streaks of grape jelly pushing through now and then. And pretty soon it's one big mushy kind of tan paste squishing between his teeth. Then he stops chewing for a minute, swallows, takes a gulp of milk, and starts all over again. It's amazing.

But after a while you get bored with watching, or the sandwich is gone and all there is to do is look at the ball game on television. Allen can stand it longer than I can. I just get antsy and have to leave. Mrs. Moyer always says, "Leaving so soon?" and I always answer, real polite like, "Yeah," and let myself out.

So I guess I was friends with Charlie. I mean, we were in the same grade, and he probably would have invited me to do stuff with him and his friends all the time if it wasn't for the stupid fact that I was a girl. I didn't act like a girl. I didn't even look that much like a girl, because I kept my hair real short and wore boys' clothes any chance I got. It's just that I was a girl, and it made it kind of weird.

Anyhow, a couple of days after Mary's stupid talent show I went over to the Moyers' to find someone to play with, and Charlie had his friend Brent over. Brent lived in a different neighborhood, so he wasn't over all the time like some other kids, but I think Charlie and Brent were best friends.

Since Brent was over, I decided to see what Allen and Will were up to, but Brent called me back to Charlie's room and said, "Hey, Carolyn! Want to see Charlie in his jockeys?"

I was so embarrassed! I mean, Mrs. Moyer was right there in the dining room. Then he did it *again*. "Hey, Carolyn! Come here! This may be your only chance! Charlie's *naked*."

I just stared at Brent and said, "No! I don't want to see!"

He teased me some more and finally I told him to shut up and leave me alone. I mean, what was he thinking? That I've grown up with two brothers and have never seen a naked boy before?

Finally Charlie came out, all dressed, and told Brent to knock it off. He said I could go in his room if I wanted, but I just stood there like an idiot while he ducked into the bathroom to brush his teeth. Then Brent came up to me and said real nah-nah-nah-like, "Everyone knows you've got a crush on him."

That made me really mad. "Do not!"

He just grinned at me like only Brent can grin. It's a real nasty grin, and it made me want to punch his lights out. Instead I said, "Do not!" again, but when Charlie came out of the bathroom, I couldn't stand hanging around, thinking that he thought I had a crush on him. I ran out the door and scraped myself all up climbing over the back fence into our yard.

After that I went straight to my room and stared at my pillow for the longest time. I wished for a friend I could talk to. Like Allen had Will; like Charlie had Brent; like Jack had Billy. And I thought about the girls I knew in the neighborhood and how stupid it was being a girl. And I just stared at my pillowcase until I did what any sensible girl would do.

I cried.

chapter 3
Midgets and Mischief

The Freekos aren't the only ones in the neighborhood who are a little strange. It's just that with the
Freekos it's obvious. With the Hilberts you have to
look a little harder.

The Hilberts live around the corner, right next
door to the Moyers, and we never spy on the
Hilberts. Their curtains are always drawn, even in
the middle of the day, and they have this wrought-
iron fence that goes clear around their lot. Most
people don't fence in their front yards. Sure,
between yards there's some kind of divider, but up
along the sidewalk? No one but the Hilberts has
that.

I've never seen Mr. Hilbert. I don't even know
if there is a Mr. Hilbert. But I've seen Mrs. Hilbert
lots. Mostly in her car. She has this big brown car.
It has power steering and seats and windows and
everything, which she needs because she's so short.
She might even be a midget—I don't know. I don't
think I've ever seen her just standing. Well, there

was the time that her gate was actually open and I went up on a dare to ask if she wanted to buy Girl Scout cookies, which she didn't, but she was real nice about it. She answered the door and she was short all right, but I was down a step so I don't really know if she's a *midget* or not.

So when you see Mrs. Hilbert in her big old car, puttering up the cul-de-sac or back down the cul-de-sac, she always looks straight ahead, clutching the wheel with all her might, concentrating real hard on what she's doing. Mom says she's propped up on a stack of pillows so she can see out the window, and I've always wondered how she reaches the pedals.

Now, Mrs. Hilbert has a daughter, and her daughter goes to Bradbury Elementary just like the rest of us. She's in Allen's class and her name is Prunella, if you can believe that. Prunella Hilbert is not a name I would want for myself. It's bad enough being a girl without having a name like that. Anyhow, Prunella is short and pudgy, and she has one of those noses where the holes are up and out. You know, like a snout. When you look at Prunella, you can see right up her nose almost clear to her brains. If I had a nose like that, I'd worry about it being clean all the time. I don't know what I'd do if I had a cold. Probably stay home a lot.

Prunella isn't someone who comes out to play with the rest of the neighborhood kids. We play kickball at the end of the cul-de-sac, right in front of her house, and she never comes out, even to watch. I can't really picture Prunella playing kick-ball anyway. It can get pretty dusty, and you know what *that* does, even to a regular nose. Besides, I don't think she has any kickball clothes. She's always wearing these lacy dresses and Mary Janes. Shiny black Mary Janes. And she has all this hair. It goes past the middle of her back, all curled in ringlets with a bow somewhere or another. If my mom ever did that to me, I'd take the scissors to it myself! Lucky for me my mom likes my hair short. Sometimes when it's getting kind of long, she'll want to go and curl it, but I always throw a fit, so she winds up cutting it instead.

Long hair's okay, I guess, if you're into dolls. Seems like all girls with long hair play with dolls. Dolls are the most boring thing in the world. Even in the winter. Don't tell anyone, but I tried it once. I got a doll for Christmas from some aunt who didn't know me very well, because she thought I was just "precious." Anyhow, I tried playing with it after I was supposed to be in bed, but let me tell you, it was a waste of time. It wound up under my bed, and it stayed there until my mom came along and made me clean up my room.

I always figured Prunella had dolls—lots of dolls. And while the rest of the neighborhood was out playing kickball, she was probably in her room dressing her dolls and fixing their ribbons. So you can understand why I was pretty surprised one day when she pounded on our door and rang the door-bell nonstop at the same time.

I couldn't understand a word she was saying. Partly it was that nose, all flaring in and out like it was. Partly it was that she was just *babbling*. I wanted to get Mom, but she hadn't been feeling well and was taking a nap, so I wanted to make sure it was an emergency before I woke her up. I said, "Prunella! Stop it! What's the matter?"

She said, "Allen and Will!" and then a bunch of really fast words that I couldn't understand.

"What about them?" I asked, thinking she'd gone nuts.

"The car! They crashed the car!"

I just stared at her for a minute. I mean, it was

awfully warm out and I was thinking that maybe she just needed some lemonade. Finally I asked, "What do you mean? Whose car?"

Up and down jumped Prunella in her Mary Janes. "The Moyers'! Their new one!"

Well, Will's family *had* gotten a new station wagon a few days before, but I still thought she was nuts. "Prunella, what do you mean 'they crashed the car'? How could they crash a car?"

Those Mary Janes were flying. Like someone was turning a jump rope way too fast. She practically screamed, "They just did! They crashed the car. Right into our fence!"

Well, this I had to see. That would be some trick. I mean, Allen and Will were too *short* to crash a car. *I* was too short to crash a car. Then I remembered that Mrs. Hilbert had crashed their car once, so I thought, Well, if someone who was probably a midget crashed a car, then maybe Allen and Will did figure out a way to crash the Moyers' car after all.

I looked at Prunella stomping up and down and decided that she probably wouldn't be wanting any lemonade. I said, "Come on. Let's go," and closed the front door tight.

She came flying after me, squealing, "Wait! I'm supposed to get your mother."

I just hopped down the steps and said, "She isn't home."

"She isn't home? Where *is* she? She *has* to be home!"

I swear she was going to go back and take a look for herself, only I cut right across the front yard and hollered over my shoulder, "Well she's not," so she decided to chase after me instead.

We turned the corner, and from the top of the cul-de-sac I could see the Moyers' brand-new station wagon popped up over the curb with its nose scrunched into the Hilberts' wrought-iron fence. Mrs. Moyer was a little ahead of us, walking down the sidewalk really fast, and Allen and Will were scuffing at the rocks at the edge of the road looking like they'd already been whipped.

When we got down to the wreck, Prunella disappeared inside her house and Mrs. Moyer took Will by the ear and hollered at him a few minutes before spanking him. Right there in front of all the neighbors, *whack!* He didn't cry, but he came pretty close.

I ran up to Allen, who was pretty glad to see me, and whispered, "What *happened?*"

Allen looked sideways at the neighbors and said, "We crashed the car."

I knew that, but I tried to be nice about it and asked, "How?"

Allen was just about crying. "I don't know! We got in and started pushing all these buttons. It just started rolling! I tried to steer, but . . ." He looked at the fence lying there on that perfect lawn and just kind of shook his head.

So I said, "We'd better go get Mom," and we were starting up the street when Mrs. Moyer stopped us.

"Carolyn, where's your mother?" She was upset in a big way.

"We're going home to get her. Right now."

She looked at me and kind of raised an eyebrow. "Right away?"

I took Allen by the wrist and started pulling. "Yes, ma'am." Grown-ups always pull you by the wrist when they mean business, and I guess Mrs. Moyer liked the way I was tugging on Allen, because she let us go.

Well, Mom was already up, making herself a pot of tea, but she really looked like she should still be taking a nap. She didn't have any lipstick on and her hair was a mess. She just looked kind of pukey.

I asked her how she was feeling, but I guess I was too polite about it. She gave me one of those looks that grown-ups give you when you haven't said a thing yet but already they don't believe you.

She looked at us sideways while she scooped some tea into the pot. When the kettle started screeching, she poured boiling water into the tea-pot and said, "What have you two done." It wasn't really a question. It was more a statement of fact. Mothers are like that. I don't care how smooth you are, moms know when you've messed up. And this was the biggest mess any of us had ever been in.

I didn't think it was safe telling her while she was pouring boiling water, so I stalled. "Well, it's not that bad, really. . . ."

She put the lid on the teapot and looked at me with one eyebrow popped way up. "Oh?"

"It really was just an accident. . . ." I was think-ing that Allen should be the one telling her, only I was afraid he'd start crying before he got the story out. Then Mom would really be worried!

She moved the teapot over to the dining-room table, and I got her a hot pad to put under it. Allen kind of followed along, shivering like he was cold

or something. Mom said, "What was just an accident?"

She was sitting down and she wasn't pouring
tea yet, so I figured it was time. "You know the
Moyers' new station wagon?"

Mom nodded and then kind of froze, so I
decided to just come out with it. "Well, it was
parked on the street and Allen and Will were
playing in it and it started rolling down the hill
and crashed into the Hilberts' fence."

Her eyes popped right open and she said,
"What?" and pulled Allen toward her and started
asking him if he was hurt, real panicky like.

Well, that got Allen crying. Bawling, actually.
So I said, "He's fine, Mom. We walked all the way
home. He's fine. So's Will."

Mom looked at me. "How on earth . . . ?"

"He told me they were just playing around,
pushing buttons, and it started to go."

Mom popped out of her chair and looked pretty
awake all of a sudden. She grabbed us both by the
wrists, and off we went. And when she saw the
Moyers' car, she stopped and stared and then asked
me, "Did you see this happen?"

I shook my head. "Prunella came and told me
about it."

She turned to Allen and said, "How'd you get in the car?" He told her that it wasn't locked and they'd just climbed in. Then she wanted to know who was driving and Allen said *he* was.

Now, Mom can get pretty mad. She's not really that big—actually Jack's catching up to her already—but when she's mad, boy, she sure *seems* big.

And Mom was mad, all right. Really mad. I was feeling pretty sorry for Allen, only something seemed kind of weird. She was being kind of rough with us, dragging us down the street by the wrists and all, but she wasn't acting like she normally did when she was mad.

We went down to the bottom of the cul-de-sac, where Mrs. Moyer was talking with a policeman. All the neighborhood kids were out thinking it was pretty neat that Allen and Will had wrecked the Moyers' car. The neighborhood grown-ups were whispering to each other on the far side of the cul-de-sac, and you could tell they were having a good time.

Well, Mom marched right up to Mrs. Moyer and interrupted. She started carrying on about the car being left unlocked and how Allen could have been killed, and it dawned on me that Allen was going to get out of this without so much as a pat on the fanny. I looked over at him and he looked at me, and we tried to look serious but something kept tugging at the corners of our mouths.

Now, Mom and Mrs. Moyer are pretty good friends, and I didn't like seeing them mad at each other, but it was better than Mom being mad at one of us. The policeman did a pretty good job of calming things down, and then he asked a bunch of questions and wrote down all sorts of stuff. Allen liked him, I could tell, because when we were walking home, he said he wanted to be a policeman when he grew up.

Mom didn't exactly drag us back home, but she did walk pretty fast. And when we got home, she sat and brooded for a while and drank cold tea while we tiptoed around the house. Just when Allen was starting to feel like he wasn't going to get killed, Mom picked up the phone and called Dad.

She was in the kitchen with her back turned, so we could get pretty close without her knowing we were listening. You could tell she wasn't trying to get Allen in trouble, she just wanted someone to talk to.

A little while later Dad came home, and he took Allen and went to the Moyers'. It didn't seem fair that I didn't get to go along, but Dad said I had to stay home. That turned out to be okay, because when Jack came home from Billy's, I got to tell him the whole story. And since Mom wouldn't let him go down the cul-de-sac, Jack got really mad because he wanted to see the wreck and couldn't. It made me feel kind of good. It's not every day I know more about what's going on than Jack does.

It was a long time before Dad and Allen came back, and when they did, they were laughing about something or other, so I guess Mr. Moyer and Dad came to some agreement.

The next day Dad and Allen worked on fixing the Hilberts' fence, and by the time they were done, you could barely tell it had ever been down. Jack and I went down to watch a couple of times. I was hoping Prunella would come out so I could show Jack what I meant about her nose, but I guess she was busy with her dolls.

I asked Allen if he'd been able to figure out if Mrs. Hilbert was a midget or not. He said that Mrs. Hilbert did come out to leave them a tray of lemonade, but he was busy helping Dad mix cement and didn't even see her do it. I would've asked Dad, because he *must* have seen her, but under the circumstances I figured I better not.

chapter 4
Fun in a Foxhole

For a while after they crashed the Moyers' car, Allen and Will didn't play together too much. I think our moms were trying to keep them busy with other stuff. But that didn't last too long, and before you know it everyone seemed to forget about the wreck.

So Allen went back to playing over at the Moyers', but I didn't much feel like it. Not that anyone else ever knew what Brent had said, though Charlie must've.

Charlie's always real polite to me. Of course he's real polite to everyone. That's just the way he is. I think my mom actually doesn't like Charlie that much because he's so polite all the time. Doesn't think it's natural. Anyhow, whenever Charlie sees me, he's nice to me, and that didn't change after stupid Brent made fun of me.

So one day I was in my room, minding my own business. Actually I was in the middle of this great mystery and I could've stayed there all day reading it. But when Allen came in with Will and little Andy, Billy's brother, to ask if I would come even up teams at the Moyers', I didn't have much trouble putting the book down. I mean, when three boys come over and ask you to be part of their team, it makes you feel pretty good.

What I didn't know was that they were having dirt-clod fights. And since Will and Allen wanted to be on the same team, that stuck me with little Andy. I should have told them to forget it and gone back to my mystery, but I didn't want them to think I wasn't any fun. I mean, the next time they might not ask me, right? So I teamed up with little Andy and started hurling dirt-clods.

Now, the Moyers' front yard wasn't in the best shape to begin with. They're on a corner, too, and have this big strip of ivy going around the yard right alongside the sidewalk. I always thought that was a pretty good way to keep people from cutting across their yard. It's *thick* ivy with big dark leaves, and if you want to cut through ivy like that, your screws aren't quite tight. You can never be sure what's waiting for you in thick ivy. Mom says that's where black widow spiders go during the day because it's nice and dark and cool. And it's no secret that snails and slugs get together under those leaves to rest after sliming the neighborhood all night. Follow one of those shiny trails sometime—it'll go straight to an ivy patch.

Anyhow, the Moyers had this ivy that was doing just fine. And they had some bushes along the garage wall—the kind with the real dark leaves and red berries. They were doing fine, too. So were the trees. Well, one was a palm tree, and I don't really know if you'd consider that a tree or not. You can't climb it, and you can't build a tree house in it, and it doesn't give any shade, so if it is a tree, it's not a very good one.

Anyway, all the plants were doing fine except the grass. The grass was completely torn up. With the neighborhood kids coming over all the time, it was doomed. And when we started, it seemed harmless enough to be breaking off dirt-clods and throwing them at each other. It's not like that dirt was going anywhere. We were just shuffling it around some.

Besides, Mrs. Moyer could see us playing in the yard because we could see her, sitting at the dining table, clipping things out of the paper. She never said one word about us tearing up what was left of her grass, so we figured she didn't mind.

The dirt-clod fight wasn't much fun. It's not that I got hit so much, although one got me in the back of the head, then broke up and went down my back and into my shorts. But Allen and Will got dibs on the bushes by the garage, and that left little Andy and me with no protection except for that palm tree. And since the tree was right next to the ivy, we had to step in the ivy once in a while, which was real distracting.

So we threw clods around for a while, but when I tripped on a sprinkler and fell backward into the ivy so that even my head was under the leaves, I'd had it. Little Andy was glad and said he had to go too, and since Allen and Will didn't want to fight each other, that was the end of that.

I wasn't planning to get in another dirt-clod fight the next day. Mom had made me take a bath the night before, and there was no way I was going to take a bath two days in a row. So I was just out for a ride, coasting past the Moyers' on my bike, when *thud!*, a dirt-clod broke up right in front of me. I got off my bike real quick, and what I saw was amazing.

There was a group of boys where little Andy and I had been the day before, only they were in these foxholes with piles of dirt protecting them and stacks of dirt-clods everywhere. Allen and Will and a couple of other guys were where they'd been the day before, only now they were getting their bottoms kicked.

Well, I couldn't just ignore what was going on, so I stood on the sidewalk and watched. When they called a five-minute truce and Allen and Will hollered at me to help them dig another foxhole, what could I say?

So we dug and we dug, and pretty soon we'd forgotten all about the dirt-clod fight and were building forts. *Underground* forts. The foxholes kept getting bigger and bigger, and deeper and deeper, and they were really cool inside. All you had to do was just lie against the wall and you'd cool right off. On top of that they smelled good. They even smelled clean. Now, you may ask how dirt can smell clean, and I don't know how to explain it to you except to tell you to go out in your yard and dig yourself a hole. You'll see what I mean.

Pretty soon everyone wanted their *own* hole. It's just one of those things. It gets crowded in a hole, and pretty soon you want out, but you don't want to leave. What you really want is for everyone else to leave, but they don't, so you start making your own hole.

And that's how we wound up with all these holes. Every day we'd all bring sandwiches and eat lunch in our own little fort, and sometimes we'd throw food back and forth, but mostly we just sat and yelled stupid stuff at each other.

Then one day someone had the idea of connecting the holes. We all thought it was a great idea and started digging like mad again, tunneling to the nearest other hole. It was even more work than digging the hole to begin with, but it was really exciting when you finally connected to the hole next to you. What happens is the dirt starts sounding different, and pretty soon it's sounding hollow. That's when you know you're almost there. Then you jab with your trowel and it just shoots right through, and you hoot and holler and back right out and yell that you made it. And anyone who hasn't quite made it yet just ignores you and starts working twice as hard to finish their tunnel so they can hoot and holler and get ignored too.

I don't really know what Charlie's parents thought of all this. Mr. Moyer came home every day around six. He'd open the side gate and park his car in the garage. Then I guess he'd go straight into the house. I never actually saw him the whole time we were tearing up their yard.

Mrs. Moyer, on the other hand, was home, and you'd see her peeking out every once in a while. I'm sure she knew what was going on, but she never actually came out to see. All I know is that Will and Charlie were right in the middle of the action and loving every minute of it. I think they like having as many friends as they do. They go to other people's houses like everyone else, but I think they like it best when people visit them. And all the people they ever knew had heard about the tunnels and were wanting to come over and play.

Then one day Charlie had some friends over that I'd never met before. They were getting kind of wild, crawling through the tunnels and running *across* the tunnels. Now, I know what you're thinking, and of course you're right, but you have to understand that the last thing I wanted was to sound like a whiny girl telling these people I didn't even know to stop walking across the tunnels.

I saw the whole thing happen from my hole. At first I just thought, "Uh-uh, someone caved in a tunnel"; but when Will started calling for help because Charlie was underground, I was out of my hole in a flash, helping to dig him out.

Now, he was fine. He'd gotten a mouthful of dirt

and was trying to spit it all out while everyone else was pushing clumps of dirt off him. He shook out his hair like a dog shakes water out of its coat, and dirt went flying everywhere. When we knew he really *was* all right, we kind of scuffed around a bit. Then when Charlie went inside, everyone else went home.

After dinner Allen and I decided to ride by the Moyers' to see if anything was going on, and sure enough, Mr. Moyer was out with Charlie, filling in all the holes, trying to get the yard back in order. We got off our bikes and asked if we could help. Mr. Moyer just smiled and said no. He didn't seem to be mad at all, but Mr. Moyer's like that. Always real nice and polite. We said we were sorry about the mess, and he said that it was all right—that he'd been meaning to redo the yard anyway.

Charlie, on the other hand, didn't seem quite himself. I don't think he was hurt or his father wouldn't have been making him fill in holes. He just looked like he wished we'd go away, so we did.

Now, you know how mad I got when Brent said I had a crush on Charlie. And you know he just said it because he's mean, not because there's any *truth* to it. But that night I couldn't go to sleep, thinking about Charlie under all that dirt.

And it bothered me, thinking about it, and thinking about it bothering me bothered me even more. Not that it's not normal to be shook up a bit, seeing one of your friends buried alive—it's *perfectly* normal. And I'd go to my grave swearing it would be a lot worse seeing Jack or Allen pulled out of the dirt like that. But it's not true.

And that's what bothered me so much. If it had happened to Allen or Jack, I would have been upset. But this was a different *kind* of upset, and I couldn't get it to make any sense.

And lying there thinking about it for so long didn't help. It got to the point where I didn't care if I figured it out or not. All I wanted was for it to go away.

chapter 5
The Crater

The Freekos aren't bad people. They're just slobs. And most people probably never noticed that the Freekos' stucco was all cracked and this dirty gray color. What they did notice, because you couldn't exactly *not* notice it, was their yard.

It's not like my parents had the most pristine yard, but at least you didn't walk by and say, "Geez, what a mess," like you did when you walked by the Freekos'. Their yard looked worse than the Moyers' did with all those foxholes.

The weeds came clear up to my shoulder, and in the summer they'd dry up and wave around. That was all right if you were spying, because no one from the sidewalk could see you. But when it came to having to weed our own yard, it was another story.

We were always having to weed our yard. Bags and bags of weeds. Mom and Dad had planted dichondra grass, of all things, and around the edge of the yard they'd planted decorative strawberry plants. These are *sensitive* plants, and every time you turn around, you've got to weed or water or do something to keep them going. Why Mom and Dad didn't plant St. Augustine grass is something I still don't understand. That's what they've got at the park, and it's tough stuff. Walk barefoot on it some-time and you'll see—it's nice and cool and thick. I asked the guy on the riding mower once what kind of grass it was, and he told me St. Augustine, which is how I know.

Anyhow, we were stuck with dichondra that we weren't supposed to walk on, and strawberry plants that were a double waste because they didn't give off any strawberries. They did all right in the shade right by the house, but the part of the yard next to the Freekos' was always in terrible shape. Their weeds would blow over and say, "Wow! This is great! There's *water* over here!" And when there's an army of weeds waving in the wind, tossing seed bombs in your direction, it can be downright scary if you think about all the weeding you're going to have to do.

Dad did try to reason with Freeko. He even offered to keep his yard mowed, but Freeko always said no, that he'd take care of it himself. He never did, though. Not until Jack, Allen, and I made the crater.

It didn't start out as much. Actually we were just going to make a spot to hide little Andy's cat. It was a really stupid cat, or at least we thought so because we liked dogs. I don't remember how cat snitching started, and I don't know why we thought it was so much fun. Usually we'd just take the cat and play with it up in the tree house, then let it go.

Little Andy was onto us about the tree house, though. If we pulled the ladder up so he couldn't get in, he'd stand down there and nag until we were so tired of him, we'd toss him the cat. And then he'd get all mad at us about *that*.

Well, one day Jack, Allen, and I took his cat and put it in a box. We punched lots of holes in the box and gave the cat some water and decided to hide it in the middle of the Freekos' yard.

The trouble was, when we put the box down, the weeds folded over and pushed other weeds down and you could tell something was there. So we started pulling weeds to make a flat spot to put the box while we told each other to hush because we weren't sure whether Freeko and Fattabutta were home or not.

Just when we had everything about set, the bottom broke out of the box. One minute Jack's carrying the cat in the box and the next minute it's streaking off. So we were standing there in Freeko's yard in the middle of the day with an empty box full of holes, and Allen said, "Why don't we make this spot a little bigger and turn it into a grass fort?"

We all started yanking weeds, and once in a while I'd sneak out to the sidewalk to see if you could see the spot, which at first you couldn't. It was great! You could crouch in the grass and hear stuff all around you. First just the grass rubbing against itself; then, if you sat still long enough, you'd hear grasshoppers and see bugs marching all around like you weren't even there.

But after a while it was like being in the car. There just wasn't enough room. Jack started stretching out, pigging up space like he always does. Then I started pushing back, and pretty soon Allen's sniffling that he's getting trampled. So we got up and yanked some more grass. And we got carried away, because before you know it we'd made the crater. You could see it from the sidewalk, and it looked even worse from across the street. In the middle of all these dried-up weeds was this huge patch of black dirt. And let me tell you, it looked really, really stupid.

We were all standing across the street talking about how funny it looked when Freeko and Fattabutta came home. Well, we started walking down the street as fast as we could. Freeko yelled after us but we just ignored him. It wasn't like he was using our names or anything—not the names our parents had given us, anyway.

We made it down to the Spook House and just sat under a tree and waited. Finally, Jack said we should go home through the school's playing fields, so that's what we did, keeping our heads kind of low just in case Freeko could see us over the wall. When we got close enough, Jack looked over the wall at the Freekos' yard, and he started laughing so hard he could barely talk. He gave Allen and me boosts so we could see too. It looked like something from outer space had landed in Freeko's yard.

Well, that night we were eating lemon chicken and potatoes, kind of moving our green beans from one side of the plate to the other. Jack, Allen, and I kept pulling faces at each other, hoping we wouldn't get in trouble about the crater even though Dad *must* have seen it when he got home from work.

Just as those beans were getting to be about the only thing left on my plate, Dad said, "So what'd you kids do today?"

It shouldn't have made me jump like it did. Dad asks us that every day. But the *way* he was asking was kind of too smooth. So I stuffed some of those green beans in my mouth and chewed like I was much too polite to answer with my mouth full.

The trouble was, Jack and Allen did the same thing—got real busy eating food and drinking milk and smiling with their lips together.

Dad gave Mom a funny look and said, "I see our neighbors have had some landscaping done. . . ."

Allen giggled, so Dad looked at him and said, "You know something about that, son?"

Allen straightened right up. "I saw it. I think it looks better."

Dad's eyebrows popped up. "You do, do you?"

Then Jack shot off with "Well, *I* do. It couldn't have looked much worse. You've said so yourself."

Dad sat there real quiet for a minute, which can be worse than him acting mad. Then Mom said real softly, "They came over this afternoon."

Suddenly there was a green bean tickling my throat and it made me choke. Jack ignored me and said, "Freeko and Fattabutta?" which made Mom look stern and say, "Jack!" like she always does when he calls them that.

Turns out Mom promised the Freekos we'd come over the next day and mow their whole yard. We acted like it was a big deal, but we were really thinking that we'd gotten off easy.

You'd think after a close call like that we'd want to stay home and recuperate from almost having gotten in big trouble, but it doesn't work that way. Not in the summer, anyway.

In the summertime, nighttime's the best. You can run around and not get sweaty. And it smells great out. In the daytime you go across the street to play at the school, and the asphalt about burns up your nose. Just try to play on blacktop during the day. First your sneakers melt; then your feet pop all over the place with blisters. And it's hard to play dodge-ball with blisters popping and sneakers melting.

But at night! You can run up and down the street or all over the playground and it's like you're invincible.

Anyway, we were all outside, sitting on the curb, awfully glad we hadn't been grounded, just kind of wondering what time it was. Time is one of those things I let grown-ups take care of. I have a watch, but I'm not sure where it is. I really only want to know how much time I have left before Mom and Dad call me home, and that's not some-thing a watch can tell you anyway.

We'd already been down to the Spook House, clear around to the railroad tracks, and back up to Lemon Street on our bikes, and we were trying to decide where we could still pedal before Dad called.

Then all of a sudden Jack laughed and jumped back on his bike. Well, of course Allen and I jumped on our bikes and chased after him. That is, until we saw what he was going to do.

He took his bike and rode it straight through Freeko's yard. I mean, *zing!* Straight through all those weeds, straight across the crater, and clear over their driveway. And then he did it *again* straight back at us. Well, he kept on doing it until there were about twenty trails going through the Freekos' yard and all these tire tracks across the crater. Allen didn't have any trouble helping Jack out, but I couldn't decide what to do. I mean, we were going to mow their yard in the morning, so what did it matter? But something told me to stay out of it. For once, I didn't just go along.

chapter 6
Filling Up the No-No Box

There is another girl who lives in our neighborhood. Actually, there are a couple of them.

Three houses down is a family with one girl. When I first saw her, I thought she was a grown-up. She wore grown-up clothes and walked like a grown-up. Well, except for her head, but I'll get to that.

You know how grown-ups are. They *watch* where they walk, which is okay, but it slows you down. Most kids don't really walk. It's too slow. They only do it when they're tuckered out or with their parents. If you see a kid out by himself or with a bunch of other kids, he'll be moving along pretty quick. Maybe not full-out running, but quicker than you can figure out if he's skipping or running or hopping or *what*.

One day it finally dawned on me that this girl wasn't a grown-up, because she walked by the house every morning at the same time. And when I finally watched where she was going, sure enough, she went to the high school's bus stop on Lemon Street.

The girl has a name, I'm sure, but I call her Wobblehead. She has all this hair. I know I said that about Prunella, but Wobblehead's hair is even longer. It's real long and straight. No curlicues or ribbons like Prunella. And it goes way down to the bottom of her back, which is longer than you might think because she's pretty tall.

So she has all this hair, and I think she likes the way it feels, swishing across her back, because when she walks, she moves her head from side to side. Like her neck is loose. Kind of like one of those toy dogs you see in people's car windows, bobbing back and forth. I'm sure she could fool a lot of people into thinking she's a grown-up if it wasn't for that wobbly head of hers.

The other girl who lives in our neighborhood is little Andy and Billy's older sister, Karen. To me she's always seemed pretty darn old, but I guess she's about the same age as Wobblehead. Whenever I see her, she has curlers in her hair. Big prickly ones everywhere, and then little bobby pins crossed over, curling up those hairs that come down in front of your ears. And she wears either this big puffy yellow robe with house slippers or cutoffs with thongs and a tie top.

I've always thought she was kind of fat, but you always get the feeling from her that *she* looks just fine and that *you're* just a little runt. Karen isn't very friendly, and she doesn't really count as one of the neighborhood kids, so you see why I left her out before. I don't think I'd ever even seen Karen out in the neighborhood until a few days after Charlie got buried alive, when I saw her talking with Danny.

Danny is Fattabutta's son. Freeko isn't his real dad, and I don't think they get along too well. Anyhow, Danny isn't home much. Except for about a month there when every night he and some friends would practice their guitars in the backyard by the pool. Drove my dad nuts. He hates loud music and doesn't think music with electric guitars is music at all.

The neighborhood kids would hang out, looking over the fence, trying to decide whether they were any good or not. We weren't spying or anything, we just looked. So we'd be watching Danny and his friends, and pretty soon Will and Charlie'd come out and look over their back fence, and then you'd see Billy's and little Andy's heads peeking over, clear across on the other side of the Freekos' back-yard.

I don't think Danny minded us watching. Actually, he used to say something to us once in a while, which he never did any other time. Danny and his friends would all laugh a lot, and sometimes it was probably about us, but mostly I think they were just having a good time.

I thought Danny was kind of fat, but I guess Karen didn't think so. You could see this white roll hanging out from under his T-shirt and over the top of his shorts. And you couldn't help staring at it because his belly button was so big. It wasn't big and round like a saucer—it stretched out sideways and it looked like you could lose something in it.

And of course when you see a belly button like that, you can't help but wonder how in the world you'd keep it clean. I mean I get little fuzzies in my belly button or, if I've been doing something like digging foxholes, a little dirt. But there it is—I can see it. And it's real easy to clean out. With a belly button like Danny's you'd have to lie down and hold a mirror above it just to see inside, and then, well, it'd be a big job to clean.

So whenever I saw Danny, all I really saw was his belly button. If he was wearing something to cover it up, I don't know if I'd recognize him right off. But like I said, it didn't seem to bother Karen much. You'd never see her looking over the fence, but you'd see her talking to Danny for hours right in front of the house. She'd lean against a car in the Freekos' driveway and listen to him talk. And she'd always have her hair done real nice and have toe-nail polish on.

Anyhow, Karen'd be talking to Danny there in the driveway, and we'd hide in the bushes and spy on them. They never talked about anything inter-esting, and it was kind of boring to watch them. I kept expecting them to start smooching, but they never did.

And why all this matters is Jack. You see, Jack was kind of stuck in between. He and Billy were in the same class, and that was lucky for him because they got along okay. The trouble was Billy was gone a lot. Don't ask me where to, he just was. So Jack was left kind of pedaling around the neigh-borhood by himself, and I think that's when he really started noticing Wobblehead and Karen. You know what *I* think of them, but I guess they'd look different to you if you were older. I know they looked different to Jack. As a matter of fact, I think he thought Karen was pretty, and once in a while

I'd catch him watching Wobblehead as she walked by. He'd always act like he didn't care, but I think he wished he was more grown up so they'd notice him and then he wouldn't be stuck in the middle.

So I guess that explains why Jack would do something he *knew* was wrong and that would get him in a lot of trouble if he got caught. Which of course he did. I think he was trying to be more grown up than he was and just got carried away.

I can't tell you *exactly* what they did, but I can tell you this: There are some words you're not allowed to say when you're a kid, and really shouldn't be saying when you're a grown-up. You know what they are and I know what they are and we don't actually have to say them to talk about them.

In some houses they say words like that all the time and it doesn't seem to be any big deal. For example, when the Freekos are in a fight and yelling at each other, boy you know you're going to hear some juicy words. The whole *neighborhood's* going to hear them.

But at our house we have to pay for words that most people don't even think are bad words. If I call someone "stupid," it costs me three cents. That doesn't seem like a whole lot, but it adds up. "Dumb" is two cents, "moron" is three cents, "idiot" is three cents—you get the idea. Mom thought it would be nicer if we weren't calling each other names all the time, so she started this thing called the No-No Box, and anytime you call someone a name, it costs you. When you get to swears, the price jumps to a quarter apiece, so in our house there's a price to pay for using words like that.

I don't know what they were thinking, but Billy and Jack decided to rub leaves on the side of the Freekos' house, making this green stain that spelled out a cuss word. And this word would've cost Jack a *dollar* if he'd said it at home.

Yup, that's the one.

Anyhow, they didn't get caught until they were done, and they let *Freeko* of all people catch them. There it was, in green letters two feet high. And Jack was caught with leaves in his hand, putting the finishing touches on a box that went around the word. He couldn't exactly deny that he'd done it, although he tried.

Freeko yelled at Billy and Jack so loud that the whole neighborhood could hear, and it wasn't long before people were everywhere. That included Karen and Wobblehead and some girl friend of Wobblehead's.

So there Jack was, being yelled at in front of the

whole neighborhood, and he was looking kind of small. Like he was actually younger than he was.

Then Dad showed up. Fattabutta called him to come over. Not on the phone, but from her bedroom window. She just opened it up and hollered. And you should've heard some of the language *she* used!

At first Dad didn't believe that Jack had anything to do with it, but that's just part of being a parent, I suppose. Finally Jack mumbled that all *he* had done was put the box around the outside, which of course nobody believed. It might have been true, I don't know, and I guess it doesn't really matter. He and Billy did it together. And they probably thought it was pretty grown up until all the real grown-ups started yelling at them. Then they probably felt pretty stupid. I mean, it's pretty embarrassing just being yelled at, but in front of all those people?

They tried to scrub it off, but it was stained pretty good. So Dad took Jack down to the store and they bought some gray paint, and the next day Jack painted the whole wall twice.

I don't know what happened to Billy or why he wasn't out there helping. I do know that Danny and Karen were standing in the driveway the whole time Jack was sweating away on that wall, and that they laughed and talked and treated him like a little kid.

Which I wish he didn't think was so awfully terrible. Being a kid, that is. After all, he ought to be glad—at least he's not a girl.

chapter 7
Pebbles Down the Chimney

You're probably thinking we left the Freekos alone after we got caught making the crater and after Jack decorated the side of their house like he did. And for a while we did. But then their weeds started coming back up, and it seemed like every day Fattabutta spent the whole afternoon hollering at Freeko. Fattabutta would go out in the car once in a while, and when she did, Freeko would sit out in the backyard smoking and drinking straight out of a bottle.

One day Will, Allen, and I were up in the tree house trying to figure out who to spy on when Fattabutta came storming out of her house throwing curses over her shoulder at Freeko. Well, we all kind of looked at each other and knew.

We decided to try spying on Freeko from up on his roof. We all dared each other to do it, and before we knew it, there we were in broad daylight, pushing and pulling each other onto Freeko's roof. Once we were up, we kind of crouched and told each other "Sssh!" a lot, but that was pretty stupid because anyone walking by could just look up and there we were.

We worked our way down the back side of the roof on our fannies so we could see Freeko's back-yard, because we thought we might have a great view of him smoking and drinking straight from the bottle.

Turned out he wasn't there, so we just sat there awhile, trying to decide what to do. Then, in the middle of deciding, we heard, "Jack, Carolyn, and Al-len!"

I looked at Allen. "What *time* is it?" Like he's going to know when he doesn't have a watch on either.

He shook his head and started walking *crunch, crunch, crunch* to the edge of the roof.

"Jack, Carolyn, and Al-len!"

I stood up too, and started looking for a way down, but all there was to land on in Freeko's back-yard was cement. So I followed Allen over to the side of the roof, *crunch, crunch, crunch*, and did what he was doing—looked down.

Now, that's a scary thing, being on someone else's roof with your dad calling you, and not knowing how to get down. But when we heard it again, "Carolyn, Al-len!" we knew we had to do something.

So *crunch, crunch, crunch* we went to the front of the house and finally wound up just jumping off the stupid roof into all those weeds.

We raced to our front door and tried to look real calm, and when Dad came back from checking the Moyers', we acted like we'd been there all along.

Dad *was* home early, and he was acting funny. He told us that he was going to make dinner and asked us to set the table real nice and maybe even use a tablecloth. Said he wanted to surprise Mom.

I don't know where Mom was. I thought she was in the house, but I didn't want to go find out because Dad was acting like something special was going on. I kept trying to remember what I had for-gotten. I knew it wasn't their anniversary—Mom helps us keep real good track of that—and I knew it wasn't her birthday.

So I got out a tablecloth and I was setting the table, kind of throwing looks back and forth to Allen, when Jack came out from his room looking grumpy. At first I thought he'd gotten in trouble, but Dad was being nice to him, asking him to peel some potatoes instead of making him help with the table.

So when we had the table set, I went over to help Jack with the potatoes because he was being so slow about it. Also, I figured he was grumpy because he knew something I didn't.

Well, that wasn't the reason he was grumpy at all. He whispered, "I saw you guys on Freeko's roof."

I stopped peeling and looked at him, trying to figure out how much trouble I'd be in if he told. "You did?"

"Yeah. What were you doing up there?"

I shrugged, "Nothing."

He snickered. "Boy, are you going to get it if Dad finds out."

I froze. "Are you going to tell?"

He looked at me like I was brain damaged, so I started peeling potatoes again real fast while he worked at getting this one potato perfect. Finally he said, "Wonder what would happen if you shone a flashlight down the chimney."

I looked at him. "A flashlight?"

He kept working on that potato. "Sure." I looked

at him like *he* was stupid, and finally he said, "At night, dummy."

Well now, that was a thought. And it was one I couldn't stop thinking about. I also thought about other things you could do on the roof. Like make scary noises down the chimney so they'd think it was a ghost or something. Pretty soon I was think-ing that we'd really missed out, just sitting up there on the roof.

Dinner turned out nice, and Mom *was* in the house. At first I thought she wasn't feeling well, because the whole time we were making dinner, Dad was telling us to be real quiet; but when Dad went to get her, she seemed fine. She ate all her dinner, too. I kept looking at Allen and Jack, trying to figure it out, but none of us could. So we just ate and tried not to lie too much when Dad asked us what we'd done all day.

After dinner Mom went into the living room and turned on her favorite record. We did the dishes and came up with a plan to go back on the Freekos' roof. The problem was that Dad had told us that he wanted us to stay home while he went to the store to get some things, and we knew if he found out, we'd be in big *big* trouble.

But you have to understand that we'd been talking about this for *hours* and we were all worked up to go. So we went down to my room and set up the Monopoly board and made it look like we were in the middle of a game. Then we changed into our spying clothes and climbed out the window.

This may sound risky to you, but we really thought we'd only be gone a little while. We figured the minute Dad came driving up, we'd jump off the roof and be in the house before anyone knew we were gone.

So we tiptoed out to the side of the house and then pushed and pulled each other up onto the roof. Jack was the one with the flashlight, and he led the way, crunching right across the roof to the chimney.

It doesn't look like it from the street, but the top of the chimney is pretty high. We couldn't see inside at all, which was pretty disappointing, so we wound up tossing pebbles down the chimney.

At first we did just one, but Allen didn't hear it go down, so we tossed another one. You know the kind of pebbles I'm talking about—all roofs have them. Kind of gray and black and smooth.

Then we all decided we wanted to throw our *own* pebbles down, and before you know it, lots and lots of pebbles were going down that chimney. We would've kept right on going, too, but Fattabutta started screaming up the chimney at us.

She was up to about three *dollars'* worth when Dad came driving down the street. We hunched over real quick and went crunching across the roof and got back home as fast as we could.

So we were in my room, barely out of our spying clothes, when Dad came looking for us. We smiled and acted like we'd been playing Monopoly, and he said, "Your mother and I are calling a family meeting in the living room."

We'd never had an official family meeting before. Usually when Mom and Dad want to talk to us, they just talk to us. None of this official business. I was thinking we were in trouble, but Dad wasn't acting mad. He was acting really nice. So we all looked at each other and raised our eyebrows and followed Dad into the living room.

Now, usually your parents are just your parents. You don't really pay much attention to the way they act or the way they look because you're used to them. And if they change, well, you see them every day, so you don't really notice.

Like Dad—he's always been real tall and skinny

and I never even noticed that he was going bald until Will said something about it. It's not like I don't know what my dad looks like, it's just that I see him every day and I didn't really pay attention to the hairs when they fell out one by one. Sure, all those hairs add up, but the point is I didn't really notice.

So you'd think I'd have noticed, but now maybe you won't think I'm so stupid for *not* noticing. We were all in the living room, feeling kind of weird for having an official family meeting, and Mom was just sitting over in her chair with a cup of tea on her lap. Then all of a sudden something happened and she spilled tea all over herself.

Dad rushed over and asked if she was hurt, but she just laughed and said that it was barely warm and didn't hurt a bit. Dad helped her clean up the tea, and then he cleared his throat and asked, "How would the three of you feel about getting a new brother or sister?"

We didn't say much. We just stared. And all of a sudden Mom looked like someone I hadn't seen in a few years. She looked real *different*.

Mom said, "Carolyn?" because I guess my eyes were bugged out, staring at her stomach.

I stuttered, "A baby?" and all of a sudden I started to cry. It's the weirdest thing in the world, but that's what I did. Mom put her arms out like good moms do, and I got a hug. She stroked my hair and said, "I thought you'd be happy."

Well, I *was*, even though I was crying, and I told her so.

She smiled and looked relieved. Then Dad said, "Now kids, I'm really counting on you to help your mother out. Things are going to be a little rough on her for a while, and I want you to give her a hand as much as you can and do your chores without her having to beg you to."

We all nodded and said sure we would, and then the doorbell rang. We looked at each other like "who could that be?" thinking it was too late for Will or Billy to be coming over. Dad said, "I'll get it," and a few minutes later he came back into the living room with a policeman.

You may think from the things I've told you that policemen would be at our house all the time, but it's not true. This was the first time a policeman had been in our house, and at first I didn't know what he was doing there.

Then it hit me. I tried to keep a straight face and

not give us away, but I was thinking over and over, "I'm dead. No doubt about it—I'm dead."

So I was really surprised when my dad said, "See, they're right here."

We started smiling a little bit. Not too much, just enough to look like we hadn't done anything wrong. The policeman squatted down and said to us, "You haven't been outside tonight?"

We opened our eyes wide and said, "No sir. We were playing Monopoly in our room."

Dad nodded. "I can show you if you'd like."

The policeman smiled and roughed up Allen's hair a bit. "No, that's quite all right. I'm sure they just got the wrong kids."

So Dad showed him to the door, and when he came back, Mom said, "What was all that about?"

"Oh, nothing. The neighbors complained that some kids were up on their roof tossing rocks down the chimney." Then he mumbled, "Probably just soused again."

Dad wound up the family meeting, but the whole time Mom looked at us with one eyebrow up just a little. We went back to my room and were in the middle of counting our lucky stars when Mom came in and closed the door behind her. We all froze. She said, "Monopoly, huh?" and walked straight to the window and closed it tight.

We looked at her and she looked back at us. There was no doubt about it, she *knew*. I was thinking, "I'm dead. This time I'm really dead." But what she did next is the most amazing thing I've ever known my mother to do. She said, "I hope you heard what your father had to say. I need your help and I need you to stay out of trouble." She saw our beanies on the floor by the bed and picked them up. "Do we have a deal? Or would you like your father to find out about this?"

We all stared, stunned that she was black-mailing us. Then we kind of nodded and told her sure, we had a deal.

She just smiled—a real pretty smile—and closed the door tight behind her.

chapter 8
Bunk Beds and Batteries

After I found out that Mom was going to have a baby, I really did try to stay out of trouble. I helped her more with chores and tried to keep Jack and Allen from being too loud when she was trying to take a nap. I even tried going to bed when she said it was time.

Actually, I didn't hate going to bed quite so much after we got bunk beds. Allen and Jack used to have them in Jack's room until a few weeks after we found out about the baby and Jack decided he wanted a room to himself. I said it was fine for Allen to share my room as long as we got the bunk beds and I got the top bunk.

That was fine with Jack, and it was fine with Allen, too. He liked the bottom bunk, and there *is* lots to be said for sleeping down there. For one thing, you can make it into a terrific fort. All you have to do is take one of your blankets and push it under the edge of the top bunk mattress and let it hang down.

Another good thing about the bottom bunk is that if you're mad at the guy in the top bunk, you can push your feet up and bounce them around some. They can't exactly ignore you, because they're flopping around pretty good, and they can't get you back. All they can do is hang over and holler at you to stop, or try to catch one of your toes in a spring. Pretty much they just have to wait for you to quit.

So the bottom bunk is pretty good, but the top bunk is where I want to be every night before I fall asleep. Maybe it's just my imagination, but if you sleep on the top bunk, you have better dreams. When you're up off the ground and the moon's peeking through the window, not real bright—just enough to light up the walls a little—all of a sudden it feels like you're in a secret fort way away from anything that's ever bothered you. And when you feel like that right before you fall asleep, you have the best dreams. Sometimes you barely remember them, but they stick with you the whole day, making you smile for no reason.

I've tried telling people about my dreams, but it's not a smart thing to do. Mom is always polite, but you can tell—to her it's just some mixed-up story.

And then I feel kind of stupid for being so excited about it.

So the secret to good dreams is to not tell anyone about them. You can tell them about nightmares or funny dreams, but when it comes to dreams like you get when you sleep on the top bunk, well, *don't*.

Some nights it's time for bed and you're just not ready. You may be tired, but that doesn't have much to do with it. You're just not ready, and that's when it's important to have a really good flashlight.

You may think I'd use a flashlight for spying, but I don't. Flashlights give you away and get *in* the way. Flashlights are for reading. Of course they're also good for putting in your mouth and puffing up your cheeks and lighting yourself up with, but mostly they're for reading.

And when it's time for bed and you just don't feel ready, and your mom's come in three times to tell you to quit giggling, and she's finally sent in your dad to tell you the same thing, that's when you need a good flashlight. There's nothing worse than being in the middle of a really good part of a book and having your flashlight turn that yellow color. Pretty soon it's brown, and everyone knows brown's just a step away from black.

Ever since Dad told us that Mom was having a baby, we were going to bed before we were ready, so my flashlight was going yellow and I was all out of books. Good books, anyway. When I asked Mom if she could take us to the library, she said she wasn't feeling well and I could tell it wasn't a good time to ask about new batteries. I guess that's why I did what I did. I didn't plan it or anything—it just kind of happened.

One afternoon we were riding around, not going anywhere, when Jack said we ought to go down to the Cornet. Well, that sounded like an adventure. The Cornet's this dime store clear past the railroad tracks, down near where they're putting in the new freeway, and I'd never been to the Cornet except in a car. When I told Jack, he laughed and said that he'd been there lots of times on a bike and that it really wasn't far at all.

So off we went, Allen and I pedaling like mad to keep up with Jack. It was fun, screaming down the street on our bikes with all that wind rushing over us. And it *was* easy. No standing up to pedal, no burn in the legs, just moving your feet as fast as you could before the pedals didn't grab anymore.

Then, before you know it, there we were, at the

Cornet. We walked inside and it hit me. I'd never been shopping without Mom or Dad before. Never. That may not seem like a big deal to you, but it was to me, and I think to Allen too. Jack took off, heading for some corner of the store away from us, but Allen and I just stood in the entrance right under the air conditioning vent, feeling the buzz of the fluorescent lights, and all of a sudden we realized— we could do anything we wanted!

What we did was run. We ran from one end of the store to the other, stopping here and there, saying, "Lookit! Lookit!" and going mad finding stuff we didn't even know existed.

Finally we wound up in the toy department, and that's where we stayed. We looked at everything and played with anything that wasn't in a box, and argued over what would be better to get for Christmas.

After we'd been there awhile, I noticed Jack. He was over by the books looking through a *Mad* magazine kind of grinning that grin of his. I got up off the floor because I wanted to see what kind of comics they had, but when I got close to Jack, he said, "What d'ya want?" without even looking up.

So I moved over to look at the books, and the

minute I saw they had some mysteries, my heart started to pound a little.

I mean the books at the library are fine books, but it feels like I've read *all* of them. These books looked great. And I'd never seen any of them before in my life.

I didn't know what to do. I picked one up and read the cover. Then I picked up another and read some out of the middle. Pretty soon I had all these books I wanted, but no money.

No money and no mom. I looked at the prices and found the cheapest one and stared at Jack. I thought about asking him for some money, but you know how Jack is, so I wound up *not* asking him. What I did instead was take a quick look around and tuck that little book under my T-shirt and inside the elastic of my shorts.

I put the rest of the books away and straightened them out, but my hands were shaking and I was worried that someone had seen. Finally I backed away and looked around, and it felt real funny, this book in my pants.

Then I heard "Carolyn!" and I about died. I mean I just knew—I was going to jail. Then I heard, "Allen!" which made me wonder what *he* was slipping inside the elastic of *his* shorts. My mind was going crazy. See, his voice didn't sound right. Nothing sounded right—like everything was underwater. Everything except those fluorescent lights buzzing away. They were really loud.

Maybe he was just trying to sound older, I don't know, but when I realized it was Jack calling us, I was so relieved, I could've cried.

He looked at me kind of mean and said through his teeth, "Let's go," and then started walking to a checkout counter. I followed him, but by the time I got to the check stand, my stomach was feeling funny and my knees weren't holding my legs together too well. Jack put the magazine on the counter and paid for it, and the lady smiled and thanked us for coming, and before you know it, we were walking under that big air conditioning vent and out into the burning sun.

I didn't wait around for someone to take me away to jail. I got on my bike and pedaled to the stoplight as fast as I could. Once we were across the street, my knees quit shaking and all of a sudden I felt great! That lasted until I was about halfway home. The book was cutting into me like crazy, and I hadn't realized it on the way to the Cornet, but it had been so easy getting there because it was all downhill.

So going home was no fun at all. I didn't even like bumping over the railroad tracks. It was hot and my legs were burning from all that uphill, and I was last in line with this book cutting me up.

I could have taken it out and moved it, I suppose, but I was really afraid that Jack or Allen would see me, so I just left it there. When we finally got home and I was safe in my room, I took the book out, and it was all wet from sweat and curled at the corners. I looked at the cover a few minutes and tried to dry it off, but when Mom called me, I shoved it under my pillow and went to see what she wanted.

And what's funny is I didn't want to go to my room to read it. I helped Mom all afternoon and made dinner almost all by myself and just stayed away from it.

But that night when it was time to go to bed, there was my new book, kind of wrinkled and smelling not at all the way a book should, waiting for me.

After a while I pulled it out and started reading it, but I couldn't concentrate. Now, it wasn't the book—it was a good book. And it wasn't the batteries—they were yellow, but not *that* yellow. I just kept thinking about standing in line at the store and the way the checkout lady had smiled at me so sweetly, and I just couldn't read it.

Finally, after Allen was sound asleep, I crawled out of bed and put the book on my bookshelf in between a bunch of other books where no one would ever notice it. Then I tried to go to sleep.

But I couldn't. I tried not to look at the bookshelf, but somehow I always wound up staring at it, and no matter which way I turned, I could hear it calling, "Carolyn ... oh, Carolyn." I swear, I didn't sleep at all that night. Or the next. And the third night I had the most terrible dreams.

I thought about throwing the book out, but that seemed wrong. Here I'd stolen it and I hadn't even read it. Besides, Mom would probably see it in the trash and ask me about it, and then what was I going to do? I thought about giving it to the library, but how was I going to do that without Mom noticing? Besides, all the books I'd ever checked out had hard covers and a plastic wrap over them. They would know right off—someone was trying to get rid of a stolen book.

By the fourth day I couldn't stand it anymore. I took the book, put it in a bag, and got on my bike. I pedaled to the Cornet and went inside to the checkout counter. I put the bag on the counter and said, "This is yours," and left before they could throw me in jail.

I pedaled like mad all the way up the hill, looking over my shoulder the whole time for a police car to come tearing up to take me away.

When I got to the railroad tracks, I stopped and looked back down the hill, trying to get my legs to quit shaking and get my breathing back to normal. Finally I headed home, kind of slow, and by the time I was parking my bike in the garage, I was thinking that maybe Mom would be in the mood to take me to the library, and that she might even stop on the way home to get some new batteries.

chapter 9
Rodents and Reptiles

It seemed like everyone in the neighborhood had a dog. Everyone but us.

Even the Moyers. Theirs just showed up at their door one day, and boy was it cute. Charlie named him Jinx, and Jinx used to sleep on his bed and follow him all around the house. I thought it was really neat, him having a dog. I also liked Jinx because Jinx liked me, and whenever I'd go over to the Moyers', he'd jump in my lap and give me kisses.

Now, you may think that a dog's a pretty normal thing for a kid to have, and you're right. It is. But Mom was worried about us taking responsibility for a dog. "Responsibility" is one of those words my mom says like she's sure you don't quite understand the definition, even though you swear to her that you do.

Mom didn't start saying no to getting a dog just because she was going to have a baby. She'd been saying no for a long time. We had a goldfish for a while, but we'd forget to feed it. Then one day

Mom found it floating on its side and told us we couldn't have another pet until we learned about responsibility.

But after a few months we got up the nerve to ask for another pet. We started out asking for a dog and wound up begging her for a lizard. At first Mom said no. But then we came up with the idea of using the old fish tank lined with some of this orange sand Mom had made Dad haul from the desert. As soon as we mentioned the sand, Mom started thinking a lizard might be okay after all.

The sand really was very pretty, but Dad was tired of it leaking all over the garage. Not that it was making that big of a mess—I think it just reminded him of getting a flat while he was getting us lost in the desert. Most moms bring home jewelry or key chains or something from their vacations. My mom brings home rocks. Or sand. Or pine cones. Dad doesn't really say much, especially if it's something she's found while he's fixing a flat in the middle of nowhere.

Anyway, Mom kept telling Dad she was going to find a use for the sand, so when we thought of a lizard, she shoveled that sand right into the old fish tank, and the lizard house was set up in no time.

The problem was keeping the lizard fed. Lizards like flies, and they don't seem to like much else. They don't like dead flies, either, and you can't just go down to the pet shop and say, "I'd like three dozen flies, please."

We were responsible for a little while, but it wasn't long before we were fighting about who had to go out and catch the lizard some flies. Then one day when we were all roller-skating over at Bradbury Elementary, we heard Mom hollering.

Of course the lizard was dead and Mom was mad at us for weeks, and it took us a long, long time to get up the nerve to try asking for a puppy again.

When we did ask about getting a puppy, she brought up the lizard, and when she was done with that, she started about the goldfish, and we just stood there not saying much.

But every time we brought it up, she'd spend less time talking about the fish and the lizard and start demanding to know who was going to feed the "animal" and take responsibility. Well, it took a long time, but finally one day she said it was okay for us to get another pet.

We didn't know she was talking about a guinea pig. I don't think *she* knew she was talking about a guinea pig until she read in the paper about some-one giving them away. That afternoon she went out and came back with this thing that looked like a cross between a rat and a gopher. She told us his name was Scamper and that he was our new pet.

Great. A guinea pig. But before you know it, Dad built a cage for it in a corner of the backyard and it was all moved in. You couldn't take it out to play because it would run away and you'd have to spend the rest of the day trying to corner it. And it didn't learn tricks. We tried, but it wouldn't do a thing. Not even sit. The only thing it would do is squeak. And boy, could it squeak! Not like a mouse, more like a little pig—which I guess is why it's called what it's called.

Mom decided Scamper needed a friend, so she went out and came back with *another* guinea pig and told us her name was Scooter. And she was right. That shut Scamper right up. He liked Scooter just fine. It was Scooter who hated Scamper. She'd bite him and kick him and run like mad to get away from him, but before you know it we had a cage full of baby guinea pigs.

All of *them* learned to squeak in a hurry, too. It didn't take long before there were even more of them and Dad had to build another cage—one for the boys and one for the girls. And all those guinea pigs spent the day squeaking and eating and messing up their cages, and pretty soon we were fighting about who had to clean the cages. After a while Mom said she was tired of begging us to take care of them and packed them all up and took them to a pet store.

So anytime we even thought about asking for a dog, Mom would give us that Remember-the-fish-and-the-lizard-and-the-guinea-pigs? look and we'd know it was hopeless.

So just when I was thinking we'd never get a dog, Jack got real mad and told Mom he didn't want fish or lizards or guinea pigs—or rabbits or snakes or cats or goats for that matter. He wanted a *dog*. A dog's what a boy's supposed to have, and no other animal would make up for not having a dog. Except maybe a monkey, if she wanted to give him that.

It seemed pretty dangerous, Jack talking like that when Mom was in the middle of starting a roast. But Mom just threw that piece of meat around in this big orange kettle, singeing one side for a few minutes, then another. And it spattered and popped and acted like it was going to explode, but Mom calmly threw it around not saying much of anything.

Allen and I were watching from the corner of the dining room, lying low. Then Jack did something I'd never seen him do before. He waited. He didn't run off mad or say anything else. He just waited. And when Mom was finally done wrestling with the roast, she didn't say a word about responsibility. She just looked at Jack and said, "I'll talk it over with your father."

Jack couldn't believe it, and when Mom asked him to set the table, well, I've never seen him do it so fast in my life. He even remembered to put out the salt and pepper and then volunteered to help Mom with the potatoes.

All through dinner we were pretty quiet, and Dad knew something was up, but he didn't ask. When dinner was over and we were cleaning up, Mom took Dad into the living room, and before you know it Dad was telling Jack he'd take him to get a puppy in the morning. Allen and I had a fit because we wanted to go too, but Dad said no, it'd be a family dog, but he'd only take Jack.

So the next day Jack and Dad went to the pound and came back with this cute little puppy that Mom named Kocory.

That's how we finally got a dog, and he's been great. He's soft and furry and lets you use him for a pillow if you feel like taking a nap in the backyard, and he doesn't squeak or run away, and you don't have to catch him flies.

And he's the one who gave me the idea of trying to touch the moon.

chapter 10
Touching the Moon

Touching the moon was a secret for the longest time, and it's not something I'd tell just anybody about. But since it's not a secret anymore and I officially know that it can't be done, I guess it's okay to try to explain it.

See, Kocory loves to howl at the moon. And I thought him howling at the moon was really neat, so sometimes I'd go out and try to get him going. I'd get down on the grass and start howling like a dog, and pretty soon he'd be howling away, too.

One night it was so hot out that you had the choice of being miserable indoors or being miserable outdoors. I'll take being miserable outdoors anytime. People are just nicer to each other when they're miserable outdoors.

So I was out in the backyard with Kocory, lying on the grass looking up at the sky. It was so beautiful out. Kind of like when you're camping and everyone else is asleep and you can see out your tent and there it is—the *sky*. It's all glittery, and if

you look at it long enough, you feel like you're one
of the stars.

It's not something you talk about. It's kind of a
secret between you and the stars. People may say,
"Wasn't it beautiful out last night?" or "Did you see
the stars last night?" or something like that. But no
one'll ever mention the magic.

So that night I was out in the backyard with
Kocory, feeling like one of the stars, when I noticed
the moon. It was just a little crescent moon, but that
night, lying there looking up, I thought it was the
most beautiful thing I'd ever seen. Partly because of
the stars all around it, but also because it was so
white and thin. And for some reason I stretched my
arm way out and put my finger up and tried to
touch it.

If I held my finger just right and looked just
above the tip of it instead of right at the moon, it
really looked like I was touching it, and it felt like
it, too.

It's not like feeling the grass or a piece of wood.
It's like feeling rain when you're inside, nice and
warm and dry. Or like music. You can't really touch
music, but think about your favorite song. Boy, can
you *feel* it.

And that's what touching the moon's like. Only better. It tingles right down your arm to your spine and makes you want to stay there all night.

I probably would've, except Kocory got tired of being used as a pillow, and then Mom came out and asked me what I was doing. At first I said, "Nothing," but when she sat next to me on the grass, I decided to tell her.

And that was a mistake. I didn't tell her the way I told you. What I said was "I'm touching the moon."

Mom got this look that moms get when they're all panicked but they're trying to stay calm, and she said, "You're touching the moon?"

I just smiled and nodded. Well, she reached over and felt my forehead and asked me if I was feeling all right, and it hit me how stupid I sounded. Touch-ing the moon. Right.

And I didn't want to explain it, and I didn't want to show her how. I didn't want anything but to take my secret back.

But that's the problem with secrets. Ones you have with yourself or ones you have with the stars. The minute you tell anyone about them, the magic disappears. Even as you hear yourself say it, *poof!*, there it goes. No more magic.

And even when I explain it right, it doesn't *feel* the same. Somewhere there's this little doubt that takes over and makes you not even believe yourself. Pretty soon you think there really isn't any such thing as magic.

Pretty soon you're all grown up.

chapter 11
Picking Weeds and Porching Papers

For a while I didn't care about having a job and earning money. It was always the older kids in the neighborhood who got the jobs anyway, and if you wanted some extra money, you had to make a deal with your mom and dad to get it. Unless you were Mary Moyer and decided to make some money by putting on a stupid talent show.

Anyway, one day Allen and I were standing in the wading pool, cool all the way up to our ankles, when we saw Charlie and Will working their way up the cul-de-sac, knocking on doors. Turns out they were asking everyone if they could wash their cars for a dollar. That got me thinking that if Charlie and Will were old enough to make money from the neighbors, then I was, too.

The trouble was being a girl; people don't think to give you a job they've been wanting a *boy* to do, so I wound up begging Mom for extra work, and all she could come up with was picking more weeds.

So I picked weeds for*ever*—sacks and sacks of

them. And when allowance time came, Jack saw my extra money and it really bothered him. That's when he decided to get a paper route.

I thought it was great fun, him having a paper route. Every day this man would come and drop off a big stack of papers, which Jack would have to fold before he could deliver. At first he wouldn't let us touch even one of his papers, but after a while he got tired of folding them and didn't mind that Allen and I wanted to help.

We folded them all up into themselves so that they made this neat little square that you could just fling. Underhand, overhand, sidearm—any way you tossed it, *zing!* It would slice right through the air.

Allen and I used to follow Jack as he tossed those papers all over the neighborhood. At first he didn't want us going with him, but after a while I think he liked having us around, because he would ask us if we were ready to go, and the three of us would pedal around together.

It was about this time that Mrs. Cranston asked Dad if Jack would want a job doing her yards once a week. Well, Jack didn't want the job. He was too busy making money as a paper boy. So I shot up with "I do!" which Dad thought about for a minute and said, "Why not?"

He took me to meet Mrs. Cranston, who I already knew, but I guess she didn't know me. Funny how grown-ups are about that. I mean, all the kids in the neighborhood know all the grown-ups. If you saw one go driving by, you could say, "There goes Mr. Kingston," or "Look! Mrs. Holt has a new car!" I mean, you just know them, whether they have kids or not.

Grown-ups aren't that way. I don't think they want to know who you are. It's too complicated for them or something. And if you wave and say, "Hello there, Mrs. Gabel," Mrs. Gabel will look up and smile kind of nervous like and wave back. And you can tell she's trying to figure out who you belong to, but she'd never dare ask. As you pass by, you can feel her wishing you'd never say hi to her again because she doesn't really want to know who you are and it bothers her when you make her try to figure it out.

So I knew who Mrs. Cranston was. She lived across the cul-de-sac from Prunella. And I could almost hear her thinking, "Well, what have we here?" as she peeked at us from behind a curtain.

But after Dad explained, she smiled at me and said, "Why not?"

So I had a job, and right away she wanted the yards done. Mr. Cranston was pretty nice. He got the mower out for me and showed me what he wanted done, and before you know it, I was pushing and pulling on that mower making the blades go *wack-wack-wack-wack-wack!* It was a fine sound, and their backyard had a lot of shade, so I didn't sweat as much as I could've.

Then I noticed Mrs. Cranston peeking out a top-story window, just keeping an eye on me. Well, that felt kind of funny—like I was getting *spied* on or something. But I kept on going, *wack-wack-wack-wack-wack!*, and before you know it, I thought I was done.

Mrs. Cranston didn't. When she saw me winding down, she tapped on the window and pointed. I'd missed a spot. So I pushed the mower over the spot she was tapping at—not that it looked like it had been missed—and then she did it again.

It would have been nice if she'd opened the window and talked to me, but I guess she didn't want to let the air-conditioning out, so she just tapped and pointed until I was ready to scream.

Finally Mr. Cranston came out with a big glass of lemonade and told me that Mrs. Cranston liked having her lawn done in two directions. I'd never heard of such a crazy thing, but I just smiled and thanked Mr. Cranston for the lemonade and got back to work mowing the other direction.

By the time I was done, there were about ten extra pieces of grass in the catcher and a big smile on Mrs. Cranston's face.

I put the mower away, and Mr. Cranston came out and paid me and said what a good worker I was and that he'd see me at the same time next week. I thanked him and took the money, and thought as I walked home that it had sounded like a lot more money before I'd started working.

But I wasn't going to let Jack know that. Ever since he'd gotten the paper route, he'd been taking out his strongbox and counting all his money right in front of me. Sometimes three times. Out loud.

Anyhow, when I got home, Jack was out front folding papers by himself. He tried to ignore me, but when he saw the money sticking out of my hand, he couldn't. "They gave you *that* for mowin' a yard?"

I just smiled and said, "Yup."

Jack looked at his mess of papers and then back

at me and said, "So are you going to fold papers or what?"

I was tired and didn't feel much like folding papers, so I asked, "Where's Allen?"

Jack scowled. "Watching TV."

Well, it wasn't too long after that that Jack told Allen he'd *pay* him to do the papers twice a week.

Delivering papers is kind of fun. You get out there on your bike and sometimes you make some amazing shots. I know, because Allen let me help him. He'd take the left side of the street and I'd take the right. And we already knew which houses liked their papers porched and which houses didn't care from all those times we'd pedaled around with Jack.

When we'd get back, Jack would see us and get all upset because we were done so soon. Then one time when we got back really early, he told Allen that he wouldn't get any money unless he did the collecting too.

It didn't take long to figure out why Jack hated collecting so much. Sometimes I'd go around with Allen, but I couldn't actually help him collect because the *Daily News* had this stupid rule about girls, and Jack was afraid if they found out he'd lose the job.

Anyhow, we'd go around one night and half the people weren't home or didn't answer the door because they saw us coming. Then we'd go around the next night and half the people said they didn't have the money and to come back later. So we'd come back later and they'd spend twenty minutes searching the house for their pocketbook and usu- ally they'd come back with an "I'm sorry, come back tomorrow." Collecting's the worst. It takes forever.

After a while Allen was doing all the work, and Mom stepped in and said, "Whose paper route is this, anyway?" That's when it came out that Jack didn't want the job anymore. I guess he was just tired of folding papers and counting his money.

I also think he wanted my job, because every week when I'd come home from being tapped at by Mrs. Cranston, he'd act all grumpy and try to find out if I was planning to quit. I'd just smile like Mrs. Cranston was the nicest lady in the world to work for and set about counting the money in my strong- box. I never told him that Mrs. Cranston made me edge the lawn with hand cutters or that she wanted the mower scrubbed and dried before it went back in the garage. Or how she'd tap at me if I mowed too *fast*.

And I was getting to the point where I would've let Jack have the job, but one day Mrs. Cranston actually opened the window and told me that they were moving and there wouldn't be any more work for me. I tried not to smile too much, but there are some things that you just can't help.

So the only person with a job was Allen, and he was getting pretty sick of it. I mean delivering papers is something you have to do every day whether you feel like it or not, and by the time you go through all the trouble of getting money out of people, well, it takes up a lot of time.

And I guess that's why we started taking turns. Every other day I'd slap on a baseball cap and fling those papers all over the neighborhood. No one ever complained that a *girl* was delivering their papers. And when it came time to do the collecting, I would wear that cap right up to the doorstep and say, "Collecting." They knew what for, and were probably thinking so hard about how to get out of paying that they didn't even notice I was breaking the rules.

Sometimes they'd look at me funny, but most people didn't even notice or didn't dare ask. Think about it—"Aren't you a girl?" is a pretty risky thing to say to a kid, especially if they're not!

But one time this lady answered the door in her bathing suit and was mad at me for bothering her. She was having trouble keeping her stupid dog inside. It was yipping and snapping and in general acting a lot bigger than it was. I'm sure you've seen the type—small with a bow holding up its hair so it can see. Dogs like that always act like they're going to tear your foot off. Probably all they really want is a decent haircut and to get rid of that bow, but their owners don't seem to understand that.

Anyhow she scowled at me from behind this white lipstick and said, "You're a girl!"

I did my best to look insulted, but she just laughed and slammed the door in my face.

That shook me up. I was tired and thirsty, and that lady just ruined my day. So at the next house I took off my cap and said, "Hi. My name's Carolyn and I'm helping my brother collect for the paper."

And you're not going to believe what happened. The lady said, "Now isn't that the sweetest . . . Harold! Come here! I want you to see this!"

So her husband came to the door and she told him what I was doing and made him pay for the paper *and* give me a fifty-cent tip.

Well, that put a smile right back on my face.

And you can bet what's in your strongbox that I said the same thing at every house I went to. And you know what? I liked saying it. Made me feel like I didn't have to cover my hair with a hat, or try to talk a little different so I'd sound like a boy.

And that's when I started thinking that maybe it wasn't so stupid being a girl—that maybe what was stupid was the rules that went along with it.

SCHOOL

chapter 12
Getting Ready

You'd think I'd be used to the way it happens. I've been going to Bradbury Elementary since kinder-garten, and it always feels the same, so you'd think I'd be prepared, but I never am.

Things start to quiet down. Even the Moyers' house doesn't have as much going on. It's not that there's nothing to do—you just don't feel like doing it. You just sit on the porch and wilt. Even the Freekos seem boring.

And even with everything so slowed down, it still always catches me off guard when September rolls around.

And when it does, boy! Everything happens all at once. Cars show up in the parking lot at Bradbury Elementary. The guy with the riding mower cruises around cutting grass that's already been cut quite nicely. Busses start going through that big bus lane—they don't have any kids in them, they just come to the school and sit there with their motors running for fifteen minutes and then leave.

Don't ask me why, it's just what they do.

And then one day you hear that the doors are posted with who's in what classroom. The whole neighborhood races over to see who they got for a teacher and if their best friend is in the same class or not.

Will and Allen got the same class, which made Allen pretty happy. Charlie and I got the same class, which I was glad to see, though I don't know why because he never talked to me much at school. He didn't talk to any girls at school, so it didn't hurt my feelings too much. I just thought it was dumb.

Every year, right after the doors at school are posted, Mary comes over wearing a brand-new out-fit. She stands there on our front porch kind of turning from side to side and leaves a couple of bags of hand-me-downs for me to sort through and wash the smell out of.

Now, don't get me wrong. The clothes aren't *dirty*. They're washed and folded, but you can smell that they've been someone else's clothes right through all that soap and bleach.

Anyhow, I dump the bags out on the floor in my room, hoping that there's something I'll like. I go through everything and pull out the few things that

I might actually want to wear. And then, as I'm stuffing everything else back into the sacks, Mom shows up.

To my mom, everything is usable. I'll be standing there in this awful dress with yellow and green flowers and birds, and she'll say, "Hmmm. We could take it in here ... hem it to about there ... it'll be fine." Yeah, and I'll be looking like a walking pet store.

But there's no arguing with her. Before you know it, it's taken in and hemmed and I'll have to wear it to school every time she asks, "Why don't you ever wear that nice dress with the birds on it?" Telling her you hate it doesn't do a bit of good. Mom likes the word "nonsense" and uses it whenever I say how ugly something is.

After the doors at school get posted, you wind up spending a lot of time in your room. Parents somehow think that cleaning out your closet and drawers is going to make you do better in school. The trouble with that isn't so much straightening everything out, it's the pile of stuff you have left when you're *done* straightening everything out. A pile of stuff that doesn't actually belong anywhere.

When I was younger, Mom let me have a junk

drawer. Anything that didn't have a real place of its own wound up in the junk drawer. Nowadays she won't let me get away with that. So I work really hard at cleaning up, but I'm still always left with this pile of junk on the floor.

Probably most of it's stuff I could throw out and never miss. But it's neat stuff, or could be neat if only I'd fix it. Like this Pinocchio puppet I have. It's the kind with the strings hanging from a cross of wood, and you can make him walk and bend at the waist and wave. I used to have him hanging from the ceiling in my room until one day he fell and broke his nose. I was pretty upset and decided right away to glue his nose back on, but there was no glue in the whole stupid house. Well, maybe there was, but I couldn't find it. And I was afraid to ask my mom, because he fell when I accidentally hit him with a ball right after she'd yelled at me to quit bouncing it in the house.

So I hid Pinocchio in the closet along with his nose, and before you know it he was all tangled up and his nose was missing. I've looked real hard for that nose, but so far I haven't found it, and every year right before school starts, Pinocchio's right there in the middle of the pile, all tangled up and staring at me. I don't know what to do with him. I can't hang him back up with that hole in his face, but I would feel terrible throwing him out just because he has a little problem with his nose.

Eventually I take one last look around for his nose and then put him back in the closet and try to forget about him. About that time Mom comes in and stands there for a while, staring at the pile. Finally she sighs and helps me until it's all put away.

And after the closet and drawers are cleaned out and the pile's finally gone, there's no sense in even trying to get anyone to play with you. Everyone's too busy getting ready for school. At least that's what their mothers tell you when you knock on the door. I think it's more that the *moms* are getting ready for their kids to go to school, and the kids are in their rooms trying to decide what to do with a pile of stuff that would fit quite nicely into a certain bottom drawer if only they'd be allowed to put it there.

chapter 13
The Dragon Lady

When school finally does start, you're almost glad because you're so tired of getting ready that going to school almost sounds like fun.

Usually you know what a teacher's going to be like because someone you know has had them before. This year, though, I didn't know what to expect, because my name was posted on the door of this brand-new teacher—Mrs. Rennalds.

At first I thought Mrs. Rennalds wasn't going to be bad. She spoke real soft and was nice as can be. Then she caught David looking up Julie's dress.

At Bradbury Elementary the girls have to wear dresses, and I'm sure you can guess what I think of that. I mean, how are you supposed to play on the monkey bars or play kickball or do *anything* fun in a dress? Even jumping rope is dangerous in a dress.

Most of the girls don't seem to mind. Especially girls like Julie. Julie wears party dresses to school. Her mom does her hair up with ribbons, and she's got curls like a stupid doll. If my mom did that to me, you can bet I'd have the ribbons torn out before I crossed the street and I'd be wetting my hair down in the bathroom. Not Julie. She *likes* looking that way.

And I swear she has ten pairs of Mary Janes. The shiny kind. She has black ones with bows and black ones without, she's got white ones that never have any scuff marks on them, and then a red pair and even a *green* pair that she wore at last year's Christmas play. Who's ever heard of a green pair of Mary Janes?

So Julie's always dressed like she's going to some fancy party, and everyone's used to that, but this year she wore lipstick and *nylons* on the first day of school. Boy, did she get a lot of attention— especially from Helen Lison. I don't like Helen. She's always whispering about people and lying about things.

Julie doesn't wear nylons or lipstick anymore, so I think maybe Mrs. Rennalds had a talk with her, but she still wears those stupid party dresses. And they do kind of flip up when she sits down, so it's no wonder that David was trying to look up her dress that day.

If she'd been wearing shorts under her dress like

I always do, it wouldn't have been any big deal. Shorts let you do anything you want and not worry about your underwear showing. I don't know why all the girls don't wear them. Debbie and Gail are the only other ones who do, so as far as I'm concerned the rest of the girls are just plain dumb.

Anyway, the minute Mrs. Rennalds saw David looking up Julie's dress, our teacher with that soft, sweet voice turned into a monster. Scared the daylights out of all of us. She swooped down on David and grabbed him by the arm so hard he yelped. Then she got right in his face and hissed and snapped for a few minutes until he was just about crying. Then she yanked him up by the arm and dragged him out of the classroom, and we could hear her through the door hissing and snapping some more.

Well! We all looked around at each other, too scared to say anything. But when she came back in, she smiled real sweetly and said in that soft voice, "Now, class, get back to work," like nothing had happened.

Turns out David spent the rest of the morning waiting for the principal to punish him, but all Dr. Berrywine did was talk to him about his Little

League team. Then right before he left, he told him that he shouldn't look up girls' dresses.

After that we started noticing things about Mrs. Rennalds. For one thing, she likes to chew gum when she drinks her coffee. She keeps a coffee cup and a thermos on her desk next to the jar of pencils we're not allowed to borrow. And since *we're* not allowed to eat or drink in class or chew gum at all, this didn't seem fair to us.

I wouldn't have minded so much except she never washed the coffee cup. You'd go up to ask her a question and you couldn't help but stare at that cup, all black on the inside and smudgy red from lipstick on the outside.

And it's not just that she drinks coffee; she also eats cookies. She probably thinks we don't know about the cookies because she sneaks them, but she's always got chunks of chocolate stuck in her teeth and she's always sucking or picking at her teeth, trying to keep them clean. She keeps the cookies in one of her desk drawers, and you can hear her rolling the drawer back ever so quiet. If you look up through your bangs, you can see her check that no one's watching, and *pop* there goes a cookie, right in her mouth.

This is a good time to raise your hand and ask if you can go to the bathroom or out for a drink of water. She can't talk with that cookie jammed in her mouth, so she just smiles and nods and off you go.

As long as Mrs. Rennalds has her coffee and we stay pretty quiet, she's okay. At least until right before recess. If you're going to do something to make her mad, it's best to do it first thing in the morning. She doesn't seem to mind so much in the morning. But if you do it right before recess or lunch, boy, does the monster come out!

It takes a few weeks to figure out what a new teacher's like and when you can get away with what, but after a while you get the hang of her. Then you start wondering *why* she does what she does. At first I thought the monster came out because she was hungry, but that didn't make sense with all the cookies she goes through. Then Debbie told me it was because she needed a cigarette. Debbie says that her mom gets cranky just like Mrs. Rennalds if she needs a cigarette. And sure enough, I started noticing that after recess or lunch, you could smell that cigarette smell on her, right through her perfume.

So everyone started calling her Dragon Lady.

No one ever called her Mrs. Rennalds unless they were talking to her or to the principal. Mom and Dad wouldn't let me do it at home, so I called her "D.L." until they were so used to it, they didn't even think about what it stood for.

Usually I can do my work on my own, but sometimes I don't understand something and neither does anybody around me. So someone's got to go up and ask the Dragon Lady to explain it and then get permission to explain it to the other kids. Usually that person is me.

When you go up for help, she gets her face right up to yours and whispers because she doesn't want the class to be disturbed. And out of her mouth come words, but sometimes they don't quite make it into your brain because her coffee-gum-cigarette breath just about makes you gag. And her mouth does this funny twitching thing as she tries to move her gum out of the way, only it won't go because it's stuck on a tooth right there near the front of her mouth, all full of cookie crumbs, kind of stretching between her teeth like dirty green taffy.

After a while, no one even talked about her gum or the cookies anymore because everyone'd seen it and talked about it so much already. But what no one had ever noticed was that she wore a wig.

At first I wasn't sure. But as she bent forward to work out a math problem for me, I could see this little bald spot at the back of her head. Only it wasn't bald like my dad's head—it was bald like a rug. You could see this open weave where hair was supposed to be.

I must have been staring at it pretty good, because it took a while for her voice to register. "Carolyn . . . Carolyn!" she was saying.

I jumped and said, "Yes, ma'am?"

Well, the Dragon Lady came out fast. "You haven't heard a word I've been saying!"

I jumped back a little. The whole class was looking at me—even Charlie, which was real embarrassing.

"*Have* you?"

"I'm sorry, ma'am," I whispered, and peeked up at her as she tried to decide what to do with me. Finally she said, "Well, just sit down and figure it out for yourself then!"

I was so relieved. And when I got back to my seat, I leaned forward and whispered to Debbie in front of me, "D.L. wears a *wig!*"

Before you know it half the class was raising

their hands wanting to go up and get something explained, and she was helping them in groups, not knowing that they were pointing to her bald spot trying to keep from laughing.

By the time recess came around, everyone was so excited about the Dragon Lady's wig that we all ran around the blacktop telling everyone we knew, "Dragon Lady wears a wig! Hey! Have you heard? D.L. wears a wig!" I'm sure that by the end of recess, even the first graders knew about it.

And, it turns out, so did the principal.

chapter 14
What to Do With Miss McPew

Before I tell you what the principal did to me, I've got to explain: I never get in trouble at school. I get in trouble at home all the time, but I have two brothers and it's just something that happens when you're outnumbered like that. But at school I get good grades and I'm pretty quiet and teachers like me fine. No teacher's ever sent me to the principal's office. Well, there was the trouble I had with Miss McPew last year, but she wasn't really my teacher.

Miss McPew is in charge of the orchestra, and I've known her since the third grade. Every year I joined because my mom said I should and because you get out of class once a week. What I didn't like about orchestra—besides Miss McPew—was that none of my friends were in it. Debbie didn't play an instrument, Gail was only in band, and Charlie— well, Charlie liked baseball a lot better than music.

Playing flute wasn't that bad. All I really had to do was figure out how to blow into it. The string people had a lot more to worry about. They were

always holding their bows wrong or something.
And some of those things get pretty big! Poor
Cathy Tunn had to carry her cello to school and
back, and Miss McPew would yell at her over and
over not to drag it on the ground. So the flute
wasn't as bad as you might think.

Trombone would have been better, though.
With trombone you don't really hit bad notes. You
slide around until the right note comes along and
then stay there until you have to go to the next
note and then you just slide over to it. There's no
sliding around on the flute. When you hit a bad
note, everyone around you knows it and they look
at you out of the corners of their eyes, wondering
what in the world you're doing. I know, because
I've done that myself with Penny Mercantile.
Penny's first chair and has always been first chair
except for the time I stared at her out of the corner
of my eye while I was challenging her. It messed her
up so bad, she blew it and I got to be first chair for
a whole month.

Ever since then, anytime I hit a bad note, Penny
Mercantile's eyes scoot over in her head, and she
stares at me until she loses her place and has to look
at the music again. I try to ignore her because it's

my trick and I don't want her using it on me, but sometimes I get messed up so bad that I just pretend to play.

And that's how the trouble with Miss McPew started. She was always so busy yelling at the strings that she never noticed when I was faking it.

Then one day we were in the middle of some song when she tapped on the podium and hollered for everyone to be quiet. When everyone had finally squeaked to a stop, she turned to me and said, "We can't hear the flutes!"

Well, I wonder why. The flutes there that day were Sharon Zimmer and me, and Sharon Zimmer's only in the third grade and so small that you forget she's there at all. Besides, I think she was faking it too.

Anyhow, Miss McPew tapped on the podium and we all got ready to play, only I didn't know where in the world we were. I didn't even know what piece of *music* we were supposed to be playing. I faked like I was playing and looked over at Sharon Zimmer's music, trying to figure out where we were. The trouble was, what Sharon was playing sounded so terrible that I was sure she was looking at the wrong piece of music too. Maybe the reason we all sounded so terrible was that nobody knew what piece of music we were on, and everyone was playing something different.

So I was all caught up in thinking this when Miss McPew hollered at us to stop again. Everyone jumped. Miss McPew is scary! She's short and really fat and has eyes that go in different directions. On top of that she sprays all over you when she yells.

She didn't yell at me this time, though. Instead she slammed down her baton, walked over to Cathy Tunn, and yanked that cello right out of her hands. For a minute we all thought she was going to hit her with the bow, but instead she pushed Cathy out of her chair and sat down.

Playing the cello is hard to do gracefully if you're a girl. You've got to spread your legs out and pull the stupid thing up to you, and if you don't watch out, your underwear shows. And if you're as fat as Miss McPew and you sit on one of those folding chairs and play the cello, it's amazing what you show off. She was wearing these nylons that snap onto straps, only the nylons couldn't make it much past her knees. Fat was coming out *every*where.

But she didn't seem too worried about her underwear. She just sat there tapping a foot, running that bow back and forth across Cathy's cello, bobbing her head from side to side. When she was done, she looked at Cathy and said, "There. That's how it's done. Now do you think maybe you can do that?"

Cathy gulped and nodded, but you knew darned well that she wasn't going to be able to play it right. When Miss McPew got back up to the podium and tapped her little baton, Cathy burst into tears and ran out of the room.

Miss McPew just ignored her and flipped that baton around from left to right like she was swatting flies. Half of us were still staring at the door Cathy had run out of, so even if we did happen to have the right piece of music on our stands, we didn't know where we were supposed to be. We just sat there, faking it.

Then all of a sudden she banged the baton on her podium so hard, it sounded like it was going to break. Everyone jumped again, and Sharon Zimmer started hiccuping like mad, popping up and down in her chair like a jack-in-the-box. Miss McPew turned to me and shouted, "We still can't hear the flutes!"

I looked down at my music and nodded, but she walked over to me and said, "Maybe you can play it so we *all* can hear."

I nodded and mumbled something, expecting her to walk back to her podium, but she didn't. She squinted at me and shouted, "NOW!"

I gulped and whispered, "By myself?"

She looked at Sharon Zimmer, bobbing up and down in her chair, gasping for air, and said, "Yes, by yourself!"

I started playing softly because I was sure I had the wrong piece of music in front of me. But after a while she started nodding, and it dawned on me that I did have the right music, so I played a little louder. Pretty soon she stopped me and said, "Now play it that way with everyone else. Nice and loud!"

I was so relieved that I didn't notice how badly Sharon Zimmer was shaking until we were halfway through the song. I looked at her sideways and saw that she was crying, so I put down my flute and whispered, "Are you okay?"

She just looked at me with tears running down her face and hiccuped really loud. That was enough to make ol' McPewy bring the orchestra to a grinding stop again. She put her hands on her hips and said, "What *is* the problem?"

I thought poor Sharon was going to turn inside out with those hiccups, and she might have if the lunch bell hadn't rung just then. I tore my flute apart and stuffed it into the case without even drying it. And I was planning to grab my music and run, only poor Sharon Zimmer was hiccuping so bad, she couldn't take apart her flute. She finally let go of it and let me do it for her.

The whole time, Miss McPew was just picking up her music and pretending she didn't hear Sharon Zimmer turning inside out. When Sharon finally quit shaking enough to hiccup her way out the door, I looked over at Miss McPew and decided— I quit.

I didn't go up to her and say, "McPewy, I hate your guts and I quit," like I should have. I left school right in front of the lunch monitor, went home, and made a petition with big letters that said: WE QUIT UNTIL YOU'RE NICER!

Mom raised her eyebrows and scratched her cheek. "Are you sure you want to do this?"

So I told her about Cathy Tunn and Sharon Zimmer and everything, and she said it was fine if

I quit, but did I really want to do this? I was so mad that I said, "YES!" which made Mom smile this funny little smile and kiss me, of all things.

When I got back to school, I barely had enough time to show off the petition before the bell rang. And then nobody wanted to sign it. *Nobody.* I couldn't believe it. Then Jeff Rice told me that nobody wanted to sign it because nobody wanted to sign it *first.* I put my signature down and pretty soon the whole paper was full of names. What I didn't know was that the person who signed first was the one who would get in trouble.

The next time we had orchestra, only the people who were too chicken to sign the petition went to practice. Everybody else stayed in class. Everybody except me. I had to give the petition to Miss McPew.

When I got there, McPewy was looking around and you could tell—she was wondering where everyone was. I almost turned around, but instead I went up to her podium and put down the petition. Then I ran like mad to get out of there.

When I got back to class, I felt really, really good. That lasted until a messenger came to our classroom with a note that said I had to go straight to the principal's office.

Now, maybe you've been to the principal's office a bunch of times and think it's no big deal. Not me. I wasn't even sure where the principal's office *was*, and by the time I found it, I was thinking that maybe it wasn't such a hot idea, me putting that petition together.

Dr. Berrywine didn't say much at first. He sat back in his chair and played with a pencil—twirling it around, chewing on it, doodling with it. And while he was doodling, I was sitting on the edge of my chair, shaking about as bad as Sharon Zimmer. Finally he said, "I suppose you know why you're here."

Well, of course I did, but what came out of my mouth was "No, sir."

He bit his cheek and nodded and started playing with that stupid pencil again. Then I noticed that right there in front of him was my petition. He shoved it forward, real slow like, and said, "Did you have anything to do with this?"

There was my name, right next to the number one, getting me in trouble. So I studied my hands, shaking away in my lap, and just kind of nodded.

"Hmmm," he said.

Now, *Hmmm* can mean a lot of things, but when

a grown-up says it to you just right, it means you're in trouble. And after they say it, they just sit there and you know that what they're doing is deciding. Deciding exactly how they're going to punish you. And all you can do is sit there and wait for them to come up with something.

That's what Dr. Berrywine was doing, and he was taking the longest time doing it. Finally he leaned forward a little and said, "Miss McPew isn't that bad, is she?" I just sat there, looking at my hands. "*Is* she, Carolyn?"

I looked up at him, and he looked like he really did want to know, so I said, "Yes."

He laughed a little—not mean or anything—then sat back in his chair and picked up the petition and shook his head. "Tell me what she does that's so bad."

That caught me by surprise. I sat up a little and blinked a lot. "She's just mean."

"How is she mean?"

So I told him. At first I was whispering, but after I got going, boy! I told him about Sharon Zimmer's hiccups and *everything*. And he stayed real still and listened. When I finished, he just sat there, chewing on the side of his mouth.

Finally he looked at me and said, "Carolyn, why don't you give orchestra another try? I think you'll find that Miss McPew is really a very nice lady."

I stared at him for a minute. I wanted to say, "She is not!" but I stopped myself because I could tell he was going to let me go without yelling at me or standing me in a corner or doing any of the other things they say that principals do. Instead, I just stared at the pen-and-pencil set on his desk until he said, "What do you say, Carolyn?"

Well, what *could* I say? I nodded, and that was good enough for him. He stood up and said, "Why don't you get back to class now?"

So the next time we had orchestra practice, I went, and Miss McPew was sweet as pie to everyone. And just when we were starting to relax, thinking maybe orchestra wasn't so bad after all, Miss McPew made her way over to me.

I smiled at her and she smiled back at me. At least I thought it was a smile, so it scared the daylights out of me when she grabbed my ear and turned my head and whispered, "I'd better not get any more trouble from you, little girl!"

My ear was burning from her yanking on it, and I looked up sideways as best I could. There she was with that smile on her face, looking like she was going to kill me.

She finally let go of my ear, and I rubbed it and watched her go back to her podium like nothing had happened. Everyone started playing. Everyone but me. I was watching her and realizing that she was just as mean as ever and I got mad. Really, really mad. I took my flute apart, threw it in the case, and left. Just like that.

And I never went back. Dr. Berrywine never said another word about it, and I pretty much stayed out of trouble after that.

Until the business of the Dragon Lady's wig came up.

chapter 15
Back to the Principal's Office

I don't know how they traced it back to me. Someone must've told on me, and I bet it was Helen, because she's always tattling on people. She probably marched right up to the principal's office and said, "Excuse me, Dr. Berrywine? Carolyn's making fun of Mrs. Rennalds' wig, and I think you should stop her."

This time when the messenger came, the note said that I had to go to the office. It didn't say anything about the principal. That happens sometimes when you forget something and your mom brings it to school for you, so on my way to the office I was trying to figure out what I could have forgotten. I couldn't think of anything, and even if I had forgotten something, I didn't think Mom would've noticed, because she was getting kind of close to having the baby and was pretty distracted.

I'd actually forgotten about the Dragon Lady's wig until I got to the office and was told Dr. Berrywine wanted to see me.

If a principal was really smart, he'd call kids into his office to tell them what a good job they were doing, or to congratulate them on their grades, or for winning a race or something. If principals did that, they'd keep you guessing.

But principals don't do that, and the minute I found out Dr. Berrywine wanted to see me in his office, I knew I wouldn't be leaving with any ribbons. So into his office I went, and the funniest thing happened. I sat down in the same chair I'd sat in before, and Dr. Berrywine looked the same as he had when McPewy got me in trouble, so my hands *should've* been shaking, but they weren't. I just sat there and looked at him.

He gave me a little smile and said, "Hello, Carolyn."

I swung my legs a little and smiled back and said, "Hi." Just like that, "Hi."

He said, "How are you?" and actually I was feeling okay, though I didn't really know why. I mean, I was in trouble, there was no doubt about it, and here I was swinging my legs, feeling fine. So I said, "Fine, thank you."

He kind of chuckled to himself and said, "Do you know why you're here?"

I opened my eyes real big and said, "Not exactly, sir."

He played with his pencil a minute while I just sat there looking at him. Finally, he said, "Does your mother have a wig?"

Well, my mouth just kind of took over. "Yes, sir, but she never wears it. She says it's hot and makes her head itch and I'm glad, because it looks pretty funny on her anyway." My legs were pumping away, having a good old time.

Dr. Berrywine bit the side of his cheek. "It does, does it?"

I nodded and said, "Besides, it's kind of red."

Dr. Berrywine didn't have much to say to that. He just sighed and said real quiet, "Carolyn, it's not nice to make fun of people the way you've been making fun of Mrs. Rennalds today."

I looked down and said, "We weren't making fun of her. We just didn't know until today."

"You don't think calling someone 'Dragon Lady' and 'Carpet Head' is making fun of them?"

Well, Dragon Lady I'd called her a million times, but Carpet Head? Boy! That was a good one! It took everything I had not to bust up right there. I opened my eyes real big and said, "Carpet Head? I've never called her Carpet Head."

He looked at me the way Mom does when all the cookies have disappeared from the cupboard. "Oh?"

"No sir!"

"I see. Well, maybe you could spread the word that if I hear of anyone calling Mrs. Rennalds Dragon Lady or Carpet Head, they'll be in to see me after school."

"Yes, sir."

He stood up, so I stood up too. "Carolyn, Mrs. Rennalds doesn't know why you were called to the office, and I'd like it to stay that way. It's hard being a new teacher, and I'd appreciate it a lot if you could help make her feel welcome here."

That caught me off guard, him asking me to help him out. So I looked at him and nodded and told him I would try.

On my way back to class I didn't run, I didn't even walk fast. I stopped and had a long drink of water at the water fountain and wondered if Dr. Berrywine's wife ever wore a wig.

chapter 16
Roy G. Biv

Some teachers are fun to answer questions for. Take Miss Emigh back in fourth grade—when she'd ask a question, I'd raise my hand whether I was sure of the answer or not. Whenever I got the answer right, she'd say, "Wonderful!" or "Very good, Carolyn!" And if I didn't get the answer right, she'd find something right about it anyway and say, "Thanks for contributing, Carolyn," and call on somebody else.

Answering questions for Mrs. Rennalds is not fun. If you get the answer right, she'll give you a little smile and say, "That's right," but she'll always find something else to add to your answer, so you wind up feeling like you didn't really get it right at all.

And if you get the answer wrong, she gives you a little frown and says, "Hmmm," and then, "Anyone else?"

So I don't raise my hand much in Mrs. Rennalds' class, and I never volunteer things without being called on. But one day during art she was writing the colors of the rainbow on the chalkboard, explaining about their order and how we should memorize them because they'd be on a test later that week.

My dad taught me the colors of the rainbow a long time ago, and I've never forgotten them because of Roy G. Biv. That's not a person—it's the first letter of the colors of the rainbow broken up into a name. You know—Red, Orange, Yellow, Green, Blue, Indigo, Violet.

So I raised my hand. And I held it up for a long time. When she finally noticed it, she was in the middle of talking about indigo and interrupted herself to say, "What is it, Carolyn?"

I said, "My dad taught me a way to—" and that's as far as I got.

"Carolyn, I'm in the middle of an explanation! I'm sure your father is a very smart man, but please, listen to what I have to say!"

When we finally got to work on our art project, I told Debbie and Gail about Roy G. Biv. They thought it was a great way to remember the colors of the rainbow, and wound up telling some other kids.

Mrs. Rennalds never did ask me what I was trying to tell her. And after school while Allen and I were riding our bikes to our piano lessons, I realized that the reason she didn't ask was because I was just a kid. She figured I didn't know anything she didn't already know. Anything important, anyway.

Then Allen said, "Race you!" and I forgot all about Mrs. Rennalds and Roy G. Biv and concentrated on catching up with Allen. Our piano teacher, Miss Melby, lives way down Lemon Street, and Allen had never beat me there. Even when he had a head start, I always caught him.

I don't mind piano lessons because Miss Melby's nothing like Miss McPew—she's a real nice lady. She wears pointy glasses with sparkly little designs on them and dresses that are always busting with flowers. But the thing about Miss Melby that makes you keep watching her from the corner of your eye is that she sweats more than any lady you've ever seen.

While you're in the middle of your lesson, she sits on a stool by the piano bench, blotting away. It comes streaming down around her hair and down her neck, and if she doesn't keep moving that hanky, pretty soon it's dripping all over the piano keys. She doesn't give piano lessons during the summer, and it's probably because she'd float away.

I get my lesson first while Allen sits in this big puffy chair in Miss Melby's waiting room, and then he goes while I sit.

You can hear the piano from the waiting room, but you can't tell what Miss Melby's saying unless you sneak up the hall and listen. I've done that a couple times, but pretty much all she says is "Coming along . . . coming along," just like she does with me.

Anyhow, I was sitting in the puffy chair, waiting, when Miss Melby poked her head in and said, "Carolyn, come here a moment. I'd like you to hear this."

I followed her, and there was Allen looking pretty proud of himself. Miss Melby said, "Go ahead, Allen," and his fingers started flying around, playing one of the songs out of *my* book. He hit hardly any bad notes, and when he got done I stared. "When did you learn to play that?"

He just smiled. "I've been practicing!"

Now, as far as I knew, Allen never practiced. I knew he went down to little Andy's and banged on their piano in the garage, but I figured he was just messing around. But after hearing Allen play one of *my* songs, I knew something was going on down in little Andy's garage besides "Chopsticks."

And I was just thinking that I'd better start practicing a little harder if I was going to stay ahead of Allen when Miss Melby said, "I think maybe we should have a little contest next week. Perhaps on identifying notes? Allen, you're still having a bit of trouble with that—maybe this will make you study them." She turned to me, "What do you say, Carolyn? Are you game?"

Well, that caught me off guard. I mean, Miss Melby's not the kind of lady to have contests. You come in, play, hear "Coming along . . . coming along" a few times, get your assignment, and leave. But Allen asked, real excited, "Is there going to be a prize?"

Miss Melby laughed. "Sure, we can have a prize." She thought a minute. "How about a rubber lizard?" And then she pulled this huge rubber lizard out of the piano bench. "This little fellow."

Allen's eyes bugged out, and mine must have too, because Miss Melby laughed, then blotted some sweat. "So you practice, Allen, and if you know your notes better than Carolyn, this little fellow will be yours."

Normally I wouldn't have been worried about winning the contest. I know my notes pretty well. And I would've been sure I knew them better than Allen except for the fact that he knew how to play one of my songs. If he knew that, maybe he also knew his notes.

There are two sets of notes: EGBDF for the notes on the lines and FACE for the notes in the spaces. FACE is easy to remember, but with the notes on the lines I have a little more trouble.

So every day after school I'd practice my lesson and then I'd practice my notes. I don't know if it was that I wanted the lizard so much or if I just didn't want Allen to beat me.

After about the third day of practicing, Allen came in, sat next to me on the bench, and said, "Eebie geebie back da freezie."

I looked at him like he was nuts. "What do you want?"

"Eebie geebie back da freezie."

"Leave me alone, would you? I'm in the middle of practicing." I figured he was just trying to wreck my concentration.

He finally left, and I spent a few more minutes pretending to practice, but I was really thinking, "Eebie geebie back da freezie? How stupid can you get?"

When our next piano lesson rolled around, Allen and I got on our bikes and raced to Miss Melby's. I had my lesson, he had his, and when it was finally time for the contest, Miss Melby sat us both down on the bench. "Are you ready?"

She put up a piece of sheet music that neither of us had ever seen before and pointed to a note. In my mind I'm going, "E-G-B..." really fast, but before I could say the note, Allen said, "D!" I couldn't believe it. Then it happened again, and again. I got some of them faster than him, but by the time it was all over, he was jumping up and down waving the lizard around and I was standing there, wanting to cry.

Miss Melby said, "Excellent job, Allen! You too, Carolyn, but Allen has really improved!" Then she asked, "What did you do to study?"

Allen pointed to the sheet music and went up the staff saying, "Eebie Geebie Back Da Freezie."

I stared at the music and was thinking, "Eebie Geebie Back Da Freezie . . . EGBDF!" when Miss Melby laughed and said, "Every Good Boy Deserves Fudge didn't work for you?"

We both stared at her a minute, and finally she said, "Didn't I teach you that? I teach all my students that."

"You didn't teach *us* that!"

She just laughed and blotted. "Looks like Allen figured it out for himself."

When we were outside unlocking our bikes, I thought about how I'd told Allen to get lost when he interrupted my practicing with Eebie Geebie Back Da Freezie. It never even occurred to me that it might mean something.

Then I remembered how mad I got at Mrs. Rennalds about Roy G. Biv. And I was standing on Miss Melby's walkway feeling really stupid for not thinking I could learn anything from Allen when I heard, "Race you!"

I looked down the street and knew—this time I wouldn't be able to catch him. I was already way too far behind.

chapter 17
Smack, Squiggle Squiggle!

Helen Lison is a tattletale and I don't like her. She's also the biggest show-off in the world. Whenever we have to get up in front of the class and give a report, or even if we just have to work a problem at the board or be in a spelling bee, Helen Lison does her little squiggle thing.

She'll be spelling a word like *chocolate*, and she'll put her hands behind her back and bounce up and down and move from side to side. And she gets this look on her face like she's so smart, which she's not. Then her mouth smacks together and makes this sound that most kids only make when they're sucking on a milk shake.

Smack, squiggle squiggle, "C!" *smack*, squiggle squiggle, "H!" *smack*, squiggle squiggle, "O!" *smack*, squiggle squiggle, "C!" *smack* . . . And then she forgets where she is and has to start all over again. It just about drives me nuts. She never gets it right, even if it's a short word, and when the teacher tells her, "Sorry, Helen," she giggles and squiggles her way back to her seat.

I've been in the same class as Helen since the first grade, and it really gets to you after a while.

Every year Helen signs up for the talent show. Well, I do too, but that's only because my mom makes me. I hate it. I get all shaky and nervous, and I never win. I usually play the piano, which is what half the kids wind up doing. When you sit down at the piano, you can almost feel the audience yawning and thinking, "I wonder what's after this."

I'm not just imagining this, though that's what my mom thinks. Every year she comes to watch. Every year she tells me how proud she is of me. And every year all the kids who play piano lose.

Last year two sixth graders got up wearing torn-up old jeans and T-shirts and sweat bands, and they played electric guitars and shouted into the microphone so you couldn't understand what they were saying. And their guitars were so loud that all the mothers put their hands over their ears and shouted, "What?" back and forth to each other like a bunch of old people.

When they finished, one of the guys said, "We wrote that song ourselves."

And then the other guy said, "It took us ten minutes." Then they walked offstage and everyone clapped.

I think Dr. Berrywine was the one who liked them so much, because he clapped and clapped and clapped. Then he announced *me* and I had to do my piano piece, which I don't think anyone even heard because their ears were still ringing from those electric guitars.

Then came Helen with the same stupid act she does every year. Helen twirls a baton. She wore this white cowgirl outfit with fringe everywhere and a red tie and red boots. And she dropped the baton about ten times and giggled every single time. And when she was done, she took this grand bow and blew kisses to the judges. Can you believe it? I just hate Helen Lison.

After Helen was done dropping her baton and blowing kisses, the judges announced that the winner was the guys with the electric guitars. All the mothers shook their heads and all the kids who'd played piano swore they'd never play piano again. And Helen Lison played with the fringe on her outfit and giggled.

One night in October Mom shooed us out of the house because she had a headache and we wouldn't quit making noise. Jack went over to Billy's and Allen went over to Will's. I didn't know what to do—nothing seemed fun, especially by myself. So I climbed up into the tree house and just sat there for a while.

And that's when Charlie came over. Charlie hardly ever comes over, and if he does, it's because his mom needs to borrow something from my mom or he's selling candy bars for Little League. He never comes over to play with me.

So I watched him from the tree house. He walked clear around on the sidewalk instead of cutting across the grass, and then he walked up to the front door and stood there awhile. I decided to say hi, and he smiled and waved, and before you know it he was up in the tree house with me.

It was kind of weird, but I liked it. I don't think Charlie had ever been up in the tree house. Not with me, anyway. Anytime I played with Charlie, it was at his house or down the cul-de-sac if he wanted me to field grounders for him. Everyone always went over to the Moyers'. It was like headquarters or something.

But there was Charlie, in the tree house, just talking about stuff. And I was still trying to figure out what he was doing there when he asked, "What do you think of Helen?"

I blinked. "Helen? Helen *Lison*?"

He looked out between the slats of the tree house and nodded.

"I *hate* her!" I said.

He was still looking between some boards, at what I don't know. Finally he asked, "How come?"

So I told him. About her stupid cowgirl outfit and how she giggles all the time and about the way she acts when she's in a spelling bee and everything else. I was getting really carried away, telling him how stupid Helen Lison was, when all of a sudden I had this terrible thought. "You don't *like* her, do you?"

He shrugged. "No, I was just wondering."

That made me feel a little better, so I talked about her some more, and then all of a sudden we didn't seem to have anything to talk about and Charlie left. I watched him walk down the sidewalk and around the corner, and I felt kind of funny. Like I shouldn't have been so mean about Helen Lison.

Then I remembered how she blows kisses, and I decided that I should have pointed *that* out to Charlie, too.

The next day Debbie came racing up to me at recess. "Did you hear?"

"Hear what?"

"About Charlie and Helen."

"What about them?"

"They're going steady!"

I just stood there and stared at her until she said, "Carolyn?"

I kept right on staring, which is not something I usually do. I mean, when Debbie told me that Darrell had asked Julie to go steady because he liked her *feet*, did I stand there and stare? No. Did I say, "*What?*" and blink like an idiot? No! I said, "Boy, is he dumb!" like anyone would.

But there I was, staring at Debbie, blinking like I couldn't see right. "*What?*"

And Debbie said it again, "Charlie and Helen are going steady!"

I don't know what came over me. I could tell I was going to start crying any minute, and that made me mad. So I stared some more and said, "Are you *sure?*"

Debbie rolled her eyes. "Of course I'm sure. She showed me his St. Christopher!"

"His St. Christopher?"

"Yeah, she's wearing it around her neck. Go ask her!"

Well, I didn't need to ask her. She was showing

it off to everyone, and squiggling and giggling and just being Helen. I wanted to punch her.

For the rest of school I didn't talk to anyone. I hid in the bathroom because I was going to cry any minute, and then everyone would be whispering, and who knew what stupid things they'd say! Like I had a crush on Charlie or something dumb like that. And sitting in the bathroom thinking about it made me even madder. Why in the world would Charlie want to go steady with *Helen*? He knew she squiggled and giggled and was the world's biggest show-off. He probably even knew about the way she blew kisses.

And Helen would never play kickball in his backyard. She'd probably show up in a *dress* or her cowgirl outfit and just watch and squiggle the whole time. And there's no way Helen would ever play in underground forts or field grounders in the street. So what good was she?

I sat there in the stall, swinging my legs back and forth, looking at the scabs on my knees from when I tripped playing hide-and-seek. It suddenly hit me that Helen probably had perfect little knees with no scars or scabs anywhere. Helen probably didn't even *own* a pair of shorts she could wear under a dress, and Helen probably had a room full of dolls and curtains of lace.

And Helen Lison had probably never wished she was a boy.

It turned out that Charlie and Helen went steady for four days. Now, I didn't know it was only going to be four days, so it seemed like a long time to me. That doesn't mean I was stupid about it or anything. I went to school and acted pretty normal. I even tried to be nice to Helen, which would've been easier if she'd quit twirling that St. Christopher for thirty seconds.

And when I said hi to Charlie, I tried to act like nothing had happened, but that wasn't easy either. I was feeling really dumb for having told him what an idiot I thought Helen was. I wanted to say I was sorry, but I wasn't sorry, which is a confusing way to feel.

Then one day I was walking home from school and heard, "Hey, Carolyn! Carolyn, wait up!"

I was in the middle of crossing the street, but I turned around anyway, and when I saw it was Charlie, I stopped. Just like that. In the middle of the street. I stopped and waited for him to catch up.

When he did catch up, he didn't say much of anything. We got to the corner where my house is and I had to go one way and he had to go the other. So we just stood there, looking at the sidewalk. And it hit me that we weren't acting like we'd known each other since before kindergarten. We were acting like we had when we first met.

I don't remember leaving our old house and moving into this house. The first thing I remember about moving was standing on the corner with my mom, meeting Charlie. I don't think I said much of anything. I just hid behind my mom and peeked out every now and then at Charlie peeking at me from behind *his* mom. I remember Mrs. Moyer and my mom talking and laughing, and I remember spending a lot of time staring at the cracks in the sidewalk.

I don't think I'd noticed the cracks since then, and now suddenly there they were, hypnotizing me. I couldn't do anything but stare at them and wish my mom and Mrs. Moyer were there so we'd have something to hide behind.

Finally, Charlie said, "Helen and I broke up."

Well, that made me look right up from those cracks. "You *did*?"

He nodded and started digging in his pocket. "I guess you were right."

I didn't say anything, but I was thinking that it was about time he got some brains about Helen Lison. Then he pulled his St. Christopher out of his pocket and kind of held it up and straightened it out right there in front of me. And for a second my heart started going really fast because I thought he was going to give it to me. I watched it twist and sparkle in front of me, and I was thinking that it was the most beautiful color blue I'd ever seen. Then he put it over his head and smiled.

Well, what was I supposed to do? I smiled back and tried to ignore that my heart had just about beat out of my chest when I thought he was going to put the chain around *my* neck. And it made me mad at myself, because I don't *want* my heart to do that around Charlie, and lately it's been doing it more and more.

Then Charlie laughed, like all of a sudden he felt real good. He said, "See you later!" and ran home.

I stood there on the corner watching him as he popped into his side gate, and after I stared at that gate for a while, I sat down on the curb and stared at the cracks some more. I just sat there and stared and wondered what the first thing Charlie remembers is.

It doesn't seem fair that it probably doesn't have a thing to do with me.

chapter 18
The Christmas Choir

I wish I could say that Mrs. Rennalds quit wearing that wig and that the Dragon Lady never came out again, but it wouldn't be true. What happened was we all got used to her. She still drank coffee and smoked and chewed gum with cookie crumbs in it, and that bald spot on her head seemed to get bigger every time you looked for it. But after Dr. Berrywine called me to his office, I quit calling her D.L. or Dragon Lady, and even though some kids still called her Carpet Head, most of us just called her Mrs. Rennalds.

And the day she told Helen Lison to quit giggling, I actually started to like her.

We all had to give reports on what our mom or dad did for a living. When it was Helen's turn, she was up there squiggling and giggling, and after about five minutes of her not getting anywhere with her report, Mrs. Rennalds said, "Helen! Stop that incessant giggling!"

I didn't exactly know what incessant meant, but

I figured it out pretty quick. Helen did stop giggling for about ten seconds, but she started up again, so Mrs. Rennalds sighed and said, "Helen, sit down!" and that's when I started liking Mrs. Rennalds.

I also like her because she's so excited about choir. Every year Bradbury Elementary puts on a Winter Pageant, and a big part of the show is the choir. People in the choir get to wear neat purple robes that go way down to your feet. Only the sixth graders can be in the choir. The fourth and fifth graders are in the Christmas play, and everybody else just has to watch.

I didn't like being in the play because there are too many kids and not enough parts, so most kids wind up just working backstage. And if you do get to be a cow or shepherd or something, you wind up wearing a costume that makes you sweat and you don't do much but go *moo* or *baa* every now and then.

Being in the choir is better than being in the play because you're almost always doing something. What I don't like is being told I'm a soprano when I know I'm not, or having to sing a harmony part when I'm standing right next to the alto section. It messes me up and I wind up singing the wrong part.

And I don't want to fake it. I like to sing.

Anyhow, Mrs. Rennalds was in charge of the choir, and you could tell she really liked doing it. She'd work with all the different sections and try like mad to teach us our parts. When all three sections would get something right, she'd jump up and down and say, "Yes! Very good! Wonderful!" And if we didn't get it, she'd just try over again. The Dragon Lady never came to choir practice.

And Mrs. Rennalds could *sing*. That really surprised me, because when you think about Mrs. Rennalds' mouth, you don't think music, you think coffee and cookies and sticky green gum. But she knew all the parts, and it really helped to have her sing along with us. She'd sing one part and then she'd switch over to another without hitting one wrong note. There's no way you can fake that.

So we practiced and practiced and practiced. And when the night finally came to do it for real, Mom surprised me with a new dress and some shoes. It seems stupid, but I got real excited, because Mom had never bought me a dress like *that* before. It wasn't full of bows and lace or anything, it was just a white dress with a couple of tiny reindeer on the collar, and I thought it was the best.

Only trouble was I couldn't wear my shorts. Mom said you could see them right through the dress even after I put on a slip, so I had to take them off.

Mom was running behind because I actually gave in and let her curl my hair a little. And Dad was running behind because he was having trouble convincing Jack to go see us in the Winter Pageant. Jack said that he had hated being in the choir when he was in the sixth grade, and that they did the same play every year and it was the boringest thing in the world. And you should've heard the way he said it. Like it was such a long time ago that he was in the sixth grade or something. And when I said, "Nuh-uh! You liked being in the choir! Besides, Allen's one of the *kings*," he looked at me like I was a stupid kid.

So Allen and I headed over to the school by ourselves, and right away Allen started looking for Will. Will wasn't hard to find, because he was sitting with his parents and Charlie in the same place they always sit, which is right next to where my parents always sit. Will seemed real happy to see Allen, and the two of them raced off to get into their costumes, which left me standing there feeling kind of uncomfortable.

Mrs. Moyer looked at me and sort of backed

away a little and said, "Why, Carolyn! Don't you look pretty tonight!"

That made me blush pretty good, because she was looking at me like she'd never seen me before. I thanked her real polite like, but she didn't leave it at that. She reached over and shook Mr. Moyer's arm. "Bob, doesn't Carolyn look lovely tonight?"

He glanced at me and said, "Mm-hmm."

I wanted to get out of there, but I didn't know where to go. It was too early to get into our robes, so I just stood there and blushed, looking at everything but Charlie. Finally Mrs. Moyer said, "Are your parents coming tonight?"

Okay. That gave me something to talk about. So I told her about Jack not being ready, but that sure, they were coming.

"Good, we'll save a couple of chairs for them."

I finally looked at Charlie out of the corner of my eye, and he was looking right at me. I blushed all over again and wished for a pair of shorts so I could at least go out and play. Instead I excused myself and started walking around like I had someplace to go.

When Mrs. Rennalds finally called that it was time for the choir to get ready, we all put on our robes and lined up on the bleachers. And before you know it, it was time for us to start singing. That's when Julie decided she should be standing where I was standing so she could be next to Darrell. Mrs. Rennalds' hands were up above her head just twitching to start scooping and cutting air, when Julie started whispering to me. I tried to ignore her and watch Mrs. Rennalds, because I didn't want to mess up, but Julie started tugging on my robe and whispering really loud, "Switch with me! Switch with me!" She'd already moved over about three places, and I suppose I could've just switched with her, but I didn't want to. Not because I didn't want to ever, just not right then. I was concentrating on Mrs. Rennalds' hands, trying to remember what I was supposed to do.

The whole cafeteria was really quiet because they knew we were about to start, and that's when Julie started pulling on me. Not just tugging on my sleeve. *Pulling* on me until it felt like my new shoes were going to slip out from underneath me and I was going to fall off the bleachers and show everyone my underwear.

I turned to her and said, "Stop it!"

And she said, "Switch with me! Switch with me!" like a record that needs you to stomp on the floor so it'll keep going.

So I hit her in the arm. Not hard or anything, just enough to get her to quit bugging me.

Julie must not have any brothers, though, because she thought it was real hard and started crying right there on the spot. She crinkled up and just *bawled*.

All of a sudden everyone in the cafeteria was trying to look around the heads in front of them to see what was going on, and the other kids were wobbling on the bleachers trying to get a better view. Mrs. Rennalds' hands quivered because she didn't know whether to start scooping and slashing or stop and find out what was going on in the soprano section.

Julie finally quit bawling, and what did she do? She looked at me and said, "Switch with me!"

I really wanted a bucket of water to pour over those stupid curls of hers. But I switched with her, and while I was doing it, I stomped on one of her stupid Mary Janes. She didn't seem to care, though; she just stood there, holding hands with Darrell.

Before you know it Mrs. Rennalds' hands scooped down and we were off and singing, turning pages and trying to get it just right. After a couple of songs I looked around for Mom and Dad and Jack, but when I finally spotted the Moyers, my parents weren't with them. And I could see empty seats next to the Moyers just waiting to get filled up.

That threw me off and I lost my place in the music. I wasn't about to look over at Julie's, so I just flipped the music back and forth, trying to find the spot with one eye and Mom and Dad with the other.

Mom and Dad always come to see us in plays and stuff, and I figured they had to be somewhere, so I sang on my tiptoes, twisting and turning, trying to find them.

It wasn't until after "Jingle Bells" that it hit me where they must be.

chapter 19
Nancy

I'd never really thought this through, and I don't think Allen or Jack had either. So when it happened, it jumbled up my feelings, and I know Allen and Jack were feeling peculiar, too.

Mom and Dad had told us not to talk about it too much. I think they wanted to make sure everything turned out all right and didn't want people asking them a bunch of silly questions.

I'd heard Mom answer, "It doesn't matter, as long as it's healthy," when people asked her whether she wanted a boy or a girl. And I heard that same answer over and over again, so I figured that it was the right answer.

But when Dad told me the baby was a girl, I started bawling my eyes out. It took me a long time to figure out I was crying because I was so happy. Happier than I'd ever been.

If anyone had asked me if I wanted the baby to be a boy or a girl and I'd stopped to think of my own answer, I don't know what I would've said.

There are two ways you can look at that question. First, did I want it to be a boy or a girl because it's better to *be* one or the other and what would I want for the baby's sake?

The other way of looking at it is what do *I* want it to be, which isn't really fair to the baby. But sitting there bawling, I realized that I wanted a sister more than anything in the world. Think about it— I've already got two brothers. You know how Jack is. And don't tell Allen, but he's going to be able to beat *me* up pretty soon. Besides, even though Allen and I play together a lot and you'd think he'd be on my side most of the time, he's not. Jack can be mean to him for weeks, and all he has to do is be nice for about thirty seconds and *whoosh!*, there goes Allen, over to his side.

And you get to an age when you don't want to go running to your mom just to have someone on your side. So you sit in your room wishing you were a boy so your brothers wouldn't do that to you. I never once thought that one of *them* should be a girl.

When Mom and Dad first brought Nancy home, we weren't allowed to breathe on her, let alone hold her. Mom was worried about us dropping her or hurting the soft spot on the top of her head, so mostly we got to watch Mom rocking her and feeding her. And since Nancy spent a lot of time sleeping, we had to do a lot of tiptoeing and whispering, which Jack and Allen didn't like too much.

I didn't mind, though. They'd go off and play, and sometimes they'd even invite me along, but most of the time I'd stay inside and watch Nancy sleep. You may not think that's too exciting, but she had the tiniest little fingernails and the most amazing little ears, and I didn't want to run around the neighborhood—I wanted to watch Nancy.

Then one day while Nancy was taking a nap, Mom asked me if I'd mind keeping an eye on her while she took a shower. I said, "Sure!" and about two minutes after Mom got in the shower, Nancy woke up crying.

I tried shaking a rattle, and I tried saying, "Sssh, sssh! Don't cry, Mom'll be right here," but that didn't work. So very carefully I reached into the crib and picked her up.

Then I sat down in the rocking chair and put her in the crook of my arm. And as we went back and forth, I sang her a little lullaby, and in no time she was quieting down. And as I looked at her and she looked at me, I knew—I wasn't going to be lonely anymore. I had a sister.

After a while Mom and Dad asked if we'd mind having the girls share one room and the boys share the other. I thought that was a great idea, and so did Allen. Trouble was Jack. He didn't want to share a room with Allen again and wound up talking Dad into letting him sleep in the garage.

So Jack moved his bed and dresser out there and then hung these bedspreads from the rafters for walls. I thought it was the greatest fort ever, but I didn't tell Jack that. I just told him the spiders were going to come back and get him.

So Allen's got Jack's old room and Nancy's crib is in mine. At night I look at her sleeping in the crib and I talk to her. I tell her about all the stuff that happened before she was born, just to catch her up. And I tell her what to look out for, being a girl. How being a girl is actually all right once you figure out that you should break some of the rules instead of just living with them.

I also tell her about the things I'm going to teach her the minute she's big enough—like touching the moon and spying and why you should stay away from ivy and girls who wear too much lace.

Now, you may think that's silly, talking to someone who's too little to understand and who's sleeping, but we learned in science that your brain stores away stuff it hears when you're asleep. If that's so, she's going to be pretty darned smart in no time at all.

And if you don't believe in stuff like that, I have proof that I'd tell you all about, only I'm thinking maybe I'll head over to the Moyers'. Allen said they were roasting hot dogs, and he said that Will said *Charlie* said I could come over if I wanted to, so I think maybe I will.

I like hot dogs. I like them a lot. And I'm thinking maybe Charlie's saving me a chair.

Wendelin Van Draanen lives on the central coast of California with her husband, two small sons, and two large huskies. She is a high school computer science instructor, and when she's not writing, computing, or running the dogs, she enjoys performing and recording with a local rock group.

She grew up in Monrovia, California, where she spied on her neighbors, threw rocks down chimneys, and learned about touching the moon.